Praise for 'SEO'

"SEOin2024 is set to be a landmark publication in the field of digital marketing, expertly edited by David Bain. This book is not just a collection of theories but a well-curated compilation of practical insights and strategies shared by some of the most influential SEO professionals in the industry. Each contributor in this book is a trailblazer, making significant strides in shaping the digital landscape. Their chapters delve deep into advanced SEO techniques and emerging trends, offering a panoramic view of what it takes to dominate search engine rankings in the coming year. Bain's editorial acumen is evident in the coherence and clarity he brings to complex topics, making the book an accessible yet comprehensive guide. From innovative keyword strategies to evolving algorithms, SEOin2024 covers a broad spectrum of topics, offering invaluable insights for both seasoned professionals and those new to the field. It stands out as a must-read for anyone aspiring to excel in the competitive world of SEO and digital marketing, promising to be an indispensable resource in navigating the ever-evolving landscape of search engine optimization. It is a must for every desk of my team!"

JOSEPH KAHN
President, Hum JAM

"I can't even imagine how much time David has put in to compile a phenomenal resource for the industry - year after year. Get your hands on this book and take the time to learn from so many experienced SEOs."

ITAMAR BLAUER
Senior SEO Director, StudioHawk

"The Majestic book series is the go-to resource for SEOs of all levels. SEO experts cover all important topics, from the basics of SEO to the most advanced techniques. The book also provides practical advice and tips that you can use directly."

SARA MOCCAND-SAYEG
SEO Specialist, Liip

"SEO is an ever-changing beast, and this book gives incredible insight from some fantastic minds into tried and tested methods that you can implement on yours or your client's website in 2024 and beyond."

ED ZIUBRZYNSKI
Global SEO & Content Manager, Swoop Funding

"Collecting so many different interesting SEO related POV's into one book is a difficult task that has been executed perfectly. Even as a seasoned consultant, the book has provided me with numerous new insights. You never stop learning and this book can't be missed in your yearly collection!"

JAN-WILLEM BOBBINK
Freelance SEO

""SEO in 2024" is hands-down the best resource on the internet, for summarizing the latest trends, sentiments and viewpoints around SEO. If you want to get up to speed for the year ahead, and get advice from the top experts of our industry, look no further!"

AMIT RAJ
Founder, The Links Guy

"I think the last few years have proven that SEO is neither dead nor ruining the internet – and this book is a great contribution to an industry that has grown so much and is now a recognized profession. It is ever-evolving and that is one of the reasons why I am proud of being an SEO consultant and for the existence of this book SEOin2024."

JULIA-CAROLIN-ZENG
SEO Consultant, Charlie on the Move Ltd

"Keeping up in the ever-changing world of SEO is hard. SEOin2024 collates great, actionable advice from some of the brightest minds in the industry to help make it a little bit easier!"

ANDREW OPTIMISEY
Founder, Optimisey

"A great book of tips and tricks from some of the best SEOs in the industry!"

NATALIE ARNEY
Freelance SEO

"This is the most actionable book in SEO! A must-read to go through the top tips for the year."

ALEYDA SOLIS
SEO Consultant & Founder, Orainti

"Whether you're a seasoned marketer or a novice entrepreneur, this book is a must-read, offering practical tips, real-world examples, and a fresh perspective on leveraging the latest SEO trends. A definitive guide for anyone serious about standing out in the digital crowd!"

TAYLOR KURTZ
Owner, Crush the Rankings

"SEO in 2024 is a wonderful collection of SEO expertise and an indispensable must-read resource for SEO experts and digital marketers alike. There's always much to learn and the books, podcasts are a great way to channel your time in the most focused manner."

ANDREAS VONIATIS
Founder SEO Consultant, Artios

"In 2024, strategically collaborate with influencers to craft content that not only resonates with your audience on essential social platforms and media outlets but also attracts targeted traffic, boosts conversions, and fosters brand advocacy."

MARIA WHITE
Global SEO Lead, Kurt Geiger

"There is NO better resource for the latest up-to-date (and ahead-of-the-curve) SEO advice than this book series! Don't start your new year without this book!"

PAM AUNGST CRONIN
President, Pam Ann Marketing & Stealth Search & Analytics

"David does an amazing job showcasing the thought leadership of outstanding SEOs. I'm honoured to share my insights amongst some of the world's finest SEOs. Thank you for the opportunity, David."

AUSTINE ESEZOBOR
SEO Consultant, DemocratizingSEO.com

"I'm glad to have been a part of this long-running series and contribute my thoughts on SEO. Excited to be a part of this book with many of the biggest names in SEO."

ANTHONY BARONE
Co-Founder, StudioHawk

"A must-have for your bookshelf if you aim to stay ahead! This book is undoubtedly one of my favourite releases every year. Offering insights from a diverse range of global SEO experts across various industries and backgrounds, it equips you with the knowledge to stay ahead of potential changes and disruptions. It's an invaluable resource to kickstart the year on the right foot while also enhancing your knowledge."

SARA FERNÁNDEZ CARMONA
International SEO Consultant

"You could argue that this past year has been the most aggressively vivacious in the world of SEO since Panda. David and the team at Majestic have done another fantastic job collecting insights and perspectives from around the globe by leaders of our industry. It's a privilege to be included in such a fantastic (and important) edition of SEOin2024."

GARRETT SUSSMAN
Demand Generation Manager, iPullRank

"SEOin2024 is the single best source of finding relevant, actionable tips from the people you should be listening to and taking notes from. It's a who's who of experts in the industry and there's nowhere else you get all of these brilliant minds and insights in one place."

JACK CHAMBERS-WARD
Marketing & Partnerships Manager, Candour

"This is a powerhouse collection of actionable advice. SEO has evolved quite a bit and the perspectives included are equal parts useful and empathetic to the fast-paced changes of the industry."

NAVAH HOPKINS
Evangelist, Optmyzr

"Reading through these insights is like attending a rapid-fire conference featuring the brightest SEOs in the industry. David's extensive follow-up with each contributor means you get more than just an off-the-cuff tip—you're getting real, actionable advice from folks who normally charge the big bucks for their time!"

KAVI KARDOS
Director, SEO, Uproer

"It's always an honour to participate in the yearly SEO industry trends and forecasts. David does a priceless commendable job in gathering information across so many talented people with so many insightful pieces of advice."

PEDRO DIAS
Technical SEO Consultant, Visively

"The recommendations on this book are gold for SEOs. They will help solve any issues we may come across during 2024 and, even, beyond then. This is an excellent reference book containing some technical advice, as well as tips that that may help us work more efficiently and be happier doing what we do. All coming from our own experience. Do let the SEOs on this book know if their recommendation has helped you or your work!"

MONTSERRAT CANO
Consultant and Trainer

"This is an insanely awesome collection of tips and information from most of the top minds in digital marketing. Instead of the generic "SEO for Dummies" approach, it's real-world tactics and tips from ridiculously smart marketers, so it's a book that's literally packed with immediately actionable information that can change how you work TODAY!"

GREG GIFFORD
Chief Operating Officer, SearchLab Digital

"It's easy to get behind in SEO with everything constantly changing, and evolving. But SEO in 2024 is a must-read because it's full of nuggets to accelerate us ahead of the game. Don't just keep up with organic search. Feel free to challenge things, yourself, other people in a constructive way, and work smarter to be better at SEO for people, for business, not for Google."

KATIE MCDONALD
SEO Specialist, Kaweb Marketing

"SEOin2024 is a super valuable resource for the industry as we enter what looks to be a period of big significant change. Our industry thrives on varied opinions, and this book is a collection of some of the very best!"

JAKE GAUNTLEY
Senior SEO Account Director, KINESSO UK

"If you're looking to stay up to date with the constant and immense changes in SEO, I highly recommend reading this book! It's jam-packed with expert info and well worth the read!"

ADRIANA STEIN
Founder & CEO, AS Marketing

"I thought I'll browse through the book super-quickly, but then couldn't stop reading it. It's so well structured and engaging. I didn't know you could make an SEO book so reader-friendly. Recommendations there are super-actionable and fresh. I'll need to have a few more books for my friends!"

OLESIA KOROBKA
Director, Fajela

"I'm honoured to be featured in SEOin2024 alongside such remarkable professionals. David excels as an interviewer, and this book stands out as a comprehensive guide in the SEO field. This Book is the Bible for Modern SEO."

ARPAD BALOGH
SEO Consultant, Slothio

"A major benefit of this book series is David Bain's commitment to showcasing a range of SEO strategies and perspectives. I'm honoured to lend my expertise alongside other seasoned professionals. Together, we're able to produce a comprehensive guide that delivers real value for readers. Whether you're new to SEO or have years of experience, The SEOin2024 offers something for everyone. The clear explanations are perfect for beginners, while the cutting-edge insights give veterans fresh ideas to stay ahead. As SEO changes, each yearly edition evolves to address the latest algorithm updates and industry practices."

DRE DE VERA
Chief SEO, PaulAndre.com

"SEO continues to expand into an all-encompassing field that touches all aspects of marketing, technology, communication, branding, psychology, and more. That's a vast field - and one that's increasingly hard to keep up with."

JONO ALDERSON
Independent Technical SEO Consultant

"SEOin2024 is a really diverse book, where we all can read so many different approaches and points of view. That's what makes it really rich. A must for everyone in the SEO industry."

FILIPA SERRA GASPAR
SEO Consultant

"SEOin2024 offers a fresh take on staying ahead in the SEO game by sticking to the basics while keeping an eye on the future. In a digital landscape that's always shifting, this book brings you tried-and-true methods from top SEO pros. It's about understanding what never changes in SEO and combining it with smart, future-focused strategies. Perfect for those who appreciate the power of fundamentals but also want to be ready for what's coming next in the world of search."

ALAN SILVESTRI
Managing Director, Growth Gorilla

"SEO in 2024 is a well-curated powerful knowledge base featuring some of the top industry experts. There is only so much research one can do online, getting practical insights and proven techniques paired with real-life examples is invaluable for anyone looking to take their SEO game further."

KERSTIN REICHERT
Head of Marketing, SeedLegals

"It's reassuring to know there are resources like SEOin2024 which can help dissect the huge changes and new opportunities that are facing the SEO industry. This book is a must-read for anyone wanting to take their SEO strategy to the next level!"

ANNIKA HAATAJA
SEO Director, Seeker Digital

"This book is one of my highlights every year. It includes so many different brilliant recommendations from state-of-the-art industry people that you shouldn't miss it. Throughout the year this book can be like a helping guideline. No matter what situation you must deal with - you will find some inspiration for your work. Thanks to all who contributed to this outstanding collection of wisdom and knowledge."

ANDOR PALAU
International SEO Consultant

"What distinguishes this book is the direct insight it gathers from practicing SEOs and marketers, providing a unique freshness. The diverse range of topics covered ensures there's something for everyone, making it a valuable resource for those looking to get a real picture of SEO trends in 2024."

ANNA USS
SEO Lead, Synthesia

"Even as an experienced SEO, I find it fascinating to read what other SEOs have shared. I find it so educational to learn from other SEOs through this book."

BILL HARTZER
CEO, Hartzer Consulting

"David has done a great job of producing a fantastic amalgamation of opinions from some of the best of our industry, a great way to broaden your SEO horizons."

MARK WILLIAMS-COOK
Director, Candour and Founder, AlsoAsked

"It's all in here! This is the reference book for anyone who wants to expand its knowledge on SEO and keep up to date with this rapidly changing topic."

ADELINA BORDEA
Team Lead, Freepik & Freelance SEO Consultant

"Few other works encapsulate the newest, cutting-edge advice from venerable titans of SEO. There are always goodies weaved throughout, if you read nothing else - read this."

NIK RANGER
Senior Technical SEO, Dejan Marketing

"ChatGPT can answer most of your questions these days, but when it comes to SEO and learning from the experts to prepare yourself for a successful SEO year ahead, "SEOin2024" book is all you need. I really enjoyed reading "SEOin2023" and looking forward to the 2024 edition of that!"

NITIN MANCHANDA
Founder and Chief SEO Consultant, Botpresso

"If you want to piggyback on the braintrust of the SEO community and really dive into a pool of SEO knowledge, you have it right here at the tip of your fingers. This book is absolutely packed with everything you ned to know about SEO for 2024."

ULRIKA VIBERG
CEO and Senior SEO, Unikorn

"Listen up, all you SEO nerds out there. If you're still trying to figure out how to rank your website higher than your grandma's cat videos, then you need to get your hands on this book. It's like having all the top SEO experts in the world gathered around a virtual bonfire, letting you in on the saucy SEO secrets that'll make the search engines swoon in 2024."

BIBI THE LINK BUILDER
Agent of Chaos, Bibibuzz

"The increased accessibility of AI this year has caused a lot of buzz within the SEO community (and beyond); however, core tenets of creating human-focused content that provides value remain intact regardless of who or what is doing the writing. The way you leverage new AI tools is what will separate a good SEO from a great SEO in 2024, and the fantastic group of experts who contributed tips to this book provides many unique perspectives on how to do so efficiently and effectively."

IAN HELMS
Director, Growth Marketing

"There are priceless and expertly curated new tips in SEOin2024. But at a time of unprecedented change in the industry, there are also some home truths you need to hear."

BEN HOWE
SEO Director, SEOMG!

"If you're looking for a book that provides clear and direct guidance on SEO in 2024 and beyond, then you've come to the right place! David has done a tremendous job by interviewing over 100 experts and categorizing their ideas in a way that allows readers to gain expert insights supported by essential context."

ALEXANDRA TACHALOVA
Chief Executive Officer and Founder, Digital Olympus

"Majestic's annual book series stands out as an indispensable resource in the ever-changing world of SEO. It offers a rich collection of diverse voices, bringing together seasoned veterans and emerging talents, each sharing unique perspectives shaped by their varied roles, levels of seniority, and backgrounds. From foundational strategies to advanced techniques, the 2024 book contains a ton of practical tips and insights, making it an irreplaceable tool for SEOs, regardless of the stage of their career. Whether you're a beginner seeking to grasp the basics or an experienced practitioner aiming to stay ahead of the curve, this book offers something for everyone, challenging readers to broaden their understanding. A must-read for anyone serious about organic marketing."

LAZARINA STOY
SEO & Data Science Consultant

"Another year, another great edition of the latest insights in SEO from the people doing the work day in and day out. This book provides opinions, actionable advice, and the real issues we face in the search landscape."

BILLIE GEENA
SEO Consultant, Uptake Agency

"This book is a testament to the knowledge and experience of its contributors, and I am so honoured to be able to count myself among them. It's been truly fulfilling to share my thoughts and experience with others and has been a pleasure to work with David Bain on this book."

EMMA RUSSELL
Founder, Oxford Comma Digital

"This book is my new go-to resource for inspiration and early validation of SEO ideas before they go on my roadmap. It's amazing to be able to pick up so many great SEO brains in one place!"

GUS PELOGIA
SEO Product Manager, Indeed

SEOin2024

101 of the world's leading SEOs share their number 1, actionable tip for 2024

DAVID BAIN

Copyright © 2023-2024 Majestic-12 Ltd

All rights reserved.

ISBN: 9798870062389

TO THE SEO AND DIGITAL MARKETING
COMMUNITY –
THANK YOU FOR YOUR CONTINUED SUPPORT

(This says "Habibi" → trust me :-D)

Habibi, my dear friend!

I know, you probably don't need any of the advice in this book! Yet getting others' input, sharing ideas and finding inspiration is always very useful. Hope you will find something to get inspired by in this book.

And, no, I am not here, unfortunately!

With love, Rad   29-April-2024

CONTENTS

Foreword		1
Opening thoughts		7
CHAPTER 1	*Be Human*	11
CHAPTER 2	*Introducing AI*	33
CHAPTER 3	*AI Technology*	55
CHAPTER 4	*AI in Action*	79
CHAPTER 5	*The SERP*	111
CHAPTER 6	*Build your Entity*	137
CHAPTER 7	*EEAT*	163
CHAPTER 8	*The Customer Journey*	213
CHAPTER 9	*User Intent*	237
CHAPTER 10	*Content*	267
CHAPTER 11	*Internal Links*	327
CHAPTER 12	*Link Building*	347
CHAPTER 13	*Technical Health*	379
CHAPTER 14	*Diversification*	407
CHAPTER 15	*Collaboration*	437
CHAPTER 16	*Data and Analytics*	465
CHAPTER 17	*SEO Workflow*	515
CHAPTER 18	*Focus*	543
Closing thoughts		575
INDEX		579

FOREWORD

It seems like only yesterday when David Bain pitched the idea of sponsoring a contributor-led multimedia series which documented contemporary industry practice.

A lot of discussion and collaborative thinking followed. At some point, we decided that if we were doing this, we wanted to do it in a way that captured the essence that we work in an amazing, dynamic, and ever-changing industry. The decision to give the first book the title "SEOin2022" was in some ways brave. It meant that if we wanted to commission a sequel, that a revision wasn't really an option. Instead, we would once again have to reach out to leading figures in the SEO and Digital marketing industry and seek new material to ensure that future editions of the book would maintain the philosophy that gave rise to the first.

This series seeks to provide a platform to share contemporary actionable advice from leading industry figures.

On behalf of all at Majestic, I would like to express our gratitude to all of the contributors who have generously given their time to create a new book, "SEOin2024", once again capturing industry insight, actionable insight and best practice. It's wonderful to see so many experts contributing their knowledge and experience for the benefit of the community. We are massively appriciative to David Bain who has once again invested hours of time, inviting guests, interviewing and compiling this book, and the associated audio books and podcast.

I'd also like to thank my colleagues, who have worked tirelessly to support David and ensure the contributions are read, seen and heard by as wide an audience as possible.

Back in 2021, when preparing the first forward, I shared some of the motivations behind sponsoring this project. We were, and remain proud to be associated with it. Now in our third year, I find myself looking back over SEOin2022 and SEOin2023 and reflecting on how our industry has changed as a result of the impact of the AI revolution.

The "SEOin…" series gives an interesting perspective on this change. If I am to be slightly introspective, I have to admit to a delight and amazement in the way these books and guides have become somewhat of an accidental almanac, capturing how our roles have adapted to the brave new AI-assisted world, the opportunities for change, and benefits discovered.

As this series is about actionable advice for today, I'm not going to fall into the trap of making predictions. Instead, I'd like to look to the past, and in particular about the relationships between human and machine in a different way.

I've been a longstanding fan of a paper by Japanese roboticist Masahiro Mori who is credited for proposing a model of how humans feel or empathise with robots. The theory focuses on how this sense of empathy changes as the design of the robot becomes more and more human like. Mori suggested that with significant exception, human beings generally felt a greater and greater affinity with robots as they become more human like.

The exception was somewhat shocking. Human beings DO feel greater affinity with robots as they become human like. However, at a point, when a reasonable degree of likeness is achieved, the sense of affinity disappears, possibly turning to revulsion, or eeriness. The sense of affinity only returns when the likeness becomes very close. The region of unease is known as the "Uncanny Valley".

The paper, available at https://spectrum.ieee.org/the-uncanny-valley is well worth a read.

The uncanny valley is not somewhere you want to be. Invoking a sense of eeriness and unease is unlikely to delight your client. Fortunately, two ways are suggested to escape from the uncanny valley. One could invest a great deal of time and effort to make a near-perfect facsimile of the human form. The alternative route is perhaps slightly less instinctive. By accepting that the effort required to overcome the uncanny valley is overly burdensome, and performing a slight tactical retreat one can instead gain a better result than failing to leap the chasm.

The notion of uncanniness, and recognising the value in sometimes opting to know when to stop is a lesson I try to apply not just in work, but also to my wider life, as a home owner, husband and father.

Returning to our world of search, I find the scale of modern search phenomenal. Everywhere you look, the level of innovation is intense. The volumes of information collected, processed and speed at which SERPS can be returned is amazing.

To highlight this magnitude of human effort it might be helpful to focus on one example. For instance, processing the search query intent. Search engines work well on just a few words. What happens behind the scenes can be easy for a user to take for granted, but is in practice very complex. When you enter a search term, your query will be analysed, the likely intent determined, and code created to effectively interrogate the search engine indexes. This all happens before results are returned and sequenced. This concept was explored in the paper "Deep Search Query Intent Understanding" by researchers from LinkedIn. They suggested that "Understanding a user's query intent behind a search is critical for modern search engine success". They go on to discuss the difficulty of predicting a user's intent from what is an "incomplete query".

Pausing to think of the incomplete query, it's worth contemplating on how a search engine might fill in the gaps. What data can be used to ascertain what the user requirement might be from partial information?

Another way to look at the world of search is to look at the online world and see where search, or personalised information retrieval impacts our experience. The classic web search engine is just one way in which tailored information is served to us.

Everywhere we go on the web, we are exposed to another form of information retrieval – advertising. If a search query is "incomplete", and requires substantial processing, then the how do we describe the targeting algorithms that drive advertising? Perhaps a queryless search based on behaviour? Advertising is targeted like never before, technology giants analysing our real lives in more and more detail in an attempt to create models of our behaviour, indexing our lives in a way that seems disturbingly familiar to the indexing of the web.

As these digital selves grow in realism, I wonder if the principal of the uncanny valley found in the study of robots could also apply to our interactions with an increasingly personalised web?

Given the scale of the world wide web, a guide of some kind is essential for effective navigation. It's hard to find anything on the web without search or recommendation. I've been involved in the web since the mid-90's. It feels fair to say that algorithm led Search has been our primary guide since the very early 2000's.

However, as Martin MacDonald observes at the start of SEOin2023, traditional web Search Engines are seeing increased competition for eyeballs from social platforms. I can't help but reflect upon Google's initial rise to dominance, when the no-nonsense way of connecting search users to articles saw off competition from competing products and the portal paradigm of the late 90's. To think of it in the terms of the uncanny valley, I wonder if the no-nonsense approach of connecting people to content generated by people represented an increase in positive emotion by applying less in-your-face technology?

As a parent, I see younger generations consuming information in new ways. Some suggest that attention spans are shortening. I question if that's a fair assessment. My kids are more than able to sit down through a film IF it's one they are interested in. A part of me suspects they just have higher standards than I did at their age.

I have to admit to observing them watch YouTube shorts and TikTok with a sense of bewilderment. The effortless way in which they navigate huge volumes of streamed multimedia is amazing. Their ability to perform this task on multiple devices simultaneously is beyond my means, if not more than a little frustrating.

Looking beyond information access and into the social dynamics at play, it could be suggested that the virtual mentors of search in search engines appear to be losing ground to humans. This made me wonder. To what degree does the competition between the increasingly portalised search engine and the human influencer for attention retention reflect our desires to connect to people rather than uncanny automata?

I wouldn't wish to try to push any one theory to try to explain what are complex trends. There are other parallels. Earlier, I mentioned that the shift away from an increasingly personalised search which seeks to retain traffic in some way reflects the rise of Google as a no-nonsense search engine back around the turn of the millennia. The early Google search, powered by page rank, connected people to blogs, websites and retailers. It didn't aim to get in people's way. It just presented relevant results for your search query.

At the time, other search engines had started to introduce more and more content. In the late 90's the likes of Altavista and Infoseek were switching to what was referred to as a portal model.

History suggests that the "one stop shop" approach didn't work then.

With today's search engines incorporating more and more information one could ask how much information can Search Engines consume and process before they stop looking like a web search, and instead become bespoke personalised information portals?

It is with some sense of slightly morbid curiosity that I wonder how close search can be to reflecting a likeness of our digital self before triggering a negative emotional response reflected by Masahiro Mori's uncanny valley.

Regardless of the cause of change, change is upon us as AI assisted search and navigation aim to engage with us and present "user generated content" in new ways while funding hugely complex computational machines with revenues from advertising B2B and B2C services.

These are interesting times to be involved in digital marketing. Attempting to decipher which rules have changed and which remain constant in dynamic times is a challenge on which our industry was built.

Foreword

One of the aspects of SEO and digital marketing that I find most endearing is how those involved thrive on change. Our industry derives strength from the generosity of those who drive it.

Earlier, I reflected on the notion that SEOin... has become an accidental almanac. If previous editions highlighted metadata, information architecture and competition from social and new streaming platforms, I suspect 2024 will capture the rise in AI.

I've rabbited on enough. It's high time I pass the proverbial baton over to David Bain, for his opening thoughts on SEOin2024.

All the best,

Steve Pitchford
Operations Director
Majestic.com

OPENING THOUGHTS

SEO is continuing to change at an alarming pace. And yet, in some sense, the principles of good SEO remain the same.

Hello, and welcome to *SEOin2024* – a significant repository of current thinking from many of the world's leading SEOs.

I'm pleased to be able to welcome you to the third book in this series, now well and truly an annual tradition, brought to you by Majestic.

Back in 2021, Majestic tasked me with producing a podcast, video series, and book that interviewed the world's leading SEOs, all on their number 1 tip for the coming year.

The results were astounding. Not just from the perspective of the quality of knowledge shared, but from the breadth of that knowledge as well. Who would have thought that, by inviting so may SEOs to answer the same question, it would result in so many different views?

This year, that same 'number 1 tip' question still delivers a phenomenal array of answers. A set of answers that I'm proud to be able to share with you right here in this book. If you prefer, of course, you can also consume the content in audio or video form. Check out *SEOin2024.com* to get all of the same excellent advice in the medium and platform of your choice.

I mentioned in my opening paragraph that SEO is continuing to change at an alarming pace – and yet, in some sense, the principles of good SEO remain the same.

The significant challenge is to know what should change, and what should remain the same. There is so much knowledge in this book alone. How do you determine what's important for you? Personally, I'm a big fan of systems, models, and frameworks to help you along the way.

For instance, I like to describe the 5 'knows' of successful SEO as:

1) **To know what to do**
2) **To know how to do it**
3) **To know when to do it**
4) **To know what *not* to do**
5) **To know when to review what you do**

Let's dive into what I mean by this, and how this framework might be able to help you figure out what to prioritise from SEOin2024.

(Please note that, at this stage, I won't mention any specific tip that resonated with me. I don't want to sway your thinking before you consume the content yourself. Each reader will prioritise the tips differently – and to achieve the maximum possible from the book, I'd like to encourage you to do the same.)

1) To know what to do

A lot of SEOs used to start by determining specific keyword ranking opportunities, and measure their success based upon rankings and traffic. Now it's generally considered best practice to first decide what products are most important for your business, and then determine the content that is likely to resonate with your target market.

2) To know how to do it

Next, you're never going to be particularly good at SEO unless you figure out the best way to carry out the specific activities that you have determined to be essential.

3) To know when to do it

Everything has an optimum order, and everything should have a priority. This is where you decide on the optimum time to carry out specific SEO activities, based upon their impact and the value they provide to the business over a specific period of time.

4) To know what *not* to do

Just as important as determining what you should be doing is collating a list of things that you shouldn't be doing. I.e., just because the value of an SEO activity is generally seen as solid by world-renowned SEOs in other organisations, it doesn't mean that it's the right things to be doing in your business.

5) To know when to review what you do

How often do you lift your head up from the grindstone to benchmark what you're doing against the latest SEO tips and tactics? Perhaps there's a new way that you can save yourself a significant amount of time, or perhaps there's a new piece of code that you can tweak on your website to provide your brand with significantly more SERP presence?

I'd like to encourage you, as you make your way through this book, to select a few tips that fall into the above 5 categories. You can't implement everything. No tip will be the top priority for everyone. Decide upon what's most important for you, then decide to follow through on it.

I have my own selections that I believe are right for me – and no peeking! I'll share those at the end!

So please – proceed, select, prioritise, and implement what's right for you – and let me know how you got on!

I firmly hope that we meet in the same place at the same time, next year.

David Bain
Author, *SEOin2024*
Founder, *CastingCred.com*

Opening Thoughts

1 BE HUMAN

Become more adaptable so that you can take advantage of change – with Rebecca Berbel

There's no doubt that 2024 will see the wind of change continuing to strike the SEO landscape. Rebecca Berbel from Oncrawl believes that adaptability will be key.

Rebecca says: "We are going to need to be increasingly adaptable.
A lot of things, particularly in technical SEO, are still the same. We're still doing the usual things – crawlability, redirects, JavaScript, internal linking, automation, site speed, etc. – but we have seen so many changes which mean that people in the SEO space need to adapt to a new way of doing those same things.

We've seen the appearance of traffic from Discover (which has become highly prevalent for certain sites), the inclusion of ChatGPT and other large language models, and how we use AI in what we do every day. We've seen the SGE being promoted by Google, how that changes the SERPs, and what that means for SEO. We've seen major core algorithm updates recently, including the second stage of the helpful content update. Earlier this year, Universal Analytics was phased out and replaced by GA4, and so on.

We are still trying to do the same things, with what we hope is the same data, but those have evolved in ways that we couldn't have predicted a year ago. They're things that are logical, but we still can't predict what's coming next year. You have to be ready for the changes that will impact how we do things."

Does the fact that changes are happening more rapidly as time goes on mean that you need to be more adaptable?

"Some of the things that have really impacted our users at Oncrawl are technologies. We mentioned AI, and both websites and search engines are using different technologies today – including in how they render things. We've also seen a lot of headless CMSs and different ways that you have to adapt to that data itself. Search engines are providing different data and we need different data from them.

A lot of our users have access to different data within their companies, so they might have more data from other departments. They could have more data on pricing, general company-wide data, and different supports for big data. None of this is particularly new, but what is new is how broadly it's impacting SEO.

For example, not every SEO is using BigQuery but, given its implications in Looker Studio and Search Console exports, that is a tool and a type of data organisation that's much more important today than it was before. Rather than learning new formulas in Excel, maybe you should be looking at SQL."

How would you summarise Google Discover and what websites and industries can take advantage of it?

"Basically, Discover is a type of result that is fed to certain users. It's highly customised, and the feed is made up entirely of articles. [At the time of the discussion] only articles are eligible for this, and it's a sort of news feed for an individual. Media sites that publish news are extremely interested in this because, when an article is featured on Discover, it essentially goes viral. In some cases, you can get much more traffic from that.

At Oncrawl, some of my co-workers have been looking into how you get an article on Discover and how that relates to SEO. In terms of our adaptability, when we started this, we thought it was going to lead to product development at Oncrawl. We assumed the tools that people need to look at Discover and how it relates to SEO would need to be new things that needed to change [within Oncrawl].

In fact, we saw that the platform that we already have allows you to look at that yourself. We can use Discover information in Oncrawl as it is. There are correlations to certain SEO elements, although they not always exact or across-the-board. What stands out is that, if you rank well, you will do well in Discover. If you don't rank well, you have no chance. Even for a single website, articles that immediately do well in search results will also do well in Discover and vice versa."

What has the transition to GA4 meant for SEO?

"GA4 is a complicated subject for SEOs. That is one of the best examples of why adaptability needs to be one of our key focuses in 2024. We have seen so many people (my team included) struggle with how to change their mindset from sessions and users to events. That is one of the main differences between how analytics information was captured and reported in Universal Analytics and how it's captured and reported in GA4.

Again, this is not different information; it's still analytics information. It still gives us the same learnings and insights in the end, but we've had to figure out how to learn what the best resources are to understand this, and then adapt our processes to that.

At Oncrawl, we did update our analytics connector for Google to support GA4 information and it brought us new metrics, but we've kept all of the old ones. That sort of adaptability allows you to have continuity, but not everyone's using GA4 – which is something that I actually really like about this change. It forced us all to look at what information we are capturing as analytics, what information is useful, and how you can get that particular part of the information that you need for your SEO.

We've seen people move to Matomo and a couple of other analytics platforms, and they are still able to use the same analytics in Oncrawl. Our objective at Oncrawl is to make sure that you can blend analytics data with SEO data to understand which SEO metrics have an impact on the traffic that comes to your site and which optimizations you should be prioritising for that traffic.

That traffic element is something that you can get from analytics. When we look at analytics for technical SEO, that element is what we really want to preserve, and that hasn't required product development or evolution. That hasn't required SEOs to abandon the entire idea of analytics. Instead, it has asked us to be adaptable and to look for other tools or other ways to collect that particular information."

How does an SEO adapt and be able to measure the traffic or brand awareness that comes from an AI result in the SERP?

"That's the key question that is going to come up in the next couple of years. If you step back and look at what have been the key metrics for SEO success, in the first evolution of the internet, the internet was just a bunch of connections between content. Those connections are links, and links were the main money-maker for SEO. You needed links and, without links, you got absolutely nowhere.

However, that was the first iteration. There is a whole debate now over whether links are still a major ranking factor. Maybe they are, maybe they aren't, but it's very clear that, even for Google, that's not the way the world operates anymore.

In the second period, we got to the Web 2.0, social elements, and shareability – and content itself became king. The key element was to have shareable content that could be transformed, reused, and shared. That desirability is one of the things that you look for in SEO. You have a lot of clickbait titles, listicles, and blogs supporting that content.

Then, we moved into the hyper-personalisation of search results where you get re-ranking algorithms in Google, the influence of search intent, and a machine understanding of what the content represents. In addition to links and shareability, what is more important is how we communicate the core of the information that is on the page. Why are you talking about this subject and what is your expertise in that?

The elements that facilitate that are already present. We already look at schema; schema has been around for ages. We already look at EEAT; it's been around for years and it's even changed from EAT to EEAT.

When we look at SGE and personal adaptation – where you're searching from, the type of device, the time of year, the time of day, events around you, and all of those elements that inform this personalised search experience – they all require Google to have a very good understanding of what is on your page in order to serve it in the right context.

To me, the technical elements behind how Google is understanding your page are the key to making sure that you place well tomorrow. However, they have restructured the SERP. A search result isn't 10 blue links anymore. That is going to impact how we need to adapt to the ways that content and content sources are surfaced in organic research."

What soft skills are required in order to be more adaptable?

"We've done a ton of user research this year, and a ton of market research. One of the things that has come up again and again is that the model of the SEO or SEO team that works alone and has to reach out to other teams is much less prevalent.

We're seeing more and more people who aren't working alone and are embedded in other, cross-functional teams. Often the marketing budget has been reduced so their dedicated SEO team members have moved to other projects.

As an SEO, the best way to do things is to learn from your co-workers, because your co-workers today won't necessarily have always done the same things that you have, in the same ways that you have. They are often developers, web designers, or product managers for a web product – and they have a different way of looking at things, different priorities, and different ways of measuring things."

If an SEO is struggling for time, what should they stop doing right now so they can spend more time doing what you suggest in 2024?

"Stop doing absolutely everything manually. Automate, automate, automate – but automate the right things. In a Google Webmaster Hangout recently, somebody's homepage was blocking Googlebot, so it wasn't indexed. They would probably have caught this in their next audit, but you shouldn't be doing manual audits.

You need to be able to free up that time to ideate, to look deeply into certain subjects, and to create new processes by being critical of your own processes. A manual audit of your basic technical elements shouldn't exist today. You should be scheduling those. You should be setting up notifications that pop up in places where you will see them when things aren't working as expected – before you get to the massive manual action (or Webmaster Hangout question) that would reveal those issues.

The more adaptable you are, the more you'll see other priorities and opportunities that you really want to be spending your time on. To me, that's the future of technical SEO. Free up your time by automating what you can, so that you can be receptive to areas where you can adapt."

Rebecca Berbel is Product Marketing Manager at Oncrawl, and you can find her over at Oncrawl.com.

Emotional intelligence can be your superpower – with Petra Kis-Herczegh

Following on from Rebecca's emphasis on personal adaptability, Petra Kis-Herczegh from Kameleon Journal believes that your emotional intelligence might make all the difference.

Petra says: "Your emotional intelligence should become your biggest superpower in SEO.

Trying to sell emotional intelligence to SEOs is like trying to sell SEO to your executive board. It receives the same response. We put it on our low-priority list and ignore it until there is a problem. We're very familiar with this cycle for our SEO strategies and tickets. Unfortunately, if we decide to ignore it, there will be a problem.

The superpower is to tune into those emotions and understand that everything we do is driven by how we feel about what we're doing – and we're working with people.

There are two sides to this. You're creating your own SEO strategies and what you should prioritise, so you should be aware of how you're feeling about those things and what's driving that. On the other side, you're managing relationships with clients, stakeholders, board members, etc., and how they feel will be key to their decisions.

You can be an incredibly knowledgeable, technical SEO, have all the data, and have everything that proves that your strategy should go forward. However, if you're unable to communicate that in a way that makes the other person feel comfortable or confident with your strategy, they are not likely to prioritise it or go ahead with it. No matter how good you are, your emotional intelligence will have an impact on what you can actually achieve."

Is the key win getting more buy-in from stakeholders?

"That is a very tangible element of success that you will achieve if you decide to prioritise emotional intelligence.

I say 'prioritise', but emotional intelligence is not a trade-off. If you spend time on soft skills, empathy, and improving your communication and listening skills, you can still play with SGE and improve your technical skills. When you look at how you divide your time, it can feel like a trade-off, but it's not. Emotional intelligence underlines all our cognitive abilities: how we focus, how we learn, how we adapt to changes, etc. It's a foundation. If you prioritise it, then everything else will become easier.

A lot has changed in the last year or so, with ChatGPT, generative AI, and how Google is experimenting. Your emotional intelligence will help you cope with that change and decide what's important and what's not by understanding your feelings and the input that goes into them."

Can being more emotionally intelligent tangibly make us better SEOs?

"100%. In general, focusing on emotional intelligence makes us better human beings, and therefore better SEOs. However, there are tangible elements that you will see as well, like improved relationships with your stakeholders, getting things signed off, and having fewer headaches.

You put so much work and effort into things that you present and don't get prioritised or implemented. That causes a lot of frustration, stress, and headaches as you try to figure out why. To you, there is clear evidence, according to your logic, that something should be done.

If you're not focusing on the emotional side, you might be missing the point. There is probably a reason why other human beings and decision-makers in your team didn't feel comfortable and didn't buy into your ideas."

You highlight four elements of emotional intelligence – self-awareness, interoception, empathy, and compassion. Do they all have a measurable impact on SEO?

"In SEO, it can be really difficult to directly attribute certain results to one specific change that you've implemented. If rankings go up, can you prove whether changing meta titles or sorting out faster navigation was what achieved that change? It's the same with emotional intelligence.

For example, interoception is the sixth sense of tuning into your bodily sensations and having an awareness of everything going on inside you. There is so much going on, like feeling tired, cold, stressed, etc. Understanding that can really help your SEO. Many studies have shown that when people are tired or hungry, they often make poorer decisions. You might get into an unnecessary argument over a project or an SEO ticket with someone because you are tired or stressed and realise the next day that you should have had the conversation when you're feeling more balanced.

Of course, you can't be balanced all the time. You can't just never be tired or stressed. It's impossible to not have those sensations. However, if you are aware of it, that really helps. Develop a practice where you're more in tune with those basic feelings so that you can dissect them, pause, and take a step back. That will help you to understand what decisions to make or what to focus on.

It's very simple and it doesn't require a lot of investment. This kind of practice has been around in yoga for 5,000 years. The term interoception has only been around since the 20th century, but it's very similar to the concept of mindfulness. It's about understanding the different elements that go into your decision-making."

How can an SEO use their emotional intelligence to get a project on track or get buy-in from internal stakeholders more effectively?

"Firstly, it's about understanding that other people have different perspectives and different ways of doing things. Diversity is beautiful and it's very important. Not everyone is like you. You're unique in the way you're thinking and the way you feel. There are patterns and similarities but you're still unique.

In terms of how this can help you, if you know why this project is important to you, you will be more aware of your own bias. That's already helpful, especially if the first response you get is a 'no'. Instead of getting upset or feeling like they're unreasonable or they don't see your logic, you can think about where they are coming from. Do you need to reflect on your own bias? Did you take something too far? Do you need to look at the other side of the evidence? We should be doing that with SEO anyway. We try to look at all sides of things, but it's natural to have a bias and push our own agendas.

They might say that they want to focus on social or put more money into paid advertisement and less into improving the site. Look at where the company stands. Are they right to say they need to get in front of a wider audience before these issues are fixed? Do you need to reflect on that?

You can also try to understand the other person. If you've checked on your bias and you still think you should go ahead, you can think about why they are saying 'no'. Do they feel uncomfortable about it? Do they not understand it?

You don't need to categorise people, but you can consider where they are coming from. This CMO could be incredibly passionate about the brand and has been with the company for 10+ years. They live and breathe the brand, they focus on how the customers feel about the brand, and that connection is super important to them. Therefore, when you present technical SEO, they just don't get it. You might want to explain how Google is also a customer that focuses on trust, authority, and expertise, and if Google doesn't see the brand in that way, it won't show the brand in that way to your audience. You might need to change your story to reflect what's important to them.

Equally, that CMO could be super knowledgeable but, at the end of the day, this is a job to them. They want to get home to their loved ones, and they want to use their free time. They want to go with the decisions that are safe and won't cause them additional questions from investors. Consider their motives.

Of course, motives can be very difficult to discover because we don't often have the time to sit down with our C-level and investigate their personality types. Become more in tune with your own emotions and patterns, recognise the emotions and patterns of others, have more conversations, and ask around to other teams and find out how C-level reacted to their idea and what they said.

Then, you will be better at recognising those patterns. If someone wants to play it safe, then that's what you need to focus on. Find a way to explain what you are doing in a way that makes them feel comfortable. Present the risks in a way they will still feel safe about so that they feel like you understand the risks and will be able to manage them. Build that relationship."

How can SEOs benchmark and improve their emotional intelligence?

"Just as no two websites are the same, no two people are the same. We all have our unique wiring, so different things will work for different people. Something we can all start with is personality tests. There are many out there and a lot of companies use them for their employees. It doesn't really matter which one you do. Just do something that will give you a description of your personality.

The higher the quality of the quiz you do, the more insights you get and the more scientific it will be. You could do a Myers-Briggs, a DISC, or 16personalities which is free online and really easy to use. You could even ask your family and your closest friends or a bunch of different people to give you feedback about specific things.

The important part is to read it and analyse how you feel about it. Why are you feeling the way you're feeling about it? Are you rejecting certain things or disagreeing with certain things? Why? If that was the personality trait of a friend, would you be as judgmental? That sort of thinking will already give you some insight into what you like, how you feel about certain things, and your patterns. Patterns is a key word here. What sort of behavioural patterns do you follow? What behaviours do you default to when you're stressed?

To improve your interoception, it's about tuning in with your bodily sensations. Are you tired? Are you stressed? Have you drunk enough water today? Do you need to unclench your jaw because you're so focused and tense? Questions like that can be really helpful. When you look up interoception or listen to podcasts about it, they suggest that you do an exercise where you try to feel your heartbeat. How quickly can you do that? Is it fast or is it slow?

Repetition and consistency are key. For the next three weeks, if you wake up every morning and feel your heartbeat, you're going to notice some changes. On a day when you present to C-level, how does that compare to a weekend or a day with friends and family? You can start to see patterns from small things like this, which is really powerful.

Everyone will find that different things work for them. You have to experiment. Also, remember that everyone needs a different level of investment. Some people grow up in an incredibly healthy environment where being in tune with these emotions is supported, or they might already be naturally very self-aware. Other people will have grown up in different environments or experienced a toxic work culture, which will have an impact."

If an SEO is struggling for time, what should they stop doing right now so they can spend more time doing what you suggest in 2024?

"Take a break. Everyone will say, 'I can't do that!' but taking a break will help you reflect on things. Pick a day and do nothing – and see how your brain reacts. That can be really powerful for understanding those patterns. When your brain is bored, a lot of thoughts and creativity come to the surface that otherwise didn't really have space. You give your brain space to think.

More practical advice, that comes from a neuroscientist, Andrew Huberman, to manage stress, is to try breathing exercises. A very quick, specific exercise is called the physiological sigh. Take two inhales straight after one another, so you take in as much oxygen as you can. Then, you exhale very slowly. It resets the breath and it's proven to help with stress. Doing an exercise like that can bring down those stress levels and give you a bit more headspace."

Petra Kis-Herczegh is SEO Strategy Consultant at Kameleon Journal, and you can find her over at KameleonJournal.com.

Be human in order to sell to humans – with Jess Joyce

SEO Consultant Jess Joyce shares that your humanity can give you the edge in multiple SEO disciplines.

Jess says: "Be human, which is just two words, but it's also a lot more. It sounds simple, but it's not.

When I talk about being human, I'm talking about the fact that we're still selling and marketing to humans on the internet. All of our optimizations and all of our SEO efforts are aimed at a human. The middle point is Google, and that's a robot, but the person that's going to end up converting, buying, or doing whatever you're trying to get them to do to make those numbers go up and to the right, is still human.

We should be trying to be as human as possible. If that includes leveraging a little bit of AI, then I'm a big fan of doing that. However, there should be editorial processes included in that because it's not yet where it should be for a human audience. Until we're selling to Googlebot or Bender from Futurama, then we still need to be human."

Why and how does being human give you the edge?

"Firstly, for all those lovely Quality Rater Guidelines: the EEAT of Expertise, Experience, Authority, and Trust. They're not directly in the algorithms, but they are the leading indicators, which is a big thing that SEOs and all our marketers are always touting. They are leading indicators of growth, conversion, and whatever you want people to do.

Including those and surfacing them as much as possible are human traits. You're surfacing the fact that you're working with a PhD, or that you are a PhD, or that you're a forager with 15 years of experience knowing which plants won't kill you if you eat them. That's important and it's human. We're not yet at the point where you can trust an AI or a robot to decide whether or not something is poisonous."

Does being human take more time?

"It can do. I've started to roll out some AI drafts of content with a few clients, to speed up that process, because writer's block is a legitimate thing that every writer struggles with.

I like using a service called Lex. When you get a little bit of writer's block, all you have to do is type '+++' and it will help fill in some of the content. Then, you can go through and self-edit to make sure that it's in your voice and using your tone, and it's not saying anything incorrect – like telling you to eat poisonous mushrooms.

It helps to speed some things up, especially with content like marketing landing pages. It's really helpful to get a first draft out there. Then, you need to make sure that your internal stakeholders are reviewing everything to ensure that it is up to snuff."

If you're outsourcing content production, can you check whether it has been edited adequately or not?

"It's easier today but it is going to get more difficult as the AIs get better, faster, stronger and learn more.

Today, there are a whole bunch of services that you can use to double-check things. ChatGPT uses pretty standard before and after phraseology so, if they haven't edited it, you'll be able to tell. It's less obvious when someone spends hours writing drafts and then feeds ChatGPT with so much information that it takes an hour to kick back some sort of content. That's feeding the dragon in a more comprehensive way to get exactly what you want out of it, but most of us aren't using it to that expert level.

At the moment, it is going to be obvious when content is written with AI because it's pretty elementary compared to something that was written by an expert.

As SEOs, we need to make sure we define what we want out of the AIs as well. We need to know our target audience. We're working closely with the stakeholders so we should know what stage of the funnel we're trying to target and what kind of expertise the reader is likely to have. If you're reaching a CEO as opposed to a tech support person, then you will use different terminology."

Are humans satisfied with reading content that they know has been created by AI or do they want their content to be created by humans?

"Ideally the latter but, in the world we're living in, this technology isn't going away. As marketers, we would be remiss if we were not leveraging it to some degree. Being human, we're also fallible. We're stretched by time, and we're always asked to do more and more and more. Using a little bit of AI to help with that is good.

That's also why there always needs to be an editorial process or somebody making sure that it reads like a human. At the end of the day, you're still selling to a human. For example, adding in a 'What Is…' section is dependent on what you're actually selling to somebody. That's usually pretty amateur and answering those questions is not often going to help you convert in the end."

Are there any specific elements in a text that tend to be created by humans?

"Definitely. Every industry has its own lingo going on, just like SEO. When I take on a new SEO client, I'm not going to bombard them with DA PA, SERP, and all the other words that come as second nature to us.

However, the person you're writing content for wants to see that kind of lingo in there. They understand it and it's their language. Ensuring that kind of language is in there helps it to read properly. If you're reading an SEO article and it doesn't include the things that you're expecting, you begin to suss out whether or not this person's legitimate by the way that they write.

The first step is ensuring that you're using the right terminology within that industry, which is where those experts come from. I'm not an expert. I say that out of the gate with all of my clients. I'm learning about their industry as much as any new person. I come in with a fresh perspective, which is cool, but I need them to make sure that whatever we're writing comes from their perspective, with their knowledge and expertise."

Is it important for every brand to have a set of brand guidelines, to ensure that the tone is consistent across any content that is produced by humans or AI?

"Definitely. This all leads back to traditional marketing. Every brand should have brand guidelines, writing guidelines, or tone documents. When you're a writer, these things are a gift, and you're able to write within these structures. Then, you can layer in SEO structures on top of that, such as ensuring that you have a TL;DR paragraph at the start to satisfy the featured snippet.

That's another thing that we have to teach clients about. Most people don't know what a featured snippet is. That's our language, not theirs. It's our job to help them layer out the content so that it feeds search engines but it also satisfies humans.

In the Semantic Web and the knowledge graph internet that we're all moving towards, especially with SGE, that kind of knowledge is going to be more and more important. Schema, knowledge graphs, and all these things are extremely important to get that prime real estate at the top."

Do you think that schema has peaked, and Google is increasingly comfortable understanding what's on the page without it?

"That idea balances out the automation part of it because schema isn't human. You're marking things up to automate and scale that out into a programmatic SEO approach.

However, schema is still incredibly important because it's the introduction to the knowledge graph. That's the human part of it: building your knowledge graph and building that up for clients as well. You are making sure that you have all those checks and balances throughout the web. Some of them are really boring but that's what we do.

Whether or not we still use the attributes and markup of schema is to be determined in the future, but the act of doing that for the humans searching the web is still going to be important."

What elements of SEO don't require the human touch anymore?

"Internal linking is something that I like to use tools for, and I have a couple of subscriptions. Ahrefs has a lovely tool that is getting better at internal linking, and they have a great tool for meta descriptions as well. They ran a study which showed that Google changes the meta description 60-70% of the time, and it's dependent on the search query.

Excluding meta descriptions completely is not the way to go but automating them to see how they perform out of the gate is really helpful. Then you can start measuring the click-through rate for humans instead of robots."

If you've designed the first couple of lines of text on a page for a featured snippet, could that also be used for the meta description automatically?

"You can use the same text for both, as long as they're both satisfying the search intent for both the page and the keyword that you're targeting. Odds are, Google's going to change it if the user searches for something that's also on the page but isn't part of the meta description. They'll try to pull in that text and make people click on it regardless. We can only control so much, as humans, but we can try to satisfy that as much as possible."

If an SEO is struggling for time, what should they stop doing right now so they can spend more time doing what you suggest in 2024?

"The speed of your site is the most difficult thing to get buy-in on, it's a long play, and Google's changing those Core Web Vitals metrics as well.

If you have time to put in a dev ticket that can sit in the backlog for them to get to at some point (as long as you're not in an extremely competitive market where you need every last inch of room), your site's loading speed can wait for the time being, because there are a lot of other things that you can focus on."

Jess Joyce is an SEO Consultant, and you can find her over at JessJoyce.com.

Keep a human eye on your AI-generated content – with Adelina Bordea

According to Adelina Bordea from Freepik, another key use of your human intuition is your ability to differentiate between AI-generated content and human-generated content.

Adelina says: "Keep a human eye on AI-generated content.

Google has accepted AI as a content generator, but AI can make really big mistakes and it can rephrase the same things over and over again. Sometimes, it will just make things up.

You want to have people proofreading everything and making sure that the content is accurate, it's good for your users, and it suits your product."

Can you get AI to produce the content initially?

"Absolutely. I used to think that Google was not going to accept AI-generated content. Now, though, they are saying, 'it's important to recognise that not all use of automation, including AI generation, is spam. Automation has long been used to generate helpful content, such as sports scores, weather forecasts, and transcripts.'

That's from Google's guidelines, and it applies to more content as well."

Will Google soon get to the point where they're not able to tell whether the content is AI-generated?

"Google has many clues they can use to detect AI-generated content, so I don't know if it won't be able to recognise it anytime soon. I know that AI repeats the same things over and over again, and it says the same phrase using different words. That's not great because it is basically repetition.

For me, I'm using artificial intelligence for my project and it's working very well. However, you have to be very careful with the prompt you give to your AI tool – whether that's Jasper, OpenAI, or whatever. You have to make sure that it's not repeating the same things. I am creating descriptions in different formats for my project and the AI would just say the same things. It wouldn't take into consideration that it's a different format.

You need to be very careful and give that AI tool the right prompt if you want to get good content in exchange. Using the right prompt will improve the quality of the final piece of content."

How do you improve your prompts and what do you need to incorporate into them?

"There are some tricks that work a lot of the time. Sometimes, though – even if you give the right prompt and you've checked it down to the smallest detail – it won't work. In those cases, you can go heading by heading, asking the AI for something very specific. It's like asking for that same content from a person, but much faster.

There are three main things that you can include within your prompts to ensure the quality is as good as possible. First, you have to give the AI a specific role. It will work much better if you ask it to act like a marketing professional or a professional copywriter. Then, you want to set a tone. You can tell it that you want an informal blog post, for example, or an informal article.

Then, you can give it the structure that you want the AI to follow. That's something that you should investigate prior to giving that prompt. Create a final structure and give that to the AI tool. Then, you can work on the final draft that it gives back to you. The role, the tone, and the structure are the three main things that you should give to an AI tool.

If you asked for a blog post and the AI is not quite giving you what you want, you can tell it to correct that issue or keep something particular in mind that it has done incorrectly. For example, you can tell it that the title it has used doesn't work for local SEO, and explain how you want it to be done differently.

To make sure that the content is accurate and correct, you need to ensure that the AI has a professional proofreader, or a person who does whatever you are writing about – or at least has specific information on the topic."

How do you ensure that the AI is structuring the content properly?

"You can give the AI a specific title, heading 2, heading 3, heading 4, etc., on that particular topic. That way, if the first draft doesn't convince you, you can tell it to change the content under specific headings or include different information in specific places within the article. Then you can go over it again.

You're probably going to be targeting a keyword phrase with your content, so you want to ensure that the content is relevant, it's targeting the right audience, and it's using the right phraseology. If you've researched the questions and keyword phrases that you want to target, you can give those to the AI. Instead of just giving it one topic and asking it to produce the whole article, break it down into subheadings and have more control over what it includes.

I still like to manually add the keywords to the article myself. I've tried telling the AI to add them in a natural way, but it's not natural at all. I do that myself and I work on the links, the anchor text, and all the rest. AI is a very powerful tool, though, because it allows you to create that content in 10% of the time that it would have taken before."

When you're editing, do you ask AI to make those changes, or do you take the nearly finished article from AI and finish it off yourself?

"I take the nearly finished piece and then add extra keywords, the anchor text that I want to use for the links, and everything else.

I don't give it back to the AI again because it usually does the job worse than I would do it myself."

How do you incorporate EEAT into AI-assisted content?

"There are different ways of doing it. Firstly, the author should always be someone who is actually a professional on that topic. For example, I am an SEO professional and I'm the copywriter for my articles, so it's 100% real.

As the author of that article, I'm going to incorporate the basic EEAT elements into that. I'm going to link everything on my profile that reveals to Google that I'm a professional who is dedicated to SEO. I'm going to keep providing my experience – because AI only gave me a draft. I'm then going to be finishing that and giving my personal experience and knowledge.

That should happen with every article that you write. Have a specific author for each topic. That will show Google that you are using AI, but you have real people behind every piece that you create, taking care of that content.

No matter what type of business you are in, you should be able to do this yourself. You will usually have people who are specialised in a specific topic as authors. If you are a coffee shop, you can have a barista as the writer of your articles. They are professionals with knowledge and expertise. Equally, you can be an SEO professional or an IT technician and have an online profile.

As long as Google can find out that you are a real person and that you have experience and authority, then you are going to lend credibility to that content."

What's the best way of demonstrating that you are a real person with authority?

"As part of your author bio, you want to link to an author page on your own website – and have social profiles that are linked to that as well. It's social signals, website signals, the author description, and any mentions on the internet about you as a professional in that sector. All of that works.

Ideally, if you want to be seen as a professional in your niche, you want to get out there and appear in other places beyond your own website. You can include those mentions on your own website, of course, but your website should also have different mentions on other blogs, and on other social media. Social media is a very powerful signal for SEO.

There are people who are already very public about their profession and what they do, and they have more authority. However, it doesn't mean that you – as a person who is starting a career in a certain environment – can't do that as well. Google actually understands that smaller profiles are worthy as well. Your LinkedIn profile, for example, is a very powerful tool for Google."

Can you format the About section in your LinkedIn profile to increase the likelihood that Google will incorporate it into the knowledge panel? Does writing in the third person help?

"That's something that I've never really thought about. My About section is written in the first person because, for me, LinkedIn is also a tool for finding jobs as a freelancer. I would rather have a person reach out to me through that platform, instead of through Google, in this case.

I think it depends. What I do know is that Google is not taking my description, so it may have something to do with writing in the third person. I do have an introductory paragraph about me as a professional on another website, and that's written in the third person, but that's not appearing either. I think I'm just not famous enough to have a description on Google yet."

If an SEO is struggling for time, what should they stop doing right now so they can spend more time doing what you suggest in 2024?

"Keep that human eye on the AI – and don't stop doing that because we don't know what is going to happen with AI in the end. Right now, Google is happy with it – or at least tolerates it and is trying to make it part of one of its own products.

However, you should keep your content as original as possible. AI is helping us make things faster, but keep that human eye and don't leave it to run by itself."

Adelina Bordea is SEO Team Leader at Freepik Company as well as a Freelance Consultant, and you can find her over on LinkedIn.

2 INTRODUCING AI

Stay ahead of the game by embracing AI – with Nitin Manchanda

Although the first chapter emphasised the need to retain your human touch, we can't ignore the elephant in the room – AI is changing many aspects of SEO, fast. That's the message that Nitin Manchanda from Botpresso would like to share with you.

Nitin says: "Embrace AI and stay ahead of the game.

AI is becoming more and more important for SEO, and any other marketing channels for that matter. It gives businesses the tools and insights they need to stay competitive in the digital landscape. At Botpresso, we're using AI for data analysis, content production, optimization, translation – you name it. We do everything with the help of AI, and it gives us 10 times more efficiency. We're also writing a lot of Python scripts to solve complex SEO problems.

Businesses can leverage all of these opportunities and much more. AI is evolving, and you should embrace that."

Do SEOs need to use AI to make themselves more efficient?

"Absolutely. In whatever you're doing right now, you will see patterns. Wherever you see patterns – in data analysis, producing content, translating content – you can think about using technology. It brings a lot of efficiencies – and it's cost-effective as well.

If you're paying a content writer 100 euros to write a content piece for you, you can probably do that at half the cost or less with the help of machines like AI. It's also efficient. You can produce a lot of content in a single click, which could take months or even years to create manually."

What is the best data to analyse with AI, and what software do you use?

"If you want to compare your crawl data to that of your competitors, you can feed it into an AI tool. You can train the AI to understand that data and give you insights. This is the main thing we are using it for. You can give the AI that crawl data and ask it to identify the differences between them and the strengths of one brand versus the other. That's the data analysis I'm talking about.

However, you feed in any kind of data. You can feed in data about the events that might be affecting your seasonality and ask AI to give you a forecast, for example. For everything that used to take a lot of time, where you were looking at hundreds of parameters, you can now just feed that data into an AI tool to help you understand what is happening and how it could affect things. It does the magic for you.

Currently, we use a lot of software for different applications. For data analysis, we prefer to write our own Python scripts because that gives us flexibility. Right now, there are people in my team with zero engineering experience who are all engineers with the help of ChatGPT. They're all writing Python scripts to solve complex SEO and data analysis problems."

How much involvement should AI have in the creation of content?

"I have been doing this for many years now. AI is still new, but I started content production at scale 6/7 years ago. I started with normal templates, then conditional templates, then we used a machine called RosaeNLG (a natural language generation machine), and then we started using more advanced technologies.

Now, ChatGPT is definitely my go-to tool when it comes to content production, but I'm also using some more sophisticated and advanced tools like Jasper and Writesonic. These tools are great if you prefer a nice-looking UI and a more structured way of producing your content.

I've been using AI for content translation as well. I have been using DeepL, which is a brilliant translator that's 100 times better than Google Translate. Now, we are also using ChatGPT because it gives the flexibility to train the machine. I can give it the content and tell it that I need a more expanded version, along with the translation. I have everything in one place. However, it does need some manual intervention to train the machine and control the outcome."

Do you still need to have human involvement in that content creation process?

"You definitely do because, at the end of the day, it's a machine. The machine doesn't understand a lot of things, like your brand guidelines. It is just generating content based on whatever data it has processed and spinning another version of that.

Ethical considerations are also very important. For example, I'm living in Germany and data privacy is a big topic here. AI can give you a lot of sensitive information, and how you use that can create problems.

On top of that, when you are writing this content, you are not only writing for machines. Gone are the days when you were writing content for the machines and that would make Googlebot happy. Now, the content should be more user-centric. If a user is happy, you don't have to worry about making the search engine bot happy, because they will be happy already.

You definitely need to include personalisation and a human touch – and ethical considerations and data privacy are also part of that. To do this, we have someone who understands the product we are writing content about sitting on top of the process and controlling everything that is generated with the help of AI.

It's all about the initial quality of your prompts, ensuring that the content is sticking to the brand guidelines, and making sure that the writing style is correct to begin with. Then, you should have a knowledgeable specialist to review that content and tweak it before it is published. We published an ebook on this recently (which is available at Botpresso.com/AI-prompts-for-SEO). It covers a lot of the great prompts that are working like magic for us, and much more besides."

A direct translation often won't read fluently to a local audience, and it can miss important context, so should a local specialist review that content as well?

"Again, you should follow that same process. There should be someone involved who is a domain expert – a native speaker, who understands how people in that location think and communicate about what you are offering. That person should be involved in the whole process, from the beginning. They can then tell you that what you would call buses in Germany are sometimes called coaches in the UK, and football in the UK is a different game altogether from football in the US.

With the help of a local expert, you can train the machines to understand these nuances. Then, your machines will produce or translate content that is of a much better quality than it would be without that training. Once the content is produced, the domain expert can take a look at it again and give their final approval.

When we were using DeepL, it was working pretty well for most European languages. Interestingly, though, there were languages that it was not as good at. English to French translation was not that great, and neither was English to Swedish. For English to German, English to Italian, and English to Spanish, it was close to perfect. The native speakers who were reviewing the content were happy and they were hardly making any changes.

However, our French native speaker was disappointed by the content that DeepL produced in the beginning. We trained it, and we got better at the process as well."

How are search engine algorithms evolving with AI, and what do SEOs need to do to take advantage of this?

"The SERP has been changing forever. I can't remember a year where we didn't see significant changes in the SERP, and that will continue to happen. Now, with SGE, users can ask for something (particularly informational intent content) and get the answer in the SERP itself. They don't have to click anywhere.

I think this is more of a problem for search engine bots, and how they show this content, than it is a problem for SEOs. They want to make money and, if they provide the information without the user having to click anywhere, how do they make money? They want to keep the links there – both the paid links and the organic links.

The businesses that are serving more informational intent, like blogs, will probably suffer because most of their content will be available without any research. I used to go and do detailed research on things like what the maternity policy for a company should look like, or how the RICE model of prioritisation works. Now I just go to ChatGPT, give a command or two, and get the answer I'm looking for. That makes life very easy. Before, I would probably have been given five links to different websites but that has now reduced to zero.

However, when it comes to transactional queries, I'm still going to Google and searching and transacting in the same way that I was before."

Is it still important to publish blog posts and pages targeting long-tail queries to gain that initial traffic?

"I think you should definitely still be doing that. Look at how the SERP is changing. Along with the detailed answers that the search engines are giving, they're also providing links to where that content was extracted from. In that case, you will gain brand visibility. If someone is searching for something and the answer appears, and it was covered in your blog, you can be mentioned there. People would know that they got that answer and it was covered by you. That is brand visibility.

Also, if you're afraid of what is happening with SGE, you can block the AI bots from using your content. Right now, I wouldn't advise doing that for transactional businesses, but more news-centric businesses might consider it.

Currently, I'm working with a business that talks about everything to do with startups (funding, news, etc.), and they have a lot of content that is behind a paywall. If all of that content is accessed by AI crawlers, and it's being pulled and published for free, then their revenue model will be compromised."

If an SEO is struggling for time, what should they stop doing right now so they can spend more time doing what you suggest in 2024?

"Start with the basics and try to understand how AI works. Try to understand different types of prompts (and you can find all the information you need in my book). Then, you also need to play with different machines that can help you do what you want to do.

ChatGPT is pretty awesome, and so is Perplexity AI. Then, if you want to go with more sophisticated solutions, you can try Jasper or Writesonic for content production.

It's important to understand the SEO use cases that you want to try. You can't just get comfortable with ChatGPT; you need to understand what you want to solve with it. Once you have those solutions, then select the AI tools or platforms from those that are out there, and the hundreds of new platforms that are coming. Try those tools, train the machines, tune them, and test them out. You won't get the ideal outcome on the first try, so iterate and refine.

Then, it's very important to keep ethical considerations and data privacy in your process, especially when you're producing content. A machine is producing content for you, so it will not think about your user. They do not know what users are looking for. Also, those machines might produce some content that you might not want to show on your website for data privacy reasons. Make sure that is also covered."

Nitin Manchanda is Founder and Chief SEO Consultant at Botpresso, and you can find him over at Botpresso.com.

Prepare for the AI-fuelled duplication epidemic – with Billie Geena

Billie Geena from Uptake would like to add a warning though – don't run full-speed into the unknown with AI without being aware of the potential consequences.

Billie says: "Prepare for the duplication epidemic caused by AI content generation.

"We've all seen how AI has become the lifeblood of digital content; everyone's using it now. It's now getting to a point where the AI is getting dumber, according to many tests. That's because it's using the same data source to generate content for different websites; the data sets haven't been updated since 2021, but when they do, they'll be flooded with potentially incorrect AI-generated content.

It will create a big cycle of slightly dumber/more misinformed content based on an old data source. The more this happens, the more we'll see a mass duplication issue, which we'll need to treat like an external cannibalisation project. Everyone's creating the same content on the same topics, and we'll need to rein that in at some point."

Is it Google's job to deal with duplication?

"Yes, but if everyone's applying the same tactics and not enough people are creating unique and helpful content, then some of that duplicated content is going to rank.

We often see lesser information appearing highly in Google search. At some point, it needs to become an SEO's responsibility. Otherwise, it will become a mass project for us all and we'll no longer be worrying that SEO is dead because we'll be so busy trying to fix the quality of our clients' content. It's better to future-proof yourself from an early stage and generate helpful human content.

I'm not 100% against AI (it's very helpful) but, if you're creating something for an expert or anyone within a specific industry, it needs to have real insight to still be successful."

What should and shouldn't AI be used for?

"I use AI to generate outlines and for generic pieces of information/facts that aren't going to change massively. I will get AI to generate some content for me, but it would then be edited by a human, and have insight from a human added.

Try to include, 'This was my experience doing this work/using this product' or 'This is why the product was created/how it was created/who it's for.' Adding those real insights that only a business owner or someone who works within that niche could have is what will set you aside from generic AI content."

What should an SEO do if their website is filled with generic, bland AI content?

"I wouldn't recommend removing the content completely because it can still be beneficial. Depending on when you started using AI and how successfully it's been implemented, you could have generated a lot of backlinks. That content piece may have been successful at some point, so you wouldn't want to get rid of it.

It's about optimizing it further and going back to the SEO basics. Do your research, look at what your competitors are doing, identify the extra insights you can provide, and determine how you can make your content better than what it's competing with. However, you need to be a human to be able to see that.

There are all sorts of tools and checklists out there that can give ideas for what you can do to improve content and make it stand out from other AI content, but it needs that human aspect. It's really important that we bring that back. For an SEO practitioner, the fantastic thing is that the people who don't consider SEO best practice from the onset are the ones using AI for everything. That could be category work, product pages, B2B pages, SaaS websites, blog content, etc.

Such a wide spread of content is now being diluted by mass AI generation.

In a year or so, we're going to be very busy fixing this and it's going to be interesting to see that breaking point when we get there."

Are there tools for identifying which pages on your website are too similar to other pages that are out there?

"Yes and no. There are tools for identifying whether a page has been generated with AI but they're not great. I've been testing quite a few and I've literally written content myself, using Grammarly, and it's convinced that it's AI content. They're very hit-and-miss.

We've had tools for a very long time, but there's nothing I've come across that can do it en masse. You'd need a massive web scraper to actually be able to do that, and you could be breaching Google's guidelines if you're trying to scrape content at scale like that.

There are also plagiarism tools out there, which have been used by universities and schools forever. They're very handy for running a piece of content and seeing how many other pages it matches and how much of it appears to be plagiarised. There are several steps to it at the moment. Hopefully, some very smart person out there will come up with a solution."

Can automated tools mislabel your content as being written by AI when it's not?

"That is a concern, and I don't think there's anything smart enough to be able to teach that at the moment. With AI, we're learning to do certain things. If I see an article that's really long and has a conclusion at the end, my brain automatically assumes that it was written by AI. That is not a set rule, of course, because lots of people end with a conclusion.

If we're not 100% able to identify AI ourselves, it's going to be really hard to create a tool that can reliably do it for us."

How can EEAT help ensure that your content is better than the competition?

"Again, it's about adding that human experience. Talk about who the product is for, why it helps, and how it was made. Bring in things like how you've used it and specific use cases for it. That will add experience and trust in the product.

A lot of people have found 'helpful content' and EEAT stressful because Google's not 100% clear about how that works within their guidelines. They are creating these algorithms and talking about them across so many niches that they can't go into much detail.

However, if you take a look at the Google Search Quality Raters guidelines, they show examples of EEAT. It's not a secret sauce or anything, and it's not telling you what you need to do, but they've got several niches and examples. It's very easy to access that information and apply it to your own strategies. If that's what they're telling their raters to look for, it's definitely going to be helpful for us."

How can you generate unique content ideas using client data?

"Go on Google Search Console and Google Analytics and look at live data that's trending. You could also look at what's being searched on your website. Has something started being searched one day that's come out of nowhere? Search that, have a look on social media, and try and figure out the reasons why this has suddenly become successful. Potentially, you can start generating content about that topic yourself.

That way, you can stay ahead of what's happening and be much more reactive with your SEO. SEO is often seen as a long-term strategy, and link-building and digital PR are more reactive. Really, we can use the same research tools they use to create data stories to generate content. We can examine why something is popular, talk about it, and then try and dominate by optimizing the products and category pages and creating blog content about whatever the trend is. There's so much opportunity within the live data we get from a client.

This also works on a seasonality basis. If you know something becomes really popular once a year, start generating content and creating hype for that."

How do you take these trending concepts and turn them into pieces of content?

"Let's say you're Lush, the soap shop, and you have a shower gel called Snow Fairy that comes out every single Christmas. You know this is one of your most popular products and there's going to be a lot of data there. It's going to be successful, and people are going to be searching for that term.

What you can do is start generating additional hype. You can create additional content around that topic so that you stand out and don't get caught in the mass cannibalisation that's happening outside of your website.

You're a big brand, you're a leader in the industry, and a lot of businesses try and duplicate what you create. There are candles with the same scent as this shower gel, and other shower gels too. You're going to rank reasonably well because of your brand name and branded terms, but people are selling these duplicate products year-round while you only sell them at one time of year.

You need to think about how your content shows that you are more than just a brand name. Talk about why this was created, why your product is better than the rest, and what people's experiences with it are. Bring in reviews – because you're a big brand and people love this cult classic product, there are lots of reviews. You're not just talking about this product; you're talking about the experience that comes with the product. It shows that you are the owners, the experts, and the wave maker for this thing.

Anyone can talk about a product. Instead of just saying, 'This is a glittery, pink marshmallow-scented shower gel', you can tell the user everything. You can tell them it's vegan and cruelty-free and you can tell them how loved it is. It's about building a bigger story. It's not just saying what you do, it's showing what you do. Then, you're going to rank better."

If an SEO is struggling for time, what should they stop doing right now so they can spend more time doing what you suggest in 2024?

"Stop worrying about certain rich results like knowledge panels. I'm seeing a lot of demand for (and a lot of SEOs promising) people to get a knowledge panel for their name. Not everyone deserves a knowledge panel for their name. Susan, who lives five doors down and walks her dog at the park, does not need a knowledge panel.

SEOs started to develop the attitude that anyone can achieve them. It's not something that needs to be sold right now. A knowledge panel should belong to notable figures, and a lot of time and energy is being spent on these, and other rich results. There are many more beneficial things that are going to benefit your client quicker.

It depends on the client. If you're working on someone's personal consulting site, they probably should try and build out their online portfolio. However, the owner of Claire's Pet Shop probably doesn't need it."

Billie Geena is an SEO Consultant, and you can find her over at Uptake.Agency.

Stop worrying about the future and start optimizing for it – with Jake Gauntley

As Billie emphasised, you can't expect AI to solve all of your content production woes automatically. But as Jake Gauntley from KINESSO shares, that doesn't mean that you shouldn't be harnessing AI's power.

Jake says: "It's okay to not know exactly how generative AI and SGE are going to change the long-term future of search – because none of us really do. Google have already admitted that they are acting boldly and reimagining their core search product.

However, while we are stepping into the unknown, you should still be forward-thinking about the future of the data you use and how your search strategy will be impacted."

What's likely to be impacted by SGE initially?

"A common theme with organic search over the last 5-10 years is declining organic click-through rates. If you think about how SERPs have evolved since the early days of 10 blue links, there's always been a decline in traffic going to sites through organic links – whether through increased paid spots or search engines catering to user intent as soon as they land on that SERP. Declining click-through rates and a decline in organic traffic aren't anything new. SEO, as a discipline, has evolved and adapted from that.

This isn't one of the 'SEO is dead' scenarios which seem to happen almost every month. We need to think about how we adapt, and how our strategy adapts as well. SEOs have a lot of very useful skills that provide benefits outside of SEO. When you're working with clients, think about how you can adapt those skills to show benefits outside of search, as well as trying to get traffic from search itself."

Is optimizing to appear in the number one AI-driven answer different to optimizing for the number one SERP result?

"To win in organic search right now, you're not necessarily optimizing a page for a keyword; you're optimizing the digital experience for users. Over the last 3-5 years, with Google algorithm updates, there has been this shift toward providing holistic optimization of your website. That can be through page experience and site speed, providing genuinely useful, in-depth content, making sure that the media in your content is tailored towards user intent – or even off-site signals like building out a positive brand perception through digital PR.

All of these holistic signals come together to improve search rankings, whether that be in the classic blue links or within generative AI results. Realistically, that's what Google and other search engines have shown that they like to rank highly. It would be quite a significant shift if that were to change within generative AI results."

If your brand does get featured within an AI-driven answer, how do you track that?

"This is another area in which we need to adapt. The data that we have used in the past to talk about SEO and benchmark performance is not going to be the same within these generative AI answers.

If someone types a question and someone else types the same question in a slightly different way, it might give a slightly different answer, which might be pulled from a different source. It's going to be really hard to track performance within those results over time in the way that we've done it historically. Although it fluctuates, classic keyword rank tracking is a little bit more stable; it's just 10 blue links, not generative AI content.

It's going to be interesting to see how the SEO industry adapts to that – and I don't have the answer. We won't know until we start getting that data through third-party suppliers or even Google themselves. Google haven't been open and honest about the kind of data we are going to get from SGE, so we're stepping into the unknown there as well.

One of the USPs of these generative AI features within search is that it can be a conversation with the user. They can ask things that are bespoke to their need, so everyone is going to be getting slightly different answers. Tracking that is obviously going to be a big job because there are going to be so many variations. I do not envy the person whose job it is to try and come up with the right data there, but good luck to them."

Do SEOs need to start having focus groups and direct conversations with users to understand the funnels that they take?

"It would be a really interesting concept to have people come together in a focus group, give them something that they need to do in search, and see the differences between the information that they get.

Obviously, that might not be a cost-effective way of doing things, but it will be interesting to see how the information that people get differs, and the brands that they see through those experiences within SGE."

How do you compare your performance with AI and SGE to how you used to perform on a more traditional SERP?

"The value of position one with SGE is not going to be the same as the value of position one pre-SGE. If you're still ranking position one on a ranking report, but you're getting significantly less traffic, there is going to need to be a pre- and post-comparison there. The data is not like for like.

If you still rank one but your traffic has decreased, you could pull a CTR curve for your rankings and see just how much your click-through rate has decreased over time. That's something that we've done for clients and businesses, even pre-SGE, when new SERP features get added for a keyword that is really important to them.

We would then be able to show them that their ranking may have remained stable, but the average click-through rate for a set of keywords might have dropped. Although things are looking good on paper, because of things that are outside of our control, the click-through rate has dropped. You can show them the data to back that up."

Can SEOs be doing anything now to future-proof their site for appearing in AI-driven results?

"The whole strategy of being an authority on a topic, and providing information about a whole topic or entity, is still going to be important. Show Google that you know what you're talking about and the information that you have is worth being shown in any type of result. The tactics that have come out of things like the helpful content update and EEAT are still going to be very important.

However, there is an additional step as well. You need to future-proof yourself for organic search success, which is always going to include making sure you have the content, making sure you're doing great with your tech SEO and UX, you have the links, etc. Now, though, you also need to think about how your search strategy can change to take customers outside of a search interaction with your brand. Then, you can own that customer interaction through different channels."

Can SEOs utilise GA4 for all of their analytics or do you favour other analytics packages for understanding the user journey?

"GA4 is what it is. I'm not a huge fan of it right now, but a lot of brands and sites are stuck with it because of their historical data and the ties that they have. I don't think any analytics package is perfect. GA4 has its flaws and that's fine; we'll get by with what we have.

In terms of understanding that customer journey and future-proofing, you want to start gathering your zero-party or first-party data through whatever channel people come to your website. Then, you want to be taking more ownership of using that data so that you can have direct contact with your customers through your CRM.

If you've created a positive brand experience through your search strategy, and you can give your users some sort of value when they land on your site, they will want to give you their email address or whatever it be. You can cut out the middleman of organic search and invest in trying to foster that relationship directly with them instead."

Are customers going to rely on chatbots and other forms of online communication, or will email still be key over the next few years?

"Chatbots are interesting because there could be a lot of potential there, if they can get the technology to provide a really authentic and genuine experience. From my experience with chatbots, I've typically not been able to do what I've wanted.

If a brand invests in something like chatbots, but it's not done well, that can break the relationship between the user and the brand because you're not providing a great experience there. However, as we've seen, it's changing so quickly. There is a possibility that those AI-led chatbot experiences could be a lot more authentic pretty soon.

You need to think about what the customer prefers, and a lot of bigger brands have the different options that users are looking for. There are more and more brands operating through WhatsApp, including big companies. Even things like TV shows and radio stations now have the option to contact them through WhatsApp. Organisations and companies need to adapt to what a user wants rather than forcing them to use one form of communication or another.

If you have the infrastructure in place to offer all possible options, that's great, but you should at least be offering the specific options your users want."

If an SEO is struggling for time, what should they stop doing right now so they can spend more time doing what you suggest in 2024?

"As I said at the very beginning, stop worrying if you don't know how AI is going to change your SEO strategy and what the future looks like. It's okay. The industry doesn't really know either. The more that you stop worrying about that, and take ownership of the fact that you don't know, the more you will start to think about what it might look like and what you can do to try and future-proof yourself.

That gives you the power to then make decisions based on what you do know or the assumptions that you've made. Hopefully, that takes at least some of the worry off your plate."

Jake Gauntley is Senior SEO Account Director at KINESSO, and you can find him over at JakeGauntley.com.

Consider how AI will impact user behaviour – with Annika Haataja

According to Annika Haataja from Seeker Digital, one of the key questions that you should be asking prior to implementing the use of AI in your workflow is "How might AI impact user behaviour?"

Annika says: "Consider how AI can impact the different stages of the user/buyer journey and search intent, moving forward.

Search is going through a massive transition, and we're experiencing more personalisation, which has been part of SEO for a long time now. As we're moving towards AI searches and AI assisting users to find the right solutions, we need to consider how that search behaviour itself will change moving forward.

We often look at the user/buyer journey in three core stages: awareness, consideration, and decision. All of these stages could be impacted by AI in the future – especially looking at Google's plans. AI isn't going anywhere. It will continue to become more and more prominent in search. You need to get ready for it and you need to start understanding it from the user's point of view."

How do you analyse AI's role in the different stages of your users' purchase journey and search intent?

"A lot of these AI tools (such as SGE) are still in the testing phase. A lot of

SEOs are using them to figure out how their search queries are showing up and what different elements appear in the search results. That's going to be one part of your content research and content strategy building.

When doing keyword research, we carry out SERP analysis to understand what Google thinks the user intent of the keyword is, and what types of results they're showing. Now, you have to do the same with AI searches. There are a lot of layout shifts happening, almost daily. Also, because of personalisation, different people see different results and different elements in the result pages. You need to understand what's available and what you can see with things like SGE.

BARD and Bing are showing similar results. They give a bit more informational content in the synopses at the top. You might have links to blogs or other informational articles, product descriptions, product listings, and perhaps even product suggestions that might be relevant. It's quite full-on for the user.

Some of these buyer journey stages, awareness and consideration stages in particular, will take a bit longer on Google. Instead of doing that on the website by consuming your content, these two stages will often be conducted on the SERPs themselves. You might see an impact on click-through rates, especially for certain types of queries – which could actually relate to higher conversion rates. You will potentially have less traffic to your site, but the research has already happened before the user lands on the site, so you might see better conversions."

Will SEOs have less control over the intent they are serving, as AI is able to pick what it wants from different pieces of content?

"Absolutely. What's going to be even more important now is to try and serve those different user intents with your content. A lot of people focus on commercial or transactional keywords, which is great. However, which keywords are definitely commercial? When you do that search with SGE or BARD, your intent might not be very clear.

You might search, 'I want to buy a raincoat' because we're moving towards conversational language. However, you might not want to buy it straight away, even though your intent says that you do. You might be trying to find information, and you might even stop the journey completely. You might decide it's not the right time of year and you don't need one.

The results that we get from AI combine different types of information, whether it's informational, commercial, or even navigational searches. If you search for 'Nike sneakers', you might get different sites selling Nike sneakers. However, when you click on a result, you might not even get to the page; there might be a pop-up. Things are moving around a lot.

Make sure to target those different user search intents for bottom-of-funnel, middle-of-funnel, and top-of-funnel keywords. It's not enough to just optimize your product descriptions. You want to be the result when it comes to the synopses as well through blog articles providing assisting information for the user to help them make that decision and compare different features. It's a holistic way of writing content."

Will AI be able to deliver all aspects of the customer buying journey?

"Yes. It's important to consider the future when it comes to data as well. Previously, when looking at transactional queries, it has been quite easy to determine which keywords are transactional. Now, you need to branch out. You can't just trust the data that you see in the SERPs. You also need to analyse the data after the consumer has been to your site. Combining data from AI searches in tools like Keyword Hero, you can determine the click-through rates and conversion rates for certain keywords as a combination of different metrics. Analyse that data and use it to build a better content strategy.

As SEOs, we now have different information and different data which can be utilised for content strategy. Even when you do searches on SGE or Bing, they give you suggested follow-ups. When you read those long-tail queries you might be able to determine a wider strategy for your content on that topic. What kind of article should you be writing? What does the AI consider important? Therefore, what do they assume the user will consider important?

You can learn a lot from these searches, even though they're not perfect. When you search for something in BARD, the synopses is quite a good overlay of the different features that you should be looking at for these sorts of searches where the user is trying to purchase a product. The products they offer might be from an article which lists the best products of 2023 for that specific category, without actually analysing whether they are the best for a certain reason.

However, search is changing, and all these different large language models are improving as well. You need to keep up. You need to understand how they find the information. When you write content for different user stages and intents, use clear language and make sure that the AI understands it – as well as the user. Structure it so that it is easy to find those nuggets of information that will be a bit more prominent in these synopses.

Creating helpful content is never going to go out of fashion. It's going to be even more important moving forward. To get your article to be top of SGE and get that link, create really helpful and unique content. Google has been giving us these hints for years now."

Will Google Perspectives be a great opportunity over the coming year?

"Definitely. Perspectives will expand your opportunities when you're writing and building content. Working with influencers in your industry can help boost your EEAT and showcase that you are a prominent brand in your field. If you work with influencers who have a lot of prominence and visibility, it can only help you.

To gain visibility through Perspectives (or any other important area, like Google Discover) you need to branch out from traditional searches and understand how other searches work. We're moving towards a more multi-modal search. Images and videos are going to be more and more important to enable you to stand out and showcase your expertise."

Are more traditional searchers going to be comfortable using AI?

"It's difficult to say. There have been ups and downs with adoption, and some surprising results as well. Younger generations have been quite open to AI searches, even though they are relatively new and can potentially provide false information. Usually, younger users are against that. However, studies have shown that 18 to 25-year-olds are quite open to these searches.

As an SEO, if you don't use AI search that doesn't mean your user won't. When you're optimising for AI searches, you're not only doing it for the AI. Even your traditional search will be better when you optimize your content and make sure it is helpful for different user behaviours and user intent. You're not going to lose in traditional search; you're still going to do great.

However, when you look at these different metrics, you need to understand what the impact will be. What will your KPIs be? Will you be focusing on click-through rates? Will you be focusing on conversion rates? What will your new benchmarks be? Even if AI searches don't immediately become as popular as they were originally predicted to be, you never know what will happen in five years."

What does this mean for content production strategies and the type of content that SEOs produce moving forward?

"As we mentioned before, looking at the different buyer journeys and how to satisfy the user intent for those is key. When you're doing research, you need to branch out and make sure that you're analysing longer-tail conversational keywords as well.

When you're looking at content strategies, it's not only from a content production point-of-view. Can you utilise this for link-building in the future, for example? Searches on BARD or Bing often serve results from listicle articles as well. How do you make sure that you're visible in these articles, get a link, and get a mention? How does your content strategy support that?

Obviously, everything is connected: content, UX, links, and technical. When you try to optimize for AI searches, the different elements of SEO will help each other. When you're creating great product content, you want to boost that with product schema. When you're creating assets or informational content, that can boost your digital PR and link-building efforts. The basics of SEO won't change massively. It's just where we focus our attention and how we can become more strategic."

If an SEO is struggling for time, what should they stop doing right now so they can spend more time doing what you suggest in 2024?

"Some SEOs chase for 100% technical site health, which can be great. It is especially great for when you're starting and trying to learn SEO and figure out what optimization does and how it improves your site.

The key thing is to consider what your competitive advantage is. You might have a very strong brand, a very strong link profile, or very strong content. Analyse your key advantage and figure out how to leverage that.

With content, you can do really well even if you don't have a strong brand or the perfect link profile. Content can help improve your conversion rates. Links won't improve conversions as much and a strong brand builds trust but, with content, you can drive conversions. In 2024, having a strong content strategy is where the money is. Focus on that."

Annika Haataja is SEO Director at Seeker Digital, and you can find her over at Seeker.Digital.

3 AI TECHNOLOGY

Familiarise yourself with the capabilities and limitations of large language models – with Bastian Grimm

Just as we need to get into the nuts and bolts of SEO, we also need to take the time to understand the technology that powers AI, as Bastian Grimm from PeakAce explains.

Bastian says: "Get familiarised with large language models.

This is one of the foundational elements of AI. Marketers need to understand how they work and what capabilities they have, but also what limitations they have, so they can become more efficient and utilise them in the best way possible."

How would you summarise the way that large language models work?

"Essentially, it's a huge amount of data that has been put into a specific type of database, and with that data, you can fulfil certain types of tasks. For example, ChatGPT is an interface for a large language model provided by OpenAI.

It's important to understand that these models don't write anything. They have training data and, based on that training data, they predict the likelihood of what's supposed to happen next. This is how they generate text.

If you give the model a task through prompting (formulating something via the interface), there is no creative magic happening. Based on the data that has been ingested in the training process, the model simply creates a new output."

What should and shouldn't LLMs be used for?

"There's a whole lot of new tech around AI, including on the generative AI side, and it's moving extremely fast. The biggest issue is that a lot of the stuff that's currently being shown off is predominantly in a beta state. Most of it is not really production-ready.

People are fascinated by the topic (myself included) and there are a lot of gains to be found already. On the other hand, we need to be cautious. Things are changing fast and what is currently there has limitations.

Say you task the model with creating a piece of text around the Audi A3. The Audi A3 has different features in different countries. In Germany, it might have different dimensions, or it might come with a different default package than it does in the UK or France. If you just task the model with producing a piece of content around that, then you might end up with mixed facts. The dimensions might be wrong, or the default pricing might be wrong, for example.

It's extremely important to fact-check, double-check, and triple-check the output. It can be used for research, and it can be used for drafting things but it's by no means meant to produce content without double-checking. That is one of the biggest misconceptions with ChatGPT, Jasper, or any other model right now."

If your prompts are higher quality, do you need to fact-check less?

"You can increase the quality, but errors will still happen. The model is predicting things and predictions can be wrong.

Using the Google search generative experience (the AI-based snippet on top of the search results), I was inputting queries about tech companies. I asked, 'How many unicorns are there in France?', and it said, '27'. When I gave it a slightly different prompt for the same question it said, '36'. This is what we call a hallucination.

The issue is that the model doesn't know. There is no exact number and there is no precise data source that says exactly how many unicorn companies are in France. Therefore, it's trying to 'guesstimate' what the right answer could be. That is very dangerous. That was a soft example, but a lot of important research relies on information being accurate, especially from big companies like Google. You have to be mindful and cautious about blindly trusting that info.

On the other hand, they're fantastic for speeding up certain processes and tasks that you're doing in your day-to-day. If you are doing research, you could now use a large language model where before you would have needed to go to 10/20/30 different sources. You still have to check it, but you would have needed to check your 20 sources as well. In that regard, you're becoming more efficient.

We have a huge client that does corporate training within their organisation, and they previously had to do recordings in person, in a studio. It's expensive, it takes time, the person needs to be there, etc. Now, they're doing it with an AI avatar. They recorded the speaker once and recorded their voice, so they have voice samples from previous trainings. Now they only need to produce scripts and the AI avatar is going to be in the video.

It's even cooler because they're a multilingual organisation. With AI, they can scale that because they just use a different avatar or voiceover and they have it in French, Spanish, etc. Some people are not as fluent in English as others, and this helps to ensure that their experience is included and onboarded. There are already massive gains to be found in terms of efficiency and even satisfaction."

Can using a tool like Jasper be more effective than using ChatGPT natively?

"It depends on the use case.

It's also worth noting that there are different large language models as well – like Neuroflash which is popular in the German region – and they all have different training and different types of feedback mechanisms. Some are better suited to certain types of tasks than others. Med-PaLM is a large language model specifically for pharmaceutical and medical information. It is much more accurate in those areas, but it has only been trained on that kind of content. It couldn't give you an answer about the best chess strategy, for example.

Having specific models for specific tasks does make sense but we're currently using large language models for a lot of things they are not meant to be used for. In the future, those models may start to rely on third-party tools through APIs or a different type of architecture so that they can then pull data from other sources when they're not confident enough to properly answer a question.

There are a ton of smaller tools right now, which is mainly because they are trying to solve certain specific tasks. As an SEO, this is great, especially if you're on the freelance or consulting side. You can use these tools without having to spend tons of time and/or money on implementation, which is a massive efficiency gain. However, there's a high chance that 80% of those special interest tools will die out in the next 18/24 months and be absorbed by the bigger models."

Are there any specific SEO tasks that you would definitely use LLMs for at the moment?

"It can already really help with things like meta descriptions and page titles when it comes to working at scale. I would still have someone handcrafting the meta description in a more manual way for the homepage or the meta description template for a certain specific type of content.

However, if you're talking about thousands or millions of pages, then the next best thing after templating it would be to use an LLM. You can dump in a URL (or even scrape that through a ChatGPT plugin), and then it's going to pull the data and create meta descriptions within certain limitations. For that kind of content generation, and suggestions at scale, it's great.

It can also produce more lightweight content. An article about a certain island in Greece might be relatively easy to do compared to a very specific guideline for XYZ because that's not based on common knowledge. It's also great for classification. If you need a new hierarchy for internal linking, you can map out and classify pages through an LLM. It's much more efficient and it can ingest much more data than you would ever be able to do manually.

It is going to get crazier in the next few years, from a variety of standpoints. Google has the SGE snippet on top, and that's obviously going to change search results quite significantly. Not only is something pushed to the top, but that may have an impact on metrics, and we need to consider how to ensure our clients or brands appear in the snippets.

There are also going to be huge advancements on the tooling side. Running your own LLM is not rocket science anymore. Google's Vertex and some others have created relatively simple, ready-made solutions already. With a bit more time, a lot of the tool providers will move towards that direction."

How are LLMs likely to change and how can SEOs prepare for those changes?

"Sadly, there's no one answer to that. Most LLMs are transformer-based right now. That's the architecture and the underlying foundational technology. They are great for what we're currently using them for, but they also have limitations.

For example, to input more knowledge into an LLM, you need more training data. That means the model will grow in size, which also means that you need more hardware. If you query a transformer-based LLM currently, from a tech standpoint, you need to go through the entire model. That obviously doesn't scale endlessly. It scales to the extent that you can throw more and more hardware at the problem (you've probably seen the insane numbers that NVIDIA released recently and the stock market's reaction to it), however, it can't scale endlessly.

Therefore, we will probably start seeing different approaches, and some projects are currently researching different directions that could be taken.

From an implementation standpoint, as an organisation, you need to build some middleware.

You might currently be in the position to use an LLM for your SEO, which is fantastic. You can take all your knowledge and your content, put it in an LLM and then run certain types of models on your own. However, the LLM model itself might change. If you build a middleware API layout then, moving forward, it will be much easier to adapt to a new model. You can just move over the data and then instantly benefit from the work that you have already done.

We know that the models might change. I can't say how this might look in practice (I'm coming from a practitioner's standpoint, not a researcher's) but this would be a logical approach to take. We're seeing a lot of large organisations do this because they want to reap the benefits right now. There are fantastic gains to be had. You can make customer service more efficient and share knowledge internally more efficiently if you can collect all your knowledge from different sources and put it into these types of models.

Don't just sit on it and wait two years. Taking a hybrid approach, and being prepared to shift over, is a much better way to do it."

How should SEOs use LLMs to enhance their knowledge and stay up-to-date?

"The big difference is prompting and how you actually interact with the LLMs. This is going to change too because we're moving towards a more multimodal world, where we will not only have the ability to prompt using text but also combine different types of inputs.

BARD now allows you to upload a photo and ask, 'What's in this image?', and it will give you a description of the photo. It's like a combination of Lens and BARD. We're also seeing multimodality with things like gestures.

You need to understand how you can prompt the model to ensure that you get what you want out of it, keeping in mind that there are certain limitations such as hallucination. You might use a plugin to bring in external data or do certain calculations. Even if you're not using it in practice, I would strongly recommend at least having a play.

Also, don't forget about the code interpreter in ChatGPT Plus. As SEOs, we do a ton of analysis, looking at numbers and trying to figure out what's happening. From an agency perspective, if you look at a new website that you're not familiar with and you're seeing ups and downs and dips, you can overlay that with different types of data sources. You can ask a model like this to generate ideas about what might have happened. That is a really cool way to use the LLM as a research assistant before you do it yourself to double-check. Again, it's about the efficiency that you gain from utilising it.

Experimenting and having a play will help you to understand what is happening, even though it's hard to say that you understand how AI really works. Even engineers don't understand it completely, in a way, because the machines are reiterating and learning by themselves. However, you can understand how to utilise it, play with it, and figure it out.

That has always been part of SEO. When I started out, we learnt by tinkering and playing, and this has never really changed. If you're not naturally curious about things, then you will have a very hard time. That is going to be even more true in the future."

If an SEO is struggling for time, what should they stop doing right now so they can spend more time doing what you suggest in 2024?

"Stop worrying so much about all the possible ranking factors. People spend so much time trying to figure out isolated, tiny things. Changing a title here or a meta description there is not going to make a huge difference. It might make a difference for that page specifically but, in the grand scheme of things, it's minor.

Move away from the small nitty-gritty stuff. Don't buy cheap links and don't buy cheap content. That's a massive waste of time and money. Instead, zoom out. Try to understand what Google actually wants to rank, because that's a big question for the future.

This is going to be a very hard realisation for some but, if you look at the current Google SGE implementation, it's becoming much harder to acquire certain types of organic traffic. In the past, a lot of people relied on churning out generic content, but that's essentially common knowledge. There's no reason for Google to rank an article that is just a rephrasing of something that has already been put out there 100,000 times. They will just do that themselves and keep the traffic.

Moving forward, you need to figure out how to become more of an expert and much more well-versed in a certain topic. Just saying, 'Here's how to do XYZ', is not going to cut it in 2024."

Bastian Grimm is CEO at Peak Ace, and you can find him over at PeakAce.Agency.

Use LLMs to improve your forecasting and save you time – with Arpad Balogh

Once you have an understanding of how they work, you can start using large language models to improve your forecasting and save you time, according to Arpad Balough from Slothio.

Arpad says: "Start using ChatGPT (or any large language model) to save you time. This applies to SEO agencies, freelancers, or anyone who touches SEO.

Specifically, one of the best things you can use it for is forecasting for your clients. Forecasting is basically showing your client how much traffic, how many leads, and how many rankings they can expect based on their budget, their current website, their current traffic, market trends, how competitors are doing, and any other data that you have.

Forecasting also shows you what is achievable in that specific niche and whether you may need to go into a more specific sub-niche. If you have a real estate client, 'real estate Massachusetts' is probably too big and you may need to go into a more specific location to be able to generate results. You can do forecasting for different types of topics, clusters, keyword intents, etc.

Essentially, though, you can either forecast based on keyword data or historical data. Using keyword data, you're looking at that specific niche or cluster and using a tool like Ahrefs or SEMrush to get the search volume for those keywords, and forecasting SEO growth based on that. Then, you use different formulas for calculating the click-through rate for that specific keyword and rankability. Using those metrics, you can calculate what is possible in that niche.

I would say that the better way to do that is based on historical data. That means you're looking at your client's Google Analytics, Google Search Console, or any other analytics tool, and forecasting SEO growth based on that. You are looking at the query count, organic traffic, seasonalities, market trends based on branded or non-branded traffic, etc.

If you do that manually, it will take you a ton of time. It takes a lot of effort and time to make it accurate. For a small client, it would take at least 10-15 hours to go through all of the data and accurately create a prediction for them. This is where the ChatGPT Code Interpreter comes in. ChatGPT Code Interpreter is a ChatGPT model that is capable of data analysis, and you can upload any type of data – whether that's a DXT, a CSV, or an Excel file of your client's data. Once you upload that data, it uses Python to do any type of data analysis you want.

The key is to not just upload your client's data into ChatGPT, but use a system prompt that makes ChatGPT act as a specific agent. With a system prompt, you are telling ChatGPT (before you begin the conversation) how it should think, what it should say, and what type of questions it should ask – and there are a lot of system prompts out there. You can go to the custom instruction section where you can add them.

To do this in ChatGPT, first, upload all of the data that is necessary for your forecast. Then, start the chat with that system prompt in place and ask ChatGPT to create an SEO forecast. You will need to give a very detailed picture of the result that you want to achieve and a ton of explanation as to what data you uploaded, what each column contains, and what exactly is said in that TXT, CSV, or Excel file. Then, ChatGPT will basically act as the appropriate agent – like a data analysis agent, which loads your data and tries to understand what that data is about based on your explanation – and it will ask you more and more questions until the task is done.

Once it is done, you can get your data in a CSV and make a chart or graph out of it manually. You could also get a Python script that you can implement on your computer, or you can ask ChatGPT to run that Python script and generate a PNG image of the graph for you.

This method integrates with the bigger SEO picture because it will help you sell more SEO retainers – while saving you a ton of money and time. If your client sees that you know the true possibilities for their business or website for the next 12 months, they will trust you more. If I told you that you could lose X amount of weight in the next 12 months, you wouldn't necessarily believe me. However, if I asked you a lot about yourself and gave you a great prediction that explained your body weight and exactly how much you can lose if you do certain things, and I gave you a graph showing the data, you would believe me a lot more.

The best way to measure the success of this is by the amount of time you have saved. If you sit down and try to go through and organise all of the data that is needed for that forecast, you will realise that you never want to do that again."

If an SEO wants to use this forecasting strategy to sell retainers to clients, what are the best data sources for that?

"It really depends on what data the client gives you. Before we sell any client on a retainer, we ask for access. We ask for Google Search Console, Google Analytics 4, or even Yandex Metrica or Microsoft Clarity if they are using them. We want access to any type of data that they have, including their goals or CRM data, that we can use to predict what type of results we can get from SEO.

If you can get all of that data, you can more accurately estimate what SEO growth you can achieve. If you don't have access to that, most SEOs create a prediction based on keyword data. You can look at how they are ranking now and what type of traffic they could be getting if you increase those rankings. Then, based on the niche click-through rate, or the specific click-through rate for that keyword, you can predict estimated growth. However, I would always try to use historical data.

When you present that to clients, they usually love it. For clients, SEO is unpredictable, and it's something that they don't really understand. They need to see where they are now and where they could be in the next 12 months."

Can you use ChatGPT to identify opportunities that haven't necessarily been present historically?

"Absolutely. You can ask ChatGPT to look at correlations between past events or any types of data that stick out. You could have Google Analytics data that has been corrupted by spam traffic, for example, and you can ask ChatGPT to identify that rather than ruling it out manually. You can tell it that an event is going to happen and ask it to predict how that is likely to affect traffic, based on the historical data it already has.

For future events, you can also look at other types of data and other data sources, like Google Trends, that you can feed into ChatGPT. The most powerful thing you can do is feed it with as many documents as possible. In the context window of ChatGPT, you can feed as many documents as you want, creating a mesh of all of that data so it can pull out what is relevant and create an accurate prediction for you."

If every SEO agency starts doing this, how do you differentiate yourself from other agencies?

"It's not necessarily an area in which you have to differentiate yourself. Right now, a lot of agencies don't even do this manually. They often say, 'Based on how much you pay us, here's what we can provide, and this is the result you might get.'

Not a lot of agencies actually look at data, analyse it, calculate an accurate prediction, and then present it in an attractive graph that shows the client what they can achieve. They just sell you on a guesstimate.

A better way of forecasting is not something that's competitive; it helps everyone."

Do you think that it is still necessary to have the human touch involved in content creation?

"Definitely. As Michio Kaku says, ChatGPT is basically a glorified tape recorder. It really is, if you're just using the tokens that it's fed with. It's only been trained up until 2021. If you just ask it about a topic, it will just spin the information it has been fed until it becomes something unique, but it's not really containing any current or unique information.

There are ways to use ChatGPT to create unique content. Again, one of the best ways to do that is to use custom prompts. There's a way to use ChatGPT that allows web browsing. You can either use a web browsing plugin or a plugin that can pull data from sources like medical studies, for example. Then, you can ask it to give you an article about the topic, making it NLP optimized, while also pulling data from a specific study and/or the top five results for a query. That way, it creates much better content because it will be factual, and it will be current.

Don't just type in, 'Give me an article about the best dog shoes'. Ask it to go on the internet, look at the results that are there, and find some studies (if there are any). Try to use plugins. You can also directly feed it the factual information you want it to use, and it can write content based on that."

Is it best just to use ChatGPT natively or are there other AI tools that you'd recommend?

"HARPA AI is a browser plugin that connects to ChatGPT, and there's a lot of GPT-4 API you can access from the playground. There is also a ton of SEO writing software – recently I've been using ZimmWriter a lot and getting great results. For ChatGPT, I would recommend HARPA AI. It's a Chrome plugin that can pull data from any web page and do a lot with it.

Honestly, I usually just use ChatGPT by itself, while utilising system prompts. ChatGPT by itself is good, but it's better when you give it a system prompt so that it asks you a lot of questions, and finds the right agent persona, like a data analysis agent or an image visualisation agent.

Based on that, it has instructions and takes on the persona of that agent. It's like pulling an expert out of the crowd to help you with the job you want to achieve."

If an SEO is struggling for time, what should they stop doing right now

so they can spend more time focusing on chatGPT in 2024?

"Stop doing things manually that can be automated or sped up by large language models. Most SEOs do things manually because they are used to it. A lot of people haven't even touched ChatGPT yet, which I think is insane. Obviously, there's a fear of missing out in the market right now, with a ton of AI software being released recently, and you have to pick out the best from the crowd.

These types of data analysis tasks are where ChatGPT is most powerful. You don't have to sit in front of an Excel sheet or Google sheet and look at each piece of data and cluster them; you can ask ChatGPT to do that. Whatever can be automated or sped up by AI, try that instead of doing things manually."

Arpad Balogh is an SEO Consultant at Slothio, and you can find him over at Slothio.com.

Learn how to tackle generative AI in search – with Jason Barnard

Jason Barnard from Kalicube is focussed on another side to the technological capabilities of AI. He delves into the ways that generative AI is also impacting search results, and what to do about it.

Jason says: "I have lots of tips about generative AI in search, Google's search generative experience, and Bing Chat.

Interestingly enough, there isn't much difference between Google and Bing when it comes to generative search. It mainly comes down to presentation, but they both function in more or less the same way.

A few months ago, Gary Illyes said that most search engines rank results in much the same way. That remains true today. What we can learn from Bing, we can mostly apply to Google as well."

How do SEOs prepare for generative AI?

"First, we need to understand what generative AI is and how it works. In Google's case, generative AI is simply a summary of its knowledge and recommendations. It takes the SERP, the knowledge panel, and the recommendations on the left, and summarises all of that to save the user the time of jumping between multiple websites to gather the information themselves. It's a dynamic knowledge panel.

To understand how the search generative experience is going to work, you need to understand how Google and Bing are summarising their SERPs and what follow-up questions they suggest to keep the conversation going. The purpose of this, as Fabrice Canel from Bing pointed out to me, is to bring the user down the funnel to the point where they're ready to buy. At that point, they send the user to the website."

What elements are missing from the current knowledge panel that will feature on the next-generation knowledge panel?

"The current knowledge panel is a statement of facts. Google is saying, 'These are the facts I've understood. Here's a description that I'm confident is true. Here are the related entities and people also search for… Here are the social media platforms this person/company is on.' It gives you a summary of the person or the company.

The search generative experience does that on the fly, instead of pulling it all out of the knowledge graph, and also offers you the opportunity for a conversation. It's a conversational dynamic knowledge panel."

How do you control that conversation with the user?

"You need to make sure that Google and Bing understand your funnel, and how to bring your audience down that funnel through their SERP. You need to educate these machines about who you are, what you do, which audience you serve, and what your funnel looks like so that they can replicate it on the SERP.

It feels like you're giving control away to Google and Bing because you are. It doesn't feel fair, but you can't change how they're going to evolve. We're going to have to bite the bullet and do it. Ensure that the funnel they recreate on the SERP is the same as, or as close as possible to, the one that you have on your website and within your organisation."

Should you adjust your funnel for generative AI?

"We've found that this process is hugely helpful for our clients. As soon as I ask them what their funnel is, how it works, and what questions people ask as they go down, the business will struggle to explain it. They are never very clear about their own funnel.

This forces people to identify what their funnel looks like, what the questions are, and who the personas are – and then lay it out on the website in an easily digestible manner. That's helpful for users who come to their website from another platform (Facebook, Twitter/X, Medium, etc.), but it also helps the search engines understand that funnel so they can guide their assistive engines to bring that user down the funnel.

Don't forget that users on Google are Google's users. They might be your audience but, when they're using Google, they are Google's users. Google is recommending you to the subset of its users who are your audience.

This new experience forces brands and companies to create the content that their audience needs and wants, in the funnel and post-funnel, and set it out clearly on their website."

What does the process for educating search engines about your funnel look like?

"It can include the use of breadcrumbs, better internal linking, navigational headlines throughout the funnel, and schema. However, the biggest chunk of the work is in your FAQ. It should have one question and answer per page, with simple answers to simple questions, and it should cover every single question your audience might be asking.

You also need to include FAQ schema markup, not for rich snippets in the SERP but to make sure that Google is confident it has understood the content. Google's given us the carrot of stars or accordions in the SERP, but schema markup is really there to translate what you're saying on the page into

Google's native language. Schema is Google and Bing's native language. The role of Schema is to reassure the machine that it's fully understood what it's seen on the page. Schema markup is supporting evidence; it's reassurance and it's confidence-building in the content you've got.

I will bet my bottom dollar that your FAQ is way too small right now, and it doesn't even answer 5% of the questions that people ask on the way down the funnel or post-funnel."

Can you format your FAQ pages to indicate which stage of the funnel the question relates to?

"Yes. Within the FAQ, you can clearly describe where you feel the user is in the funnel by the way that you word what you're saying. Are you talking to somebody who hardly knows who you are, somebody who knows who you are and is ready to buy, or somebody who's already bought?

At Kalicube, we're integrating FAQs into our process with every single client. The Kalicube process is to create knowledge and understanding in Google's brain and make sure that the recommendations about the company are relevant and helpful to your audience. Together, those two elements will feed into generative AI, as long as we're answering all the questions down the funnel.

Our process nails knowledge, recommendations, and Google's summary of its own results – i.e., its assessment and judgment of the SERP. If you're a brand, that's hugely important. What does Google truly think of you? That's what it will produce for your branded search with generative AI."

Would you break up your FAQ with headings/subheadings?

"You're not going to have a lot of headings because you should be giving a short, succinct answer to a simple question.

If you search for 'plugin for multiple authors on a WordPress blog', you'll see results like, 'Do you want to create multiple authors on a WordPress blog?' and 'What is the technical implication of creating multiple authors on a WordPress blog?' However, you just want to know how to do it. You don't want all that introductory information that SEOs have created for context.

You already know what you want; you want the simple answer to the simple question, 'What plugin do I need?'

From that perspective, FAQs should be short – and they can be as short as 100 words. I've ranked FAQs for a tiny French company above Apple with just 100 words. The trick is to categorise correctly. Each stage of your funnel should be in a specific category that has a descriptive name that makes sense to your users.

I would also suggest having two main categories: one for branded questions and one for generic questions about your topic. Then, you can build them out with multiple categories, making sure that you identify every category at the beginning so that it's infinitely scalable. If you're thinking ahead, you should never be answering a question that does not fit into one of the categories that you created right at the start."

In 2024, should you bin the blog and have an evolving FAQ section instead?

"I wouldn't bin the blog, but I would focus on the FAQ – at least for 2023-2024. The blog has its own role. If I want a quick answer to a simple question, I need 100/200 words. If I want to delve into a topic, I need 1,000/2,000 words. That's a blog. If I really want to dig into a topic, I'll buy a book or download a PDF white paper that's 8,000 words. At Kalicube, we've got FAQs, blogs, white papers, and books."

Is generative AI going to kill SEO?

"No, but SEOs are going to have to adapt. You need to create a digital marketing strategy that covers all of the different channels where your users hang out. You need to stand where the audience is looking (Facebook, Medium, LinkedIn, Forbes.com, etc.), package your content on those platforms for Google, and create content that helps Google and Bing to bring your audience down your funnel, on their platform, and buy.

There's an enormous amount of SEO work to do, but SEOs are going to have to learn that the job is no longer standalone. By necessity, it's part of a wider digital marketing strategy. In my opinion, SEO is simply packaging great branding and great marketing for Google and Bing."

Do you need to be everywhere all at once?

"You don't have to be everywhere; you have to be where your audience is looking. At Kalicube Pro, we analyse your digital ecosystem and your market's digital footprint so we can identify where your audience is hanging out. Then, we can focus your marketing efforts on the platforms that make sense to your audience and ensure that you're creating the right content that helps your audience understand you have the solution to their problem.

You need to stand where they're looking, show them you have the solution to their problem, and then tell them what to do next."

How do you know whether or not to use a platform?

"In Kalicube Pro, you can look at the market template. If Facebook is dominating your market, you focus on Facebook. If LinkedIn is dominating your market, you focus on LinkedIn.

We prioritise it. We will give you six major platforms that you could potentially focus on and you can say, 'I don't have the team to do that, let's just focus on the top three.' You need to do each job properly, so it's better to focus heavily on three platforms than do a bad job on six. It's obviously even worse to do a bad job on ten. I can't imagine any company needing to be on ten different platforms.

We have lots of free tools on Kalicube Pro so you can have a general look at which platforms are dominating. The most basic way of doing this yourself is to use your human intuition and intelligence. Search your own brand name and look at which platforms come up on pages one, two, and three. Then, search your competitors and just look at page one. Look at the correlation and correspondence between them.

By looking at 20 competitors, you'll probably see repetition, where one platform is dominating. That will be the platform to focus on because that is what Google perceives to be the most valuable platform for the majority of your market."

If an SEO is struggling for time, what should they stop doing right now so they can spend more time doing what you suggest in 2024?

"If you consider that Google and Bing are going to keep the user on the SERP for longer, and bring them down the funnel, site speed and page speed become less important.

From an SEO perspective, page speed is significantly less important in a generative AI world, but site speed remains important for your users. From an SEO perspective, push site speed down in priority. However, from a user perspective, bear in mind that your users do need a fast site.

Focus on cornerstone entities instead: the Corporation Entities (website owner) and the Person Entities (content creator, author and CEO). This is the key to maximizing the effect of the EEAT credibility signals which, in turn, is key to appearing in Generative AI search results on Google, Bing, Bard, ChatGPT et al."

Jason Barnard is CEO of Kalicube, and you can find him over at Kalicube.com.

Understand how generative AI is affecting SEO content – with Itamar Blauer

Expanding on what Jason shared in the previous tip, Itamar Blauer from StudioHawk adds that, if you want your content to appear on the AI-driven SERP, you'll need to tweak your content strategy.

Itamar says: "My tip revolves around content, particularly related to what Google is doing now. The introduction of the search generative experience and having generative AI in search results is going to have a lot of implications on SEO and content. It's probably going to be the biggest shift we've seen in SEO in the last 10 years.

My advice is to try and understand more about what Google is trying to surface when it comes to generative AI results. As soon as it's rolled out worldwide, and a lot of queries start utilising AI within their answers, it's important to understand what Google is actually looking for.

When it comes to the content you're making for your website, try to think about all the areas of the funnel, everything that's relevant to your niche, the synonyms, the types of language people are using, and the different areas of your business that somebody might want to know about. Then, think about the content that will help weave users down the funnel and help serve the more colloquial searches that will utilise generative AI.

Google is going to be able to understand more about nuances and context. As long as you've got a lot of content that can relate to that and help answer those more comprehensive queries, then you'll be getting more clicks.

The results we're going to see from AI are going to be a lot more saturated. We're not exactly sure what proportion of clicks are going to be from the other organic results when AI results start showing up. It's really important that you're able to manage that and put yourself in a better position to get those clicks."

Is the search generative experience going to be focused on certain types of intent and certain types of keyword phrases?

"If we think about the traditional types of intent (commercial, navigational, informational, transactional), the AI results are probably going to have the most impact within informational and commercial searches. A lot of businesses will have informational content about their niche on their website, even if they do sell products. People will be asking about what they do, and they will have other queries related to their industry or their offerings.

It's probably not going to affect navigational searches as much. Most people are essentially using Google when they want an answer to a question (informational), or they want to buy a product (commercial). Those two intents are where AI is going to be utilised within the search results, so they're the ones you should focus on."

How do you make your content more likely to be picked up by Google's SGE?

"Language is very important. Google continues to get better at understanding different nuances within language. MUM, for example, can understand the context around the words that people are using which may have multiple meanings. Within certain types of searches, a word might have a meaning that's more relevant to that particular area, which can get very complex.

For your content, you need to make sure that you've reached out to the experts within your team and your industry. You need to fully understand all the different areas and hit all the different points that people might be asking. For example, if you're on the e-commerce side, you can reach out to customer service and ask them what sort of questions people ask. You also need to be up to date with the language and terminology people are using in your industry, because that's going to be important.

Make sure that you hit all of the different points within your content and address all the possible stages of the funnel. You might predominantly have bottom-of-funnel content at the moment, for people who are trying to buy stuff. That's very common for businesses because they want to make content that will make people buy. However, there are loads more stages involved.

The more comprehensive you can be – in terms of the types of content you put out, the language you're using, and making sure you're up to date with everything that your industry entails – the better position you will be in. You will have more ammunition for Google to crawl and utilise to your benefit. Then, somebody who's searching for something very particular will have a better chance of seeing your content, no matter what stage of the funnel they're at."

How do you go about mapping content to different stages of the funnel?

"Take a traditional look at the funnel. Top-of-funnel, people don't know who you are, but they're also not sure exactly what they want. They might be asking questions about a certain term or concept related to what you do, or about their use case or the problem that they're trying to solve. They might not even be sure about the terminology around what you do. Top-of-funnel content will help people who either don't know exactly what they need and are trying to solve a problem or people who have a rough idea but need to know more.

Middle-of-funnel is more precise. People already know what they want, but they want to do some more digging and maybe make some comparisons. They are generally looking for more information in that area.

Bottom-of-funnel is people who are ready to convert. That could be content that's answering any big questions that might divert somebody away from you and towards a competitor, or vice versa. This content should be focused on your USP and why they should pick you over somebody else.

Content that fits around these different areas of the funnel will do well. The amount of content you should create really does depend on your industry. Talk with people from customer service, go to industry events, and get the gist of what people are actually looking for – but always keep the areas of the funnel in mind when you're doing that research."

Do you still look at the four traditional areas of intent or do you try and break it down even further?

"You can break it down even further but, for most websites, businesses, and industries the four traditional areas (commercial, navigational, informational, transactional) are quite useful – and quite accurate.

There are certain niches where you might want to delve a bit deeper but, from an ideation perspective or for a glimpse into how you should approach intent, they are the easiest way for most people to understand."

What are the more comprehensive searches that will be relevant to SGE?

"We've seen different examples of SGE. A traditional Google search is typically very straightforward and a few words long. If you want to buy a red Ford, you put in 'red Ford for sale', or something like that. Now, you can make that search more comprehensive and add, 'I'm a father of three. I've got one kid who's two, and I require lots of space in the boot.', and Google will understand that context, so it will be in a better position to give you the right answer.

However, that does rely on your content matching different types of use cases. You can scale your content and branch it out a lot more. If you're selling cars, you could have potential use case pages for 'Best Cars With a

Large Boot' and 'Best Cars for Fathers of Three'. That will help Google to get those answers directly to the people who are searching for them.

There may not be many people making these types of searches, but they are going to be a lot more ready to buy. It's not so much about the volume and the demand here; it's more about making sure you hit exactly what somebody who's ready to buy your product or service will be looking for."

Would you recommend creating longer content with subheadings answering each long-tail keyword phrase or having individual URLs for each question?

"I don't think that one way would be better than the other but it's worth experimenting. SGE is going to be smart enough to extract the context within your content, even if it is on one page that contains loads of different content split up under different subheadings.

If you're putting the pieces on separate pages, you want to make sure that it's comprehensive and high-quality, and that it makes sense for it to be its own page. Don't have a page without much on it. From a user's perspective, they might stumble upon that and want to know more about the topic."

Should SEOs give up on attempting to rank for short-tail, high-volume keyword phrases?

"You don't need to give up. Google still cares about understanding your website in terms of the topics or areas you write about and your topical authority. It's still important to have general types of content so that Google is able to crawl it and understand what your website does and what it's useful for.

You shouldn't completely scratch trying to focus on more generic terms, but what I'm suggesting helps to support that. It helps strengthen Google's understanding and solidify yourself as an expert and authority.

This is linked to what we've seen with AI. ChatGPT has come into play, and we've seen a lot of people using it – even to write content, which I personally think is quite dangerous. With SGE and the Perspectives filter, it's clear that Google wants to display real people and new perspectives on things.

However, ChatGPT doesn't have any knowledge from after September 2021.

You should be making sure that you have real people writing your content, who know what is happening in your industry right now. That is going to be a lot more potent when it comes to content creation."

Should SEOs not be using ChatGPT at all?

"It's not that you shouldn't be using ChatGPT at all, but you shouldn't be using it to write your content in its entirety. It's useful for creating briefs and trying to get ideas. You can ask it hypothetical questions about how to make a post appear a lot more authoritative, what you should be mentioning, etc.

If you've got ChatGPT writing the content for you, but you don't have somebody there who can edit it and fact-check it, that's a problem. Think about the volume of low-quality content that can be produced by AI at the moment. If it's all uploaded to the web, Google's going to have to sift through all of that and improve its models to detect it and know exactly what to surface.

I'm not saying don't use ChatGPT at all but use it with a strategy in place. Don't just go and blindly create a bunch of content."

If an SEO is struggling for time, what should they stop doing right now so they can spend more time doing what you suggest in 2024?

"Stop getting ChatGPT to write content. That sounds counterproductive because that's the easiest way to save time but, fundamentally, if your content's not going to rank then you've wasted time doing that in the first place.

Just have a plan. Take a moment to think about what your strategy should be, if you want it to be comprehensive and sustainable, especially with all the things that we've covered in regard to SGE and AI. Have a plan, have a think, and then you can utilise AI to help make your life a bit easier."

Itamar Blauer is Senior SEO Director at StudioHawk, and you can find him over at StudioHawk.co.uk.

4 AI IN ACTION

Learn to think, and only automate when it makes sense – with Kristina Azarenko

One of the key challenges with uncovering new automation opportunities is the temptation to automate before thinking, shares Tech SEO Trainer Kristina Azarenko.

Kristina says: "Learn to think, automate when it makes sense, and don't when it doesn't make sense. Don't rely on AI.

Know when you need to rely on the alerts from different SEO tools because we are bombarded by them all the time – and we are bombarded by everything AI. Two years ago, AI wasn't a thing, so it was easier for SEOs. Now you suddenly need to rely on it a lot. However, the best thing that you can do is start relying on yourself first and automate when it makes sense."

When should you use AI and when should you rely on yourself?

"AI is a great help, as an assistant. It's not someone who can replace you; it's your assistant. If you need to create a technical SEO process for a website, for example, the first thing that you should do is think over the business goals of this website, their current tech stack, and what their goals for the site are. You can't ask AI about that.

Then, once you have created a process, you might have specific tasks – like generating structured data. You can use AI for that, or other tools that can help you. You can also use tools for the checking and auditing of the website.

Use AI as your assistant, but the backbone of what you're creating and the final delivery of that is something that you need to think over – before you delegate some of the tasks to AI.

So many people were afraid that they would be replaced by AI. However, if you're doing strategic work at a high level (instead of just generating a couple of title tags for a website), then you will not be replaced. AI is actually going to be your assistant and friend instead of someone who will take over your job.

I don't want to go deep into the specific prompts here. My point is that you should use AI when it makes sense and use it as an assistant. Rely on your common sense."

What challenges are SEOs having with thinking correctly?

"In some ways, SEOs aren't thinking enough, and they are relying on tools too much. It's not the fault of SEOs; it's just the way that many things are built. For example, SEO tools will send so many alerts to you. Even Google Search Console will send you things like, 'your page is not mobile-friendly' when, in many cases, it actually is. It's not SEOs' fault that so many things are on their shoulders.

Also, when you have the core SEO knowledge, and you can rely on that, then you are not turned in different directions by an alert telling you that there is a JavaScript issue on the website, or some structured data is not correct. You can identify if the issue that a tool sends to you is actually an issue or not – and if it's high-priority or low-priority. If it's of low priority and impact, then just ignore it. We are not striving for perfection here. Perfection is impossible in SEO.

The bottom line is that you should learn SEO to the level where you can rely on your knowledge, instead of relying on alerts or SEO tools, and know exactly when you need to act on these alerts and when you can ignore them."

How do you prioritise and decide what needs to be done first?

"I know people will hate me for this, but it depends. For websites that have huge issues with duplicate content, a proper canonicalization strategy is going to be a high priority. For another website that has client-side rendering and Google can't see any of their content, even though they might have a bad canonicalization strategy, it's not going to be a priority right now. They need to make sure that Google can seek and render the content so that it can rank in the search results. It really depends on what the issues on website are.

Another thing to consider is the type of website: is it a B2B website or an e-commerce website? E-commerce websites are more likely to have duplicate content and pages generated that you don't actually need. Also, you need to think about the business goals. If the goal is Black Friday, maybe something needs to be done with the seasonal pages, and that should be the priority.

In order to know what to prioritise for a website, you need to understand the business and SEO. There is no one-size-fits-all strategy. You can't work with 10 different clients and recommend the same things to all of them. They'll be at different stages of their business, their business goals will be different, their websites will be different, and the current issues on their websites will be different. It will depend on a variety of factors that you should consider, as an SEO, when providing any recommendations to your clients."

Do you need to have conversations with leaders in the business to truly understand the key products, goals, and objectives of the business?

"100%. When I was just starting and talking to clients for the first time, I was terrified to ask questions because I thought that they would think I was stupid or that I didn't understand something. I quickly realised that not asking the right questions made me a bad source of help for these clients because I couldn't recommend something that would be better for them in their particular situation.

When I changed that mindset – when I started asking questions, rephrasing, and asking the same questions again to make sure that I had all the pieces of the puzzle – it made a huge difference. Don't be afraid to ask questions. You will look good to your clients and the boss. Even if you have just been hired as an in-house SEO, ask the questions. It will show that you're interested and that you actually want to bring results instead of working in a silo and not seeing what's going on around you."

What does an SEO need to do better in terms of interacting with clients, presenting to clients, and listening to clients?

"I love that you mentioned listening to clients because that was the first thing that I thought of. Listen to clients and make sure that you know the language that they use and what they care about. Then, when you are delivering your recommendations, you can tailor them to what your client wants. Obviously, make sure that it makes sense. Sometimes it doesn't, and you need to communicate that to the client in a nice way.

Once you have all of your recommendations and you need to present them, don't ever say that it is for SEO. From my experience, when you just say it's for SEO, nobody cares about that. Stakeholders will not hear you because it doesn't mean anything to them. It's not for SEO; it's for increasing the number of people who are willing to buy products from this company or order their services. It's not just for SEO.

Also, don't use jargon. Don't say, 'We need to create a redirect map'. Nobody cares about the redirect map except for you. Instead of that, you can say, 'We want to make sure that, whenever people come to our website, they can access all the pages that they care about so that they can complete a purchase' – or whatever the main conversion of the website is."

If we're using AI for the work that's traditionally done by SEO execs, what does this mean for newer SEOs coming into the industry?

"Honestly, I think that AI can be used for good by just replacing some of the things that you can do.

If you're just starting in SEO, one of the things you will be learning from is keyword research. Many people start with that, and that's totally great. You're learning keyword research, and then you're learning how to optimize the metadata and the headings on the page. If you don't learn how to do that first, you will not be able to evaluate whether the results you get from AI are any good.

For me, learning SEO doesn't change. You still need to learn all the steps and go through them all. When you're comfortable with them, and you know what helpful output should look like, then you can delegate that task. If you're generating title text, and you know what they look like when they are generated properly, delegate it to AI. Choose the best options and use them for your work with clients. However, you still need to learn what it should look like when it's done properly."

Would you be in a dangerous position if you're asking AI to do something and you don't know how it's delivering that and putting everything together?

"Absolutely. As humans, we are always looking for some magic wand that will help us not work and just make money. That's what all humans want. To my knowledge, though, that's just not possible at this point. AI is not going to help you just lay on the beach, drinking cocktails and not doing anything, while it does the audits, sends the recommendations to the client, and then implements everything. It's not going to work that way.

You need to learn first and then use AI as an assistant. Ultimately, a magic wand is a short-term shortcut. It may work for the short term but it's certainly not going to be part of a long-term business."

If an SEO is struggling for time, what should they stop doing right now so they can spend more time doing what you suggest in 2024?

"Stop stressing out about the huge number of things that you could potentially do. You can use prioritisation for that. Also, specialising really helps.

When I started in SEO, it was so easy to be an SEO. You needed to know on-page, link-building, and technical SEO. Now, in SEO, there are so many different specialisations. There are people who do content strategy, there are people who specifically talk about algorithm updates and EEAT, there are technical SEOs, and there are international SEOs. If you can find the niche that you want to go into and only choose the battles in that niche, it might save you a lot of time.

The third thing that will save you time is creating processes. Even experienced SEOs will start everything from scratch all the time. If they're doing a technical SEO audit, they will start from scratch. That doesn't help because it leads to procrastination and stressing out about what you need to do next.

Start creating processes for your workflows – and then see which parts of the process can be streamlined using AI. You want to at least have a process that you can follow every single time, then you can improve it with each and every client."

Kristina Azarenko is a Tech SEO Trainer, and you can find her over at TechSEO.pro.

Utilise AI to save you time with your content creation – with Isaline Muelhauser

As previously touched upon with Itamar, Isaline Muelhauser from Pilea.ch would like to emphasise that AI can and should be used in the content creation process.

Isaline says: "Content marketers and SEOs: let's start using AI to save time."

Does this apply to all content?

"It applies to most content. Basically, I'd like to share my experience testing a tool called Reword. It claims that it is designed to empower content marketers. It's not trying to take your job but to help you with your job. I wanted to see how much it could help me, how much time it could save, and how successful it would be for the long-term clients I work with.

How it works is you feed the tool with either your idea or the URL of your website, and you can connect it to Google Search Console. If you connect it to Search Console, you have the advantage of keyword data as well.

First, I'll start with how the tool is helping me. The first thing I noticed is how it can help when you have a new idea, but don't know exactly where to start. For instance, I had the idea of starting a podcast for clients in French, and it was really hard to find a good title and make sure that I had the right content for the episodes. Reword gave me a succession of ideas. They weren't all 100% good ideas, but I had 5 to 10 title ideas that I could rewrite and use, which is easier than starting from a blank page.

The second way that it helped me was by giving me a list of titles and blog post articles that I could compare to the content of the episodes I had already planned to see if I was going in the right direction or if I had missed something. That gave me confidence to know that I was moving in the right direction. When I fed the tool with what I was doing and the audience it was for, it went in the same direction that I was going. That sped up the process, in that case, when I didn't want to spend hours researching, carrying out customer interviews, etc."

Should you tell your clients that you're using AI to augment content? If you're connecting the tool to their Google Search Console, should you be transparent about what you're doing with their data?

"There is a distinction between when you're working for the client and when you're gathering ideas and trying to make a plan. Before I work directly for the client, I'm making shiny new ideas and trying to move quickly. Onboarding a client and getting that lead to become a client takes a lot of time, so I need to be fast. In that case, I think it's okay to not inform them because it's just a tool for me and my workflow.

When it comes to connecting the tool to the Search Console, I would not do that for a client without asking them. That data doesn't belong to you. For some tests, you can insert the URL, which is public information. If there is an existing blog, for instance, instead of connecting the Search Console you can insert all of the URLs for a topic on the blog to show you if there are any content gaps or how their articles can be improved."

Do you feel that SEOs should incorporate their intention to use AI as

part of everything they do for the client within their contracts?

"Since I'm still testing, I don't 100% have an answer for that yet. For my own contracts, I intend to include the fact that I use the tool but be really specific about which tool I would use and in which scenario I would use it.

Presently, I'm not comfortable using Reword to generate content because, as far as I have seen, the quality of information is not adequate. You would expect that, since you feed the tool with the URL of a website, the tool would produce high-quality content. That's not exactly the case.

I have been working with many of these clients for a long time, so I know the industry. When I read some of the auto-generated content, I don't trust the key facts. I don't think this is a function I would use. I would rather use it to generate ideas and check what I have already written, which is the third interesting capability of the tool."

Do you have a process for creating articles before using Reword to optimize them?

"At the moment, I'm using AI to check that I'm going in the right direction. I use Reword like a colleague who would read what I have done so far and give me ideas. Either it gives me more ideas, or it will quality check the content and highlight what could be improved and how.

This functionality is a little bit like Yoast. When you use Yoast, you have highlights in the text that tell you very basic information that a human could tell you if you had someone re-reading your work. It's saving you time because it's doing the quality check for you. My job is to balance the suggestions. The tool gives all its suggestions at the same priority level. You need to balance which of those are really important.

It will give ideas about the style, it will highlight a sentence that may be confusing and could be more precise, and it will give ideas about further content you could add or what you could explain in more detail. As a human, you need to prioritise these.

Before, I would write the text first, then pause for a day and come back to the text with fresh eyes, a fresh brain, and a little bit of distance. The tool saves me that time because I can ask someone (the tool) to quality check and proofread the text for me, and then I have suggestions that I filter and choose to follow or not. This is the second feature I find very interesting: the idea of having a colleague proofread your work. It's a very thorough colleague, too, who is highlighting a lot of things, so you have to filter."

Have you used AI detectors to check AI-assisted content? If an article is mistakenly perceived to be 100% produced by AI, is that a concern?

"That's why I don't get the tool to write for me, and why the writer needs to filter. Most of my clients are established brands with established branding, so they have ways of saying things that I have to use when I write the article. They always use specific words for certain things, for instance, so I wouldn't write what the AI tells me to write.

It's more about using the tool as a hint for where it could be better, but really filtering the suggestions that it gives. When we write an article, we write a certain way that is correct for the brand. When I tested the auto-generated content, I found that the quality of the text sounded off. It's not only the information, but something is wrong. That's where I think it's really important that a human manages the content and filters what is necessary and what is not. You need to navigate a tool according to the brand universe of the clients you're working with."

Does Reword produce facts and do you have to verify the accuracy of these?

"At this stage, I wouldn't trust the tool to write for you. I have tried it and it's not something I would propose. If you actually use an AI tool to create content, that is something that you should discuss with the client.

Right now, I'm using the tool to help me quality check and benchmark. It is like an exterior pair of eyes. At the beginning of my career, I used to work with my dad sometimes. He's retired, and it was really helpful for me. In French, we say, 'Four eyes are better than two'. When you're a solo consultant, you are often on your own, and content is expensive. You might not have four eyes. I used to ask my dad for his help and take him out for lunch in return because it would give me confidence and because he's really good at spelling. That is how I would use the tool. It does not replace my dad (nothing ever could, of course!), but it gives me an extra bit of confidence by highlighting what is good and what is bad.

It is similar to when a client comes to me and says, 'In your text, I can see that you have/have not done such and such.', which does sometimes happen when the client starts using tools themselves. They will do an automatic audit in Ahrefs and ask me why I haven't implemented what it suggested.

Reword gives suggestions like this as well, but it's really a question of prioritising what is good, what is not, and especially what is suitable for that client in that context. You need the human brain to do that."

Why did you choose Reword as the tool that you wanted to test?

"Through word-of-mouth, mainly. Someone I knew was trying it out and said that they were having fun and I decided it was worth a try.

I have been testing it on several projects and I feel like, if I want to have a good overview, I need to test it for a while on different topics to better understand its shortcomings. We need to understand the shortcomings in order to manage them. I need to test it for long enough to understand it before I test another tool."

If an SEO is struggling for time, what's one thing they can start doing now so they can spend more time doing what you suggest in 2024?

"This is particularly a tip for consultants who have to create offers. For offers, you need to feed your clients with something interesting and something shiny. Sometimes, you don't have an awful lot of time to do research. Depending on the clients, you need to be fast. In those cases, this tool is useful for getting things going so you're not sitting in front of a blank page.

It will give you suggestions. They may not be 100% perfect, but it is something you can start working with. It's a way to unblock, sometimes, and it can save time – especially in idea generation. Other tools can help in the same way too; you don't have to use Reword for that."

Isaline Muelhauser is an SEO Consultant at Pilea.ch.

Employ AI to improve your quality, not your quantity – with Joseph S. Kahn

It's easy to get grand visions of how much content you can create using AI. However, quality over quantity should be your aim, according to Joseph S. Kahn from Hum JAM.

Joseph says: "My number one SEO tip for 2024 is to focus on quality, not quantity, by using AI to harmonise user intent and coming from the perspective of the writer and creator of a web page."

How do you focus on quality and avoid the temptation to produce a lot of quantity with AI?

"One thing that came out with the ChatGPT craze was everybody thinking it would replace writers, and people were scared of losing their jobs. They were focused on the old world of SEO, which was creating tons and tons of content. Most local SEO agencies that we work with are compensated based on quantity – on how many blog posts they make, etc. When ChatGPT and other AI tools came out, everybody rushed to produce more quantity for free.

Keep in mind that Google's EEAT had already been changing the algorithm for well over a year. Google's been moving away from a spammy, quantity-based algorithm and moving towards a focus on the user. Social media now shows everything from engagement to happiness signals. Reviews show up on Facebook, Google, and different platforms now. Google is looking for what's going to make the user the happiest, so that's what we are using AI for.

We're the harmonising people. If you learn a little about me and HumJAM, we focus on harmonising things. With ChatGPT we know that Google doesn't need more content. The other thing that people are scared of is that Google's going to replace the need for SEO altogether. People will type in, 'How is weather created?' and Google will provide the answer with chat. It won't be a webpage; it won't be that kind of thing But guess what? Google doesn't need you to mass-create more information because they already have it. Eventually, AI will take care of it.

What they need is information that's going to engage the user or reader. You can take ChatGPT and say, 'Rewrite this from the perspective of Bugs Bunny.' If you're a business, you can take a children's storybook and say, 'Write this from the perspective of Richard Branson.' Nobody wants boring content anymore. We're in the information space, we're in the social media space, and people want to be 'enter-trained'. They need to be entertained and trained at the same time."

Does Google want to rank content that's purely written by humans above AI-generated content?

"100%. To get around that, we use another tool called WordAi, which we've been using for a long time. It's a great tool that will take any content that you've written with another AI tool, rewrite it, and remove the AI signals. Once WordAi is done with it, the content will present a 98% chance that it was written by a human.

There are watermarks that can be recognised in AI content. The LLM (which stands for large language model, such as ChatGPT) is choosing next-sentence phrasing when it's writing, which follows a pattern that can be seen by Google or another tool. If there's a repeating pattern, we might not see it, but Google or another tool can say that it's probably AI because of the way the sentence structure was written.

WordAi will remove that repeating pattern, so it appears more natural. We've tested it out and it really does make a difference. With side-by-side testing, 'WordAi' and 'human' rank about the same but ChatGPT by itself doesn't rank that well at all. If you're using ChatGPT, even just to reword something, try to throw it in another tool. There are many out there.

We haven't run into a limit for how much content WordAi will produce, and we will put complete 4,500-word articles through it. If we do any AI work at all, WordAi is the last filter we will put it through."

Do you rewrite articles from another website or are you simply refreshing your own existing content?

"We're always refreshing our own content, not somebody else's. Neil Patel was recently in the news because he was showing how you can take something that's already ranking, rewrite it using WordAi, and then use that on your own page.

Some people think that's okay and, in my personal opinion, it can be – as long as you're making it better. If you're rewriting it, adding more graphs, adding facts, etc., you're taking what someone else is doing and improving it. It's no different than what Led Zeppelin, Jay-Z, or any musical artist might do. You're just improving it. If Google rewards you for improving it, then the original person shouldn't be upset because you simply did it better.

Is that okay, ethically? I'll let the readers decide. I wouldn't personally do it, but you can."

With this content, are you creating a new URL on your website or are you refreshing an existing article on an existing URL?

"We're mainly refreshing existing URLs because we're very keyword-centric in our processes. We don't do any SEO that's not driven by keywords, which is driven by user intent, which is driven by a dollar or a goal that we're trying to achieve. We're not just ranking for vanity purposes.

My partner calls the keyword 'the treasure map'. If we rank for these keywords, we're going to make money or get leads or whatever you need. That keyword is going to tell us if we're already ranking. Does our website already have content on that? If it doesn't, then we're obviously going to create new content to fill that gap.

If there is content already, we're going to check and see where we're already ranking for that keyword. If we're within the top 10, I'm going to do very little editing or updating. I might take the first paragraph and rewrite it: add two more bullets, throw it in WordAi, double-check it, and then put it on the page. I might analyse the top 10 and then make sure that I'm at least matching what the competitors are producing, which is basically a refresh or revamp of existing content.

If you want to rank and you're on page two or page three of the SERPs, then you should revamp or refresh. We use Surfer SEO to do that but there are a lot of tools out there. It will say, 'Here's all the keywords you're missing. Here are the paragraphs you're missing.' Then we'll edit or update it and republish.

We might change the title, but it depends on what we're ranking for and what the competition is doing. The slug, however, will absolutely stay the same because we're not changing the keyword.

When we revamp or refresh, ChatGPT can add flair; it can add a new perspective and harmonise with user intent. You can add creative things like local information. You can literally say, 'What are the concerns that homeowners with families in the Norcross area have about service technicians in the air-conditioned industry?'. ChatGPT will give you all of those very specific concerns, which makes for great content on a refreshed page in that industry.

You can ask ChatGPT flair questions, and it will help you rewrite your content to match the user's intent. You can tell it to rewrite your content from the perspective of a specific user to make them want to engage. It could be the perspective of a homeowner, an art collector, a cartoon enthusiast, or any client's perspective. You can even instruct it to write 'in a way that will make the user want to engage'. You can be very specific, and it will harmonise your content with that user intent.

When Google recrawls it, they won't see it as information-based content. It will look like experience content, which is EEAT content. It's about the user experience. Are you making the person who wants to buy from you have a good time? That's what AI can help you with.

You can also add video, add an FAQ, add an index that you can click to get to sections, etc. There are lots of different things you can do, but you're just refreshing it, making it better, and bumping it up – with the help of a tool."

Are you seeing any trends in the elements that you should be including that Google wants to rank?

"The secret one that I've noticed is for triggering 'near me' searches (which is probably most relevant to local SEO in 2024), and that is FAQs. FAQs are great additions to most content. For a local service, the first question can be, 'What is the best [fill-in-the-blank] near me?' Some SEOs will be thinking they've been doing this for years but there is a secret here if you want to be in the 'near me' search and trigger that really easily.

You put your FAQ at the bottom of your service area pages, and the number one FAQ question is, 'What is the best [plumber/carpenter/main keyword] near me?' The answer is your company, but you point to a map pin. If you put that FAQ on a service area page, then that map pin is saying, 'We're the best company near you'. The 'near you' is then linked to that service area map pin, which will get you within the top three 'near me' searches in the Google search map.

That's one little secret but, to go a step further, Google loves your frequently asked questions section. Go to AnswerThePublic or wherever you can find frequently asked questions for the keyword you're targeting, and make sure to include and answer all of them in your content. That will go a long way. Even Surfer SEO will show you those questions in your briefing when you're updating your content. Make sure you answer them, and an FAQ is an easy way to do that."

Can you use AI to determine the questions you need to answer and generate content based on that or is there still a lot of human involvement?

"There doesn't need to be a lot of human involvement. I can't tell you how many FAQ items I have saved in my ChatGPT. There are lots of helpful tools you can use. You can find browser extensions that will read a webpage and consume it into the ChatGPT database. You can tell it to read a URL into ChatGPT and then ask it to create FAQs based on that page. It will basically give you the FAQs and you can then tell it to write a paragraph answering each one of those questions.

Alternatively, you can then take your keyword and throw it in a tool like Surfer SEO and it will tell you the frequently asked questions. Grab those, throw them into ChatGPT and say, 'Answer these questions in a unique way that would appeal to the search engines.' You can literally phrase it like that. You could also say, 'Answer these questions from the perspective of the owner of a plumbing company.', or 'Answer these questions from the perspective of Bugs Bunny.'

Your FAQ can become something that people will be interested in and stay on. Engagement is another ranking factor that's coming into play here. FAQs will keep the person on the page looking through those questions – so will an index, intriguing videos, and things like that. Anything that gets people to stick, stay, or share is key."

If an SEO is struggling for time, what should they stop doing right now so they can spend more time doing what you suggest in 2024?

"Stop doing quantity. Stop working for the sake of working. Ask ChatGPT what you should be doing when it comes to a website, an issue, a challenge, or whatever you're working on. Having mentors and other people in your life, or reading books, can also help with that but stop just creating content.

Also, stop getting Fiverr gigs. We saw someone doing citations for Fiverr gigs and it massively messed them up, because they went and created thousands of junky citations which were then really hard to get rid of. Stop the quantity game. Google is going to get rid of that game. They've already been deprecating and de-indexing a lot of stuff that's poor quality.

Up your quality game. Use the AI to harmonise that quality and write from different perspectives. Write from the perspective of the owner, and use EEAT and these algorithms to create the content that Google is looking for right now. They're not looking for knowledge-based information, they're looking for user-based content that a user wants to read and consume. That's what we've got to start modelling our content towards, and AI can help us do that."

Joseph S. Kahn is President and Co-Founder of Hum JAM, and you can find him over at HumJAM.com.

Improve your success with AI by building a prompt library – with Garrett Sussman

How do you ensure that AI is able to deliver in a brand-appropriate, consistent manner? You need to build a prompt library, says Garrett

Sussman from iPullRank.

Garrett says: "Build a prompt library for AI content.

The reality is that these LLMs (ChatGPT, BARD, etc.) are here to stay. They're incredibly valuable for being able to generate content, depending on your resources, but you want to use it as efficiently as possible. Learning these tools now is going to future-proof you for SEO and in any other marketing capacity. You absolutely need to learn that skill set."

Where does a prompt library live?

"It depends on your use case. ChatGPT has recently released an enterprise version of their software where you can save prompt templates. However, you could use something as simple as a Google Sheets spreadsheet and copy and paste all of your prompts in there.

You can also use tools like AIPRM, which is a prompt management tool. It allows you to build your prompt libraries and organise them. The whole purpose of this is to be more efficient, and that's a great way to make efficiencies within the efficiencies."

What kinds of prompts should SEOs be using?

"There are so many and, again, it depends on your use case. You might be using it for ideation or building out topic clusters, though I'm not saying that you should use AI to identify keywords and search volume because it can't do that. You have to understand the limitations of these tools. It's best for coming up with ideas, idea-building, and writing content.

You need to make sure that you're checking your content so that it's factually correct and accurate. These AI prompts can be really efficient for getting that first draft out on paper, paragraph by paragraph and section by section. For SEO, the most important areas are headlines, meta descriptions, and regex formulas for technical SEO and research.

When you're building your prompts, you need to understand your constraints, understand the tone and your brand voice, and have prebuilt prompts that you can add to other prompts. That way, you're saving time and maintaining a consistent output. Having brand tone instructions for your prompts will give you great output."

How do you phrase a prompt to ensure that the output is consistent?

"I scaffold my prompts and I stack different components. Start with the role you want your LLM to have, whether it is acting as an SEO or as a subject matter expert in the home services industry. Then, the task. What type of blog post do you want? Do you just want a few short paragraphs, or do you want an entire blog post? I would recommend working piece by piece rather than creating a whole blog post from scratch.

Then, provide context and constraints. That's where the tone and voice come in. You may want it to use a certain style, use a certain number of bullet points, or avoid using emojis. Finally, look for an opportunity to give examples of the type of output you want to see. The more specific the prompt the better the output, then you can fine-tune it with different variables to make it reusable across other tasks."

How did you establish this formula?

"There are a few different large language models out there – OpenAI has ChatGPT, Google has BARD (which is based on PaLM), Meta has Llama, and Anthropic has Claude. They all have their own best practices for prompt engineering. As you read the documentation and listen to other people (such as myself) who spend hours and hours testing through trial-and-error experimentation, you start to get an intuition as to what works and what doesn't work.

I can now generate a much more effective prompt much quicker than I did six months ago. When you're getting started, you have to get a sense of the nuances. Equally, even when you are more experienced, there's no such thing as a perfect prompt. There is always trial and error, and you can never completely predict the outcome. You still have to be prepared to tweak it so that you can get what you're ultimately looking for."

If an AI model starts hallucinating, can you start a new conversation without having to re-teach everything that you've been working on?

"You can pre-train them. For instance, OpenAI introduced custom instructions so that, if you have the tone really well mapped out, you can pre-train the model by simply installing those custom instructions. AIPRM does the same thing with custom profiles, where you can have a profile pre-trained so you don't have to do it from scratch.

If you're in a conversation, the model will remember what you've already talked about in the conversation. However, that degrades over time, the more that you write. At some point, it is going to forget the instructions that you gave. Therefore, there will always be an element of retraining.

I do want to emphasise that we are at the very beginning of this technology. Things that we're dealing with now are probably going to look vastly different in six months, a year, or two years. Take everything that you're learning with a grain of salt. It's more about learning how to use the tools and being able to adapt as they get better and better.

I believe custom instructions are currently available for free on OpenAI. Obviously, they will probably offer extended capabilities in the professional version, but the most basic custom instructions are there. For some tools, like AIPRM and Writesonic, you typically have to pay for custom profile options."

How do you establish the right tone that you should be using?

"You can combine your prompts with existing brand guidelines, but you still have to do a lot of the hard soul-searching work if you're a business owner or a marketer. You have to understand your brand and you have to develop your brand identity.

These tools are effective in the same way that Photoshop is. If you're already a great writer, it's going to help you. However, it's not going to turn you into a great writer overnight. You still need to be able to effectively communicate what you want. You'd be surprised by how many people don't know what they want or how to articulate it. ChatGPT might help you ideate some of that, but it's not going to solve that problem.

If you have brand guidelines, you can take all of those and use them to pre-train the model, then you're good to go. That's easy. However, if you don't have clear, effective brand guidelines, you should consider building them out first."

Does giving a novice a great tool just allow them to shoot themselves in the foot even more quickly?

"Absolutely. That's why the education around these tools is critical going forward.

These tools hallucinate and they make up facts very confidently. If you're not a subject matter expert on whatever content you're producing, you have to assume that it's not always going to be correct. You have to double-check, or get a subject matter expert to review it, to make sure the output is accurate."

How is Google dealing with AI-generated content at the moment?

"They have publicly encouraged it, in the sense that you're not going to get penalised strictly for using AI content. They're currently skirting the issue by saying that, as long as the content is helpful, then you can potentially rank. If your content will help users, then that's the type of content Google wants.

They're not saying 'yes' or 'no' to AI content. They're saying it's how you use the tools, and they're trying to avoid letting spam, unhelpful, factually inaccurate content rank the highest.

Google's under the gun anyway, when it comes to the performance of search results in general. They've done a lot of work over the last few years. One thing to pay attention to (that's adjacent to all of this) is the search generative experience. That is Google's version of integrating AI into search results and it will certainly impact SEO going forward, which is a whole other can of worms."

When you're using AI, what part of the process should humans keep for themselves?

"There are two major areas where humans are always going to be valuable in the content creation process. One is editing. Editing has already become so much more of an important skill than it was before. AI will continue to get better, but it doesn't understand anything. It's a very sophisticated piece of tech that can predict the next word based on its training data. Right now, it doesn't actually think.

The second key area is subject matter expertise that is unique to people, which is based on EEAT – specifically experience and expertise. It's about being able to infuse your content with real experience from real experts. AI doesn't know how to actually fix a kitchen sink. If you're a plumber, you want to talk to a plumber who deals with the latest tools, techniques, and technology. You want to get that specific expert to inform your content, and that's what Google's going to care about going forward.

As you see more and more AI-generated content, new ideas that are helpful for users are going to help content surface to the top. Supplementing your AI-generated content with expertise and experience is going to be the best combination for SEO going forward.

The technology is amazing, but it has a lot of problems. When e-commerce first came to the internet, none of us wanted to put a credit card in to buy something online. Yet here we are, a couple of decades later, and you have trillions of dollars online.

With any of this technology, it's slow. However, this isn't like Google Glass or even VR. AI-generated content is here, and it is going to disrupt a ton of industries, so don't put your head in the sand. At the very least, learn about it and understand what it can do."

If an SEO is struggling for time, what should they stop doing right now so they can spend more time doing what you suggest in 2024?

"Don't get too sucked into the trends that are being parroted on social media. It's very easy to chase a new trend, but SEO is still all about fundamentals. It's all about being helpful. It's all about internal linking. It's all about making sure that your content is easily consumable and discoverable.

Ultimately, don't spend too much time getting caught up in what people are saying about SEO and just learn for yourself. Every situation is unique; that's why we always say, 'It depends.'"

Garrett Sussman is Demand Generation Manager at iPullRank, and you can find him over at iPullRank.com.

Build your own prompt libraries for your clients – with Victoria Olsina

SEO Consultant and Speaker Victoria Olsina says that having a single prompt library might not be enough. You need multiple prompt libraries, one for each client.

Victoria says: "Build your own prompt libraries, using AI and the voice and instructions of your clients, to produce the different content typologies that they need."

Why does an SEO need to do this?

"Right now, AI can't do this. I don't know if, in a week's time, we will have an AI that can automatically act like a client and replicate how they write, their tone of voice, and their unique selling proposal. It is possible, but I can only talk from my perspective today. So far, I haven't seen any AI that can do that.

You can use the link reader plugin in GPT-4 to read different URLs, and therefore prompt the AI to write like a client by giving some samples – but you still need the samples."

What does a great prompt library look like and what content are you building prompts for?

"Great prompt libraries are instructions that aim to produce their most popular content typologies faster. For example, newsletter intros, blog posts, and social media posts.

For B2B, the most important social media platform is LinkedIn. When you are creating your LinkedIn prompts, you need to consider how you would write about a topic. What's your tone of voice? How does this brand talk to their audience on LinkedIn? For that, you need to define the audience. It's not the same for a client in crypto compliance as it is for a client in automation testing. Developers and compliance officers talk in a different way.

Another very popular content typology would be product pages. Different clients talk about their products differently. The way that the CTA displays and the USP are different. Press releases, reports, and guides are also important. If you have the Ultimate Guide to Crypto Compliance or the Ultimate Guide to Automation Testing, they will look quite different.

Each type of content will need different prompts because the output is different. A LinkedIn post is different from a quarterly report or an Ultimate Guide to…"

Where would you keep this library and how often would you update the prompts?

"The most basic place to host these libraries would be a Google Doc or within Notion. It's basically a Word doc.

As for how often you update them, it depends on the client's needs. It's very rare that the prompt is 100% perfect the first time that you try it. You have to refine it up to the point where the client is happy, then iterate and use it for one or two months. Then, if the client has feedback, you can incorporate the feedback and alter the prompt."

How do you decide on the right prompts and the right way to use AI for a client's content?

"It's in agreement with the client. It's a joint effort and a joint decision. You say to them that you can create a model, a framework, and a prompt that will help speed up the process of creating the kind of content they produce all the time.

In order to create those prompts, I sit with the client and ask them what their content is. I ask if there is any piece of content that they don't like doing or they feel takes a lot of time and they could be doing something else that is more valuable to them.

For example, newsletter intros. Clients might say, 'I really don't like doing them. It takes me a lot of time, and it takes me away from things that are more important and would deliver more value to the business. Can you help me create them, so I don't have to?'"

Do you use these prompts at the beginning of each conversation that you have with AI?

"It depends on how the prompt is structured. If you need to give examples, you can give them before or after, but the prompt has instructions for that."

How do you 'prime' the AI?

"Priming the AI could be to say, 'Act like X persona', and X persona has a number of attributes and gives certain context. What's more important, though, is to give examples. If you have a client who wants to automate the process of creating newsletter intros, you need 3, 5, or 10 examples of the introductions that they like. If they don't have their own, then ask them to give 5 examples of their competitors' newsletter intros that they like.

This is even more important than saying 'Act like…' because, if you give examples, the AI can identify the tone of voice, whether they are talking about a certain matter in an informal way or a formal way, etc. It can infer a lot of things from the example itself.

When you're giving an example, providing a link is often faster than copying the text into the tool. You can give a link to 10 Google Docs, and each Google Doc could contain 10 client pages with 3,000 words on each page. If you try to copy and paste that same amount of content, it might stop working."

Is this just for GPT-4 or is it for other AI software as well?

"You can create your own prompts on most platforms. Jasper and Writesonic have the ability to create your own prompt, and they have had this functionality for a long time. I mostly use ChatGPT because it's the most flexible, and you can use them with the AIPRM plugin.

AIPRM is a Chrome extension that gives you a collection of prompts and allows you to store your own prompts as well. If you save your prompts there, you can then send the link to the client. The client doesn't even have to see the prompt if you don't want that."

Once the AI starts creating content that you're happy with, can you keep coming back to the same conversation and get the same results?

"I have had varied results with that approach, actually. When it's reading or using a file that you upload, it tells you that it has to upload everything again. However, that could change.

Currently, whenever you use Code Interpreter to read priming information from a spreadsheet, you have to redo the process. It tells you that it has to run everything again to get to the same point."

What downsides of using AI would you discuss with your clients?

"Firstly, crafting prompts will often require a lot of iterations, and we have to use our time wisely. For example, I might ask the client how long it takes them to write a newsletter intro. To have a prompt that looks excellent might take 5-10 hours. I need to check whether that is something they want to spend their budget on, or if they would rather have me spend that time on something else.

Besides that, AI can sometimes seem repetitive or use words that the client generally wouldn't. However, you can take those words and put them into the instructions, telling the AI to avoid using those terms.

The other problem is with fact-checking. We all know that AI hallucinates and makes things up, and that cannot happen in certain regulated industries. If I write product pages for a solicitor that have errors, they can get suspended. Manual fact-checking 100% has to happen. It's part of the quality control process."

Do you use additional software to rewrite or improve what the AI initially produced?

"I have used Page ReWriter in the past and it has an option to make it sound more human-like. I haven't used it recently so there may have been big changes to that tool but, when you check it manually, a content writer or someone that works with the product will add words that AI would not. That gives it a layer that sounds a bit more human (particularly for Google), in terms of the writing patterns.

What AI does is it gives you the word that is most likely to follow after another word. When a human comes in, they will interrupt that pattern and bring more human life to the writing."

If an SEO is struggling for time, what should they stop doing right now so they can spend more time doing what you suggest in 2024?

"SEOs, particularly freelancers or consultants, often try to do everything ourselves. Try to outsource to another SEO or a VA. If you're unable to do all of the things that you have to do in your day, outsource a small, manual task, and partner with another SEO consultant who will help you deliver different services.

Also, try to automate the manual and repetitive processes using tools like Zapier, IFTTT, or Make (formerly Integromat). You can create a trigger or an event for an RSS feed or Help a Reporter Out (HARO) emails, for example. Then, use a ChatGPT model to receive instructions from that trigger and create something with that output.

HARO is a resource that SEO people use a lot. If you want to be a thought leader, it's a service that allows you to provide a quote to a journalist as soon as possible, so you're more likely to be featured in their story. However, it's very hard to reply to journalists' requests every day. It's very time-consuming. Recently, I created a workflow where, the moment a HARO email arrives that's related to SEO, marketing, or AI, Make takes that query and generates a reply.

HARO sends 3 emails a day, every day, so use automation or a VA to help you with that."

Victoria Olsina is an SEO Consultant and Speaker, and you can find her over at VictoriaOlsina.com.

Watch out for better, AI-powered technical SEO tools – with Pam Aungst Cronin

In addition to using services like ChatGPT natively, you should also keep an eye out for better, AI-powered technical SEO tools launching in the near future, says Pam Aungst Cronin from Pam Ann Marketing.

Pam says: "Keep your eyes peeled for new, better technical SEO tools that utilise AI.

There are a lot of great technical SEO tools out there. That includes tools like Screaming Frog, that crawl and gather every bit of technical information about the site for you, or some of the more all-encompassing platforms where you can manage everything in one place, both technical and on-page. There are great tools out there now, and maybe they're utilising AI a bit, but they're still traditional SEO tools.

I would love to see some truly impressive AI-driven technical SEO tools. When you run a Screaming Frog crawl, you get every bit of technical data about a site you could ever possibly collect. You're basically recreating Googlebot. Then, it's up to your eye, and real intelligence, to figure out what to do with it.

In this age of AI, why do the tools stop there? Why can't they use AI to go further, reverse engineer Google's algorithms, and tell us exactly what our biggest wins would be?"

Would you like to see a Screaming Frog plugin for ChatGPT?

"Something like that would be incredible, but maybe not just for ChatGPT. Everybody is tunnel-visioned on ChatGPT – because it's amazing and it's breaking barriers that haven't been broken before. However, I think it's too limiting to constantly think of AI as just ChatGPT.

I've had some software developers ask me to review their new AI-driven Google Analytics tools. There are a bunch of different ones, but they're all very ChatGPT-driven. They're trying to mimic ChatGPT by giving you the ability to chat with your data (you can ask it how many visits you got in X time frame from Y source, etc.). It's not that impressive to me because AI could do so much more. In the SEO and analytics world, I want tools that utilise the machine learning aspect of AI, more than the chat aspect of it.

I'd really love to see something along the lines of a Screaming Frog AI that learns from all of the SEO professionals who use Screaming Frog. It could be a SaaS software, all online, that anonymously collects all sorts of information (with consent) about how the best-performing sites are technically configured versus how the worst-performing sites are. It could understand which technical changes created the most improvement and which were useless.

Imagine all that knowledge from all those SEOs using Screaming Frog, all collected into one AI that's constantly learning. That would basically reverse engineer the Google algorithm."

Could that AI eventually identify where the issues are in your site, and make site performance improvements for you?

"Eventually, yes. I would not trust it to that degree yet. A lot of the AI tools that I've seen thus far are not that impressive. It would probably take several years of verifying with real intelligence that artificial intelligence is making the right suggestions before I would trust it to make those changes for me.

The final stage of this would be auto-tuning the site based on Google's algorithm changes. The AI would notice that your site needs an edit because of an algorithm change, and just do it. That would be very interesting. It would become a constant, rapid, iterative race between the SEOs and Google whereas, currently, when Google makes a move and it takes us a while to catch up."

Could you let AI loose on a relatively unpopular category in your blog and allow it to make some minor tweaks to attempt to rank it more highly?

"I would be more comfortable with an approach like, 'Don't fix it if it's not broken; only tinker with the broken stuff.' If it could be limited to that, I would feel a bit better about it.

I would also want a way to roll back changes – like a really good changelog, where you can monitor it and see what the AI did and why. Then, if you don't agree with it, you could just roll it back. I think that would be necessary.

Unfortunately, I think we're incredibly far away from that at this point. As rapidly as AI is evolving, I can't imagine it getting to that point in 2024. What I'm excited about for the coming year is that tools will hopefully start to come out that utilise the learning aspect of AI, as opposed to the 'chatting with a bot' aspect of AI."

Are there any AI tools that you would recommend for SEOs at the moment?

"Not with regard to technical SEO tools. That's what I'm excitedly waiting for.

As far as content goes, ChatGPT is just amazing for content ideation. However, not for writing your full content and publishing it with ChatGPT as the author.

If AI knows exactly how to make a website perform, will all sites end up performing equally well, making content and experience more important than technical SEO?

"That's an interesting thought experiment. I can't think too far beyond that without thinking in circles. It's a chicken or egg issue at that point. At that point, Web 3.0 might have taken over and we'll all be focusing on that instead. At the moment, we have to optimize both the chicken and the egg."

Is there anything that should never be automated?

"Content production. Content ideation – planning and strategising – is what I recommend automating with AI. The content production part should never be automated, especially considering the new E in EEAT. Google has told us specifically that they want us to add experience to expertise, authoritativeness, and trust.

I think that's because EAT can be mimicked by AI but personal, firsthand experience can't. ChatGPT can make it up, but it can't create a genuine case study about something that you did for a client that worked. Nothing can replace that first-hand experience. The full content production, with the injection of personal experience, should probably never be automated.

Your process and project management, however, can be automated. I've implemented some things using AI that have provided tremendous improvements for us, from an automated process perspective. Tools like ChatGPT can write conference call summaries based on a transcript or create an automatic report review.

I have created a prompt in the GPT for Sheets add-on where I put all my thoughts about what I look for when I review a report before it goes out. It checks the report summary for all of those things: Did we say anything that sounds like we're making a promise? Are we using non-committal language? Are we using relatively positive terminology, while still being accurate? Everyone should be trying to use AI for their own internal process optimization."

Do you share with clients that you're using AI to assist you?

"It depends on what it's for. If it's for their written report summary, no. It's the same as using Grammarly to double-check emails before sending them out. For a more specific application, though, we would tell them.

For example, we had a client who purchased an old magazine that had been produced for around 40 years. The magazine had given them all the content and pictures on DVDs, and they were turning that into a website, and each picture had a really robust caption. In the process of turning this old-school print magazine into a well-optimized website, we needed image alt text tags. The captions were too long for that, but they were so accurate in their descriptions of what was shown in the image that we told them we'd like to use AI to shorten the captions into img/alt text tags.

It was tens of thousands of articles, so it didn't make sense for a human to do it, and the cost would have been extremely prohibitive compared to using the ChatGPT API. For that application, we recommended AI to turn the captions into shorter image alt text tags for SEO and ADA purposes. We designed the project around AI's capabilities.

You want to have that open conversation. I naturally end up having that conversation with clients when I talk about how they can use AI to come up with ideas but not to write their content. I'm constantly preaching about the responsible use of AI as it pertains to SEO. That's my overall theory, even when it comes to client management. If you're going to write up a report summary, and you want to use AI to slightly polish it up, that's a responsible use of AI – as long as it was written by a human in the first place.

If you're going to do their project work with it, they should know from the get-go. It should be used responsibly and selectively, for very specific cases where the benefits are almost impossible for a human to achieve."

Will it be necessary to use AI to compete in the future, based on the size of projects it can accomplish?

"Yes and no. In some ways, what's old is new again. At some point, the AI will be so overdone that businesses might seek out consultants who do things the old-school manual way with their own brains. In an AI-dominated world, the injection of real human intelligence could be the differentiating factor.

On the flip side, the scale of certain projects and the role that AI plays in scaling probably would limit competition. Another thing to consider is that it's kind of already that way. We are competing against big SEO agencies that have hundreds of employees and project management software we couldn't dream of affording. That opens them up to certain enterprise-level clients and projects at a scale that we couldn't handle.

However, that's fine because we don't position ourselves that way. We position ourselves as small, boutique, hands-on, and offering one-on-one communication with clients. That's our differentiating factor. It might end up being the same as that with AI.

We're constantly getting clients who have left a giant SEO agency and are craving that more personal relationship. Human relationships are something that will never be replaced by AI – at least in the near term. The human relationship with your clients is going to remain no matter how much you use AI in the background to scale their projects. You can't replace that human-on-human interaction."

If an SEO is struggling for time, what should they stop doing right now so they can spend more time doing what you suggest in 2024?

"If you aren't using ChatGPT for content ideation, then start doing that. Having ChatGPT come up with topic ideas, outlines, and content briefs for pieces of content will save a ton of time. I'm always going to preach that you should not have ChatGPT write the content, but the content ideation it can provide is a huge time saver.

Also, recently, we have been shifting a lot more towards reviving, revising, expanding, and improving existing content on sites that have a lot of content already. Of course, if it's a newer site, you have to focus on creating new pieces of content and building out your encyclopedia of content on that website.

However, you might have been doing the content production thing for many years – there's a lot of content on the website and you're still sitting there with writer's block wracking your brain. We have been doing SEO for one client for 10 years, and we have written about every angle of their topic that we could ever come up with. That's an extreme example but, on any large site, there's tons of content to work with.

Pick the pieces of content that aren't performing, rewrite them, revamp them, make them higher quality, make them longer, and ask ChatGPT how you can make the content better. Revise and relaunch existing content instead of agonising over coming up with new topics."

Pam Aungst Cronin is President and Founder of Pam Ann Marketing, and you can find her over at PamAnnMarketing.com.

5 THE SERP

Keep a closer eye on the ever-changing SERPs – with Julia-Carolin Zeng

Julia-Carolin Zeng from Charlie on the Move would like to share that the opportunity you are optimizing for is constantly evolving, thanks to the shifting SERP.

Julia-Carolin says: "For 2024, I recommend keeping an even closer eye on the SERPs. They are dynamically changing, especially with the integration of AI. Google is testing a lot and I expect to see a lot more changes coming."

What are we specifically looking for in the SERPs?

"We already know about the knowledge graph and featured snippets, and we've seen fancy widgets over the last few weeks like tiles and images that link directly to content.

I recommend keeping an eye on all of these things because it will have an impact on your click-through rate and the data that you get out of Google Search Console. If Google suddenly displays an image, that's still an impression for you, but it might not be displayed as your actual content.

It is also becoming more important to look at things like intent. Is it informational or commercial? What is Google showing the user? You can look at the SERPs to explain why somebody is clicking or not.

At the same time, Google seems to be doing a lot of testing, and I expect this to continue until they find the best way to integrate AI in the SERPs. I've seen lots of things appearing and disappearing a few weeks later, and then something else comes up and disappears again. Over the last three months, I've been showing screenshots to my clients and saying, 'This is what I'm seeing right now in the SERPs, but hold off. Don't do anything yet because Google might change this again.'

In some of my recent research, I put in a query like 'best internal communication tools', and the SERP had this grid of tiles showing the logos of different communication software. When you clicked one, it gave three options of articles to read.

How do users really interact with these new things appearing in the SERPs? What can we expect? Do they see a company logo, open a new tab, and then search for that company name? Do they click on the image and then click on one of the articles? Do they just scroll over it because they think it's an ad and go to the first organic result? We don't know, and Google doesn't know either. This might impact why Google is changing things every few weeks."

Is Google going through testing to land on something more consistent or do you see this constant flux being the new norm?

"I think it will be a bit of a mixture. There is a lot of testing going on at the moment, but we already have things like personalisation and geography embedded in the SERPs. When I search for something, I might see something completely different than what you would see for the same term – based on search history, personal interests, and so on.

In my opinion, this won't go away. It is what makes Google the most used search engine; the fact that the search results are so relevant to the individual.

It will never be static, with 10 links that come up for every search query. There will always be the featured snippet and different elements being pulled out for different individual users. However, I expect that the recent heavy testing will stop once Google has a bit more clarity on how to integrate AI and machine learning into the SERPs."

Do you need to optimize your pages based on intent and incorporate different elements relating to that?

"That is already the case. That doesn't seem like a new tip to me because I've been recommending this for the past two years. Look at the intent behind the keyword and what type of content you should create to serve that intent.

What I'm seeing lately, with the changes in the SERPs and the heavier use of featured snippets and knowledge graphs, is that informational queries get fewer and fewer clicks. We look at the data for a website and clicks are going down, but we're still ranking in position one, and we have the featured snippet. This is something we have been discussing in the SEO industry for years, but now it is really starting to have a heavy impact on the data.

When I am reporting this to my clients, they ask, 'Shall we stop producing this informational content?' I think it is still important to have that informational content and brand visibility on the SERPs. It's what makes the internet perceive you as an expert in your field. If you explain certain terminology in a glossary, for example, it makes the whole package of what your website offers more authoritative.

If you have the featured snippet, even if nobody clicks on it, at least half of the people who see it will recognise your brand name there. Then, if they see it coming up again for another query they search a few days later, it stays in their memory."

What is good informational content? How broad can you go with your informational content?

"It really depends on the industry, what you're trying to achieve, what products you're selling, what your speciality is, and who your target audience is. A big industry I've been working with over the past few years is cyber security. I also have a client in threat intelligence, and we see a lot of overlap there. Threat intelligence, though, is not only about cyber security. So, how many cyber security-related terms should we really target on the website?

If we focus too much on cyber security and not on other threats like protests and war – which are threats that need to be embedded in threat intelligence – then the internet will see us as an expert in cyber security and not threat intelligence. These are the things you always need to consider, and they are specific for every industry."

What does the potential move towards an AI-driven SERP mean for changes in consumer behaviour and how do SEOs need to adapt?

"That is exactly what we need to keep an eye on: how much of it is AI? I have a friend who is also an SEO consultant and they say that the only thing tools like ChatGPT is going to achieve is taking rubbish and creating more rubbish out of it. There's some truth to that. It is demotivating content writers. Why write good content and invest a lot of time and research if somebody else is just taking ChatGPT-created content that is essentially taken from existing sources?

One question is, how is Google going to remove that barrier? How will they convince content writers and website publishers that it is still worth producing quality content by doing individual research, doing surveys, using data, etc.? That is in Google's best interest, but how are they going to do that?

With that in mind, I don't think the SERPs will ever be 100% AI-generated. There will always be a link to individual content. The extent to which Google is already using machine learning (by pulling featured snippets out of content, etc.) might stay. However, original content will always be featured somehow because that's what provides quality and originality."

If Google doesn't change significantly, in terms of how the SERP operates, are younger audiences more likely to turn to other platforms for answers?

"I think it depends on the industry and the topic. TikTok, for example, is a video-heavy platform. It lives on video. We already see that appearing in the SERPs. For certain how-to queries (like 'how to clean your kitchen sink'), you get a list of YouTube videos displayed in the SERPs. Video is already there.

I think it will be similar to the discussion we had 6/7 years ago about voice search. Everybody was saying that the whole industry would move to voice search, and everything would be voice search-driven. Now, that is only true for certain queries. If you're on the street and you need directions from Google Maps, voice search is handy. If you're at home on your laptop and you need in-depth information about something, people are still reading content.

There will be a bit of a shift. There might be more video for certain things, but there will still be written content as well. I don't think platforms like TikTok will completely take over from the older, more established platforms and shapes of content."

What impact does the amount of content being produced by AI have on copyright and protecting your IP?

"That is another reason why I think Google is being quite cautious and testing so much. There have been big lawsuits over the last few weeks, especially regarding copyright.

That was one of my big concerns right from the start. When everybody was excited about ChatGPT and saying that it would take over the web and everything would be AI-generated, I had a feeling that there would also be legislation coming, at some point, that might prevent that.

A few months ago, Italy banned ChatGPT for a few weeks. I was surprised that it was Italy and not my home country of Germany because we're usually big on things like data protection. That is another thing to keep an eye on. I'm sure Google has had the technology for years. They probably could have been the first to release something like that, and there must be a reason why they didn't. I think it is exactly because of all the legal questions that are still unsolved and a bit of a grey area, at the moment."

If an SEO is struggling for time, what should they stop doing so they can spend more time doing what you suggest?

"I see too many people still obsessing over title tags and meta descriptions. I'm not saying that they're not important, they are, but if you get a list of 200 URLs from your website where the title tag is too long or too short, or there's a meta description missing, and focus on rewriting them – that, in my opinion, is a waste of time. That won't get you the results you're trying to achieve.

In most cases, Google is now dynamically overwriting title tags and meta descriptions to better match the user's intent. If Google overwrites these, it doesn't necessarily mean that something is wrong with your current title tag; it just means that the algorithm decided, in the moment, that the content could be more relevant for another query and that it has more to say than just what the title tag contains.

If you do pull a list of 200 URLs, then check it. What are these pages? Maybe there's something else that's wrong. If a page doesn't have a title tag, it might not have any content at all, it might have a noindex tag, or it could be canonicalized. Take a look at that first.

Then, if some tool tells you that something might be wrong with the title tag, check if there actually is something wrong. A page can rank without an optimized title tag and, if it ranks well for the right keywords, why spend time updating the title tag and meta description if there is nothing else that you can improve? In my opinion, and based on my experience, if something is really wrong with the title tag and the meta description, and the page doesn't rank, you need to look at more than just the metadata. There might be outdated content, there might be images missing, or so many things that could be wrong with that page as well.

In a way, I always use these lists of URLs as something to look at. What are these pages? What is their purpose? Do they even need to be there? Then, see what you need to update on these pages. Instead of going through a list of 200 URLs and updating the title tag, go through a list of 200 URLs and say, 'These pages need attention. Let's prioritise.' Work on the pages that actually have value in terms of the keyword, the traffic they could bring, and the value for the business if you get traffic to this page."

***Julia-Carolin Zeng** is an **SEO Consultant** at **Charlie on the Move**, and you can find her over at charlieonthemove.com.*

Consider Google's incentive to index your site and prepare for the next chapter of the internet – with Jono Alderson

Independent Technical SEO Consultant Jono Alderson advises that you cast an impartial eye across your site, asking why Google would want to crawl, index, and rank what you're offering.

Jono says: "My number one tip is a scary one. It's to start worrying about what happens when Google has no incentive to crawl, index, or rank your site."

Are you in trouble if your whole content strategy and your entire business model are dependent upon getting indexed? Are you saying that SEO cannot be your marketing strategy?

"It is definitely something you should think about. Almost everybody, to some degree, relies on some form of content marketing – whether we call it that or not. We do marketing keyword research, we try and spot opportunities, and then we build landing pages, we write articles, or we have a blog. The objective of all of those things is to try and boost our rankings, get traffic, and convert visitors. However, that whole ecosystem is built on the assumption that people are typing things into a search box and we can access search volume metrics for that.

Increasingly, that isn't true when you look at Search Generative Experience, AI-generated content, Google Discover, and the 'ambient search revolution', where it's not as simple as: 'type the thing, get the results.'

Also, we still assume that Google is incentivised to spend their resources trying to discover our content, index it, evaluate it, rank it, and return it in some kind of list. That's not in their interest anymore. Increasingly, for many of the things users are searching for, they don't need to be evaluating our content and serving it. They can synthesise their own results, using SGE or something similar. They understand the inherent problems well enough to be able to solve them without relying on our content.

We've seen the beginning of this for a while now, with things like zero-click searches. The balance of power has changed. This is the conclusion of the whole first chapter of the internet. It is no longer necessarily the case that Google is relying on websites as sources for answers. If we're still plodding along going, 'I will research my keywords, I will rank my landing page, I will commission my article', all of the dominoes that would have followed from that – around indexing, crawling, ranking, etc. – no longer exist.

We need to rethink what content marketing is, what content strategy is, and what our SEO is. It's probably not about trying to write pages to rank for keywords; it's probably more about brand discovery and preference, and trying to convert people in other channels when you've built those relationships."

How do you incentivise Google to want to rank your content? What does content that highlights your brand and adds value look like?

"This is the heartbeat. I don't think anybody really knows, but there are some areas you can go to. You can definitely try and work on bringing unique value to a space. Do something that no one has done before. Go deeper, go better, commission the research, and employ the experts. None of this is easy or cheap. In some spaces, it might not even be possible, but this is one of the options.

Also, don't be too unique and too out there, because misalignment from established norms might mean that you do worse. You can definitely be polarising; I think that's interesting.

For a long time, it's been trendy to say that brands need to become publishers. We misconstrued that to mean we should have a blog or commission articles. Actually, when you look at real publishers and real editorial outlets and newspapers, they do research, they are in the field, they form opinions, they have editorial policies, etc. If we do those things as brands, then we might get in front of people. Perhaps not when they're typing 'renew car insurance', but when they're on their journeys, searching for other things, or solving other problems. We start to build brand preference and association there.

It's cliché and it's tedious, but the answer keeps coming back to: be the kind of brand that users expect to see, consume information from, and trust. It does come down to EAT and demonstrating substantial experience.

Tactically, you can cheat a bit. You can compete in other verticals, where it's easier at the moment. You can double down on e-commerce, video, audio, and other areas where there's less competition and it's going to be more expensive for Google to synthesise content. That might buy you another year or two, but that's not the long game. It's all about brand."

If Google decides not to index your content, do you give up on that URL or is it possible to get them to change their mind?

"Anecdotally, I've seen more and more people grumbling on Twitter/X or Threads that, 'I've got good content. I've got some links. Google isn't indexing it. Why not? Is it some kind of mysterious technical problem?'

It's probably not. It's just that, even if the content is good, it's probably not valuable, unique, or distinct enough for Google to want to expend resources putting it in their index. I always come back to the example of lasagna recipes. What is Google's incentive to index the lasagna recipe that you publish on your blog? They have a hundred trillion of them. Even if somebody searches for a weird lasagna recipe that doesn't exist, they can synthesise it on the fly.

If you've got pages that aren't getting indexed, and you think that they're good and that you've done SEO best practices, maybe you're not fundamentally solving a problem that either the users or Google has. If the objective is to feed the beast, it doesn't matter how much more work you put into that page if you're trying to feed it content that it doesn't need.

Maybe delete them. Less is more. Find the stuff where you can make an impact and make it 10 times longer, 10 times better, or even 10 times shorter if that's more valuable. Add video and employ experts. Double down on what Google can't easily synthesise out of thin air. If that's the kind of content you're writing, you're probably not adding value to the web. Your pages have to truly add value to the corpus of the internet, in the same way that you might if you're researching a paper."

Is there a way to easily measure how valuable, unique, and distinctive

your content is?

"Not directly, which is where it gets tricky. It's difficult to build a business case for this and get buy-in when you could just show a list of keywords, search volumes, and CPCs. If you do the big shift – you stop writing pages that try to rank for keywords and, instead, start writing pages that try to solve specific user problems without going to sell or convert directly – you start prioritising the needs of the audience rather than just your customers.

Yes, you can't monetise it or quantify the impact on the bottom line, but you could do things like measure brand recall and saliency. You could do traditional surveying mechanisms that say, 'Which of these logos do you recognise?' You could put voting widgets on the bottom of your articles and resources that say, 'Was this page useful?' You can monitor upticks in that time and vaguely correlate that to engagement, then vaguely correlate engagement to revenue.

It's going to be much harder than a simplistic machine where you get a number for ranking, a number for visitors in, and a number for visitors out. That's never been how this works, though. Pretending that this is a direct response ecosystem has been a big con. SEO has only ever accidentally been a channel that converts. It's so much more powerful as a channel that introduces brands and helps people to trust and become familiar with them. From there, you convert in your other channels when you're solving people's problems, they're recommending you, and they recognise your logo when they see you in the supermarket. This is where SEO is far more powerful than other channels, but we've become so focused on the bits that are measurable.

Maybe measurement isn't what we should be optimizing for. Maybe it's audience success and recognition. You can measure some of that, it's just harder."

Is it still useful to look at what websites are ranking number one for your target keyword phrase, looking at the style and type of content it is, and taking lessons from that?

"I think there are two aspects to this. One is that looking at Google is one of the best pieces of research you can do, and the SEO industry seems to have only recently rediscovered this. Google has the best understanding of what the intent might have been and what kinds of content the user might want. In some cases that will very obviously be showing the cheapest product and the fastest way you can get it. In some cases, it might be quite nuanced. It might be a couple of videos, an informational resource, and other bits.

All of that is the product of what the SEO teams at those companies are doing. If they're all stuck in yesteryear's thinking, and they're all trying to compete on keywords, then maybe you end up aping their bad behaviours.

I think a bit of both is sensible. Look at Google search results to identify the types of things that Google does a good job of understanding, in terms of what people want, and then do better than the people in that space. That has always been SEO; ever since the first days. Look at what's ranking in front of you and do a better job than them."

You have spoken about the concept of operating in a space that's solved. What do you mean by that and what do you do if that's the case?

"I love this concept, and the lasagna recipe is a really good example of this. The lasagna, at a conceptual level, is a solved problem. Google comprehensively understands the concept of 'lasagna'. It understands what it is, it understands all the things that might be in it, how you might cook it, where you might eat it, etc. You are going to struggle to create a piece of content that adds unique value to that space.

Google has such a comprehensive understanding of the concept that, even if you did, they don't need it. They can synthesise new information based on what they've already got. If you want a recipe for a blueberry lasagna, even if that doesn't exist, Google can take a strong enough punt at it with generative processes and a bit of AI, and they can create that on the fly. There is no content strategy where you can write an article, page, or recipe and rank on 'blueberry lasagna'.

There are lots of spaces like this. More practically, every car insurance website and aggregator on the web has a page about how to prevent your pipes from freezing in winter. They've done a bunch of keyword research, they've seen that this is the kind of thing that people search for, they understand it's loosely in their sector, and they write a 500-word article that says the same thing as every other page. This is a solved problem. There is enough content out there that touches enough of the angles that Google, having ingested all of it, can solve users' problems and synthesise answers in spaces that it hasn't encountered before.

There is no way into these spaces – and there are going to be more and more of these. Anywhere where there is either a simple binary answer (which is the case with zero-click searches today) or, more increasingly, spaces where there's enough information on all the different permutations that it doesn't make sense to add another one.

This goes right back to the beginning. If your content strategy is to spot keywords, write pages, get ranked, and get traffic, all of that stops when Google has no incentive to consume your pipe tips or your lasagna recipe. It's a solved problem."

How do you limit the danger of Google not indexing your content? Are there other channels that you can work with?

"There are definitely other channels. You could go all in on TikTok, or Threads, or X, or whatever we're doing today. However, a more diverse content strategy that does some kind of hub and spoke thing is probably not the craziest idea, to spread that gamble a bit.

SEO is going to be harder and harder to do in the way we've done it. There will always be a need to have content about the services you offer and the things you do. Increasingly, though, the kinds of 'hearts and minds' content might make more sense on Instagram. Maybe you just do the hard sales stuff via page search.

SEO looks less and less like a channel that can and should convert. You can't attract and compete with that type of audience, at least not reliably. It's not in Google's interest to do that. Wherever there's a clear route to monetisation and transaction, Google is going to try and do that in the SERPs rather than funnelling to your site. We see this happening in sector after sector. They take click-to-buy, flights, hotels, jobs, etc., and they just escalate it out.

That's going to happen pretty much everywhere. It's a better user experience and it makes more sense strategically. Whilst I love SEO, and I think it is truly the best way to attract, influence, and engage an audience on any axis, it's probably not where you want to be piling all of the money that you're expecting to turn into more customers. You're going to need a more diverse strategy."

If an SEO is struggling for time, what should they stop doing right now so they can spend more time doing what you suggest in 2024?

"I'm going to get some hate for this but I'm going to say Digital PR, as an entire category. Let's go to war. If you think that you need more links or better links to get better rankings, then you're operating way too far downstream. You probably have brand, quality, product-market fit, budgeting, or political problems. Those are the reasons that you think you need the links.

Maybe it's hard to fix those, or maybe you can't fix them, but piling money again and again on campaign after campaign to keep your site yo-yo-ing in the search results doesn't feel like a smart long-term bet. If you do this right and you think that you need PR to gain recognition and build brands, etc., then that's great, but do PR. Don't do PR to get links from diverse domains. Embrace it and do proper PR. Some of the best SEO strategies I've seen are people running billboards and TV adverts because it changes how people search, what they type into Google, and which brands they recognise. Think about SEO as a more holistic thing. Let's downplay the focus on Digital PR as a magic solution.

I have seen digital PR done very well and I have seen it used very effectively. Tactically, I think that it is an appealing sugar rush that people turn to instead of doing the hard work of earning rankings, brand recognition, etc. They burn a lot more money renting that awareness over time than they would by positioning themselves in a place where they would earn it themselves. It's not inherently evil, it's just lazy and it's not a long play."

Jono Alderson is an independent Technical SEO Consultant, and you

can find him over at *JonoAlderson.com*.

Recognise the value of visual elements in the world of SGE – with Mufaddal Sadriwala

Mufaddal Sadriwala from Assembly MENA would like to emphasise that organic optimization opportunities within the Search Generative Experience aren't just about text.

Mufaddal says: "Visual elements are going to be incredibly important in the world of SGE.

We all know that SGE is being rolled out on Google. Along with the text that is presented in AI results, it also showcases images, videos, and a lot of other visual multimedia elements like GIFs and Web Stories.

Along with the text you write, and the content you create on the website, all of these visual elements are going to be very important in the world of SGE we are now entering."

Will most queries have visual elements alongside the text answer?

"When SGE was open for testing in the US and India, we saw images along with the text on the right-hand side – and other articles that were linked which also had an image shown. The featured images from those articles were brought into the AI results.

Along with that, YouTube videos were also fetched for highly informative SGE results, along with timestamps of where you could find the exact information you were looking for.

Basically, along with providing very simple answers that are pulled from the website, Google also wants to push visual elements. Those elements play a very important role in helping people understand that information easily, read more about it, or explore more of those results."

Are Google only incorporating visual elements from the web page where they source the text content?

"From what I've seen so far, the source is not only going to be your website, your articles, or your pages. These elements are also going to be fetched from other sources, like YouTube.

With the rise of YouTube Shorts, that is also something that Google can fetch for the SGE results. Also, long-form YouTube videos, TikTok videos, and your other social media platforms as well. Instagram and Facebook content does not usually get featured in the SGE, but visual elements from Snapchat can be.

You want to have a top-notch visual experience on your web pages but, at the same time, you should also look at the way your content is being indexed on other social media platforms. If someone is making a brand-related search, they might see your top trending TikTok or YouTube videos within the SGE results. It is becoming very important that you control how your brand SERP is being presented in the era of SGE.

Along with that, your images, videos, and GIFs can be fetched from the pages on your website. I also want to touch on Web Stories, which is going to be very crucial in the coming years. In the countries where it has been launched, it is booming right now. Every large publisher out there is creating Web Stories – and they are getting really great traffic from Discover. Now, Web Stories are also going to be featured in the SGE results as well."

What kind of content should you be publishing on Web Stories?

"Web Stories is your visual content. You want people to consume the visual content that you have on your website.

Let's say you're a tour operator in India and you offer tour packages to Europe, America, Australia, etc. If you were creating content conventionally, you might be writing blog posts on the Top 10 Cities to Visit in America. That post might include cities like New York, Boston, and Washington, D.C., and you would have images and video elements in that as well.

For Web Stories, your most important elements are your images and video, and there should be some text or headers that are included as part of that. If you are saying that Boston is the best city to visit in the United States, your most important element should be the imagery – of the skyline, the museums, the parks, etc. Then, you would have one or two-line descriptions of those places that people should be visiting.

That's the way around it should be. In Web Stories, you're flipping the conventional method of writing content and making it very visual-heavy rather than text-heavy."

Currently, Google says that the Web Stories carousel is only available in the US, India, and Brazil. Will it launch in other countries soon?

"John Mueller has said that they are testing it out in some other countries but that doesn't mean that it is going to be launched in those countries. They are looking at the demand from people in those countries. If a lot of people are creating Web Stories in a specific region, Google might make that a feature in Discover or Google search in that location.

However, it's not limited to only the countries that they have mentioned. I've seen some Web Stories being featured in the MENA region that I work in. It's not as common as it is in India, but some Web Stories are being featured in my Discover feed.

If you try it out in your region, Google might fetch your Web Story and put it out in Discover. That's how they can test it too. They've said that they are testing it out in other regions, but they need the content. They need those Web Stories from publishers so that they can test more of them and see how people are reacting.

This is another example of why you need to be aware of what the SERP looks like in whatever region you are working. In different countries, the SERP features can be completely different.

If you are stuck with your SEO strategy, and you need to find more avenues to get traffic, Web Stories is one of the methods that you can explore. If you're working with a large brand and you're ranking for each and every keyword (your conventional on-page, off-page, and technical methods are all going smoothly), but you're wondering how you can get more traffic, this is something you can explore. See if it works in your region and try and get the most out of it."

Will having visual elements on your web page, alongside your content, increase your chances of being the primary answer for a particular query in the AI results?

"Definitely. If your content is up to the mark, and your images and visual elements also match that, Google will have no reason to not feature your website in the search generative and AI results.

It's worth noting that, from what we have seen so far, Google won't necessarily fetch your imagery for the SGE results just because they have fetched your written content. In some cases, the content is fetched from one domain and the images and videos are fetched from other domains.

Even if your written content is not getting featured, you can dial down on your visual elements strategy and get featured with that. That can help you with discovery and get you more clicks onto your website."

How do you optimize these images and videos on your website to make them likely to be used within AI results?

"With images, the most crucial thing is having them in a certain size. There is no official documentation so far as to what dimensions they need images to be because Google does not want to show their cards to everyone. However, you can check the SERPs and look at the size of images on the web pages that are being featured. Then, you can try and adapt your images so that they have similar dimensions to the ones that are being featured.

Along with that, the alt text obviously plays a crucial role. It helps Google understand, and the description of the images can be featured as well. Image titles are also important. Whenever you upload an image, consider what the title says, what format it is in, and what the dimensions are. That is a good starting point.

For video, the popularity of your YouTube channel plays a crucial role. In the SGE results, Google is being more stringent in what kinds of results they showcase. Your popularity, and your overall domain authority, will play a crucial role in being featured.

With that being said, you shouldn't limit yourself to thinking that, if you are popular, you are going to be featured in SGE. Your strategy also needs to be heavily focused on helping the users get all the information that they need. Being featured in the SGE is not only limited to your authority but also what type of content you put out and how you are helping the users.

In the end, Google wants to deliver and showcase the information that's helping their users. You can get started with long-tail queries where large brands are less likely to be trying to rank, so medium to small brands can probably get featured in the SGE."

If an SEO is struggling for time, what should they start doing right now so they can spend more time doing what you suggest in 2024?

"With all the hype in the industry around AI, SGE, ChatGPT, etc., a lot of SEOs are scared. Many are spending time looking at other career options and trying to see whether or not SEO is dying.

Stop worrying about that. SEO is evolving, as it has evolved with every year and every decade. It's evolving over time, and we need to evolve with it. Think about how you can evolve with the changes that Google is bringing to the table. You will realise that SEO is not dying in the near future, just because AI has arrived.

AI is here and it is going to have an impact. The race is becoming more stringent, and the competition is cutthroat. The test is going to be how you can adjust to all of this right now.

Before, we had 10 search results that we had to compete in. Then we were competing to be in the top 5 positions. Now, you are competing for the top position in the SGE results. It's the evolution of what has happened in the results. Focus on how you can bear with that instead of looking for other options.

Recently, I read a study which said that ChatGPT traffic was down by 10% already. All the hype around ChatGPT when it launched has already started to die down. These AI tools are there to help us, but people are realising that they can only help us up to a point. If you need to go further, those tools have to rely on updated data from Google, Discover, social media, and all the other places where they get updated and correct information. Stop worrying about what AI holds for you, and start embracing it and utilising it instead."

Mufaddal Sadriwala is SEO Manager at Assembly MENA, and you can find him over at Mufaddal.digital.

Consider schema markup as the language you can use to build a knowledge graph – with Martha van Berkel

An important element of optimizing your content for the SERP and to be understood is ensuring that you are creating a knowledge graph. Connected Schema Markup is the building block to build a Knowledge Graph, shares Martha van Berkel from Schema App.

Martha says: "Start to think about schema markup as your language for building a knowledge graph. Don't just go after rich results. Really focus on being understood by these new AI engines – not just search engines, but AI large language models."

Does AI understand your content in a different way, and does schema markup need to be different to how it was before?

"You have to think about translating your content for it to be understood. Up until now, when people did schema markup, they focused on trying to get that rich result and hitting the minimum that was required and recommended by Google for the elements of the page that you had to translate.

Now, you need to think about what that page is about and how you ensure that it's truly understood. How does it connect to other things in the world and on the web? How does it relate to other things across the brand? We're now aiming for a comprehensive translation instead of the minimum.

This is important because large language models are trying to make inferences. They're trying to understand the intent of the searcher (or the person they're interacting with). To make those inferences, they need the context of more than just the basic pieces. They need the context of where this puzzle piece fits in the much bigger picture of all the other things that they've indexed or understood."

How do you fit into this bigger picture?

"Let's start with links. Links continue to be something that you need to have but, with schema markup, you can actually have links in context. You have a link on a page – so you know where it is, you know how often the link is used, etc. Majestic does a great job of illustrating this in their tools. However, you don't know what the link is, in the context of the topic of the page.

If I'm talking about a product, is the link taking me to who created the product? Is the link taking me to a related product? Is the link taking me to understand more about the accessories of the product? With schema markup, you can give context to that link. It also brings in the context of all the other content on the page.

If you want the page to be understood in a certain way, use the *schema.org* vocabulary. It has been around since 2011. Google and Microsoft collaborated to define all the things that they wanted to know about. The Schema.org vocabulary helps you bring context and allows you to disambiguate with external definitions.

If this is a page that's talking about all the hotels in Paris, you want to be clear that we're talking about Paris, France not Paris, Texas or Paris, Ontario. However, you can go much deeper than that, especially when you're bringing out products and trying to figure out and position where they fit.

In your marketing language, you might be talking about footprints, but you don't mean footprints in the sand, you're really talking about carbon footprints. Schema markup is a control point for marketers to make sure that the content they are building on the site is truly understood and positioned in the right place, not just for humans but also for machines."

Do you need to do anything differently to appear in the different AI-

based search locations, like SGE, BARD, Bing, and ChatGPT?

"Currently, there's very little documentation with regards to how SGE works. In fact, I just saw Gary Illyes speak and he said that he's not allowed to talk about SGE. One thing that's really great for digital marketers is that Microsoft has been trying to articulate what we need to do. They've asked us to make it easier for them to index our pages and help them understand when things are changing.

This plays to the point that we need to help them make sure they understand. If they're investing money to make sure that they're crawling the pages so that you have a chance of showing up, you also then need to make sure they truly understand it – and make it easier to understand.

If you look at any research around large language models and knowledge graphs, a knowledge graph actually grounds large language models. It removes hallucinations. It provides a standard, structured way for them to make inferences with less investment and energy. Again, we need to think about how to help them do what they're trying to do and understand it – through things like structured data or schema markup, and doing it in a really connected way. You're building a knowledge graph that will help them achieve their goal faster and cheaper. That is some of the key messaging we're hearing from other thought leaders."

Are we going to get to a stage where AI understands the meaning behind the content on your web pages and schema might not be required?

"It is a possibility. We work with mid-to-large enterprise, and there is a control point that content creators will want to have. I was speaking to someone today who was saying that it's kind of scary that we won't even own the experience. This is not just true with what we're seeing from Google and Bing, but also, who are the other innovators in that experience that are going to give us the conversion?

I'm a firm believer that, whether we're talking about search or about marketing overall, the brand is going to want to have some control over what they're consuming and where they're going. If the experience doesn't exist, then they're going to want a marketing data layer.

The knowledge graph (whether that's using the standard language of schema markup or something else) is going to be a way that enterprises can have that control. That's how they will be able to continue to play and tell these AIs how they want to be understood."

How could this position SEO as a hero in preparing marketing data for broader AI initiatives?

"Search engines are just one consumer, and we're so focused on that all the time. However, when you look at a knowledge graph and how one can be used, it can be used for lots of other things. What's exciting about the vocabulary of schema is that it's very comprehensive.

Tools like Schema App allow you to build a knowledge graph very quickly, which allows the SEO to be the hero and raise their hand within organisations that are trying to figure out how to pull data together from all these different places. You can say that you've already done it. You've done it for organic search.

We also have indications of the mental model of how this becomes a data pipeline that users consume, that you can build other applications on. When Fabrice Canel spoke at PubCon recently, he talked about how they're not using multiple data sources. They're pulling in the indexing and data all in one piece, and then building the services on top. If Bing's doing that to deliver a different level of value, other people can do that too.

My question is, what are marketers doing to make sure that they have their data in a really consumable way, which allows people to consume and use it? We're seeing innovators within our enterprise clients who are already thinking this way and using their knowledge graph as a way to inform and accelerate some of the things they are doing, even internally."

Should SEOs consider turning into analytics professionals?

"I don't know about analytics professionals, but we have to start asking ourselves how we think beyond the click as our one value piece. We need to be thinking about our business relevancy on a much larger scale. How do we help the business stay relevant to capture conversions, get appointments, and make sales – beyond how analytics are today?

We need to be thinking about the other analytics we might need to be going for. Conversions are key. As we see more and more of that data exploration and research happening off our site (or being consumed and packaged in other places), the ability to measure conversions is going to be really important. If your business is struggling to measure true conversions, that needs to be where SEOs are asking questions."

Could the internal role of SEOs be turned into an SEO consultant as opposed to an SEO manager?

"The need for the cross-functional nature of the job is accelerating, especially when it comes to content. The other big play here is unique content – that is truly tied to your authority and expertise. I don't use those words in an EEAT context, but truly what you are an expert in and why users need to go to your site and the content you're creating as opposed to anybody else.

It has to be unique, it has to be well positioned, and it has to be worth putting you in the initial position for those answers. You have to be the number one result, because the other links aren't going to exist."

Do SEOs also need to become more specialised in their expertise or can they still handle multiple roles?

"It depends on your talent. Being able to connect the dots and explain how these things all come together is going to be more important. Everyone needs to become a translator. If you're a technical SEO, you can't just say that they need to do IndexNow. You need to explain that they have to do IndexNow because, if you are costing the search engines too much money, you're not gonna even get the chance to play. You need to tie it back to the business.

Whatever role you're in – whether it be content, technical SEO, or analytics – you need to be able to think four steps ahead about how the business achieves their primary goal. That's going to become more and more important. People aren't going to just accept that you need to build links. They want to know why you build links, how that plays in the space, and how it's evolving."

How do you articulate the value of schema to non-technical or even non-marketers?

"Today, a lot of what we're talking about is how things are changing – and then we're trying to break down large language models. These days, even my mother knows what a large language model is because of ChatGPT. If you articulate that you want to play in this landscape and be understood there, someone in content can understand that, someone in the business can understand that, a sales leader can understand that, etc.

Schema Markup is a language. I've had t-shirts that say, 'This is the language of search engines' but I now say, 'This is the language of machines and AI'. This is the language that can articulate what you are about. Explain that you need to translate things so that you are being truly understood, which is the practice you're doing around schema markup.

You want to explain that it's not just working page-by-page, but how you are telling the whole interwoven story – and then talk about a knowledge graph and how all these things are connected.

As humans, we don't just read one piece of content and move on to the next. We read a piece of content and it makes us think of related concepts and ideas. Even when we talk, we're trying to find commonalities and things we can connect on – whether that be children, things that we love about our work in SEO, companies we work for, etc. That's how the neural brain works.

How the machines' neural brains work is not so different from ours. It's about making meaningful connections through different pieces – and how you can tie that changing journey to this control point or vocabulary that we can use to explain and speak to machines. We're all trying to find these connections in order to experience and make decisions. That's how I would explain it and get people bought in."

If an SEO is struggling for time, what should they stop doing right now so they can spend more time doing what you suggest in 2024?

"Stop writing really generic content. If you're just doing the basics, and things that aren't very differentiated, put that aside and go deep.

Figure out how you can articulate what you have today using schema markup so that you can tell the story. Make sure that unique content is standing out."

Martha van Berkel is CEO at Schema App, and you can find her over at Schema App.com.

6 Build Your Entity

6 BUILD YOUR ENTITY

Recognise the increasing importance of brand SEO – with Miracle Inameti-Archibong

We hear a great deal about entity SEO. Building a creditable, professional entity starts with an understanding of brand SEO, says Miracle Inameti-Archibong from John Lewis Finance.

Miracle says: "This year, I have talked a lot about brand SEO. With the onset of AI, the content market is going to become oversaturated. Indexing content is expensive and Google is going to have to be even more selective. Being recognised as an entity and having a clear brand identity is going to be even more important to earning that trust, especially for niche sites.

The younger generations don't use appointment TV, they get their news from a highly specific source. Everyone has really strong feelings about who they are, and they're looking for brands that speak to and tap into those social feelings. There is already a growing mistrust in the content saturation that's coming at us left, right, and centre.

With the helpful content update, Google is moving towards verifying sources and listening to people with experience. Recently, they started verifying medical information on YouTube because people are getting their information from a diversity of sources. There's a lot of pressure on Google to make sure that their results are credible – and this is what sites need to lean heavily into.

You can't build an audience by just focusing on generic keywords. Be hyper-focused on who you are and what your audience wants. There is too much similar content out there, prioritise what makes your business unique."

What does brand SEO mean in practice and how can it drive organic visits?

"It is about getting Google to understand your entity. What your site is about, the relationship between that brand name and the product. Which businesses are you similar too? Basically, understanding your brand entire ecosystem.

It is also about building a returning customer base, so you see brand searches and brand plus product searches grow. I did some research in the insurance and fashion industry SERPS and I saw a strong correlation between brand Plus product search demand and higher organic rankings. That's when I started paying more attention to Brand SEO.

Stick to your niche and think about what products you offer. In the past, if you offered pet insurance but you only covered single pets, you could still appear at the top of the SERP for 'multi-pet insurance'. They you could have content that said, 'If you're looking for multi-pet insurance, although we don't offer it, you can...'

You can't get away with those kinds of things anymore. I see lots of sites go after lots of generic terms that are so far removed from what they offer just because it is in the same industry and, with AI, it's only going to get worse.

When you're doing your keyword research now, go to social media see what people who interact with your brand are saying about your product and what search terms they are using.

Carrie Rose gave a really interesting presentation at MozCon about how she has been using social media to see what's trending, make sure it's optimized on the client side, go to PR with it, jump to #1, and get loads of sales from it. For my brands, I have been going to forums and Trustpilot and looking at what people are saying – not just thinking about brand reputation but translating it to content as well.

A practical example of this is Monzo. I love what they are doing with their content. They are getting their customers and employees to write about how they use Monzo to solve their debt problems, split their bills, or save for a festival. It's about getting your customers to come to you because the generic market is so flawed. In my MozCon presentation this year, I talked about searching for quotes on love and then being served 4 million results. With very similar page titles and content, how do you navigate that?

You want to instil loyalty in your customers and you want them to come directly to you. You want them to be thinking, 'I know this brand. This brand has the same social ethos as me, and it always offers what I'm looking for.' Then they come to your site and do that search. Build that trust and make them come to you."

Do you have to reach out to users for them to create content for you or will they naturally write on your behalf if you have a great product?

"Users won't necessarily naturally write for you. They might write on social media, forums, or Trustpilot and leave feedback for you.

However, there are people within your organisation (not just copywriters) who are interacting with the products that can write content for you. That's what Monzo does as well. Their employees are using their Monzo cards in ways that the general population does and they get them to write articles about their use case.

You can also look for writers who already have EEAT. If you're in the SEO world, you would reach out to someone like Chima Mmeje (who speaks a lot about content), to write content about SEO for you. That content would automatically have weight. Don't just go and look for generic writers. Search for writers who already have EEAT in that category."

How do you find a writer who has EEAT?

"Look at what they've written in the SERPS. Google a writer, look at their profile, and look at where their by-lines are. It's very important to see that they have by-lines elsewhere and that those correlate to the topics they're writing on.

Then, get your people trained. We ran a website talking about hair, and we got the writers to go on a trichology course and they became qualified trichologists. Now, they can give advice and opinions on that subject. That way, you can start building the EEAT of your writers yourself.

I encourage my writers to have at least half a day where they do some research and try to get their by-line into publications that talk about the topics they write about. It's in your interest to build their profile. Send them on training courses, and get them to have by-lines in publications that offer the same kinds of things that you do."

How does brand SEO interplay with search generative experience and AI results?

"Search engines exist to make money. There's going to be paid search, then there's going to be SGE, and then organic search results below that. Organic is going to move lower and lower.

Trust is what will make Google pull your result into SGE. It's all about building your brand's trust so that you are considered for SGE. The same metrics around EEAT will get fed into SGE. If your brand is not reputable and doesn't have EEAT, it's not going to get pulled in the SGE result.

You need to get as high as you can. Organic search results are going to drop and paid search spending is going to go up. Paid search spending is going to go through the roof because, as the organic search space gets more competitive, visibility drops. More things are taking their baseline: map packs and other features in the SERP. Google exists to send what it wants to its users, so you need to get yourself into the space where you're able to earn the SGE results.

If you're not able to earn that, you need to make sure that you're doing enough to build your customer loyalty so that people search directly for your brand. You need to get people to come directly to you.

From my rudimentary experimentation, when you search 'brand+dresses', the brand that has the highest search volume in that niche is usually in position one. If your demand is naturally high, you come out stronger in the organic SERP. Driving demand and making your brand front of mind makes a difference, and it affects organic search.

Moz has launched a brand authority metric to see the strength of your brand and how it is tracking amongst competitors. That's really interesting. Loads of people have gone after generic so much that they've literally forgotten their brand.

Search habits have changed. UX people talk about journeys but nobody searches that way anymore. If they know the brand they want to use, people will go and type that into search. Most people will now type 'brand+query' and expect the page to surface. We have become so hyper-focused on generic keywords that a lot of brands are not covering that.

As an example, I researched Expedia. They were bidding on the PPC keyword, 'how to book tickets through Expedia'. They had no organic page ranking for that keyword. They were spending money bidding on PPC, but a generic content website was ranking in position one for that query because they had created a blog post, a video, and a step-by-step process on how to book tickets through Expedia. Big brands need to start thinking about all of those things.

Start thinking about your returning customers and how to serve them – because they will have a higher conversion rate. For smaller brands, it's going to be so competitive. You need to build that niche for yourself. If anyone is saying that you need to cover everything and go after every generic keyword, you should be very suspicious of that.

I heard an interesting a talk about a tech brand generating around 500 pieces of content a year using AI. There are thousand tech brands out there, so times that by 500. We're all going to be drowning. You need to start narrowing your focus and being more specific."

If customers are coming directly to you, is this still SEO, and how do you measure the value of brand SEO?

"We've been asking what SEO is since I first started. Before, it was on-page link building, then speed became a metric and we all went tech, and then we went into the code – and everyone said it was still SEO. SEO is a fascinating industry because of how much it evolves.

This is where it's going, and you have to get on board with it. I'm collaborating with brand teams and product teams in a way that I never did before. The developer knows how to fix the thing that is broken, but the product team is creating the feature in the first place. If I'm liaising with them before it even gets built, I'm getting all my requirements in there, and then getting the developers to scope it out. The way we work will always change and evolve; that's the nature of the industry.

The SEO budget is always the first thing pulled, so we got really into tracking data. Now, we need to start thinking about the integrated search experience and doing tests with the PPC team. Think about incremental tests and the incremental value of every channel, and look at combined CPAs.

In practical terms, direct traffic, an increase in brand search, an increase in brand+product searches, the number of returning customers, the conversion rate of returning customers, etc. – those are all the things that you track. Those are the practical metrics you can look at now. For the rest, we have to evolve and get better at showing incremental value when we step away from specific keywords and specific pages."

If an SEO is struggling for time, what should they stop doing right now so they can spend more time doing what you suggest in 2024?

"Stop chasing generic keywords that are so far removed from what you do, just because they're somewhat related to your industry. That will save you a lot of time. Instead, go to your content, do an audit, and prune anything that is not adding value.

Then, focus on those things that are within your niche and are exactly what you offer, and think about how you can enhance them. If you've written a page that's ranking on position one, go and work with your media team or social media team, and say, 'How can we create YouTube Shorts for this?' That's adding value.

If you've already covered the top 20, 30, or 100 keywords in your niche, then think about how you can repurpose that content. What else can you do to add value? This is where people usually struggle because we like to stay in our lane, but we have to get more innovative – which is what SEO is all about."

Miracle Inameti-Archibong is Head of SEO at John Lewis Finance, and you can find her over at MiracleInametiArchibong.com.

Add a technical layer to your branding and start thinking of branding as a technical practice – with Ulrika Viberg

Leading on from Miracle's thoughts, Ulrika Viberg from Unikorn shares that branding through the SEO lens goes beyond creativity and messaging – you should think of branding as a technical practice.

Ulrika says: "Start thinking about branding with a technical layer. That means having a technical layer on your website, around your brand, so that AI understands who you are, what you do, and what your business does on the internet.

It's going to make it much easier for them to understand what your business is about and who you are. Start thinking of branding as a technical practice."

Is this technical layer going to include more than just schema?

"Schema is a part of it; that's a way of implementing it. We're talking mostly about entities – specifically, the entities that you and your brand are connected to or associated with. You have to start thinking about that.

Think about the kind of entities and relevant topics that you talk about and surround your name with. Here, it is very important to think about EEAT and how you become the expert to build trust and authority around you and your brand.

This also applies more broadly to wherever your brand exists online. That includes social channels and other websites as well. I'm building my brand right now, by doing this interview.

The large language models need to verify that you are who you say you are, and that the content you put online is indeed accurate. As we have seen, they can spit out all kinds of stuff. The AI models hallucinate when you talk to them, so they don't have everything covered yet, but they're working on it. One way that they are working on it is to verify the things they find on the internet for a generative answer by checking the EEAT of the entity that they're talking about."

Could SEOs be responsible for AI hallucinations if their entity information isn't consistent online?

"Yes. Up until now, we've been focusing on creating all kinds of content – and content that doesn't really relate to each other. We focus on content that is sprung out of one keyword, on one landing page, and we optimize it the way we are used to doing that. We build links between our content and links to our content, and that's how we optimize it.

Now, we have to connect everything, and make sure that it is connected, so it is relevant to our brand and our person. That way, the machines can understand exactly what it is that you want to be recognised as and what you want to be associated with so that they can see your expertise or experience."

Can an SEO influence other departments to try and ensure that they don't talk about content that doesn't immediately relate to what the brand's about?

"That's going to be tricky; we all know that. Hopefully, the company or brand has an overall digital strategy where you talk about the topics that are important and relevant to your brand. Then, you don't talk about all the other things because that would be diluting your brand anyway. It's not just for your technical branding online, but also for how you are seen in general.

As well as determining what your brand is about and how the content you write about relates to your brand, you should also be aware of the content that isn't relevant to your brand.

Typically, brands want to be seen as big and they talk about everything and do everything, especially when they're starting up. After a while, when you are rebranding, you consolidate everything that you're doing and what you're good at. You don't talk about the other stuff because it is actually not very helpful."

Are there ways of structuring, choosing, and marking up content to make life easier for AI to understand what you're about?

"There is a thing called 'entity juice', and it's about all of the entities that are connected to each other and also your entity. That juice is gained through structured data, but also nested structured data – this entity is the same as X, this person has also done X, this brand is also mentioned here, or this brand is also doing X and Y, for example.

I work with a large e-commerce for books online, where we can nest all kinds of data together, with the author, the books, the categories, etc. You can go bananas with this and try to do it as much as possible.

Structured data is a blunt tool in itself because there are not that many types to use, but use it as much as you can and nest it to other topics – where it is appropriate and where it makes sense."

Will structured data eventually be ignored or less necessary because AI will become better at determining what content is on a web page?

"I don't think it's going to be ignored, but it's going to be evolved. I'm guessing here because I have no actual insights, but that would be the logical progression.

It makes it easier for the machines to read content if it is tagged with some structured data or some language that the machines understand much better. Human language is not that easy to understand, from a machine's point of view. Around 95% of it is relatively easy, but then come elements like context. We use the same words for completely different things, for example, and the machines misunderstand us.

Structured data makes it so much easier to understand what kind of context we are in and what are we actually talking about. It makes it easier for them to understand the full text if we just point them in the right direction. I don't think it's going be ever ignored, it's just going to be evolved."

Can you automate the insertion of schema?

"Yes. I automate it with my developers. I add what kinds of schema are going to be needed into a template, in a JSON-LD file, and then they populate it with the actual content taken from different places on the page.

For example, an article is always going to be an article. The type is always going to be the type. Then you put in the author, the content, or the abstracts from the content on-page. There's an initial workload to be done, but then it's automated."

Do we need to better structure our content to make it more easily understood by machines?

"The format is, of course, important here as well. However, that is already important. That is basic SEO, so it's already part of the deal. We have to do that – or we should do that."

Best practice hasn't changed. You should do the same things to make your web page easy to understand for AI as you would for the search engine – which is to think about the user. Always have the user in front of you and always prioritise the user.

You can't go wrong when you do that. Then you put a technical layer on top of that to make it easier for the machines to understand what the brand represents."

If you were starting a new line of products, would it be sensible to start up a new website if they're not directly related to what you currently offer?

"That's a million-dollar question, and I think the SEO community is a bit divided on it. You would want to have the large website behind you – the age of it, its domain authority, and everything else that makes it easier for the new product line to evolve and develop on the SERP. On the other hand, you don't want to dilute the brand name and the products too much.

If it's something very different, maybe you should create a new brand and a new website. That would make sense. Then you connect them through the actual company behind both brands. For example, I'm from Sweden, so I live and breathe H&M. However, there's also COS, ARKET, and all the other different stores. They have different names, different stores, and different strategies, but they're all connected back to the mother company: H&M.

If you're launching a new suite of products aimed at a new target market, you could launch a new domain name and have an overarching central brand that both belong to. Then, in terms of the website user experience, they're not together. However, this is only relevant if the products differ significantly. If they don't differ a lot, that no longer makes sense.

You might have significantly different products that appeal to the same target market, which you may want to unite under a single domain. It depends on the products, the market, and the overall business strategy. You need to consider how you want to be perceived by your users and by the machines as well."

If an SEO is struggling for time, what should they stop doing right now so they can spend more time doing what you suggest in 2024?

"Stop doing SEO in isolation. Stop working on one keyword and one landing page, and building lots of links to those landing pages. Start doing semantic clusters instead and connect them with each other. Start building entity juice between yourself, your brand, your products, and your services.

Go out there and create instances where you or your brand are being talked about on other pages, and in topics that are relevant to you, so that you also can start building your thought leadership. That is super important."

Ulrika Viberg is CEO and Senior SEO at Unikorn, and you can find her over at Unikorn.se.

Become a real entity by feeding the machine the right information – with Sara Moccand-Sayegh

Both Miracle and Ulrika's tips focused on the importance of branding. However, even if your brand is spot-on, you need to ensure that you're

feeding the machine the right information, says SEO Specialist Sara Moccand-Sayegh.

Sara says: "Work to become an entity and feed the machine the correct information. You need to understand your identity, your offering, and your target audience.

You want to remove any uncertainty. You want Google, Bing, or any other search engine to understand you. In the case of Google, you want to apply your EEAT signals. If they understand you, they can better apply those signals. If you are an author and an entity, and they know who the website owner is, it's much easier to apply all those signals.

That's why it's very important to focus on becoming an entity and feed all the correct information to the machine – especially with generative AI.

What kind of content will help you become an entity?

"I recently wrote a white paper with Jason Barnard about how to adapt to generative AI. You can apply the same logic in this case: when you produce your content, you have to think about the buyer decision journey and what type of content will make sense for your company.

If you work for a development agency, it will make sense that your content has a product element because that is what you sell. However, you also have to show how fantastic your developers are – in your blog, for example. Your developers could write directly on your blog, demonstrating their experience, which is just a small part of the buyer decision journey. You have to think bigger as well, but those are a couple of examples."

What initial content will give you the best chance of a search engine understanding exactly who you are and what you represent?

"These are your key pages. The homepage and About Us page are clearly key pages, as are product pages.

Start by directly stating who you are and what you do, and that will probably be on your homepage. You want to start putting data into that page. If you can say that you've been in business for 20 years, that already helps. Then you go to the About Us page. The About Us page is fantastic because it's where you can go deep into explaining your history. There is so much data and factual information that you can put inside that page.

On the About Us page, you can speak about your structure. You can write about the owner of the company or, if you are owned by another company, you write that. Give all the information about who you really are. You obviously also need to explain what you do and your history, which is also fantastic because it gives extra information.

One of the advantages of using those pages is that you can really create the logic and structure of the website. You can explain what the brand is, who it is owned by, etc."

How do you decide what schema to use, and can you use ChatGPT to produce the schema on your behalf?

"I never use ChatGPT to produce schema because I work in a development company. I tell them what my requirements are and they produce it for me.

In terms of how to ensure that you're using the right schema, that is difficult to answer. What you can do is identify the minimum requirements that you want to have. For example, you know that you want to have 'organisation'. Maybe you can go a little bit further and be more precise about the type of organisation. Then, you create a list of things that you think you need to have.

Another option is to copy people who are currently doing it better than you. Take a look at your competition and see what they are doing. Then, you know what kind of information you may want to add. You can just go through the library, or you can check the Google documentation for their minimum requirements."

What other key places should you be present in to enhance what you do on your site, and how do you go about doing that?

"If you have a page on your website that is full of comments saying how fantastic you are and how incredible your product is, that is just on your website. Nothing outside of your site is saying how fantastic you are.

Trustpilot, for example, can be great for software companies. If you appear on Trustpilot, you have an external element confirming that you are fantastic, which is great. Those external spaces are very helpful for building your credibility. I'm not necessarily talking about backlinks, but everything that can confirm the information you are providing internally.

Making sure that your Google Business Profile has reviews on it is another example of an external source. There are tons of different sources you can utilise and, provided they are valuable, they will confirm what you are saying on your site, which builds your credibility."

Should you link to those external sources from your own website, and can you use schema to point search engines toward them?

"You can always link to somewhere like Trustpilot from your website. Why not? There's nothing wrong with that. Also, you can use schema for those external sources.

If there is a Wikipedia page that confirms what you do, for example, you can use the *sameAs* tag in your About Us page to let search engines know that this information is the same as what the Wikipedia page that you link to is saying. There are always ways that you can use schema to show that there is a connection with an external source."

How much does interacting on social media assist search engines in understanding what you do and enhance your brand's identity?

"Social media definitely has an influence. Whenever someone searches for you, there will be references to your social media profiles on the SERP, which will make a difference.

If you are a person, you will probably have a Twitter/X and LinkedIn profile showing who you are. If you are a company, you might have a TikTok or something else. Social media certainly plays a role in the sense that it is showing up in your SERP, which the search engines will pass through and try to understand you through that."

What social platforms give you the best presence on the SERP?

"At the moment, the knowledge panel for individuals is often being taken from LinkedIn – and I've also seen information being taken directly from the About section on LinkedIn.

People sometimes write their About section in the third person, and that may help as well. Either way, that information is definitely being taken from Linkedin, so there is something to be gained there."

In terms of ChatGPT and AI, what is the future of schema? Will AI become so clever that search engines won't need schema anymore because they'll be able to understand the entity without any markup code?

"That is a big discussion. To sum it up, the first thing that comes to my mind is that generative AI has a big problem with hallucination. It needs to have something to give it structure. The technology is fantastic, but it needs confirmation.

At the moment, the only thing that can confirm what AI is seeing, and help it remove the problem of hallucination, is the knowledge graph. Everything that is structured can prevent generative AI from hallucinating – and schema clearly creates structure.

AI can understand an entity, but it can understand that entity wrong, and it can invent the story completely. Everything that helps with that understanding has to stay, at least for the moment. In two years, maybe it will be perfect and there will be no more problems but, right now, everything that gives structure is still important."

If an SEO is struggling for time, what should they stop doing right now so they can spend more time doing what you suggest in 2024?

"If you have limited time, then spend less of it working on Core Web Vitals. That's never a very popular sentiment but, when your time is limited, then you should use it on something else."

Sara Moccand-Sayegh is an SEO Specialist, and you can find her over at MoccandSayeghSara.ch.

Make sure your brand-related entities are in Google's Knowledge Vault – with Austine Esezobor

SEO Consultant Austine Esezobor from DemocratizingSEO also espouses getting the right information in the right places. Specifically, ensuring that your entities reside in Google's Knowledge Vault.

Austine says: "Get your entities into Google's Knowledge Vault, starting with your brand.

Your brand-related entities will include the main brand, your products, and anything else that's brand-related, such as personal branding for CEOs, CFOs, and C-suite individuals – especially for businesses in the B2B sector."

Do SEOs often neglect their products as brand entities?

"I think so. For example, Apple is the main brand, but the iPhone and iPad are products that fall within the brand grouping. They are essentially brands themselves.

All businesses need to have their entities within Google's Knowledge Vault. You can think of entities as nameplates of things. Quite a while ago, Google mentioned that they are moving from 'strings' to 'things'. One of the reasons why they are doing this is because the traditional way that they seek information, their information retrieval system, is out of date. When you want to have an entity on a social media platform, you input your entity and you provide the information to them. This is where Google has slowly been headed over the years.

They started with logged-in users – on Android, for example. Whenever you're on a mobile phone, you're logged into Google. When you're logged out on desktop, Google prompts you to log in to your Google account. That is them having data of users. I believe they're headed into the same sort of methodology with businesses, brands, and websites."

What does the optimum entity footprint look like?

"Start with your brand. That should be the root of everything on the website. Once you have the brand on there, you should then focus on brand-related terms. The least important will be generic keywords. If you target brand, you'll be able to associate your branding with generic keywords in the long run.

In terms of what it looks like, having a knowledge panel for the main brand, that the business owns, is a stamp of approval by Google. They not only know who you are, but they also know the audience you're trying to target. Remember, the audience you're trying to target is Google's users.

Whenever you attract visitors via Google, you're essentially seeking to attain a subset of Google's users. In order for Google to recommend you, in 2024 and beyond, you need to provide Google with the understanding they need to recommend you as best as they can to their users. You must not think of SEO in terms of the users that you acquire. You're acquiring Google's users. Whichever search engine you're attracting users from, you're acquiring their users, so you have to play their game.

Google is quickly moving toward ensuring that their users have all the information that they want, seek, and (to some extent) expect on their platform. This requires Google to have a better understanding of entities."

What's the ideal source of information for the knowledge panel for Google?

"Ideally, you want it to be from a website that you own and have control of. Wikipedia, IMDB, and even Wikidata used to be ideal sources, in the very early stages of Google focusing more on entities. Nowadays, the key is to have the site you work on provide Google with the same level of confidence that they have in Wikipedia or IMDB. Those websites dominate search queries because Google has confidence in them.

Ideally, you want Google to have this level of confidence in your own website – not a social media platform that you own. It's your land that you own and control. Having this as the source of information means that, whenever you update it, you can update the way Google presents you to your prospective audience."

Why are branded keywords becoming more important than generic keywords, with the introduction of the SGE?

"Think of the overall search journey that users are taking, from the beginning right until the end. The SGE is designed to shorten that; it's designed to make their search journey a lot quicker. One of the ways Google is aiming to do this is by providing the information on the SERPs themselves, starting with generic keywords.

If a user were to search for 'home insurance', they almost don't expect to browse through different sites, find the information they want, go back to Google, and then enter another site. That is a lengthy, unnecessary process. Google will aim to provide the information that they believe their audience is seeking within the SERPs themselves. Therefore, from a business point of view, the value will be around branded, bottom-of-funnel keywords.

This is why I mentioned brand – and products are essentially branded keywords as well. These sorts of keywords will become increasingly more valuable to users because they'll be starting and ending their search journey a lot quicker. They'll be getting to those brand-led queries quicker, and they'll be using more of those brand-led queries to pinpoint what they're seeking.

You want to teach your users to use your brand keywords within their searches to educate Google about what your brand represents, and make it more likely that they're going to come back to you."

If you're producing content in other areas (podcasts, video shows, etc.) should you subtly incorporate your brand as part of that as well?

"Absolutely. These are the sorts of things that people will expect when they carry out a search. They will start from an unknown point of view and quickly become a lot more informed. Their queries will be based on those that they trust, which will be those that they see and have seen throughout their search journey.

If you target and focus on having your entities within Google's Knowledge Vault, you are automatically targeting your generic keywords, so there's no point focusing on them.

Throughout the years, SEOs have focused more on generic keywords as the richer source of traffic, demand generation, and acquisition. These days, though, it's the brand that's going to be more important. Bottom-of-funnel keywords will have a lot more value than top-of-funnel keywords and, by targeting those bottom-of-funnel keywords and having those entities within Google's Knowledge Vault, you will ensure that you capture everything that's related to what your business does and who your business is.

You can think about entities in line with your head term branded keywords. As I mentioned earlier, iPhone and iPad are top-end, branded, head term keywords, and they are the kind of entities that you're trying to ensure Google is aware of and has confidence in knowing. You want Google to have the information from your website (in this case, from Apple's website), rather than a competitor."

For a user who isn't aware that a brand exists, does generic keyword targeting still play an important role?

"It is a less important form of targeting. SEOs have historically focused on the generic term, aiming to have that generic term within the left-hand panel and be recommended when that term is searched for.

If you target 'Barclays home insurance', by having that branded ownership of that generic entity, you ensure that you're associating the brand with the generic term. On top of that, whenever someone searches for the generic term, Google already knows you're associated with it, so they serve you up – whether the user searches with the brand term or not.

To build on this, you can actively encourage users to search using your brand terms. We're already seeing a lot of this in above-the-line advertising, namely TV. I like to call it the third call to action. The first call to action is the brand, the second is usually the brand's social media platform, and the third is 'Search for X'. They explicitly tell users to search for the term that the brand wants their prospective users to be searching for.

This is a way of directing what people search for and ensuring that Google is aware that this search phrase is pertinent to this brand."

How do you establish the right keyword phrases to be targeting?

"Start with the brand. Ensure that you have a description that is shown concisely on the site that is the entity home of the brand, then look at your product-led keywords and have their descriptions in semantic triples. Then, you can start associating branded terms with the generic terms that you research.

If the business is in the maritime industry, what are people searching for in the maritime industry? Associate your branding with that generic keyword research, whichever keyword you choose. Ideally, you want to ensure that your brand is prominent within the targeting of the generic keywords."

If an SEO is struggling for time, what should they stop doing right now so they can spend more time doing what you suggest in 2024?

"Stop doing ineffective activities, such as reporting on individual generic keywords. That's a thing of the past, which is slowly evolving out. Instead of reporting on generic keywords, focus on entities and pages. Google doesn't rank keywords, it ranks pages. Pages are what matters, and they are the value that we have. If you want, you can have keywords as a secondary activity, but you should primarily be reporting on your entities and pages.

To track that, you can use all the typical tools, such as Search Console, SEMrush, SearchMetrics, BrightEdge, Pi Datametrics, etc. However, have your view focused more on your pages, which GA is ideal for. Have that focus on your pages, particularly to ensure that business leaders move away from generic keywords and start looking into pages. This will also mean that marketing teams and departments are better integrated with SEO, and vice versa."

Austine Esezobor is an SEO Consultant, and you can find him over at DemocratizingSEO.com.

Accept and prepare for the fact that Schema is becoming less relevant – with Anne Berlin

SEO is often about contrasting opinions, and that's something that Anne Berlin from Lumar offers – Anne believes that, as time goes by, Schema is becoming less relevant.

Anne says: "We've reached the point of declining relevance for schema."

What does this mean for SEOs and what structured data will still be essential in 2024?

"From my vantage point, the state of natural language processing means that structured data is no longer serving a critical role in training search engines what your content is about. Our content no longer needs to be optimized for machine consumption through the addition of specific schema markup. We've reached the end of the training period where that was a value-add.

As evidence for this, the Google Merchant Centre feed is slated to become less robust because Google has said that they can find what they need to generate product rich results directly from your page. You no longer have to structure this for them in a way that you have been previously.

I used to be the absolute number one advocate for structured data and schema implementation. Now, in many cases, it's difficult to maintain, it's poorly optimized, and it's brittle. The return on investment is just not there anymore for most applications of schema. Unless you're in the position to do a case-study-worthy, best practice, advanced implementation of schema, I wouldn't embark on the project."

Do certain sites, like recipe websites, still benefit from using schema?

"The argument I would expect against my advice is that there are still some rich results worth fighting for, whether it's a recipe rich result, a product rich result, review schema, etc.

We only have to look in the recent rearview mirror to the revocation of the how-to and FAQ rich results to say that this is potentially a moving target, and the time is better spent optimizing our content for users."

Do you still need structured data regarding what your company is, the history behind your company, and the thought leaders within the company?

"There's a lot of buzz right now about semantic SEO and semantic markup. I am really playing the cynic here but, very often, the way that semantic markup is being prepared is that you're putting your content into some sort of text analysis software, and then allowing it to tell you what the main entity of the page is. If external NLP (natural language processing) can already tell you what your article is about and understand what the content of the page is, then adding that as structured data doesn't add any value.

The other way that this type of semantic schema is being generated is by individual editors who author content for a site. In most cases, these teams are not deeply trained in taxonomy for machine learning. They may be applying taxonomy to articles in an inconsistent way that doesn't necessarily denote the core topic but instead indicates that a particular subject matter is mentioned.

Human-generated taxonomy for semantic structured data is flawed and machine-generated taxonomy is something that can already be interpreted. If you can't do best-in-class, then I don't know how much it's helping.

There is some value to doing explicit entity SEO using structured data, I just haven't seen it done in a way where it's worth the effort."

Are there any specific page or content structures that make it easier for the machines to digest?

"I am a big fan of returning to fundamentals: effective use of well-nested header tags, readable paragraphs that are informed by keyword research, etc. It seems almost as though these fundamentals are being neglected, but that is exactly what works.

Think about structuring a page so that it could be an award-winning high school essay. It should be well-outlined, and the topics and subtopics should be nested in a way that allows the reader to scan it and understand the argument. That's going to help the machines to interpret the subject matter and it's going to make it easier for a real user to consume as well."

What is your opinion on AI-generated content?

"Large enterprises that are trying to tackle content deficits at scale (having unique product descriptions, having unique and differentiated product metadata, etc.) want to try and solve that problem by using some external content generator.

However, we know that it has to be evaluated in some way by a human because inaccuracies could be introduced. I don't have an objection to using AI for content generation. The hurdle is going to be organising teams of content fact-checkers at scale. Of course, this may stop being necessary as AI improves.

It's a fascinating thing. I love that there are tactics in our industry that used to be considered table stakes but may be completely obsolete come next year."

Is content like short-form video and audio podcasts preferred now? Should you be trying to publish multiple forms of content on your page?

"That makes me think back to the Facebook-led original push towards video that ultimately resulted in a lot of teams pivoting to create in a format that they didn't have the right expertise for. In some cases, teams drew away from other areas where they could have been growing because of the influence of these tech behemoths on our access to an audience.

I consume a lot of short-form video every day, so I know that is certainly an addictive way to get information. However, I don't think every brand has the right team in place to really compete in that space. Moving into multimedia and new-format content that you are not currently equipped to handle is a risk. You are spreading your resources thinner and thinner instead of applying discipline and focusing against the buffeting headwinds to put long-term emphasis on areas where you know you can differentiate and grow."

Can short-form video be appropriate for every type of content or is it

only suitable for a certain stage of the marketing funnel?

"I've been paying a lot of attention to this lately because I am in one of those few phases in life where we do a large burst of new consumption. I just bought a home, so I have been using short-form video to learn how to do some critical home repair projects.

I feel that this kind of content is actually very bottom-of-funnel. If I'm learning how to repair a crack in my driveway, I'm going to need a product to do that."

Where and how can effective short-form video content reach its intended audience?

"Personally, I am a Reels and YouTube user. I don't usually like having targeted ads but, because of the change of address form and the new charges on my credit card, the algorithm knows that I am a new homeowner and has been seeking me out. I didn't have to go out and say, 'What do I need to know to tackle the likely challenges of being a first-time homeowner?' I've been riding that wave of suggested content and finding that it is both engaging and educational.

Of course, I am always a big fan of word-of-mouth and speaking to local experts never lets me down. I will ask the people who have inspected my home or done small projects, 'Where do you get your advice? Who do you trust?' Then, I can use that to explicitly seek out content creators so that I can learn how to safely do projects on my own and what products I'm going to need to accomplish them. It's a combination of both push marketing and pull marketing to find the kinds of credible sources of short-form video content that are useful to me.

Going back to the previous question, I don't think there are any areas of the funnel where short-form video content isn't relevant. There is a lot of transactional intent in that space."

If an SEO is struggling for time, what should they stop doing right now so they can spend more time doing what you suggest in 2024?

"Since my overall tip is to stop doing something, I'll answer it like this: Where do I think elite SEOs should be focusing in 2024?

You should be doing deeply researched competitor benchmarking. You should be strategic visioning and setting up a long-term growth plan that you can stick to, despite the buffeting winds of change. Also, you should be using experimentation to gather data and support your big, bold moves."

Anne Berlin is Senior Technical SEO Analyst at Lumar (formerly Deepcrawl), and you can find her over at Lumar.io.

7 EEAT

7 EEAT

Provide value by using EEAT as your starting point – with Ed Ziubrzynski

We've covered a great deal about the use of AI in SEO in the initial chapters of SEOin2024, but that's not where you should start, says Ed Ziubrzynski from Swoop Funding.

Ed says: "Start with EEAT and the rest will follow."

How do we start with EEAT?

"EEAT is a slightly imaginary metric that a lot of SEOs often overlook. In recent years it's really risen to prominence in terms of just how important it is. Previously, it was especially for YMYL websites whereas now, in the age of AI, it's for every website.

Starting with EEAT means having that value proposition early on in all of your messaging and making sure that everything you publish on your website has some form of value attributed to it. It also means not just publishing content via ghostwriters and not having any author bios present. Make sure that users, website visitors, and ultimately search engines can understand who is behind the content and why that content was published.

Obviously, we want to gain brand exposure, brand visibility, new customers, potential clients, and new business, but the 'Why?' will help you deliver your value proposition: I'm looking to educate. I'm looking to solve a problem for somebody. I'm looking to provide the value that has ultimately led the user to use a search engine that day."

Should SEOs be doing some kind of EEAT analysis for every existing page on a site?

"Definitely, especially for service-led pages. If someone is going to be working with a specific member of your team, making that person's information readily available on the corresponding service or landing page raises your prominence and brings the human element that ultimately drives EEAT.

From a user's perspective, they get to see the person that they might be working with. They can get an idea of who they are and why they should feel comfortable trusting this individual to support their business, offer them a service, or sell them a product.

These can be product specialists but it could be anyone who is trying to sell you anything. It could be someone giving you tech insight on whether you should choose Apple or Windows, Apple or Android, etc. For anything like that, having someone who can act as a figurehead really raises the status of the interaction. Ultimately, it's not [Company A] telling you [XYZ]; it's the person within [Company A] who has this experience and is offering you their insight."

Why should you start with EEAT at the beginning of your marketing strategy and how does that work?

"By starting with EEAT, while the rest of the strategy evolves with sales funnels, etc., the messaging stays consistent. When you are retroactively adding people in and then crafting an almost-false narrative on your website – where information has been published by the company and is then attributed to a person – 3/6/12 months down the line, there are changes in staff and there's no consistent messaging.

If you integrate EEAT at the very start of your strategy then you are futureproofing yourself, but you're also doing something that a lot of businesses overlook. Commonly, you will be looking at competitors that you're striving to beat one day, and they have the luxury of 10-15 years in the industry. There is already a level of trust attributed to the domain and the brand.

Focusing on EEAT from the very start is how you can fast-track your way into ranking prominently, especially if you're starting out. You are showing who you are and what your credentials are, and nothing's being hidden. You've got clear messaging that basically says, 'You can trust us, and here's why', or 'You can feel safe transacting with us because we're regulated, and we have all of these trusted accreditations'. Integrating that from the very start raises you at least two, three, or four steps up from the next person looking to start up in your space."

What elements of Experience are websites missing out on in 2024 and beyond?

"From an Experience perspective, everyone tends to just say, 'The company has been operating for the past 20 years'. It's all well and good to highlight that because it gives you a quantifier. X years of experience should show expertise and, if the company has been running for 5/10/15 years, there is that element of authority within the industry and trustworthiness.

However, when it comes to Experience, a lot of people overlook the journey and progression of a brand. You'll often see people saying that they've grown loads in the past 20 years, but having a real timeline saying, 'The company was founded [Here] by [Person A] and [Person B]. Over the years, the workforce has gone from five employees up to 500.' really starts to paint that narrative. It shows the scale. It gives an idea of what the mission statement was and how true they've stayed to it, but also what obstacles they've overcome and how they've managed it.

You can even include things like COVID, how you managed to navigate that, and either elevate your services or maintain consistent growth in a time when a lot of industries and businesses were struggling."

What's an element of Expertise that tends to be missing?

"Expertise can be related to awards, accreditations, partnerships, and also any third-party media mentions. Not necessarily direct PR mentions that are very self-serving, but where you've been shortlisted for an award and you have coverage on external websites. Centralise that information and make it accessible to the user and search engine bots on your website.

This can be through an In The News section, In The Media, or even a press package. It will centralise that information and create a digital business card saying, 'You can trust us. This is where we're featured. We're experts in our field and here are other people who can vouch for that.'"

What about Authoritativeness?

"Authoritativeness lends into the Experience and Expertise side of things, through having years within the industry, having awards, highlighting that, and even mentioning times where you've been shortlisted for things or you've contributed to other articles.

It can also simply be having policy pages on your website. Having a publication policy on your website shows that any writer or contributor to the website has to follow a certain set of rules and guidelines. You are ensuring that your content is of the highest quality, it can be trusted, everything is well cited, and you are referencing data and any external websites that you use. That helps to build credibility behind every piece of content and everything that the business puts out."

Does Trustworthiness blend in with other elements or are there distinct elements of trust that you'd like to highlight?

"Trustworthiness is, in my opinion, the most important aspect of EEAT. However, it is generated by all the other steps. If your website is Trustworthy, you're displaying Experience, Expertise and Authority. It takes all of these components working cohesively to form a website that efficiently achieves that EEAT strategy.

There are additional things that you can do. If you are an e-commerce brand, show what payment types you accept, have clear refunds, returns, and shipping information, and other policy pages like that. Make your contact information easily findable and basically ensure that there is nothing hidden on your website. Everything should be easily accessible, and users shouldn't have to jump through hoops to find ways of getting in touch with you if they have any sort of dispute.

You can have reviews and testimonials, including a blend of both the good and the bad. If you see a website or a business that has 500 five-star reviews and no negatives at all, you know that something a bit untoward is going on. No business is perfect, and you shouldn't pretend that it is. I'm not saying that you actively want to display one or two-star reviews but there should be a blend of five-, four-, and three-star reviews.

How you respond to them is also incredibly important. If someone offers you constructive criticism then you can say, 'Thank you so much for this insight. We'll review this and see how we can apply it to the business going forward.' That shows commitment, and that you're not just content with how things currently are. You're constantly looking to improve which, as we know, is part of Google's Quality Rater Guidelines as well. Any website that's consistently putting care and attention into the content it puts out and its relationship with customers is always going to outperform someone that doesn't.

It may take a longer time, especially when you're starting off. SEO is a long game. You can't just do these things, increase your EEAT by 20 points, and then suddenly start ranking. However, integrating it into the day-to-day business and your ongoing marketing strategy is one thing that will really solidify your business for success going forward."

Can you carry out one EEAT audit and implement those changes into the production of your future content or should you carry out further audits as well?

"Definitely continuously audit. It could be little things. If you have an evergreen piece of content, even if you don't physically update anything that's on it, at least have a note on the blog article or landing page that says, 'This page was recently reviewed on [X date] by [Person A] to ensure accuracy'.

That's another signal, in the grand scheme of your EEAT strategy, that shows you're not throwing up a singular piece of content and saying, 'Fantastic. High fives and handshakes all round. That's job done.' You're continuously making sure that every bit of content you have on your website is factually accurate at all times.

At Swoop, when interest rates change or schemes end, we have to update the website content to ensure that we're reflecting the current rates on loans, interest rates, etc. to make sure the user isn't misinformed. We're also regulated by the Financial Conduct Authority, so we have to ensure that everything we do is above board and hitting those criteria. This obviously fits into YMYL but there is no reason why any other website shouldn't be doing this to make sure that they are meeting or exceeding what is expected from an EEAT perspective."

How do you measure EEAT success?

"EEAT success is the continuous growth of your website. Obviously, this also relies on the other content that you're putting out, the feed of content, and the improvement in rankings, but the real testament to it is continuous growth. It can also be the fact that, when core algorithm updates happen or there is volatility, your website isn't impacted.

Google will always say that, when a website gets affected by a core algorithm update, it's not necessarily that they're doing anything wrong; it's just that other websites are doing something right. Starting with EEAT will ensure that your website is doing something right because you're focusing solely on white hat tactics, you're focusing on EEAT, and you're delivering that value to your website visitors."

If an SEO is struggling for time, what should they stop doing right now so they can spend more time doing what you suggest in 2024?

"Don't go too big too soon. Everyone wants to go after these high-volume keywords that offer 20,000/30,000/40,000 monthly searches. That's not immediately obtainable and, realistically, the brands that are already holding those rankings are going to hold them for a very long time.

You need to focus on the long-tail searches and weave your experts into that.

Really create a persona and a voice for your brand as an authority within these long-tail searches. Over time, you'll be able to compete for the bigger, higher volume searches that will ultimately generate a higher volume of traffic, almost as a vanity metric. We all want more users on our website, but we know that the long-tail high-intent searches are the ones that are actually going to convert. They're far more transactional whereas a seed keyword has a lot of discovery, informational, and navigational intent behind it.

Focus on long-tail. Build your authority within a certain aspect of the business. Have your experts reviewing, publishing, and vouching for content. Have clear experts listed on-site, cite their credentials, and really build them up as people within the organization. Over time, you may well see that you're ranking for that seed keyword you initially wanted to target as a byproduct of going after the long-tail keywords."

Ed Ziubrzynski is Global SEO and Content Manager at Swoop Funding, and you can find him over at SwoopFunding.com.

Prepare for a renewed and increasing emphasis on EEAT – with Kavi Kardos

Following on from Ed's advice, Kavi Kardos from Uproer believes that all SEOs should be putting renewed and increasing emphasis on EEAT in 2024.

Kavi says: "Follow Google's lead and adopt a renewed focus on EEAT, which stands for Experience, Expertise, Authority and Trust.

Google has already started emphasising EEAT in the recent messaging they direct at site owners. That suggests that they're predicting a corrective pendulum swing away from the recent swell in AI-generated content.

Not that we'll stop using AI to create or augment our content, but they're accurately predicting that people are going to have more of a thirst for user-generated content with the growth of all the AI content we are seeing in search results. Organisations need to be prepared for that swing to happen as well."

What are the useful ways of using AI within content in 2024?

"It's really important to have a process for getting AI to give you the output you're actually looking for. That means knowing the right input to give to ChatGPT or any other tool. You can't just hit copy, paste, and publish on the content that it spits out for you, without taking the time to refine your prompts and know exactly how you should be talking to those models."

Asking the right questions upfront, and letting the model know exactly who the audience is and what the content is going to be used for, is often really important. That helps to refine the voice and tone that it will use in what it spits back out. If you don't, it uses a generic tone that won't match your brand and won't sound authentic or human-written. If you feed it a little bit more information upfront, that helps to tweak it more closely to what your users actually need."

How does Google Perspectives factor into EEAT?

"The Perspectives idea is really interesting. We haven't seen exactly how it's going to play out in its final form, but the fact that they've introduced that new kind of search result suggests they're predicting people will be looking for human perspectives, user-generated content, and content from subject matter experts – not just what you see in those generic search results.

Of course, we don't know if the SGE experience is going to play out exactly as it looks today either but, if it does, we will see more people clicking through to those Perspectives results as opposed to just being satisfied with what's on that first page."

What type of content is likely to appeal to the Perspectives filter?

"Video, definitely. We're not just talking about textual content here. It's short-form videos and even longer videos of the type that you see on YouTube.

When we're learning how to write in school, we're told, 'Don't talk in the first person.' Now, we need to start thinking a little bit opposite to that. Don't be afraid to speak in the first person and say, 'My experience is this. This is why I am qualified to talk about this.'

Especially in videos, try to sound like you're talking to a person or advising a friend on the topic rather than generically stating facts. That will come across as more authentic and it will be rewarded in search results as well.

These are typically vertical videos. When I've played around with Perspectives a little bit, I've seen a lot of that. To some extent, they're looking at Perspectives as a competitor for TikTok because Google sees so much of its traffic being pulled away by TikTok right now. They're thinking that short-form, vertical video is the best way to compete with what people are used to seeing on that platform instead.

If a brand is already set up with a solid TikTok strategy or Instagram strategy, then they're probably already making content that looks quite a bit like this. Brands that have stayed away from TikTok and Instagram might have a harder time adopting the format. Speaking to your audience in a more casual, friendly way doesn't feel natural to a lot of brands but it is going to be really valuable, where it makes sense."

For a longer sales cycle, where does this content fit in the user journey and what comes before and after?

"If you're an e-commerce website, this type of content (coming from the brand itself, short-form video or text that demonstrates more authority) is probably more useful at the top of the funnel, where people are starting to learn about whatever they're going to eventually buy.

It's less relevant once you get down to the nitty-gritty of actually hitting 'Add to Cart' and making a purchase. When you get to that point, you want to incorporate more user-generated, or customer-generated, content by encouraging comments, reviews, and that sort of thing.

We already know that Google is training some of their own models on reviews at this point, so they're obviously taking a much closer look at user-generated reviews and considering those to be even more valuable than they did before."

Should brands try to incorporate users in the content on their own website or should they encourage users to talk about the brand on their own social platforms?

"Both, but if a brand can incorporate user voices in their on-site, housed content, that's something really interesting that we should start seeing more of. A lot of brands aren't doing that right now, but it demonstrates more authority and more trust from users in the brand and the product. Pushing that to your own in-house platforms makes a lot of sense."

Do SEOs need to work more closely with social media departments to achieve this?

"One of the most exciting things about this shift is that it's naturally going to lead us toward less siloing of marketing departments and more cross-department work. I've always advocated talking to your customer service representatives about what customers are asking about and how you can solve those pain points using content or SEO.

We're going to start seeing more of that on the social media side now too. SEOs should be going to the social media directors and asking, 'What are people saying about our brand on Instagram, TikTok, and Reddit right now? How can we use this conversation that already exists outside of our control, bring it within our control, own that messaging, and encourage users to contribute to it too?'

I don't think about this as social media teams giving up responsibility but simply sharing information. Social media managers can keep doing the job that they're doing while passing off what they've learned and any content ideas to the SEOs and content creators. It shouldn't create a particularly different division of labour. It's collaborative work that we get to do together, which is really exciting."

With SGE, are Google going to incorporate Perspectives into partially AI-generated results, creating an opportunity to stay on the SERP there?

"It does look that way right now. Again, once SGE is fully rolled out we don't know if it's going to look exactly like it looks right now. They're certainly getting a lot of negative feedback on it, and I've heard quite a bit of chatter around the SEO universe that SGE is relatively useless as it's just scraping language from the top few results. What's the point, when you can just scroll down and see the same thing a few results down?

However, we are going to have some version of AI-generated results in our SERPs pretty soon. It looks like Perspectives is going to live in that top bar alongside Videos, Shopping, and Images. I think we'll see some users using both and some users opting more for one or the other."

For newer SEOs, is it still necessary to learn all the traditional aspects of SEO?

"We're still going to need to rely on a lot of the SEO basics. On the blogs, at conferences, and on podcasts, I'm seeing a lot of people encouraging back-to-basics SEO at the same time as all of these new things are happening. That makes a lot of sense.

Technical SEO, for example, probably isn't going to change very much. You're still going to need to do all of the things to keep your site in good shape. Understanding crawling, indexing, etc., is probably never going to change, but we can now use ChatGPT to help us write some of those tasks and make them go faster, which is nice.

Creating genuinely helpful content that is written for users is and always has been the basic gist of SEO, and I don't think that's going to change. If anything, we're seeing more of a focus on that.

For people who are new to the industry, this is a really great time to be getting into SEO because you're coming in with a fresh perspective. You're not bogged down by the old-school focus on title tags and meta descriptions. Instead, you can bring a fresh pair of eyes to what we're doing. For younger people who are more used to TikTok and the exchange that happens on social media platforms, that perspective is going to be really helpful in this new era of SEO."

Will Google introduce some form of paid advertising opportunity into Perspectives, similar to thought leader ads on LinkedIn?

"It's definitely possible. Putting paid ads into Perspectives seems a bit counterintuitive to what they claim to be doing with that feature, but they've got to make money somehow. I'm curious to see how the paid side of things is going to be incorporated into both Perspectives and the SGE too."

If an SEO is struggling for time, what should they stop doing right now so they can spend more time doing what you suggest in 2024?

"Stop relying on AI-generated content without human intervention. We've seen GPT-4 and other large language models come a really long way in terms of creating fairly good content, but you can't just hit copy, paste, and publish. You've got to interact a little bit more.

We spend a lot of time getting to know how to use AI tools and then not using them properly. Right now, the best use of ChatGPT is for automating time-consuming SEO tasks. Focus more on that and learn how to use them for the more technical and tedious tasks that you've been doing in spreadsheets for the past five years.

Don't waste time figuring out what content you want to get out of it, prompting it the wrong way, and sending that off to your client or your publisher without putting the thought that's required into making it good and authentic."

Kavi Kardos is Director of SEO at Uproer, and you can find her over at Uproer.com.

Invest time and money into the EEAT of your website – with Taylor Kurtz

To experience the benefits that Ed and Kavi have shared, Taylor Kurtz from Crush the Rankings says that you need to be investing both time and money into the EEAT of your website.

Taylor says: "Invest your time and resources into building your website's EEAT: Experience, Expertise, Authority and Trust. If you can only invest time in one thing, that would be it. Things like backlinks are very important but, at the end of the day, if you're not providing quality information and value to the user, you're not going to rank."

Why is EEAT so important?

"Google has always put out their search guidelines. In September of 2022, they released the helpful content update essentially saying that experience, expertise, authority, and trust are exactly what they're rewarding. They want to reward people who have first-hand knowledge of whatever they're talking about.

Google's search generative experience and Bing's AI chatbot being integrated into the search results will probably lower the click-through rate for a lot of search results. Similar to a featured snippet, people will get the info they need right at the top.

At the same time, that info has to come from somewhere and, within its answer, Bing cites where they sourced that information. I want my material, or my client's, to be part of the information that's being cited."

Is AI content able to deliver the same authoritativeness as human-written content?

"It's capable of being an incredible ally, but it's not a one-stop shop. I've had numerous clients who are writing specifically about something they are an expert in. I can ask questions about that to an AI tool. I'm not going to defer to its answer, particularly when I have access to someone with firsthand knowledge, but it can give prompts, ideas, and questions that weren't in the original content piece. It's a gap filler, and it can go in a different direction to open up your thinking.

Using law as an example, AI can't necessarily cite proper legal cases or statutes. That's where you want an expert. You're just getting the background information, on a surface level, that can supplement what you are doing.

When AI first came out, a lot of people felt very threatened. We felt unsure about what the future landscape might look like. However, technology has always changed. When the car came around, the people who drove wagons panicked. AI can open up so many opportunities if you're able to view it as an ally that can aid your efforts, but it's not something to be relied upon as an expert."

How can a content writer differentiate themselves from their competitors and look like the key authority to Google?

"It comes down to first-hand experience. Recently, Google released their August core update. A common theme I've seen with this update is that a lot of the websites that are being rewarded have clear, obvious, firsthand experience. They aren't writing broad overviews of a topic. They are able to put their personal experience into it and show their expertise.

It's not easy. Most clients are busy trying to do their jobs and they're not focused on helping us with our content. However, getting that firsthand experience is great, especially through video. If you have an article where the client isn't involved in the writing, other than reviewing it for accuracy, get them to summarise it in a video, or tell a personal story on the topic. That's a very digestible and user-friendly form of content, and it's an easy win.

Say you have a client who's a dentist and wants to be the foremost authority on root canals. You can certainly write about root canals but there isn't much evolution in the root canal business so there'll be a lot of overlap and redundancy with your competitors. Get the dentist to commit a minute of their time to talk about how they've been doing it for X years, their 10 top tips, or whatever else might add that personal touch. That makes it very clear that an actual expert has their hands on the content.

It's not that every piece needs video, but supplementing your content with video is an easy win. My motto is, 'No stone unturned.' Look at your top ten competitors. Any topic they address on their page, you want to address as well. Don't leave any stone unturned, where the user may have to go to another site to find the information they're looking for."

Why is UX important to SEO and how can you measure the impact of it?

"As users, we all endure plenty of poor user experiences. Let's say I'm interested in a restaurant, and I want to see the menu. I open the website and it's loading slowly. I see the 'View Menu' button, try to click it, and the next thing you know the whole thing loads, and I've clicked on something else inadvertently. That drives me crazy. That's why user experience should be a focus.

From a search engine perspective, Google will tell us that things like user experience and web speed matter but they rarely tell us exactly what they want to see. When we are actually given a benchmark metric, we know it must be really important. For example, mobile speed needs to be two seconds or less or the Largest Contentful Paint in Core Web Vitals needs to be 1.5 seconds or less. They're taking the time to tell us to clean up those areas. Once you exceed those benchmarks, you can focus on portraying yourself as an expert, creating content, and building a beautiful house without worrying about the walls crumbling down.

Core Web Vitals are the main way to measure your UX, whether it's the Largest Contentful Paint, Total Blocking Time, First Input Delay, or Cumulative Layout Shift.

Audit your website, make sure that you're able to exceed the known benchmarks for Core Web Vitals, test them in PageSpeed Insights or your tool of choice, and then you're starting with a clean slate. You can invest time, effort, and resources into creating authoritative, quality content, knowing that its performance won't be hindered by the technical components that Google has plainly stated are important."

You've coined the term Virtual Environment Optimization. What does that mean?

"In the last couple of years, nearly the last decade, virtual reality of some form has become more accessible to the everyday person. Mobile introduced augmented reality and everyone was chasing Pokémon in Pokémon Go, Meta has their Oculus platform, and there are all sorts of new implementations. It's not going to slow down.

What might search or marketing look like in 10 years? In 2005, you could go on the internet on your flip phone, but you had to click the button and scroll very slowly. It was a nonsense experience. At that time, nobody would have envisioned that, 10 years later, the majority of web traffic would be on cell phones thanks to the introduction of the iPhone and the smartphone. Nobody would have expected that Google would come out and say that you need to have a mobile-friendly website. That was inconceivable. Now, they're working on implementing a mobile-only index.

I've tried the Oculus and it's very just rudimentary. It's not that technologically impressive, but it's in users' hands and in their homes. Soon, Apple is going to release their Vision Pro. Potentially, Oculus will be to Blackberry as Vision Pro will be to iPhone. It has the potential to change our everyday lives, even if that sounds wild right now. With the Vision Pro, you will have the opportunity to go shopping, have the storefront in front of you, and test the products in your living room. Eventually, we will have clients utilising this technology, and we're going to have to figure it out.

If we're in a virtual environment and multiple products are available, how do we get ours to the forefront and make ours the most visible and compelling? While that's not necessarily integrated at the moment, neither was mobile web speed back in 2005. It's going to keep evolving and, as it becomes less intrusive, less bulky, and easier to incorporate into your life, it's likely to become more widely used.

Brand loyalty does not necessarily exist for the younger generation in the way that it does for older generations. I could see the younger generation being able to embrace a more virtual commerce experience. How is your client's product going to be the one that they see?

Imagine, one day, you don't go to the grocery store anymore. Instead, you go to a virtual grocery store that's a hundred times the size of any store that's ever been built. It has every product, and you can pick them up and inspect them. You can look at the labels, nutrition panels, etc. The possibilities are endless and there's no way that it doesn't creep into our digital marketing/SEO spectrum, at some point."

Is it possible that SEO will become Digital Experience Optimization, Customer Experience Optimization, or something else in the future?

"I like the term Virtual Environment Optimization (VEO), but it's all on a

TBD basis. We don't know what this new world will look like. In 1989, no one imagined that 7-year-old me would be learning how to use Napster 10 years later. It all evolved so quickly.

I can't imagine consumers aren't going to try to be more in front of your face. The movie theatre is a prime example. I am very hesitant to go to a movie theatre because I can watch from the comfort of my couch. With a younger generation that has an even smaller attention span and less patience, why would they want to go to a store and deal with crowds when they could do it in their own, personalised environment?

With the metaverse, Zuckerberg wanted to create a space where you could interact with your friends. While that might not have taken off, I could very much see a world where everyone puts on glasses or a headset and enters a virtual space that's catered specifically to them. In that environment, an algorithm would show you the content that you might be interested in. That's where we would have to optimize what we are offering; to target people that fall within those demographics and their algorithm."

If an SEO is struggling for time, what should they stop doing right now so they can spend more time doing what you suggest in 2024?

"Stop focusing on backlinks altogether. If you write good content and show your expertise, experience, authority, and trust, the backlinks will come. People writing on the same topic as you will cite your article and you will get organic, valuable backlinks. That doesn't mean that you shouldn't take opportunities for valuable links, but it's not worth a significant amount of time anymore.

If you're a brand-new website, you need to get some sort of reputation, being the new kid on the block. If you have a website that's been around and is starting to perform, though, find a better way to spend your time rather than wasting an hour or two pursuing backlinks. Use that time to bolster your experience, authority, and trust.

To some extent, backlinks play a role in trust. If you're a doctor, a link from WebMD builds trust. At the same time, unless you're getting on a directory on one of those websites, the way you get those natural links is by being the expert on your topic – by people reaching out to you for quotes, your thoughts, or citing your specific content. With backlinks, it's about quality over quantity. Focus on doing things right, making your content visible because it's high quality, and getting organic backlinks that way."

Taylor Kurtz is Owner at Crush the Rankings, and you can find him over at CrushtheRankings.com.

Gain and retain visibility by demonstrating EEAT – with Kerstin Reichert

Kerstin Reichert from SeedLegals advises that in an automated, AI-driven world, utilising your expertise within EEAT should result in measurable gains in visibility.

Kerstin says: "Truly embrace building authority and demonstrating EEAT – meaning experience, expertise, authority, and trust.

With AI, there's so much content flooding the search results. The counterpart to that is building authority, being the number 1, 2, or 3 go-to source in your industry, and demonstrating that not only to your potential customers but also Google – to keep and gain visibility there."

Is the counterbalance to excessive AI content not using AI to produce your content?

"Using AI can help you do things faster, but what becomes more important is your own input, keeping an eye on actual expertise, and doing something unique. If everyone is doing the same things now, and using the same AI, content just becomes a big mess of mediocrity. Logically, Google has to differentiate between what is a good result, what is trustworthy, what is high-quality, and what is just the same old content being repeated.

Even with Google potentially using AI to generate search results with SGE, if you want to show up there and be the answer that Google provides, you can't be mediocre. You need to be at the top. You need to be the relevant source that Google goes to for their AI-generated response.

You can use AI for brainstorming and to help with writing and the more laborious tasks that you can automate and do faster. At the same time, you need to think about how you can improve the quality of what you're producing. How can you really stand out and be at the top of the playing field and not just another mediocre resource of information?"

When you look at the SERP, you will see similarities between the sites that are ranking. Can you be different to the other results and still expect to be number one?

"It depends on what your capacity is and what you're working with. You need to have the necessary resources to produce really outstanding and quality content, and that might not be the right way to go for every company. For some, it might be enough to just produce content. However, if you're in a YMYL field, EEAT becomes even more important because whatever you say has to be trustworthy and factually correct.

However, I believe that you can stand out by doing things differently. Some of it will be the same, but you can create your own insights, have your own opinion, and work with experts. Not everyone has the luxury of having experts within their own company, but you can reach out to experts and amplify what you're doing through collaboration.

Use your knowledge and your creativity to really stand out. That's not going to happen by just looking at data. Of course, data is really important, but if you just look at the numbers and who's ranking, that's not going to give you the edge over your competitors. It's really important that you also do the manual work. Go into search results, see what they are doing, and look for what you could do better. Is there anything you could add to this topic, that you can't find everywhere?

At SeedLegals, we're a legal tech company, and we're lucky that we have a lot of internal experts. We usually cover complex topics, often in the areas of finance and funding. We have lawyers and funding experts in-house, so there's a lot of knowledge for us to tap into. That means that we can use our colleagues to get unique information. We are also a platform where people do funding rounds, so we have a lot of data that is unique to us, which we can use for articles we produce and reports that can challenge what is already out there based on our data.

We can start conversations, and that is exactly the type of thing that makes you unique, so you add more value than just giving a list of basic steps. Go a step further and think about what else you can add that might be useful, apart from the general information that people would like to hear or read about. It could be data that you have or insight from experts that you have access to. Reach out to them, collaborate, and bring something new to the topic."

Should you combine the general information with those additional elements on the same piece or would you create separate pieces of content?

"We usually combine it, and we tend to do it across our content. If we work on an article around funding, it could start with an introduction that explains the trend we're seeing from our data for 2023 compared to 2022, then compare that to third-party data has been published elsewhere. We do usually give some of our own insight for general topics, if we have something interesting to add.

At the same time, almost all of our content is produced in collaboration with internal experts, so we usually feature them in the article. We display the author in the article, and we also include the experts who've contributed. We link to their profile pages, and we feature them throughout the article in highlight boxes that show their quotes or expert tips.

We tend to do that across different content formats so, even within a newsletter, you might find an expert highlight. We do reports on the state of funding or option schemes in the UK, which are very data-led, but each section has insights from an expert. That could be their own view, something they can add from their experience, or something that they are predicting for the future. You can do that with content where it's maybe not the most obvious thing to do.

Pitch deck templates are very useful in the start-up space, but they have been over-produced. When founders pitch to investors, they want to know what a good pitch deck looks like and they want to find a template online. There are hundreds of these templates already, so we looked at all of them and thought, what do these pitch decks not have?

For our pitch deck, instead of just giving the framework and design for founders to use, every step of it has insights from not only other founders but also investors. Collaborating with investors on content for founders generated a huge amount of interest and it's been hugely successful. Founders are downloading the pitch deck because it is a good template, but it is also paired with insights from investors and what they want to see during a pitch.

That's an example of using an idea that already exists but finding a way to make it better."

If you don't have access to internal experts, can you turn to external experts and get them to contribute in a similar way?

"Yes, but it involves both finding the right people and relationship building. You need to have someone who can do that, who has the time for it, and the personality to reach out and find these people to work with.

You might also have internal experts who are not recognised externally. If they're up for it, you can try to build their profile by featuring them on podcasts or other websites. That's something we've done in the past. We look for press opportunities to get coverage outside of our own website that would help establish them as experts.

Additionally, you can work with external experts. In our case, there are different types of external experts. We could be finding insights from other founders who have started or sold multiple businesses, or we could be talking to investors as well.

The content type doesn't usually matter. We work with external people on webinars and then we repurpose that into other content formats. We have an internal contact list of people we've collaborated with in the past, and we reach out to them. When our writers work on content, they can then contact the relevant experts for each topic.

Sometimes collaboration also happens unplanned. We were working on and e-book that covered funding advice and I saw a post from an investor on my LinkedIn feed that was very relevant to the content we were creating. She made shared an infographic she designed on different types of funding and fundraising stages, that I thought would work really well with our e-book content.

I shared the LinkedIn post with one of our writers who then reached out to the investor to see if she's like to collaborate with us. She agreed and we used an adapted version of her graphic and also featured her with insights and tips throughout our e-book. She's since collaborated with us on blog articles as well – and we've seen some good engagement levels from the added investor insights.

We also prominently featured her on thee-book landing page and in our social media posts. And she shares our e-book in her newsletter, and it got a lot of traction. This approach isn't limited to a specific type of content. It's about finding the right people who have great knowledge to share.

How can you make it more likely that experts will contribute?

"We've noticed that it doesn't really work when we reach out to people and just ask if they want to be featured and what they have to say on the topic. It's usually better if we schedule a call to interview them. We record the call and then draft the content and quotes from what they've said. Then, we send it back to them to see whether they are happy to sign off or if they want to make any changes.

The easiest way to do that is for us to do the heavy lifting because they don't really have time. Investors, especially, are always short on time. They usually don't have the time to sit down and write their own articles or draft insights; it's just too much of an ask.

Schedule some time for interviews and be very clear with the brief and your timelines. Send them what you are asking for and your timelines beforehand so they know what's coming, what's happening next, what you expect, when you sign off, etc. It's about good project management – and stakeholder management as well. Do the legwork and take care of all the heavy lifting."

If an SEO is struggling for time, what should they stop doing right now

so they can spend more time doing what you suggest in 2024?

"Stop working in a silo. A lot of successful SEO campaigns are successful because you step out of the SEO bubble – and that's also true for people. People are successful when they aren't stuck in the SEO tunnel. Open up, reach out, find what's important to the business, and then collaborate with other people.

A good time saver is to step back from the endless backlog and SEO roadmap. Look at what is the most important thing to do for the business at the moment, and then find the right people in the business to collaborate with you on that."

Kerstin Reichert is SEO and Content Lead at SeedLegals, and you can find her over at SeedLegals.com.

Lean into long-tail search with the added value of EEAT – with Ben Howe

Delving deeper into where these principles apply, Ben Howe from SEOMG! shares that you should be applying EEAT across all of your content, including long-tail search opportunities.

Ben says: "Use the principles of Experience, Expertise, Authority and Trust to lean into long-tail search.

EEAT elements are no longer nice to have; they are absolutely essential. Practically, showing the principles of EEAT on your site is a very long list of activities, but I will rattle through them. You'll need to show transparency as to how your material is published and show transparency about you as a business – for example, where you're based and how to get in contact.

Your material should show first-hand experience and avoid generalisations by using statistics when making claims. Your material should cite sources and provide nuggets of information that are not found elsewhere. Also, you should be doing all of this while building a brand. It's a very broad set of expensive and time-consuming considerations but there are some ways to make it easier to target your content."

Does this focus on EEAT apply to every type of content and every intent?

"It applies on a sliding scale. When these principles were first introduced, it was primarily through the lens of YMYL topics – topics and niches where big financial or health decisions were involved. In the last 12 months, guidance has come out which has made it clear that this applies to everything, but to a greater or lesser extent depending on the risk for the users.

It applies to all types of content. It applies to a site as a whole when you consider business transparency. It applies to really informational content when it comes to showing unique value. It applies through the funnel and to almost all niches, but on a logical sliding scale of importance."

Which styles of content does it apply to the most?

"I've seen clear evidence of it applying to all material, from home pages to landing pages to longer-form editorial.

To try and answer that question, the longer the form of a piece, the more opportunity there is to show these considerations – and the more these considerations would be expected. To oversimplify it, these principles apply most to longer-form content.

EEAT principles need to be baked into everything. For example, there's an opportunity in an FAQ content extract (whether that's placed on a landing page or in an editorial) and, because there's an opportunity, everybody should be doing it.

We can see the importance of this through trends in Google's algorithm updates from the past year (which haven't reached their logical conclusion), and from trends in the development of generative AI in the last year (which also haven't reached their logical conclusion). I would encourage everybody to apply these principles everywhere it's possible to do so."

Should these principles be baked in when you initiate your content

production strategy or is it an ethos to consider with each individual piece of content?

"As with many aspects of search, it is sometimes oversimplified and only applied at the level of execution. Somebody has decided they want to publish to meet a certain kind of intent, they've decided on the landing page they're going to create, then they try to show first-hand experience at the page level and bake statistics in. However, it should be considered at the absolute most abstract level of strategy as well.

If you're planning your overall content strategy for the year ahead, it's really important to consider how you can demonstrate that this is something you're actually good at. When you see car dealerships suddenly writing affiliate blog posts about window cleaning services, that is clearly a paid blog post. That dealership has no authority in this niche, so it doesn't make sense, from a strategy perspective. They haven't considered what they're a perceived authority at, what they'd like to be a perceived authority at, and whether they're giving their material a chance to succeed.

That article could be executed with all the tick-box EEAT considerations, and it would still be strategically incongruous. They haven't considered their overall expertise signals as a site, so it's destined to fail."

Does this impact video-first content that is then transcribed? Does EEAT have to be considered during scriptwriting?

"It depends on whether that material is going to be repurposed purely for traditional search, or simply transcribed word-for-word. In general, the EEAT principles conceptually apply just as much to video-first publishers.

There's been a trend in the last few months for more social search results. Google Perspectives search results put emphasis on individuals and tend to share results from platforms like YouTube and TikTok. This type of search result is ripe for a video-first format and, because these result types are increasingly prevalent in search, it makes sense to consider EEAT principles for the video medium just as much as you would for the written medium."

Why is it becoming important to look at modifiers for long-tail keywords as much as entities?

"Some of the principles of EEAT are to produce nuggets of information in your material that can't easily be found elsewhere. That is so important with the proliferation of AI-generated content.

2023 has been the year of AI adoption. There was a post on Google's developer blog which said that, in the last year, they found five times more spam content than the previous year. That can only have been enabled by the increased adoption of generative AI.

To add unique value to your content – with lots of people considering the same keyword data from the same keyword research tools – it's time to go beyond the verbatim output of keyword research tools. When I talk about leaning into the long-tail, I'm talking about changing how you approach keyword research to identify gaps in the output of your common keyword research tools.

Let's take a niche car model as a practical entity. Instead of looking just at what queries searchers modify that particular car model with, look beyond to modifiers amongst a set of similar entities in the wider industry. In practical terms, that means doing keyword research around what modifier groups people apply to all car models (colour modifiers, door modifiers, engine size modifiers, etc.). You might find that there's no search volume for your niche car model modified with "boot size", but you might see that modifier used quite frequently with established models – so it's a no-brainer to address despite lack of known search volume.

You can use your keyword research to identify what there is likely volume and appetite for, that you wouldn't necessarily find by just looking at the modifiers for an individual keyword. With your keyword research, start looking at a whole group of related entities rather than just the given entity. SEOs are used to categorising their queries by entity. Now, there's also value in categorising queries by modifier groups within an entity group to see all the relevant things you could potentially talk about where there might be zero volume in your conventional search tools."

How do you ensure that you don't put too much effort into more speculative long-tail keywords?

"Even the longest of long-tail plans will have a data-backed rationale, so it's rare to have a truly speculative idea. However, a common approach would involve testing the click-through and conversion potential of niche queries in paid search before committing too much resource into ranking organically. However, the key to succeeding in that is to use product expert knowledge to understand whether the rationale you're applying to your keyword research is valid.

When you look at the modifiers that are applied to similar queries within the industry, the key to success is vetting that output with somebody who actually understands something about the product so that you can understand the relevance of those modifiers. It also helps that you can then explain how this material was gathered in the end output. You can say that the data was gathered by going through a named product expert.

If you're looking at modifiers for certain financial products, it would be absolutely critical to go to a product expert to make sure that similar-sounding financial products are affected by some of the same modifiers that you might find in your keyword research."

How can SEOs segment organic audiences in the way that social media marketers do?

"One example (which is only really possible in more popular and common niches) would be to use audience insight tools to understand what publications are more likely to be read by certain individuals.

If you're doing keyword research for a certain niche and you have insight into what other publications they may read, you can look at queries that these related publications rank for and are also relevant to your target topic. That can help you expand your keyword research with more confidence."

If an SEO is struggling for time, what should they stop doing right now so they can spend more time doing what you suggest in 2024?

"I'm advocating for the adoption of a very different, more intelligent, method of topic organisation and using topic insights – and it does take time. You have to find efficiencies. To do that, SEOs should focus less on tiebreaker ranking factors for imperfect content.

Google has been encouraging SEOs to place slightly less emphasis on things like Core Web Vitals and page experience than we have been. Remind your teammates that these sorts of things are generally tiebreaker ranking factors. If you're spending time and expensive resources trying to fix tiebreaker technical ranking factors – when you haven't extracted all the value out of your keyword in search and applied that to content – then you might be wasting your time.

As much as we are all technical geeks in the SEO industry, and we love doing clever technical SEO things, there are definitely some instances where you can kick Core Web Vitals and page experience down the line until your content is in the best possible shape.

Consider some of those really fun technical things as tiebreaker ranking factors, rather than as key strategic enablers."

Ben Howe is SEO Director at SEOMG!, and you can find him over at SEOMG.co.uk.

Improve the experience you offer through high-quality content – with Dre de Vera

While other tips in this chapter have spoken about EEAT as a whole, Dre de Vera from the SEO Video Show prefers to focus a little more on the 'Experience' aspect of EEAT.

Dre says: "Focus on enhancing the experience aspect of EEAT by producing high-quality content that embraces content creator principles.

That means going beyond traditional on-page optimization and extending your off-page optimization strategy beyond backlinks. Brands need to start actively establishing authority by sharing experiences on social platforms like YouTube, TikTok, Instagram, Twitter/X, Reddit, and Quora.

Last year, I talked about optimizing YouTube videos to dominate the page one pixels. Now there's a cool new feature coming out on Google called

Perspectives. With the Google Perspectives filter in play, creating value-driven, authentic, and creative content across social platforms is even more important for ensuring it aligns with the target keywords and audience.

What is the Perspectives feature?

"Perspectives is a filter that will pull information from high authority websites and comments – such as answers on Reddit or Quora and social media platforms like YouTube, TikTok, Instagram Reels, and even Twitter/X.

They mentioned a few of the websites they'll be pulling these answers from in Google I.O. this past year.

The Perspectives results are going to appear for educational, question-based queries. With the new SGE, which is becoming more of a conversation, they're actually pulling the experience aspect of EEAT into the Perspectives filter. They're going to be augmenting the result with different perspectives and viewpoints from users on high-authority platforms."

How can you optimize your content on these platforms to take advantage of the Perspectives filter?

"Like I said last year, keep making those long-form YouTube videos. Think about what you're saying in them, and use content optimization tools to help you optimize your scripts to target these keywords.

At the same time, once you create these long-form pieces of content or long-form videos on YouTube, repurpose them into vertical shorts that you can then upload to YouTube Shorts, Instagram Reels, and TikTok. Google is pulling from these sources and displaying them in search results now. If you can optimize for those platforms, that content will also be pulled into this new filter."

Do you want to publish Shorts on a different channel from your long-form content?

"That would depend on how big your audience is. If you have a really huge following on your long-form content, then definitely separate things out. This is what I see bigger content creators doing. If your audience has already watched a long-form video, they're unlikely to watch a Short of the same content, which can be a negative signal for your channel.

If you're just starting out, though, one of the new features they have implemented within Shorts is that you can have them linked to the longer-form video. Interlinking your Shorts to your long-form videos is a great way to grow a new channel."

When it comes to optimizing for Perspectives, are you looking at more than just video content?

"Yes. The idea is that they want to pull in perspectives and opinions. Last year, I was talking about being able to rank videos on YouTube by optimizing my video scripts. This is another opportunity to optimize. It brings in a new form of off-page optimization.

When we think about off-page optimization, we usually just think about backlinks. Now, you should be able to optimize the content that you put on other websites, like an answer on Reddit. Think about what you're writing and incorporate your keywords, using your favourite content optimization tool if you want to. That's what I'll be doing."

Are platforms like AlsoAsked and People Also Ask on Google the best places to go to determine what you should be answering with this kind of content?

"Those are definitely some great places to look for questions. However, there are also other places, like Quora and Reddit, that you can get questions from. Look at the questions that are more popular – filter them by the most upvoted on Reddit or the ones that have the most engagement on Quora. These are great places to find questions that you can answer that could be related to your content.

This isn't about keyword volume. These are popular questions that pop up, where you're trying to help and provide your perspective."

Can any business take advantage of this?

"The importance of this tip lies in having a timely response to the evolving landscape of SEO. In particular, when it comes to the new Perspectives feature and the addition of the new E in EEAT.

As the search landscape constantly changes, businesses that want to maintain a solid online presence need to continue to adapt. This is not limited to a specific industry. It can be helpful for any business or individual seeking to optimize their online presence and establish their authority across different platforms."

Is Google more likely to feature your content if it's confident that you're an authority within a particular niche?

"This brings me back to the idea of putting on your 'VALUE CAP' as a creator, which is an acronym. The V stands for being Value-driven by focusing on developing valuable content across all platforms, like Reddit, Quora, and YouTube. The Perspectives filter will really prioritise high-quality insightful content, and being value-driven ensures that those contributions stand out and have a better chance of being featured.

The A stands for Authenticity, which is also part of EEAT. Google places great importance on genuine, credible content. Being authentic increases that trust and is a signal to Google that your content is worth highlighting. Then you've got L for Learning. I can't over-emphasise the need for flexibility and continual learning. Adapting to this type of content – from keyword-optimized Reddit comments to optimized YouTube video scripts – gives you more chances of featuring with this particular filter.

U stands for Understanding your audience. This is creating content that aligns with your audience's interests and needs, and it can really increase your relevancy in the search results. Google loves showing content that matches what our searchers are looking for.

E is for having an Entrepreneurial spirit. Treat your online engagement as more than just participation. See this as an opportunity to establish thought leadership in your industry. Approach these platforms with an entrepreneurial mindset by innovating and setting trends rather than just following them. You can build that authority and credibility in your field by offering valuable insights.

In CAP, the C stands for Creativity. The Perspectives feature highlights unique and diverse viewpoints, which further emphasises the importance of creativity and originality. Offering unique insights based on real experiences can make your content stand out and resonate more with your audience. A real experience adds a layer of authenticity to the content and makes it more relatable. This doesn't just appeal to people but search engines too.

The A means that you want to be Analytical. Start tracking your performance on these third-party posts that you're creating, whether it's Twitter/X, YouTube, Reddit, etc. They all have internal analytics platforms so pay attention to that. Use each platform's analytics section to see how your post is doing. The last thing, the P, is Persistence. Regularly contributing content and engaging in discussions signals to Google that you are an active and reliable information source."

Should you publish this content on your own website, such as embedding YouTube Shorts on your FAQ pages, transcribing them, and making them into blog posts?

"Yes. Not only that, but you should be taking it even further by going into schema.

If you're sharing a viewpoint on Reddit, make sure that you implement the right schema to show Google where that featured information is coming from. You're telling Google that this original viewpoint came from your blog post – and you can do that to other platforms as well, like Quora."

Can you take parts of your long-form content to use as short-form content too?

"Absolutely. That's what I'm doing right now as well. For anything that you put out there, if you can bring it down to less than a minute, you should definitely create Shorts, Reels, and TikTok videos out of it.

I just recently started doing TikTok because of the Perspectives filter, and I was amazed at how much more visibility I am getting there compared to what I am getting on YouTube Shorts.

It's the same content; I just uploaded it to TikTok. I'm working on the SEO

Video Show Instagram too, but I'm taking advantage of TikTok since it's the first time I've been on there. I started uploading all my YouTube Shorts, and the views I get within minutes is what I would get in a few days on YouTube."

Are you overlaying text on top of vertical video to be more engaging for TikTok?

"I do that with YouTube Shorts as well. That's the best practice for anyone who's going YouTube Shorts.

Even if you're doing long-form videos, putting a text overlay in the first five seconds is a great tip as it allows people to see that text in the previews, etc."

Is there a place for leveraging AI within your content production process?

"I'm actually using AI to help me create Shorts. There are some tools out there that will take your long-form videos and cut them down to blocks of less than one minute, and you can pick the blocks. If you're interviewing someone, it will know who's speaking and it can isolate their video. There are a bunch of tools that you can check out and some of them are even free.

One thing I would throw out there is Opus. They define themselves as AI-powered video repurposing, and using tools like that can really streamline the way you optimize for repurposing your content."

If an SEO is struggling for time, what should they stop doing right now so they can spend more time doing what you suggest in 2024?

"Stop checking where your site appears on Google and panicking whenever there's a Google update. You don't need to be checking in on your Google Search Console or rank checkers every day just to see where you're ranking. Instead, spend more time creating great content for both Google and people with the VALUE CAP mindset. That will make people happy.

If your boss keeps asking about those metrics, go into what you're working on. If you're following my tip, show them how much visibility they're getting. Your work might not directly relate to rankings, but it is generating brand visibility and it's also optimizing for the future.

You're thinking ahead. In 2024, if you want to dominate more pixels on the first page of Google, you have to create this type of content and understand the search landscape."

Paul-Andre de Vera, aka Dre de Vera, is Host and Producer of the SEO Video Show, and you can find him over at paulandre.com.

Focus on the E, E, and A of EEAT – with Andrew Cock-Starkey

Like Dre, Andrew Cock-Starkey from Optimisey prefers to break down the specific elements a bit further. He shares that you can't have the T from EEAT if you don't have the E, E and A.

Andrew says: "In 2024, more people need to focus on EEAT, as it is now.

I'm mainly referring to expertise, experience, and authoritativeness here. I read the Quality Rater Guidelines and, if you look at the way Google talks about it, trust is an overarching thing. If you don't have the E, E and A then you can't have the T. People focus a little too much on trust and not on the other things.

If you build those elements to show that you have expertise, experience, and authoritativeness then you are trustworthy by definition. If you build it, trust will come."

How do you build experience?

"You have to have it first; you can't fake it. It's interesting to look at the way that Google talks about this in those Quality Rater Guidelines (You should read those guidelines. It's about 170 pages and lots of people say they have read it, but they've only skimmed it.)

Google talks about the extent to which the content creator has the necessary first-hand or life experience in the topic. You might call your dad or aunt to come and fix your plumbing for you, but why do you call that person? You call them because they've done it before. They know what they're doing, and they have experience in that area. The difficulty is in how you prove that to a machine.

You know a lot about microphones and cameras, David, because you've got experience in those areas. I know that, as a human, because I've spoken to you. How do you prove that to a machine? How do you prove that you've got experience?

Lots of people copy each other on the internet now. We get all these spin-offs of content, and people scrape this and steal a bit of that, but they're not showing that they have experience. They're showing that they have experience in scraping, stealing other people's content, and using ChatGPT to write things for them. You need to show Google that you have first-hand experience, and that's where they're becoming much more intelligent. They can tell the difference between original content and stolen or copied content, to a certain extent.

If you want to show that you are experienced in this area, and you have first-hand experience, having original photography can really help. If you have a photo of one of your plumbers fixing somebody's sink – not just the same stock photo of a plumber that's on 100 million other websites as well, but a photo of one of your team fixing a sink – Google sees that as an original image. That is a clue.

The intelligent systems that platforms like Facebook and Google use can identify the things in the photo. They know that the photo contains a van, a dog, a sink, a tap, a pipe, etc. If you have original photos, Google knows that they haven't appeared anywhere else. It's unique to you. You are showing that you have unique, first-hand experience of doing this thing.

There are certain industries where original photos are hard to come by. Some industries lend themselves better to imagery and photos than others, but it doesn't have to be photos. Create other original things for yourself. Create logos. Don't use a stock image from a library like Unsplash. Google can detect that, and they know that that image appears on hundreds of websites. You're giving Google a clue that you're copying other stuff. It's not offering anything original, and it's not first-hand experience."

Is your Google Business Profile the best place to have your original photos?

"You should absolutely put images on your Google Business Profile, but I'm mostly talking about your website content. On the page where you talk about your sink-fixing service, heating-fixing service, or horseshoe-fitting service, you need to have those images on your website too.

It's that corpus of content: building up the chapters in the book of the things you talk about and having that kind of information across your website. If Google reads the whole book of your website, you want them to have a chapter on each thing. Then they're starting to build up a picture of you.

You say you're an expert, but everybody says they're an expert. When you say you're an expert, you have some evidence to back that up."

If you're a thought leader in a B2B business, is your LinkedIn profile key to demonstrating experience?

"That kind of information is more about disambiguation. If you've got an unusual surname, like me, there aren't many people to differentiate between. When I talk about myself, Google probably knows who I am. If you're a James Smith, Google's not going to be 100% sure which James Smith that is.

You can use things like schema markup to help Google understand which James Smith you're talking about when you use the name 'James Smith'. Also, here's their Twitter/X profile, here's their LinkedIn profile, here's where they're cited on this other website, here's their bibliography of all the books they've written on Amazon, etc. That helps Google join up those dots for that entity.

Google views people as entities, so it wants to disambiguate that James Smith from all the other James Smiths. A good LinkedIn profile that is updated will mean that, when you talk about your company, Google can say, 'Oh, that James Smith! We know who that person is. We trust them a little bit more than an unknown James Smith.'"

What's the difference between expertise and experience, and how do you demonstrate expertise?

"Google fudges around a little bit and there's a definite overlap between these two things. You can't be an expert in an area without some experience but it's about how you prove those things.

Of course, I'm going to tell you I'm an expert in SEO, but how do you know that? Who else is backing up that statement? Showing expertise in your area might include showing that you have won respected awards (not just the ones you can buy for 500 bucks). These would be awards that people love, talk about, and trust. Google's not just reading your book; it's reading all the books on the whole internet. When other people talk about those awards, Google knows which are worth having.

Have you got any of those? Have you got any certifications? Are you a member of a trade body or a guild? Have you done recent training courses? Are you registered with Companies House? All these things are ways of proving to a machine that you're an expert in that area.

If someone's offering to re-roof my house, and they are registered with a trade body, have a qualification, and have a certification, these are all things that I can use to prove that they are an expert – and a machine can use them as well. They can go and look at those awards, look through the archive, find your name, and disambiguate it from all the other people with very similar names. That is the kind of stuff that can prove your expertise.

With experience, it's more about looking at the language and the way that Google talks about it in the Quality Rater Guidelines. They're looking for that first-hand experience and some of that can come down to the way you communicate. When you talk about things that you've done on your website in the content that you write, use the kind of language that shows experience: 'We did this.', 'We found that this happened', 'We don't do it this way anymore because, when we did it this way in the past, it was more expensive', etc.

Use words and language to convey your experience to a machine that's going to be looking for these clues. They are trying to determine whether you have actually done this or you are just an affiliate website that's trying to use the right buzzwords and keywords because you want to rank and make money when people click that link.

Can social proof help demonstrate expertise?

"Again, Google's going to be looking for proof. They want to know if you can prove it. I'm saying that I'm an expert on SEO. The social proof for that might be that you're talking to me about SEO, David. You're well-known in SEO and *SEOin2024* will be another bestseller, I'm sure. The fact that you're talking to me and the fact that I'm cited in this book are both clues to Google. That's more social proof that I might know what I'm talking about with SEO, at least to an extent.

Again, it's about who else is saying that you're an expert, and that's where this Venn diagram of circles is going to overlap. We're talking about expertise and social proof, which very much overlaps with authoritativeness. In Google's words, you have to be the go-to source. Would this person be your go-to source for X? If you're looking for SEO experts, is Andrew your go-to? (Maybe not. After Aleyda and other people have said no, you might come down the list to somebody like me).

If someone is going to re-roof your house, and they say they're an expert roofer, you go and look at something like Trustpilot or TrustATrader. If the reviews all say that this person is rubbish, you shouldn't use them, and they're cowboys, then they're probably not that authoritative. If the reviews all say, 'We had our roof redone and they were amazing! Five stars, would use them again.', that's another clue that is building up that authority."

What are the key ways to drive authoritativeness?

"If you want to be known as an expert, and known as authoritative, then you absolutely need other people to be saying it for you. You saying you're an expert is a good start, but you need other people to be saying it for you.

Also, you need to help Google to join those dots and disambiguate. When other people talk about you – and say what a great job you do and how fantastic and authoritative you are – cite that on your website. Boast about it. Say, 'We were mentioned in the Telegraph's best 100 companies', or 'We were mentioned in the Cambridge Evening News's article about the best marketing companies in Cambridge'.

Reference those things and help Google understand that, when that site talks about you, they do mean you because you mentioned it too. You can put that in schema and join all those dots up, and Google will start to build up a clearer picture of who the company is, who the person is, what they do, who else talks about them, who else says they're good/bad/indifferent, etc. Those are the kind of things that Google is looking for."

Will AI-produced content ever be able to achieve the same level of quality as humans, in terms of EEAT?

"Honestly, I think that one day it might be. It's already getting very good very quickly. There are certain areas where it is going to be much harder to differentiate between AI-written content and human-written content. This is particularly true where the lines are already being blurred – with some editors using AI to write content and then going back and editing it afterwards, correcting it, and tweaking it to make it sound more human.

These large language learning models, as the name suggests, are using that all the time. When their work is corrected, they look at what a human added to make it sound more human. They learn from it and try to repeat it.

For now, though, it's usually easy to tell the difference between some of the machine-written and human-written content. Again, if you look at the Quality Rater Guidelines, Google talks about this. Importantly, they say that this content has to be trustworthy, safe, and consistent.

It explicitly says that content should be given the lowest possible rating if it's created with so little effort, originality, or skill that the page fails to achieve its purpose. That is Google's words. They're looking out for main content that is copied, auto-generated, or otherwise created without adequate effort.

They know that people are doing it and, to an extent, it was already happening. Before ChatGPT came in and wrote all our content for us, people were using RSS feeds, scrapers, and various other tools to combine bits and pieces and jigsaw together an article. Google spotted that. It's not terribly useful and it doesn't take a great deal of effort.

Like most things in SEO, if it's easy it's probably not a good long-term solution. It might work for a bit, but probably not for long."

If an SEO is struggling for time, what should they stop doing now so they can spend more time doing what you suggest in 2024?

"Stop buying links. We all get emails saying, 'I'll sell you this link for $50'. If you can set up an inbox filter to scrape all those things out, that would be useful. Stop buying links is my stock answer every year.

For something slightly different, stop pursuing trust quite so much. If you can build up and show your expertise, experience, and authoritativeness, Google will start to have a more trustworthy view of your site as a whole."

Andrew Cock-Starkey is Founder at Optimisey, and you can find him over at Optimisey.com.

Highlight your real-life authority in your online presence – with Anthony Barone

Exploring yet another aspect of EEAT, Anthony Barone from StudioHawk UK believes that incorporating your real-life authority in your online presence is a key.

Anthony says: "Take your real-life authority and put it online.

You want to develop your topical authority (entity SEO, EEAT, etc.) by taking that real-life authority and putting it online through various forms such as improving your About Us page, improving your bio pages, adding author bios, showcasing your qualifications, skills, and education, etc.

Think of it as your own LinkedIn and Wikipedia – but on your website for you to detail to Google and users that you are who you say you are.

You should still have all your stuff on social media, control those things, and make sure all of that content is correct. However, when we're talking about SEO, you want to have it on your own website. That will make sure that you're telling Google and users that the people who wrote this content and work in this business are who they say they are, and they are legit.

At the end of the day, humans buy from other humans so that's what you want to talk about."

If you have a personal brand and a business brand, should you have two different websites or can you just have a personal page on the business site?

"You could do a bit of both. Usually, you would have a page on the company website that leads to your personal site, but it depends on what you want that personal website for. If it's just a portfolio and you only want people to check it out, that's great.

However, if you really want to use SEO as a lead generator then you want to have all that content on there. Have blogs, create content for that, and treat it as a separate website. I don't see the issue with having a bit of both because, if a lot of traffic is coming to your company website, you've opened up the door for the page that's talking about yourself to lead them to your website – and you're doing SEO for your own website by building up the authority on that too."

On that page, what do you include about yourself and how should you talk about it?

"You would usually write in the third person. I also like to write the way that I talk so it's more natural. You don't want it to be like an encyclopedia, where it's too structured and stiff, because humans buy from other humans. When people are reading that, you want them to get a sense of who you are and what you do.

Include the basics, like your education, qualifications, awards, articles you've written, places you've been featured if you've done PR, and things like that. If you're an owner of the business, you want to highlight your experience, expertise, authority and trust. You want someone to read that and think, 'I want to work with this person. They know exactly what they're doing, and I trust them.'

Then, help Google to crawl that easily by having some simple, easy-to-create schema markup to clearly tell Google who you are."

Does writing this content in the third person make Google more likely to feature that content in places like your personal knowledge panel?

"Potentially. However, you don't want to over-optimize everything. Follow the guidelines and see what works, just make sure that you're conveying the message to Google and users that you're legit and you are who you say you are.

Think of it as a two-way conversation with Google. What do you do? Where did you go to school? Where did you grow up? How did you get into the game? Think of that conversation and try to replicate it online so that, when both Google and humans are looking at it, they get a real sense of who you are."

If you offer other services, like SEO, should you include that in your about section?

"100%. It's the same thing you would do as a plumber, an electrician, or a jockey. By detailing that experience, you're detailing how long you've been in the game, the companies you've worked for, the awards you've won, etc.

You wouldn't go to a doctor who had no qualifications. You're going to go to a doctor who has all their awards and certifications on the wall, and you would make sure that they're legit. People love that experience, and that's what you want to be talking about and focusing on."

Can you measure the direct impact of building your profile online and creating a great personal entity?

"Developing your knowledge panels and things like that are good indicators. Again, it's not just related to your website; you've got other social signals that you want to control and develop as well.

There isn't really a quantifiable number, but you can look at your traffic. Look at Search Console to see how much traffic is coming through. If you're adding author bios and internal links to relevant pages, are people going through to those pages? How long are they staying on the website?

You can grab some numbers but this isn't a 1+1=2 situation; it's part of a holistic approach to SEO. You're doing your best to tell Google who you are and what you do, and add that credibility. Even if you threw numbers out the window, you should be telling people that information anyway. You do it in real life when they walk through your store. Does there have to be a number attached to that? Think beyond the numbers and consider the real-world impact that this can have."

Does having your own personal entity online help to differentiate yourself from ChatGPT content?

"I think so. ChatGPT is just scraping things from the internet. We had an inquiry come through because someone had searched, 'best SEO agencies in Shoreditch' on ChatGPT, and StudioHawk came up. We didn't optimize for it; it just happened.

I think we came up for a couple of reasons. One was location-based because they were literally just down the road. Also, the intent of the keyword. They used the term 'Shoreditch' and we came up as one of five. I don't know the history of what they searched before on ChatGPT, but location was certainly one of the biggest factors."

Should you create entities for everything, including your company brand, the products that you offer, and yourself?

"100%. I really love schema markup, and some of the team will dive deep into developing that, as well as improving our content offering and our ability to create content, working with clients to get better content out there, and pushing the EEAT and entity SEO idea – especially with the advent of SGE and AI in search.

That's definitely something that we're trying to do more of, for ourselves and our clients, and schema is a big part of that as well.

Although the bots are becoming more intelligent, I think schema still helps. It's the basics, and there is no harm in doing it. Schema will have a role. As we've seen with SGE and Perspectives, Google will pull more from social signals and your presence on other channels where they can grab more information about you.

We are moving toward Google having a wider look at all these other social signals – because anyone can say anything on their website. Google will then look at other websites and other platforms to determine whether they have seen this person before and where they have come from. While schema will be a part of it, you will need to have a presence in other areas, to feed Google's knowledge of yourself or your company. Being prevalent on other social media platforms and having your business and information elsewhere helps Google get more information.

It's important to focus beyond just your own website. It's a big world out there, so why not have a presence in other areas? It will help your SEO and it will help Google understand more about your entity or your business entity."

Do you recommend that clients involve ChatGPT in their content creation process?

"You can use it to speed up your website and speed up the work that you do – it can make you more efficient and help you out with ideation and writer's block – but don't let it do 100%, and don't copy and paste it. That's what everyone else does.

Use the 80/20 rule. Use it to speed up your work, but don't let it write the whole piece. You are the expert, at the end of the day.

We tell clients that ChatGPT is not going to replicate their 30 years of experience being a lawyer. It might be able to pull contracts together and do certain things, but the client has gone through those cases, they've fought those battles, and they've dealt with clients. You need to get that point across.

ChatGPT will help speed things up, just like the typewriter and the printing press did. People have been doing article spinning since before ChatGPT. Use it to speed up your work so you can be more efficient, but don't let it do everything because it's not you. Only you can be you.

When you're creating content, it's about quality over quantity. Who is your target market? Who are you trying to talk to? Who do you want to buy from you and engage with you? Once you have an understanding of that target market, what are they searching to find you? Create and tailor content around that. Put the right prompts into ChatGPT to give you some ideas, then create content, and then you can edit, tweak, and improve upon that. Don't outsource your thinking, just let it help you."

If an SEO is struggling for time, what should they stop doing right now so they can spend more time doing what you suggest in 2024?

"Stop getting stuck into the nitty gritty when a business owner just doesn't understand SEO. You want to be doing things that will move the needle, such as good fundamentals and good basics. Work on your technical SEO: get your ducks in a row and make sure that's clean.

However, the things that can really move the needle are jumping onto your Google Search Console and finding those second/third-page opportunities that you can move to the first page. Improve the metadata, page structure, and content on those specific pages. Those are some quick wins.

I'm not going to say that you can 100% go from page two to page one just by improving the basics. However, we have achieved that for some decent brands that we've worked with. They were around the top of the third page, and we improved the title, meta description, and on-page content – and we added internal links and fixed up the heading structure of those pages. In 3-4 months, with a bit of schema markup, we've seen them reach as high as the top three on page one.

With the way Google's constantly crawling websites, you should be able to see an impact within a month or two. You can show your client the before and after of what you've done for the important pages that match up with their business goals. You can really showcase that impact through improved click-through rates, impressions, and clicks. That is something tangible that a client can see.

Don't get too deep into the nitty gritty SEO stuff, especially if you're an agency working with clients who don't understand it. Focus on things that will have an impact and, like with football, the good fundamentals and good basics."

Anthony Barone is Co-Founder and Managing Director of StudioHawk UK, and you can find him over at StudioHawk.co.uk.

Keep EEAT at the forefront of your mind – with Filipa Serra Gaspar

SEO Consultant Filipa Serra Gaspar completes our EEAT overview with a comprehensive round-up, advising that you keep EEAT at the forefront of your mind.

Filipa says: "Always have EEAT at the forefront of your mind – every time you are creating a new page or any content that you want to rank on Google or any other search engine."

How do you demonstrate the new part of EEAT, experience?

"You can demonstrate experience by giving first-hand experiences or personal experiences. That is something that really humanises what you are writing. If you include those kinds of elements, it means that you are writing from experience, of course.

If necessary, you can also provide case studies and give examples of situations you have been through, or something else that is different from all the other content you can find online. If it is very specific and concrete, that is a great way to demonstrate experience.

Of course, you should also be thinking about what search engines will find relevant to you and your brand – and you should consider the users themselves as well. You always need to have the search engines at the back of your mind. It's not only about your personal experiences.

You can also use other examples such as linking to or citing other sources. You can write something that is not a personal experience, but then use an author bio to explain that there is a person behind what you are writing. It's not always possible to write from personal experience, so it can be a mix of both.

It is hard to measure, and it is subjective but, in the end, if you have quality content and people go to you when they are looking for answers then search engines will pick up on that. They will see that it's helpful and that the content is good. As a consequence, you will also rank, and you will gain visibility."

How do you select the right sources to cite?

"You want to cite websites or sources that already have a lot of authority. It depends on the topic that you are talking about, but a worldwide organisation is usually a good source to look for.

Essentially, you are looking for sources that give you credibility. Typically, that would be organisations that are well known for their expertise, and also mentioning experts in the area that you are talking about.

You can use tools to determine the best sources by looking at metrics like link authority and relevance, but the criteria won't always be the same. You will find a lot of information online for some industries and not as much for others, so it depends on the industry.

If the content is related to health, for example, you could mention highly-renowned sources like the World Health Organization. If you are talking about an industry like the pet industry, you can mention a veterinary association or you can cite specialists in that field. You're not necessarily trying to find the most authoritative commerce websites as much as you are looking for reputable trade bodies in the industry that you can refer to."

What demonstrates that you are producing high-quality content that will appeal to users and search engines?

"Whenever you have an article that you really want to demonstrate experience and expertise, you should always link back to an author bio. That already gives quite a lot of credibility.

In terms of the structure, there isn't a perfect formula because it varies a lot. You can refer to data, statistics, case studies, and other studies that have been carried out on that subject by trustworthy sources. That's very important. If it's possible, you can also use some kind of social proof, reviews from other people, or another form of trustworthy user-generated content. Again, it really depends on the field.

You want to mention examples that really demonstrate what you are talking about, but I wouldn't say that there is a structure or formula to follow."

What's the optimal way of setting up an author bio?

"The content matters. If it's e-commerce and it's a product, it obviously doesn't make sense to refer to the author. Where there is content, the author bio itself should be a URL or a page where you can actually find information about that author, and all the articles that person has written.

I was looking at some articles last week where a lot of people were talking about how the New York Times is structuring their author bios. You can find a lot of information on them – not only about the author but also about what they usually cover, their journalistic ethics, their background, etc. Sometimes you can even contact them. Alongside each article, they have a little description, and then you can click through to visit the full author page and find out more information there.

You can also include links to the author's other platforms, including their social media profiles. If the author is active, then you can include that social proof – where you can also find an address or phone number for an institution that represents them. For a journalist, that might be a media outlet, and you can refer back to the website for the media outlet itself."

How and where can you incorporate user-generated content into your pages?

"I wouldn't recommend having it on all of your pages. Include it in topics where the users might have questions that other people would have the answer for or, if possible, where they can interact with the author.

That gives a lot of authority, and it humanises that content a lot as well. It shows that there's someone behind it who is actually reading what you are saying and getting back to you. In the case of reviews, have the author reply to the reviews your customers or users are leaving on your website.

If it is possible and it makes sense, it can be like a category of an FAQ section, where you answer users' questions as a follow-on from a piece of content. That is definitely a great practice. Of course, it has to be monitored to make sure there is no spammy content or anything like that. If it's really productive or it brings value, though, then it's a great practice.

It can even give you ideas for something new to write. If you're writing about a certain topic and a user comes up with a question that you did not answer in that article, it's probably a good idea of what you should write next or include in the content you are planning in the future."

In what ways should SEOs incorporate transparency into their content?

"If you work in e-commerce, that could be transparency regarding your relationships with providers and your supplier chains. That would be beneficial because people often want to know where your products come from and who produces them.

However, it also includes being transparent about things like the author, for instance – and making sure that there is a face and a name behind them. It works on both sides.

If the user wants to know more information, then that information should be available so that they can really understand what they are consuming. They should be able to identify if the information is biased or if it comes from a certain ideology that they should know about – and be aware of what they are reading."

Would you ever use AI to produce content, and can AI-produced content demonstrate EEAT?

"It can demonstrate EAT, without the experience – so it can demonstrate the old EAT.

AI cannot have experience. I think AI is great but, of course, Google recommends that we always have a human fact-checking that content. It can be a very helpful tool, but you should always have a human fact-checking and proofreading any content that you produce with it.

What differentiates content that comes from AI and content that comes from a human is the experience. AI content cannot have that experience because

AI does not have lived experiences.

If you have decided that AI-produced content is too good of an opportunity to miss out on, and you want to use AI-produced content, then improve it with experience to show that an individual is involved.

In that case, it is a human plus AI. You can show a bit of human experience and it becomes a 50/50 article, with the AI part and then also the human side of it. If the article is 100% AI-produced, then it cannot have the experience side."

If an SEO is struggling for time, what should they stop doing right now so they can spend more time doing what you suggest in 2024?

"AI content does not have experience, so it does not fit within all the EEAT rules. Make content for people and not for robots or the algorithm. Make content for humans. In the end, you will have more visibility and it will be more successful. Your ratings will improve, and you will start to achieve everything else that comes afterwards.

AI is great but, if you really want to differentiate yourself, the human side can play a big part in that. That can be great for your SEO strategy."

Filipa Serra Gaspar is an SEO Consultant, and you can find her over at SEOlipa.com.

8 THE CUSTOMER JOURNEY

Stand out and give people a reason to visit your site – with Gerry White

Now looking at the other side of the coin, it's time to consider your customer journey. Gerry White from Mirador Local believes that standing out and being different is what matters.

Gerry says: "As content production and other aspects of digital marketing are becoming rapidly easier, you've really got to stand out. You've got to be a bit different.

In 2024, with huge amounts of content everywhere (and AI generating, regenerating, rewriting, and producing more of it), you've got to give people a reason to visit your site and do something with your product or service."

How do you deliver a reason to visit and engage with the site?

"Every single website is different. One of the things we're trying to do at Mirador Local is get more and more people to visit our site – not necessarily just customers, but potential customers too. We're building out some tools and other elements on the website.

For example, it's not enough to just say that you need schema on the website. You could be integrating a schema builder or a QR code generator when you're talking about QR codes.

If you can create a service that is a little bit more special than just a block of text on your website then, and get people to visit you, there's a much greater chance that they'll engage with you in the future. That is what's missing from a huge amount of the marketing that's happening at the moment."

If you look at the SERP and the search engine appears to be looking for a particular type of result, do you still try and be different?

"I spent about a year building out the organic strategy for an international supermarket, Oda. I quickly realised that there are phrases and terms that you can't rank for. For the query 'nasi goreng', you can't rank unless it's a recipe. All of the results are recipes, so you have to make sure that your website features recipes.

There are several occasions where you look at all the search results and they're all fairly similar because of how Google is interpreting the intent. You used to be able to put in FAQ schema to signal that you were going into more depth. In the past, I've spoken about microphones, the value of a microphone, what you need from it, and whether or not it's the right microphone for you. Adding that bit of value to the page will differentiate you.

Understand how everybody else is doing it and then understand what else you can add to show that your page is providing more. Even if somebody visits one or two results and then comes back to yours, that is a sign to Google that yours is definitely the better result.

People start to develop a brand preference as well. As soon as they start to see one good result amongst all the others, they'll tend to click on that result again in the future. For example, Amazon has great reviews. I often search for the Amazon page of a product, even if I'm buying it from somewhere else, because I'm going to look at the reviews on Amazon."

How do you measure the impact of trying to stand out?

"At the moment, Google Analytics and other tools are increasingly more challenging to use. I often look at click-through rate in Google Search Console and try to figure out why this particular result is way lower or higher than the results of all of the other pages, and whether the conversion rate on the back of that is happening.

When I was working at Oda, we were ranking for one of the most competitive keywords with huge amounts of search volume, but nobody was clicking into it because there was a Local Pack above us. We couldn't compete in that; we were an online supermarket. I looked at the SERPs and considered how to rewrite the titles and the descriptions, and we managed to improve the click-through rate considerably. Understanding how the SERP looks is critical.

I am struggling a lot with interpreting all of the data in Google Analytics 4 at the moment. I miss the old Google Analytics data, where it was really clean and simple."

Are there any trends for page titles or meta descriptions that might encourage a greater click-through rate?

"Google has stopped rewriting title tags as much as they used to – if you have good title tags. At one point, all of the title tags on a lot of websites were being heavily rewritten by Google, but that is happening less often at the moment.

I have played around with a lot of title tags. When I was working with Oda, we would make sure that the brand was included to encourage people to recognise the product. Again, SERP analysis is critical. If you look at all the different SERPs, you can quickly tell which title tag is going to perform better based on how users would look at it and click through on it.

If I'm looking at a particular product, I'll Google that product in 20 different ways. I will add supplementary keywords like 'reviews' to see why our listing is underperforming in comparison with anybody else's. Quite quickly, you will start to see what you need. You can see what people are looking for, and how people are searching for it.

You can also look at the data to see who's getting the greater click-through rate. It's not just about title tags and descriptions; it's also the images and things like that which are being pulled into the page. Product images are often being pulled in, and that is so important. Make sure that you have a product image, and you have all of the extra bits and pieces to make sure it's truly showing up in the search results."

If you're changing the style or content on a page, should you be split testing to determine what gets the most user retention?

"Split testing can be difficult because you need a certain amount of volume. In e-commerce, you will often find that one product will have a much higher click-through rate, more traffic, etc., than anything else. In organic, it's a massive challenge to get the results that you need through split testing. You can't just split-test 2 products; you need 50-100 because so many external factors come into it.

Usually, you would measure over time by comparing the before and after. Update the title tag, have a look at it, and see whether the click-through rate has improved. Do you see an improvement? If you add '2024' to a search result, does that improve the traffic by making it look more recent? Will 'The Best Guide to Podcasting 2024' perform better than 'The Best Guide to Podcasting'?"

How do you stand out in the world of the singular AI result?

"AI is going to be constantly changing so giving any viewpoint is challenging at the moment. The Search Generative Experience – and all of the different ways Google rewrites the SERPs to give you the answer at the top instead of 10 blue links – is a challenge; not to get the answer at the top, but to make sure the answer at the top is what you need it to be.

There is a question about how much we should start blocking the AI robots from indexing the core content that you want people to come into. At the moment, you can change your robots.txt file to block AI from crawling certain pages – like the guide pages. They'll still appear in the normal results, but you might not want AI to pull from this content because want it in a different place.

AI is constantly changing, and it's almost the prisoner's dilemma. If you do it and someone else doesn't, will you lose to the person who doesn't do it? If you don't do it and someone else does, you might lose out then too.

In short, you need to make sure that you're fully pushing the brand and pushing a reason to engage further with you as a service/product, rather than just a listing of an example."

Would you recommend blocking AI at the moment?

"If you've got the unique content on a particular topic (like the guide to something or a lot of information about a particular site) and you don't want Google pulling that information out and putting it at the top, then maybe it's something you should consider. However, if everybody's got the same content and you block AI from using yours, then all you're doing is letting somebody else fill the gap.

That's why it's the prisoner's dilemma. I don't have a straight answer for what the best strategy will be yet. As digital marketers and SEO strategists, we need to ask ourselves whether we want our content to be repurposed and pushed out at the top of Google search results. The question is, will there be attribution in the right way or will Google just take it and rewrite it without attribution? If that's the case, we would be losing any value from letting Google index the content in the first place."

Is an SEO's job nowadays more about standing out on the platform that the user prefers, rather than on their own website?

"I completely agree with that. I've been having a lot of conversations about how to market on TikTok and other platforms.

TikTok is a very strange thing. As a gentleman in his early 40s, I don't spend a lot of time on it, but I see how much it is being used. People will say, 'Have you seen this restaurant?' and they'll send me a TikTok link. I do follow a coffee guy on TikTok who recommends certain scales, coffee machines, and various other things. Even though I don't use it often, my buying habits have been heavily influenced by who I follow on TikTok and other platforms. I love traveling and I will look at different places on TikTok or Instagram before I choose a destination.

Increasingly, people are putting out short promotional pieces on TikTok for digital PR services. I 100% believe that you should market where people will be able to consume it. The way in which you do that is dependent on your audience and your niche.

I like coffee and TikTok is giving me more and more coffee information. If you're a coffee brand and you're not making coffee content on TikTok, you're missing a huge opportunity. It is a challenge for a lot of B2B or SaaS companies but, if you can do a great podcast, cut it up, and get shorts out of it, put those on YouTube or TikTok. I've seen some great examples of that recently."

If an SEO is struggling for time, what should they stop doing right now so they can spend more time doing what you suggest in 2024?

"Stop obsessing over one thing, like page speed. Don't get me wrong, I'm working with somebody to improve page speed at the moment, but once it gets good enough (and you get the green lines in Google Search Console), you can't keep maximising it to the nth degree and keep seeing returns on investment.

There's a special line which SEOs need to understand, and that's 'good enough'. When it's good enough, the return on investment significantly decreases as you strive to get to 'perfect'. We're perfectionists, but that can be a killer to the commercial value of our work. If you've got a website with 20,000 pages, you don't need to fix every single broken link from a blog post 10 years ago.

Be happy with 'good enough' and understand where the commercial value lies."

Gerry White is VP of Growth at Mirador Local, and you can find him over at MiradorLocal.com.

Find your audience of one to cut through the noise – with Dixon Jones

While Gerry explained why you should stand out, Dixon Jones from InLinks tells you who you should be standing out to. He tells you to dig deep and discover who your audience truly is.

Dixon says: "Clearly, AI is going to take over in 2024 – in many, many ways. For all its dangers and its pitfalls, you won't be able to avoid it in the SEO world, whether you like it or not.

However, I do think it gives the enlightened company founders a real chance to shine. If you know why your business truly exists, and who it truly serves, then I think you can cut through a lot of the AI noise.

Write like you've got an audience of one. The idea is that you don't talk to everybody with your content. If you're talking to the founder of a small SaaS business: I'm talking to you. My audience of one for this tip is people who have their own websites and want to do their own SEO. Those are the people I want to speak to. I don't want to speak to the rest of the world. When I give that tip, I'm talking to you, Mrs. Founder-Of-A-Website-With-A-Real-Business-Purpose."

Is cutting through the noise and talking to a specific individual something that AI has a challenge with at the moment?

"I'm talking about your business wrapping itself around a central concept that will allow AI to always come back to you. 'All roads lead to Rome' is a concept that's been around for 2,000 years. Originally, all roads did lead to Rome. Rome portrayed itself as the centre of the known universe and the empire expanded from there. I think that that's the same for anything that you do.

If you're a plasterer, you're not just a plasterer – you're a plasterer in a particular area. If you're a consultant, you're not just a consultant – you're a consultant in a specific subject matter. If you're a retailer of electronic products, you've got a specific genre of products that you're selling. What you need to do is become synonymous with that concept. It's the same with any marketing principle. You either need to be number one or two or be in a position to become number one or two in your niche in the near future, or you need to get out of the game.

Now, that has transferred over into pretty much any concept. First, you've got to define what it is that you do. You've got to be so specific that, if you were to ask anyone in the world to define the best person to go to for this, then they'd come to you. Then, in theory, all the AI in the world, reading all of the pages in the world, would end up with you as the best answer to that question.

I'm not saying that's gonna happen all the time. What I'm saying is, if you don't have that mentality going into the game, then you won't get much out of an AI-driven world."

When you've found your niche, how do you define if it's possible to become number one or number two within that niche?

"One way to do it, with or without SEO, is to have a look on Google and see who the players in that niche are. Using a tool like G2 (formerly G2 Crowd) is also a good way of doing it for a SaaS business.

Really, though, it's working out the raw ingredients of your business which, to be honest, starts with you as a business. It doesn't really start with market research. There's no point in a plasterer trying to become the best electronics expert in the world. They're a plasterer. You've got to start with that.

Then, it's about what makes you different. It used to be called the USP, but now I think we need to refine that idea a little further. Your USP has to fit into a well-definable concept. Let's take Banksy as an example. His USP is that he is an artist who does graffiti art and is well known for his graffiti art. If I were doing SEO for Banksy today, I would work around the concept of graffiti art as my marketing USP, rather than art in general.

If you want to become the world's greatest website on graffiti art, then it would help to know great graffiti artists. You would want to talk about particular pieces of graffiti artwork that are famous around the world. Go and have a look at them, photograph them, talk about them, and try and find the people who painted them. Then, you're building your business around graffiti art. You would not then become a fine art salesperson because you're not going to transfer your skills from graffiti art to fine art very well. If you're creating an artist's website, you need it to become more than just a generic artist's website."

If you clearly define your USP for your business, but also for AI, could AI then write content on your behalf?

"There are two philosophies that SEOs are thinking about. My philosophy is that you can't stop AI from reading your content. Another philosophy is to block AI from interpreting your content altogether because they're stealing content. I agree; they are stealing your content – which is exactly what I felt when I started doing SEO, even before Google arrived.

People crawling your website, indexing that content, and then providing it back as their own seemed to me to be stealing. We've moved on from that, and we made a big business out of SEO, and that became okay. Then PPC came along, and we got angry about the fact that we had to pay to send people to our own content, but we adapted and metamorphosised.

There are two streams of thought right now. One is to protect yourself from the AI so that the AI doesn't steal your ideas and repurpose them. From an SEO perspective, a better approach is to make sure you are the answer to the question. Make sure that everything about your business answers one question incredibly well so that, when people want to do business, they're going to end up with you.

You can clean a carpet, or you can hoover a carpet. You want to be the 'Hoover'. You want to be the verb. That's the objective: to make sure that your content is so good that it not only becomes part of AI conversations, but you end up as the answer even when your content isn't directly cited because you are the best answer to the question. It's not an easy thing to achieve, but it is the same principle as defining your own USP and being the best in your niche, which are common marketing principles that have existed for a long time.

I'm not ignoring a lot of the problems with AI that are going to be coming forward. That's a conversation for another day. Today, we're talking about

SEO, and you've got to work with what you've got. Now, we've got ChatGPT, we've got OpenAI, we've got BARD and LLAMA, and all these different things coming down the road. We've got to understand them as the neural networks that they are.

Another way to look at neural networks is that, of course, they are mimicking the human brain. You can also expand that idea to say that the human species has always been a neural network. We have all communicated with each other since the dawn of time, in various different languages. The Chinese language didn't converse so well with the English language in the past, but now it does because we've found more ways of communicating and connecting the dots.

It was always possible that you could talk about your idea in a pub, and it could get stolen. It could be pinched by somebody else, and they could go and build the next great thing that you thought of. That could always happen. it's just going to happen a lot quicker now. That doesn't mean you should stop talking about your ideas in the pub."

Do you need to do anything differently to optimize for becoming the answer in ChatGPT as opposed to the direct answer in the SERP?

"Google is now depreciating its answers in the SERPs, as we're talking today, but I think that they're depreciating the direct answers in the SERPs to make space for a ChatGPT box. I'm sure that, by the time this book goes out, that will be live. I think the depreciation of a direct answer in Google SERPs is to allow for the Google equivalent of OpenAI to provide a summary of the answer. That's important. If you haven't answered the question, then you won't be the endpoint of that answer.

The trick, of course, is getting the customer to then buy from you, which means there has to be some kind of business model that you're applying to follow the money. ChatGPT and generative search are not there to try and grab the sale, per se. That's still up for grabs. As SEOs, we still have the obligation to try and get the customer to the point where they're going to buy your stuff instead of the other guy/girl's stuff."

How do you define your ideal audience of one, either from the perspective of your own business or the perspective of an AI?

"Through the InLinks tool, we first look at the website itself and break it down to the underlying entities that it's about. We then throw all of those back into Google Suggest, which uses Google's AI systems to generate the kinds of questions and search terms that people are looking at, based on that existing website.

Break your website down into its constituent entities, throw all those entities into Google Suggest, and then collate all of those answers and filter out the ones that are semantically distant from your business model. Then, you're going to get a big picture of the concepts that are semantically close to what you already have. In many ways, you can only work with what you've got. I'm not asking you to reinvent the wheel, as an SEO.

Let's say your website has 50 - 100 pages on it. If they're good pages, you've got a core set of ideas that you can then build on. To become a more authoritative answer to the exact audience that you've already defined, you can then talk about the things that are semantically very close to what you already are, instead of suddenly jumping from graffiti art to fine art."

Is defining what your business represents, who it's for, and what content you should be sharing a fairly individual process?

"Looking at the core of your own website and then expanding on that is a great methodology for creating a fingerprint that's unique to yourself. There's no point in getting entirely third-party data to define who you should be. It's much better for you to develop from what it is that you already are.

InLinks is based around a knowledge graph and a natural language processing tool. That makes us different from other SEO tools because we're not based around keyword research, technical SEO, etc. We need to create content that is building on that core because that will naturally give us a different fingerprint from any other SEO tool. That's our approach. Majestic's approach was similar. It was able to crawl the Internet very effectively, but it didn't index the entire content of the Internet. It didn't want to become a Google or a competitor to a beast of that kind. What it could do was invert that information and have the world's largest link index (for a long time) and incredibly impressive backlink information, and focus on that. That propelled Majestic into its niche.

I think that we can all do it. We don't have to be huge businesses to do it, but we can't just wake up one day and create the same thing that everyone else has done. If we want to survive in the world of SEO, we need to have a unique element."

If an SEO is struggling for time, what should they stop doing so they can spend more time doing what you suggest in 2024?

"I would stop using a generic keyword research database. For example, 'house' as a key research term.

'House' means a house in bingo, it means a house as in a property, and it means many other things as well. Even when you're talking about the term 'house' as in property, do you want to buy a house, sell a house, or decorate a house? These are very different things. If you just look at the search volume for 'house' or 'SEO' or any other generic head term that has large volumes, then you don't focus on the users that you are actually interested in.

There has been the tendency, for at least 25 years of SEO, to say, 'I'd love to rank for [insert big term here], so I'll get a long-tail one here and then try and build up.' That's fine. You definitely need to concentrate on that long-tail keyword and make that long-tail big. You need to get that fine definition of who you are, and then enlarge the market that is buying that product, or make more people aware of the product, and work that way round.

First, concentrate on USP, then expand that USP to a market size that you can make money with."

Dixon Jones is a Majestic Ambassador and CEO of InLinks, and you can find him over at InLinks.com.

Always pay attention to the people that matter – with Ian Helms

Like Dixon, Ian Helms from Q.Digital believes in recognising and understanding who you are speaking to. He suggests that chasing

Google is far less important than catering to your customers.

Ian says: "Stop chasing Google rankings and focus on the people that matter.

The people that matter are the folks whose pains you're trying to solve with your product, service or whatever you're creating content for online. Whether you're a bigger company or you have a niche that you're a part of, you're going to have somebody who's looking for your product. You can't create content for just anybody and hope that it'll stick.

You need to make it more personalised and find the right people at the right time for the product that you're selling or serving."

How do you find the right people that you should be creating content for, and how do you define the pain your content should be addressing?

"Assuming that you have a product or a service that offers a solution to something that somebody needs in their life, that's essentially the pain that you're going to be answering.

To use a classic example, if you're selling nails, you're not selling small pieces of metal; you're selling the fact that the nail can be used to hang a picture and make a home a more personal, happy place to be in. The pain isn't that they're looking for something to stick into their wall, it's that they need something to hang their pictures from so they can create a home for their family, display their experiences, etc.

That's essentially the way that you can think about the pain. Put yourself in the shoes of the person who's going to use your product or service and think about what they're ultimately trying to use it for, rather than what you want them to use it for. Do people use your product in the way that you want them to or are they using it in a different way? That's something you can uncover during focus groups, on social media, or by looking at product reviews online."

How do you decide which piece of content goes where on the buyer journey?

"I usually think about it as the traditional sales funnel. First, you identify what people are searching for at the top level. Put yourself in their shoes and consider how they are starting to explore. They may be thinking, 'I need a picture. How do I hang it up?' They could be going to a photographer and looking at getting portraits of their family. Then, what questions might they be asking when they're in the consideration phase? They might be deciding between nails, screws, drywall screws, etc.

In the awareness phase, you try and think about the questions that people are asking. Where would they be looking for these answers? Who are they talking to? What types of content format are they looking for and how would you want to present that? Is it a video, a picture, a piece of text-based content, or a combination of both? Is it on social media, on your website, or Google?

Think about that throughout all the steps of the buyer journey. You need to start with how they even discover that nails exist. Then you go into how they find the best brand of nails. After that, you think about how they decide that your brand or product is exactly the one that they're ultimately going to want to purchase. Those three steps also have the caveats of what questions they are asking, who they are going to (online or offline), and then how they are getting to that decision in the end."

How do you ensure that your audience is the right size?

"I'm a fan of the statement 'niches make riches'. Not everyone is going to need your product and service. Some people might want to know about it or need to know about it in the future but, if you aim too big too quickly, you're going to be up against giant companies and people who are already well-established.

If you're not already one of them, it's important to go down a couple of levels. You need to cover the basics and the bases to establish that you have expertise and authority in different topical areas. The deeper down you can go – by looking at longer tail keywords, product reviews, forums, or other places where people are communicating about products and services – you can start to identify where you fit in the bigger picture of people who are considering what you have to offer.

That could be by gender, age, socioeconomic status, or whatever else is relevant. There are different ways that your product might fit in and that is where you can start to position the content that you're creating, how you're formatting it, what form it takes, and how you're amplifying it across your platforms."

Do you start by identifying an audience, then wireframe the content, and then look for keywords after that?

"I work in the LGBTQ+ space and, at the end of the day, not all keywords are inherently LGBTQ+-related. However, when we're looking at a keyword like 'holiday gifts for men' (whatever that means, in this day and age), we're going to position our content specifically toward gay and trans men, or non-binary people who may relate to masculine energies or tendencies. We're not going to be as broad or stereotypical as another site or brand, but we're still targeting that keyword, just through our unique lens and point of view.

The more personal that you can be with your content, and the more targeted you can be with the audience, the easier it will be to create better, more authentic, and stronger connections. You will be able to establish longer relationships and get your audience to value you the same way that you're expressing that you value them. Demonstrate that you recognise your audience in the way that you're talking and writing about them and the product/service you have to offer, in relation to them and their needs."

Should you optimize the keyword phrase for your niche and incorporate that within other elements on the page or should you optimize for the generic term and showcase your niche on the landing page?

"It's a delicate balance and it depends on the topic. If the keyword doesn't already include an LGBTQ+-related term, we often try to include some sort of modifier. That might be in the title or the meta description when it shows up in Google search, to allude to the fact that the content that we're creating is for LGBTQ+ people. At the same time, it's not always inherently necessary.

I had a conversation with a former client of mine who was in the financial services industry. We were writing some content about how to build savings and invest your money. There's no keyword for, 'How do I invest my gay money?' People don't search for that, specifically. You just want to know how to invest your money. It's important to make sure that, when you're covering a topic, you're being broadly applicable and answering the general question. Then, anybody who might land on your site can still get a potential answer, and Google will recognise it as valid and worth being on the top of the search pages with everything else that's already there.

For the sake of their product and service, however, we transitioned within the content. We started with the general consensus around how to save or invest your money and then said, 'As an LGBTQ+ individual, you're probably looking for businesses, brands, or services that support LGBTQ+ people or are owned and operated by LGBTQ+ people.'

We can also get a little deeper into that conversation within the content, to insert that perspective and make that content more unique, relevant, and authentic to the audience we're looking for, while still answering the broader search intent and need that Google is looking for. It's a very delicate balance, but it's something that's achievable and that I've had success with."

How do you measure the SEO value of creating a great customer experience?

"Oftentimes, search is a more top-of-funnel or mid-funnel area of opportunity, unless you're looking at things like specific brand keywords. It can be really difficult to attribute the fact that somebody had a really awesome first touch on your site through a piece of content that they found through search.

However, we can look at how many email newsletters folks signed up for so that they could learn more or keep in touch with us. If it's a low-barrier-to-entry product, they might buy right away.

In most cases, though, it's looking at things like whether they went on to an additional page that you internally link to. These are softer, less tangible metrics. They're measurable, but they're not necessarily something that will wow a CEO. If the user didn't buy, you can still point to the fact that they found value and will, in theory, be more likely to return or remember you in the future."

Is it possible to create a wonderful customer experience from content that has been created using AI?

"I think so, yes. I've been testing some AI-assisted content. It's never 100% AI-generated, but I have been leveraging AI to outline content and even fill in certain gaps that are just general knowledge. If there's general knowledge about something, that's a great place for AI to colour in the lines so that you can spend the majority of your time on the things that matter more. That could be personalisation or, in the journalism world, conducting interviews associated with the general topic that you're writing about.

You can spend less time writing the bones of the article, let AI handle that, and then bring in a great expert opinion, an awesome social media embed, or a YouTube video. You can spend that time finding and creating those things instead of having to rewrite the fact that water is wet for the 100 billionth time. A million sites have already said that, and AI is very well-trained and aware of most of those types of things."

If an SEO is struggling for time, what should they stop doing right now so they can spend more time doing what you suggest in 2024?

"If you're writing basic content and trying to create a nice content ecosystem, work smarter, not harder. Use AI to your advantage to help create the basis of what you're doing, and then spend the time improving upon it or enhancing it with your own perspective, your unique values, etc.

Spend that time creating a video or social media assets to go along with the content. Think about ways that you can automate and improve your processes, leveraging the tools that we have. I don't think it's a bad thing to leverage AI; it actually creates lots of efficiencies."

Ian Helms is Director of Growth Marketing at Q.Digital, and you can find them over at Q.Digital.

Future-proof by focussing on the middle and bottom of the funnel – with Myriam Jessier

SEO Consultant Myriam Jessier takes a look into how you go about capturing your audience: by creating better content for the middle and bottom of your funnel.

Myriam says: "Focus on middle and bottom of the funnel content if you want to future-proof your SEO strategy, particularly when considering SGE."

How do you define the mid-funnel?

"Let me set the stage. When we talk about the customer funnel, we have the top, the middle, and the bottom.

What we mean by top-of-funnel is, 'I'm not quite sure what I need. I'm starting to look for it. I have vague questions.' Middle-of-funnel is, 'I think I know what journey I'm on. I think I need more help, and I'm refining my understanding of the problem. I'm introducing some query modifiers that completely change my expectations in regard to the topic we're talking about.' Bottom-of-funnel is, 'I'm ready. Whatever comes next, I'm ready to make an informed decision.'

When we're talking about the middle of the funnel, let me illustrate that for you. A top-of-funnel query that all of us will have at some point in our lives is, 'what to do in Rome.' It seems to be one of the cities everyone wants to visit. If we're going to the middle of the funnel, that could become, 'what to do in Rome with two teenagers.' With that query modifier, 'with two teenagers', it is no longer the same experience.

The difference between top-of-funnel and middle-of-funnel, when it comes to SEO, is that top-of-funnel is generic and vague because, at the end of the day, it is introducing you to something. An LLM can do that quite well. When it comes to expertise on a specific topic, or where two elements collide to create a brand-new starting point, they're not so good. That's something that humans are very good at because we have experience.

When someone asks 'what to do in Rome with two teenagers', what's the implication? We know that it's for a vacation. We know that there are problems because, if you know teenagers, there are always problems. If you know Rome, you know there's always traffic congestion. There are always tourists. Tie these elements together and you produce real value that a machine would have a harder time producing due to the nature of both LLMs and human expectations."

Where does this lead us in terms of bottom-of-funnel keywords?

"At the middle of the funnel, we haven't really decided if we're going to Rome, at the end of the day. We're still evaluating what's going on with the teenagers. Maybe we'll choose a different destination. In some cases, you might stick with Rome as a destination and leave the teenagers behind. It all depends. Sometimes, the person will go back to the top of the funnel and start a new journey because they can't get to the bottom of their current one; that road is blocked.

If they do continue digging deeper, though, the bottom of the funnel is where you are addressing queries beyond the initial friction. The initial friction is travelling with two teenagers. If we go deeper than the travelling companions, it might become, 'What specific activities can we do?' You start removing any obstacles that would make you say 'no' to whatever you're considering."

What is a good way to measure the success of traffic coming from a middle-of-funnel phrase?

"I love this question because it's not about better metrics. When we're talking about SGE, which is an experience that is more interactive in SERPs, we are no longer able to capture the reality through our metrics.

In Google Search Console data, you have impressions stating how many times you have been shown to users. Now, though, there are multiple things happening on that page. If you're shown, but you're not part of the main element that the user is engaged with, are you really shown? Are you really having an impact? In terms of clicks, they happen outside of Google's ecosystem, but most of the experience happens inside the ecosystem. Google doesn't report on that. It doesn't report on the engagements that people have with different elements that lead them further in their journey. We're going to be losing a lot of visibility when it comes to seeing the impact we have.

Does that mean it's all lost? No. In this context, traditional metrics – like query reporting, search volume for forecasting, etc. – are becoming a bit moot. We need to shift towards more outcome-based metrics, like revenue. At the end of the day, most websites care about getting people on the website to take an action, engage, and move closer to conversion.

Ultimately, if you want to think about SEO performance, you need to tie it to real-world performance and the bottom line. If you have C-level folks that are really focused on metrics saying, 'Domain authority! Are we number one on this?', it doesn't always translate into bottom-line metrics that really serve the company's interest. Today, we have an opportunity to focus on what happens at the end of the story.

If you're not comfortable with that, it's okay, because it ties into another metric: the brand-new bold world of your total addressable market. Since these metrics are changing, how do you define your total addressable market? How do you calculate it? How do you gauge how much you have penetrated that market in that location, for example?

For me, measuring the success of mid-funnel queries is a mix of determining whether it really brings home the bacon and, before that, figuring out what your real market value is. That's something that most of us don't do. We see volume (People are looking for Valentine's Day gift ideas? Let me enter the ring), but what is the real total addressable market? What does the ring look like? Many SEOs don't take the time to gauge this."

How would you summarise what SGE means and how it's going to impact the future of SEO?

"This is something that bothers everyone because we don't want to address it. There's an elephant in the room: SEO used to be easy traffic. No matter how much we used to complain about things getting harder, it used to be easy traffic because we were not necessarily focused on customers. We weren't even focused on product or marketing.

I've been doing SEO so long that I remember when, if we were number one on 'red shoes', nothing else mattered. We won the world. Now, we're forced to rethink this and acknowledge that, it's not only getting harder, but a machine is replacing us. A machine is giving these answers, so what's the point?

Right now, you need to focus on the customer journey. Is that part of the customer journey starting on TikTok? If so, why are you wasting budget on SEO? This is not where a majority of people are going to find you. If they do find you there, the total addressable market is probably going to be very small compared to what TikTok could offer. What I mean is, if you're only focused on SEO, you could be producing the right content for the wrong channel – or for the wrong reasons. You really need to consider, out of your entire ecosystem, where you should be putting your money at each stage.

We used to do full-funnel SEO for everything, and we would want the budget to go with it. Now, it may be an assistive channel in some cases. Maybe it's not the main focus. That is going to be a very bitter pill to swallow, but it's the truth. If search engines are fundamentally changing the search experience towards answering questions by telling people what the next question should be and offering perspectives, what does that mean for us as experts? Either we have to have a more integrated approach, so SEO makes sense in the context of the customer journey, or we need to figure out what we can do that a machine cannot, in terms of content production.

Search Generative Experience in search results means that, as an SEO, you don't dictate the rules as much as you used to anymore. This is a trend in SEO; we have less and less control over things. There is a reason for this. Previously, we used to trust Google to be a bouncer. We would produce content and say to Google, 'Find the right people for us and bring them to us.' Today, it has learned from us and it's able to do that just fine without us. The next step is figuring out what it cannot do as well. That's middle-of-funnel and bottom-of-funnel because that requires true expertise, and knowing things that nobody really thinks about telling you.

For example, nobody told me that dogs lost their teeth. When they're puppies and they grow, they lose their teeth. That makes sense, but I didn't think about it until my dog started spewing her bloody teeth on my feet. That was a terrible experience, and understanding it required experience. You have to go through it. At the top of the funnel, you don't necessarily have to go through it to explain it. At the middle and the bottom, you do. For me, that's the next step in SEO.

What worries me is that we may end up, once again, teaching machines how to replace us in the midterm. When you focus on the middle and bottom of the funnel, always keep the customer journey in mind, because this may also be taken away from us in a few years, and we will have to find our added value elsewhere."

Does the heightened importance of mapping to the customer journey mean that we do not need a traditional marketing funnel anymore?

"We don't necessarily need it anymore because it's a tool for us, internally. Does it reflect what really happens in the world? No. Some folks get to the middle of the funnel and then they go back up. Some folks exit completely. Some folks go straight from one question to a purchase.

You need to really focus on the customer journey and the jobs that need to be done. Jobs to be done could be: 'Excel is so slow and frustrates me. I need something better. Let me look at BigQuery or Looker Studio. Let me look into learning a programming language.' You try to find solutions to your problems. We're too focused on the funnel to really ask ourselves, what are the problems that people are trying to fix at each step? We want this to fit in with the way we sell things instead. That means we have blind spots in our marketing."

If an SEO is struggling for time, what should they stop doing right now so they can spend more time doing what you suggest in 2024?

"Stop stressing about the metrics that are fluctuating right now. Do your best with the existing metrics. Keep the funnel in the back of your mind, but really take the time to focus on the customer journey. That way, you can actually understand your own blind spots in the content. What's missing, fundamentally, that will help you get people onto the next stage and become customers?

Instead of focusing on how to scale your SEO content production at each step of the funnel. You really need to focus on the problems that you're fixing for people at each step, where you can actually have something meaningful to say and help them."

***Myriam Jessier** is an **SEO** Consultant and Trainer, and you can find them at **PRAGM**.co.*

9 User Intent

9 USER INTENT

Stop getting distracted and go back to the basics of search intent – with Jan-Willem Bobbink

Focussing on a different aspect the user journey, Freelance SEO Jan-Willem Bobbink implores you to think about the intent behind your users' searches and what they are really looking for in the first place.

Jan-Willem says: "Focus on the basics and don't fall into the trap of Shiny Object Syndrome.

Over the past few years, there has been a trend where more and more tools are being introduced that do not actually provide value for the average SEO, which perfectly aligns with the introduction of AI-based tools as well. We're being led into traps. Companies are starting to ask SEOs why we're not using AI to produce content and meta descriptions.

I want to focus on one important aspect of optimizing for SEO: matching your content to the search intent Google deems users to have when they are searching for specific types of keywords. Focusing on this one basic optimization aligns with all the other SEO tasks you're doing. Making sure you understand search intent helps you understand how to structure your website and where to prioritise your technical optimization.

Let's say you think you have a commercial keyword, but Google ranks Top X Lists with the best SEO rank tracking tools. Does it make sense to spend time technically optimizing your category page or do you need an informational blog article?

Understanding search intent is one of the fundamental things you need to do as an SEO. However, the new features that tools are launching, and the day-to-day discussions SEOs are having, are not about search intent. The shiny stuff that's being released usually doesn't add much value for the average SEO. Go back to the basics, see what Google is actually showing in the top 10/ 20 links, and base your actions on that."

Are you still mapping navigational, informational, commercial, and transactional intent?

"The traditional model for search intent is not specific enough in the current landscape. Google is moving towards a more dynamic way of ranking. They have much more data available for identifying specific user needs, which translates into more specific intents. We need to identify those intents and map out our actions from that.

Traditionally, we have informational intent, which is one of the biggest buckets. If you look through the content that ranks for some of those 'informational intent' keywords, you will find long-form content, short-form content, and simple definitions in featured snippets showing the meaning of a specific word. Sometimes people are looking for visuals, an image, or a figure to give them an answer.

They want to be guided to a certain form of content. Classifying a keyword simply as 'informational' is too broad to determine the actions that need to be taken."

How does Google determine specific user intent for informational queries?

"What we've seen happening over the years, especially during the core

Google updates, is that they shift intents, and they need lots of data for that. We've also noticed that, by having more advanced technology available, they better understand the content that is produced on the web. They can now determine whether something is actually the most relevant content for a certain topic.

They can get a first impression by looking at the length of the content and the form in which it is produced. Interestingly, I've been able to rank with a Top X List for commercial keywords just by being the first in the market to create that form of content for that specific keyword.

If you look at your SEO rank tracking software, you might notice a mix of content that's currently ranking. There could be informational content, tool providers, Top X Lists, etc. Lately, this has changed with every update. There is no one singular classification for each specific keyword. Those intents only exist in a certain context. You need to take into account the date, the time, and even the year.

If a user searches for 'winter jackets' in the summer, they may be focused on getting the models from last year at a discount. That's a commercial-focused intent. However, if they are searching for 'winter jackets' in the autumn, they may want to know what the latest trends will be. After the summer, Google might shift to providing more content-rich visual style guides for the same keyword. It's really difficult to say that there is one specific intent for that keyword over a longer period of time.

Some SEO tools are trying to map search intent just using the four traditional intents we previously mentioned. That's too basic to cover what's actually happening. Go back to Google, see what's currently ranking, and adapt your content to what you think will be relevant. Don't just copy what others are doing (although that may lead to a top 5/10 ranking) but also try to do it differently and test it."

Should you have multiple pages targeting different intents for the same keyword or should you adapt your content according to how intent changes over time?

"Think about it like a living organism. During the year, or during specific periods, change the focus within your own domain. You have to cover multiple intents for the same keyword. There may be overlapping content, but if there's a clear difference in the layout of the page and the content itself, it shouldn't be a problem – as long as the quality of that content aligns with the intent and what the user expects.

The challenge is in proving the value of that content and measuring success. It can be very resource-intensive to monitor 100,000 keywords, constantly adapt your content, and change your strategy throughout the year. That's where AI comes in handy if you want to do analysis at scale. There are tools that provide you with raw data from the current SERPs so that you can compare that with what was ranking half a year ago, or before or after a core update. You can check out the content of the pages that rank and use an AI tool to classify the types of content that are ranking, which helps you to do it at scale.

Even if you do it manually, if you identify a trend across a subset of 10 keywords, then it would make sense that Google will apply the same kind of logic across similar keywords in the same niche."

Does AI understand intent, and write with intent in mind, at a high enough standard?

"It's good for doing things at scale, but you have to teach it. Whatever tool you use, make it very clear what you expect the output to be. The same logic applies for content creation but, for classifying intents based on what's ranking, have the tool visit the top 10 search results. Have it check out the content on those pages, and give it rules.

For example, you can give it rules so that it can tell the difference between a list of top 10 SEO rank tracking tools and a commercial landing page from a rank tracker. You can teach the AI that, if there's a table, then it's probably a comparison piece. If there's just a list, then it's probably an affiliate suggestion list. Once you teach it to check for certain features, then it's really easy for the AI to extract the logic out of that and apply it to a larger data set."

What metrics do you use to measure whether or not your page is

serving the intended intent?

"I like to report on rank volatility, especially for bigger clients. Rank volatility is the amount of ranking movement for one specific page type throughout the year. The bigger core updates always happen at set periods so it's easy to check the volatility around those updates to see if something is missing or not matching up.

What we've traditionally been seeing is that, when you're in the top 10, rankings are quite volatile. However, once you're in the top 3, your results are usually much more stable. That's what we want to look out for. We want to push a URL into the top 3 because it's much more stable. Therefore, one of the metrics I report on is the percentage of keywords that have low volatility and a top 3 ranking.

However, anything that aligns with traditional SEO metrics will do. If you're able to compete on a commercial keyword with a Top X List informational blog and outrank the category pages that are already ranked there, you will directly see the impact in traffic and conversions."

When's the best time to change content on your page to match upcoming changes in buyer intent?

"I recommend making changes a few months before because Google needs time to collect data. Also, we can teach Google about changing search intent. If multiple websites start to publish articles about 'winter coat trends' in August, then Google will understand that this is something people are looking for and writing about. They may even want to change the search intent directly when they notice an increase in certain types of content.

You can compare it with how Google News works. If something is going on around a famous person wearing a specific winter coat, a Google News section will pop up and Google Discover feeds will be filled with that same kind of content. That's a good sign that Google is able to directly respond to both changes in intent and requests from the actual users.

On one hand, you want to try and change your content a couple of months beforehand because that also gives you time to tweak the content and make it perfect before the peak season starts. On the other hand, Google is fast enough to respond directly to any changes you make.

Let's say you have an informational section on your website dedicated to giving simple definitions of 100 SEO-related keywords. If you notice that Google now wants dedicated long-form pieces of content for these types of queries, then just do them one by one and publish them on the go. Google will pick it up immediately and see that it aligns better with what they currently want to show to their users."

If an SEO is struggling for time, what should they stop doing right now so they can spend more time doing what you suggest in 2024?

"Stop playing with the shiny stuff and focus on the basics. 95% of websites still haven't covered the basics. Why use an AI to write meta descriptions if you already have many meta descriptions that don't contain a USP? Why use tools to optimize internal linking when the main menu doesn't even contain the most searched pages?

There are so many examples where basic thinking will give you enough input to optimize already, and you don't need fancy tools for that. The same is true for search intent. I have built fancy setups for identifying search intent across millions of keywords at once, but that only applies to one or two really specific clients I have. For all the others, they just need to go to Google, see what's ranking, and do the work. Use AI or shiny stuff for ideation or when you have a mental block. Otherwise, just focus on the basics and do the work."

Jan-Willem Bobbink is a Freelance SEO, and you can find him over at NotProvided.eu.

Evolve your approach from SEO into HEO – with Ken "Magma" Marshall

Like Jan-Willem, Ken "Magma" Marshall from RevenueZen wants SEOs to shift their perspectives, and he's coined his own initialism to explain why he believes human engagement should be at the forefront.

Ken says: "Focus less on SEO and more on HEO. It's a term that I heard from the HubSpot CEO, but I am changing it from Human Experience Optimization to Human Engagement Optimization."

What is Human Engagement Optimization?

"In essence, it's a perspective shift. It's like saying you're a marketer who cares about performance or revenue outcomes, which forces you to think less about tactics and more about strategies.

When I think of SEO in 2024, I don't think about driving traffic as though that isn't humans with needs and jobs to be done. I think, 'How can we get somebody at one stage of their buying or decision-making journey to continue that journey, with each aspect of our content on our website, and take a specific action?' For us, working mainly with B2B companies, that's engaging with the sales team as part of the sales pipeline. That is the kind of engagement I'm talking about: not just with content but further into the pipeline."

How do you create web content that delivers on user experience without starting with keywords or technical?

"Google has published their helpful content guidelines now. It's not about removing the tactics that we all know and love – picking target keywords, optimizing the technical aspects, the authority, etc. – it's going a few layers deeper.

We all talk about search intent now, and commercial or transactional queries. When a potential buyer lands on a page, if that information isn't presented in a way that will take them to the next decision-making stage, then it's all for nought. You can be ranking number one and getting 800 potential customers per month but, if there isn't a price point or a good call to action or the page load speed is terrible, then you're not going to get that person to take the next step.

In B2B, that's where the money is. We don't care about rankings and traffic as much as we care about qualified opportunities. It's in those steps after they get to the site, and making sure you know what kind of decision they're going to make. You need to structure the page, the content, and the messaging that will get them to continue that engagement."

How do you go about establishing the likely user intent for each page?

"There are some easy tips and tricks that we're all familiar with. Certain modifiers – like agency, consultant, services, price, etc. – indicate that somebody's either looking to make a comparison or a purchase decision.

However, we can and should take it a step further. Carry out customer interviews when they onboard, right after the sales process is done, and ask, 'What triggered you on the site to want to reach out to sales?' Alternatively, after the onboarding customer success team, what five frequently asked questions do folks have? Put those on the page right before they convert to eliminate some of that friction and help move them forward.

We're talking about CRO, verbal identity, messaging, etc., but those steps should be considered upfront as part of a broader SEO and content strategy."

Is it customer service or post-purchase teams asking those questions or should SEOs actively be involved?

"It's a collaboration. Different teams are having to become more interdependent, and I think that's a good thing. It creates a more holistic buying experience on the site. It's a collaboration between user experience teams, brand teams, customer success teams, sales teams, and SEO and content teams.

If your customer success team says, 'This is what everybody says after they are finished onboarding.' and sales says, 'This is what they say in their customer conversation', but it's not a keyword, then does it make sense to have it on that page? If it gets 50 people to convert, even though only 150 people use the page, that's a win for most companies. Ideally, all of those teams will be working together."

How do you persuade organizations that SEOs should be involved with the whole marketing conversation more holistically, rather than just focusing on keywords and traffic?

"First, you've got to get good at the pitch to get by in an organization. Due to the black box of Google's algorithm, a lot of marketers and SEOs do not understand how to make business-focused use cases.

They might say, 'I need to take up all the customer success team's time and $10,000 to do X, Y and Z.' Instead, you can say, 'We are only converting 10% of our pipeline. The user drop-off rate is X. If we improve the time spent on the site and improve the messaging, this is the kind of revenue we're going see in the next 12 months.' Most executives' ears are gonna perk up. Get a better understanding of business metrics and map them back to the tactics or initiatives that you want to use.

Secondly, take a look at those helpful content guidelines that Google posted. SEO is moving outside of the technical. For example, AI and machine learning are a big thing now. It says right there in the documentation, 'We don't care if you use something to create AI content'. However, they also say, 'If it's mass-produced and doesn't have a quality assurance process from an expert and a trusted site, forget about it.'

Getting imaginative about rounding out that journey and thinking about what a customer is likely to engage with on the page is something every SEO can do – even if you don't have a new budget or the resources to work with other teams. Broaden your understanding of the customer journey."

Can you utilise AI even though the process is very people-centric?

"I'm pro-technology, pro-GPT4, and pro-AI tools. They've been around for a while and it's no secret. The number one thing, again, is that you can drive all the traffic in the world but if your actual buyer doesn't enjoy, engage, consume, and take the next step, it's all for nought.

If you're using it for production, what is the framework you're using to know that your output is going to be successful? We've all heard the term 'prompt engineering', but why did you create that prompt? Is it strategic? Then afterwards, who is the subject matter expert who's going to review it? What is the software that's going to do the analysis? Grammarly might handle the syntax and grammar. Is there an SME in the organization who is going to say whether this is factually correct or not?

The QA process and the prompt engineering on the front end will make the content either follow Google's guidelines or not. If you're going to use AI to produce title tags, content, major content assets, calculators, etc., follow those two steps.

Also, you can use it as an AI assistant. I do that all the time, multiple times a week. I'll bounce ideas off the tool to get outside of my limited range of thinking. That's the strength: ideating, formulating ideas, making them more concrete, and then scaling the tedious parts of production and coming up with different versions so that the expert can give their final approval quicker."

What metrics can you use to define whether your content is delivering excellent, exciting experiences for prospects?

"Look at the data. If you don't have data, stop right now. Go set up GA4. Go set up Hotjar. Go get a free CRM like HubSpot. That's step number one. Whether you are doing a good job or not depends on who's coming into your pipeline, how often they are converting, what the value is, and what sources they're coming from.

Average engagement time is a really easy one. Engaged sessions is a great metric that I love in GA4. Also, how many people from the pages that you consider bottom-of-funnel or high-purchase-intent are actually converting there? That's the point, right? You drive people to those pages so that they convert. If you're a B2B company you should be able to see that from your CRM and, if you're a B2C company or e-commerce, you can see purchases by source.

For the target terms that you're using and the target pieces of the content that you want to convert folks, is it actually happening? How often is it happening? What's the value of that to your company?

If you look at a three-month window before your optimizations, after, and then on an ongoing basis, it's easy to say, 'Do we have more people converting, viewing, and viewing for longer, or less?' It's actually that simple. The hard part is defining what led to those outcomes and deducing that. Knowing whether it's working or not should be very simple."

Do we finally have a more sophisticated understanding of attribution?

"Attribution is a dirty word for some people, but I think so. We have the tools, and the ways to build connective tissues around the tools, to get better insights. However, there is a rise in people going to sales communities, marketing communities, LinkedIn groups, etc. Some people call it 'dark social' but I just call it what humans have always done. They go to people who sound and look like them and ask them questions. They inherently trust their friends, family, co-workers, etc.

Attribution technology is more sophisticated but there's also a lot of attribution that's never going to be figured out. Trying to get to a nine or a ten when you are already at an eight is a futile exercise.

Here's an example of a real journey. Somebody read a LinkedIn profile of ours, came to the site, left, read a LinkedIn post later, Googled us to make sure we ranked for 'B2B SEO agency', and then reached out on the website after a couple of months. There's no way an attribution tool will tell you all of that.

However, having the LinkedIn profile and the website optimized enhanced each step of their journey. The most important thing is knowing where your buyers are, showing up in those locations properly, then getting that feedback as the sales conversation progresses, rather than just with tools, to really be sure how they found and purchased from you."

Do you look at the profitability of individual keywords or do you measure on more of a page-by-page basis?

"Somebody out there probably has a more sophisticated blend of tracking on the website or some UTM parameter magic that gets put into a sheet where they blend the data. For us, it's as simple as looking at the top keyword groupings per page, and then how those pages fit into conversion paths.

Take one of our services pages. 90% of the people convert on the B2B SEO Services page, and we know what our top five keyword groupings for that are. You can assign those a weight.

For us, we are thinking more broadly than taking a number of specific keywords and breaking them down to the dollar. We are thinking, 'Do we understand how people are searching for these terms and how our buyers actually speak in sales conversations?' If the whole channel is profitable multiple times over, you focus less on the dollars and cents at the keyword level.

However, understanding the keyword groupings that lead to the page and which pages lead to conversions is a helpful set of metrics to know, and it's fairly easy information to get."

If an SEO is struggling for time, what should they stop doing right now so they can spend more time doing what you suggest in 2024?

"A lot of modern CMSs (Squarespace, WordPress, Webflow, etc.) take the small technical things and bring everybody onto an even playing field. Instead of focusing on the latest JSON-LD schema type that isn't going to lead to a rich snippet, go back to basics.

See whether your messaging is resonating, and people are actually converting on those pages. See if you can get buy-in to work with cross-functional teams and improve the experience on those pages. Really consider a target customer journey.

What are they likely to do? Have you provided them with a choose-your-own-adventure on the website? Focusing more on human engagement – getting people into your sales pipeline and converting them – and less on technical tactics will pay off."

Ken Marshall is Chief Growth Officer at RevenueZen, and you can find him over at RevenueZen.com.

Think about the user above anything else – with Amanda White

SEO and PPC Consultant Amanda White also believes that the user should come first, and she suggests that this should affect how you approach every aspect of your SEO – including the use of AI.

Amanda says: "It's the same as it has been for the last 10-15 years: always think about the user.

Historically, we've had things like the Panda update (12 years ago now) that stopped people from focusing on content farms, blog networks, scraping content, and filling the web with low-quality content. Even back then, if you focused on the user, and you wrote for that user and gave them the information they were looking for, you were not going to get caught out by the Panda update.

The same was true with Penguin in 2012. Previously, you could focus on building backlinks just for the sake of building backlinks and gaming the system so that the more you bought, the more link equity you could get, and the better your results would be. However, who was following those links? Was anyone coming through those links and bringing traffic to your website? You weren't focusing on the user; you were just focusing on numbers. Then, when Penguin hit, you were likely to get caught up in the algorithm update and lose that authority, and your websites would decrease via SEO.

Even back then, you needed to focus on the user. Now, it is even more important. This year, we got the helpful content update and Google was saying that you needed to be creating content 'by people, for people'. Recently, they changed that to just 'for people'. They're saying it's okay to use AI and lean on it, and they're not going to penalise you because it is part of what the future is going to be.

Always think of the user. Always think about that customer and whether they are going to get value from that content – whether it's written by you, written by AI, assisted by AI, or written by somebody else."

How do you identify who your ideal user is?

"You can utilise user profiling to find out who your user is. That could be through research on your website and looking at your analytics data to find your demographics.

It can be as simple as having questionnaires, pop-ups, or quizzes where you ask your customers those questions to bracket them into your audience profiles and audience types."

Is that also how you should decide what content to create?

"Absolutely. If you have a search function on your website and your customers are searching for content on your website, you know what answers they're looking for. You know that you should be giving them those answers if they can't find them already.

If you've got it set up in your Google Analytics, you can see all the queries that your customers are typing in. When you've got those queries, if they're already being pushed to a page that gives the answer, you're already covered. If not, then that's content that you should be creating for them – to answer those queries."

Do you prioritise those on-site user queries over opportunities you find through keyword research, even if they don't have as much search volume?

"It should be a bit of both. If you've made the effort and you've got those customers to your website (whether that's through SEO, PPC, social, etc.), they've already shown an interest. They've clicked on a call to action and they're on your website. If they are then typing in a search term or query that historically doesn't have much data yet, that doesn't mean that it's not valuable. It could be a trending topic.

You're getting that data directly from the user before it's become popular. You might be able to get that content out first, get it ranking, and beat the competition. Whereas, when you're finding topics through keyword research, everybody else can find those topics too. You can use your own data to your advantage."

Can you take user queries from your site and ask ChatGPT to write and publish that content for you, or do you need humans?

"You always need humans. I don't think human interaction is going away anytime soon. We've had the BERT infrastructure in Google since around 2019, which already uses AI to understand language, the nuances between keywords, what the person is searching for, and what answer is being given on the page. Using AI isn't something new for Google; they've been using it for years.

If you are taking a search query and popping it into ChatGPT, and it's churning out a piece of content for you, just read it. Proofread it and see the quality of it. If it's robotic and impersonal, without much character to it, then you can start putting in extra prompts to give it character.

Using AI as a starting point to give you the bones of an article, and then using that human interaction to add personalisation and tone of voice to it, is absolutely fine. I don't want to use robots; I want to use humans. However, the future is AI."

Are users satisfied with written content or do they gravitate towards video?

"There will be more distrust in written content as AI becomes mainstream because it will become harder to tell if it's been written by a robot or a human. Users will be wondering whether they are just being given the answer that the AI thinks they want to read because it has already written every single version of said answer – the good, the bad, the ugly – and it's just giving them what they've asked for.

I was talking to some completely untechnical people at the weekend about cookies, and they said they just press 'accept' because that's what they do. Even now, people don't really understand anything about cookies. The same thing could happen with AI. People might not be able to tell whether content has been written by a human or a bot.

It is becoming more mainstream, and there is a lot more talk outside of our industry about it. As that continues, hearing real human voices (with or without video) will become more popular, as people lose trust in the written word. Then, that could be turned into a transcript for written content as well. Of course, even videos that appear to show real humans talking could be AI-produced, but that's another issue entirely."

Is it still SEO if you optimize your content to be seen on other platforms, like podcasts and video?

"SEO already encompasses things like YouTube optimization, and making sure you've got your keywords, your transcripts, your descriptions, and your titles done in the right way.

There's already an element of video and image SEO. This is just the next transition of what we always used to call SEO. It's always changing; it's never going to stand still."

What other marketing channels should SEO be working more closely with and how should they do that?

"I'm a huge advocate for PPC. The terms you can pull out of PPC are real-time. If you are seeing your customer search for something in the afternoon, you can have something written by the evening, answering that query. Utilising PPC data to influence your SEO content strategy is key for me. The data is there, and you're literally getting it from the horse's mouth, so you should use it."

Should SEOs use PPC for testing?

"It does depend. If it is a very low-investment piece of SEO content, such as something where you used ChatGPT to write it and that was as far as it went, then you can absolutely use PPC to test it. As opposed to content where you're organising interviews with people, you need case studies, or you need to use lots of data sets, and it's going to be very involved and time-consuming to get it through organic.

If your cost per click suddenly goes through the roof and it's hugely competitive, you know that putting out a quick ChatGPT answer isn't going to work. It's going to need that time and investment. Use the PPC as a testing ground to see what's out there first."

Do SEOs need to narrow their focus towards answering users' questions on their website and maybe seek the initial inquiry phrase traffic from other sources?

"The internet has changed over the years. Now, we think about answering the user's query and being the solution to problems. There is still a massive space for content that is, not just being produced for content's sake, but for people to enjoy. You're not just there to do SEO and answer the question. You're actually giving something of use or benefit. You might be portraying your brand as nice and fun, or showing that they do something with charity. It doesn't always have to be focused on SEO; looking at keywords and content, and having that as our main focus.

The internet will become very boring very quickly if all we're doing is focusing on answering keyword queries. Brands that show their own personality and shine, above and beyond answering the query, will be the ones that succeed. They might be using AI, but they're showing that there are still real humans behind it."

If an SEO is struggling for time, what should they stop doing right now so they can spend more time doing what you suggest in 2024?

"I'm still getting cold emails in my inbox on a daily basis saying, 'Do you want to buy some blogroll links?' and 'Do you want to buy guest posts on these terrible blog pages?' It didn't work ten years ago. It's not going to work in ten years' time.

If your main focus as an SEO is trying to sell low-quality content, then stop. Stop annoying me, and stop annoying everybody else. AI is likely to be the future, so maybe we'll start to see emails with, 'Buy my AI content that I'll post on my blog' instead. Cold emailing for guest posts and backlinks is done. It's over. Stop wasting your time on that one."

Amanda White is an SEO and PPC Consultant, and you can find her over at AmandaWhiteDigital.com.

Think about the user, not the search engine – with Eli Schwartz

In another warning against forgetting who your audience really is, SEO Consultant Eli Schwartz wants to remind you that the search engine is not your target customer – and it never has been.

Eli says: "Care more about the user than the search engine."

Has the way that you do that changed over the last few years?

"It has changed from a technical standpoint but not from a marketing/product standpoint. I don't think that ever changes. It's like asking a storekeeper if the way they approach sales and how they approach their customers has changed in the year 2000 from the way they did it in 1900. It's exactly the same, it's the mediums that have changed.

In 1900, you wouldn't have people coming into your store very often. You would approach them, have a conversation with them, walk them to the store, and help them buy things. In the year 2000, we had supermarkets and big box stores. In the year 2024, we're going to have different experiences. The medium might change, but the approach should never change. SEO should be the exact same way.

In the year 2000, right after search engines came into existence, people went on Google/ Excite/Yahoo, and they typed in things indicating they wanted to buy something or learn something, so you built a website with content that they could learn and buy from. In the year 2024, you're going to be doing the same thing, except the medium has changed a little bit.

The big thing in 2024, of course, is generative AI. Will Google have integrated generative AI for all users or not? We don't know. In 2025, they probably will have. Last year we talked a bit about whether there would be other search engines. I predicted that there would be other search engines. I said that it could be Apple, Amazon, or Facebook. I had no idea that it was going to be ChatGPT. Whether ChatGPT is a meaningful search engine or not, it is a search engine. Whether the Bing integration with ChatGPT is a real change to the platform or not, it is still another search engine.

Having more search engines changes the way we do SEO because it becomes fragmented. You can't just follow the rules of Google and expect to hit everyone. Right now, Google has more than a 90% market share. When there are more search engines, you change your methodology a little bit because you can't optimize for six search engines. You can't even optimize for two search engines. The right way to do SEO is to focus on the user and not the engine, which is just the medium through which they arrive on your website.

With generative AI, the queries will change and the way users experience content will change but, ultimately, the users are still the same people."

Have we reached a point where search engines can understand your content without the need for on-page markup?

"I think we've been past that point for years. There's still a debate around dofollow vs. nofollow links, and clients will ask me about it all the time. The concept came about in 2010, and we're now going into 2024. It's 14 years old.

We're in a world where we've seen what generative AI can look like. We're in a world where Google and other companies have self-driving taxis. Technology has changed. We're well beyond the stage where you need to tell a search engine what is a real link and what is not. We're even beyond the stage where you need to tell a search engine what the image alt text is.

Initially, image alt text was an accessibility feature. You tell the search engine what the image is so that it can be read out on an accessibility reader for someone who's vision impaired. Now, technology is creating images from scratch, based on prompts. On Android devices, you have Google Lens which can look at an image and parse out what that image is.

We're well beyond an age where you need to tell a search engine, 'This is about the business. This is what the image is. This is content, etc.' The engines can parse it themselves. Some SEOs get lost in these details, but I don't think they're necessary. I don't think they give you a leg up."

How do we find out why users are searching instead of what they're searching for?

"It's very simple: you just have to ask the users.

I find this all the time. I talk to businesses, and we talk about their keywords and who their users are. When I say, 'Have you asked them?', they say, 'That's a novel idea!' It shouldn't be a novel idea. Technology has allowed us to step too far back from who the customer is.

Earlier I talked about a storekeeper walking the customer through the store to understand what they want. We can still do that, even in an age of technology. You can look at your analytics and try to understand the user's journey on the website. You can even use generative AI to have a conversation with the user and learn what they want. The best way to understand users is to talk to them but you don't need to have a direct conversation. You can use technology to understand their needs. That's a representation of what they're doing when they type a query into a search engine.

Google knows this. Before generative AI, you would input a query and Google would match intent to that query. Let's say I searched for 'podcasting software', and a podcasting platform didn't know they were supposed to use the word 'software', so they used the word 'platform' on their page instead. Google would still match the user to that even though they never used the word 'software' because they understood the intent behind both the website and the user.

Now we're in the world of generative AI, which takes the entire concept of keywords away. It's about parsing what the user said and then the engine responding to that. Now, they can serve website results by parsing both the website and the query based on generative AI. The only defence you have against that is understanding the user and creating for the user."

Is there any software that can determine the 'why' behind user behaviour?

"I don't think there is a pure software solution right now. Let's say you have a bunch of keywords; those are one-dimensional. All the SEO research tools offer one-dimensional keywords. Many clients that I have worked with look at keyword research as the gospel for what they should be doing without understanding that some users are inputting those keywords and looking for something completely different from what their website or company offers.

You need to take those keywords and understand the user. There is no be-all-end-all solution for taking what the user searched, seeing their user journey, and knowing what to do. You need the human intelligence to look at what they have searched. Why did they search it? Where'd they end up? Did they buy?

Generative AI can be useful here because you can have conversations with the users. Many websites have chatbots that are useless. They're essentially search engines. Let's say I am trying to cancel my internet service. I go on the website, and it gives me a chatbot that says, 'What do you want?' I say, 'I want to cancel.' and then it says, 'Here's a good article about cancelling.' It should be having a conversation about why I want to cancel, trying to understand my needs and intents based on generative AI, and then recognising whether I should talk to a representative, read an article, receive a call, etc. Generative AI could be better used for having those conversations, but the software needs to improve."

Once you've defined your 'whys', how do you incorporate those into your content?

"You need to speak to the user based on those 'whys', whatever it is that you're doing. If you're selling mortgages, there are so many other people who sell mortgages too, but you know your users and you have a particular angle.

Before the internet age, if you were a mortgage broker, you put an ad in the newspaper or the Yellow Pages, and people called you and you found out what they wanted and offered your particular skills. Mortgage brokers specialised in that, and they should still specialise in that. Now, they need to use websites and content in an asynchronous way to show how they cater to those users.

A mortgage broker that caters to users with complicated job situations shouldn't be writing generic content about mortgages. They have an angle, they have a perfect customer, and they have a specific skill set. Their content should be about that."

Has this changed the way that SEO needs to interact with other marketing channels?

"I have always felt that SEO does not interact with other marketing channels enough. If you use an agency to do your SEO, then they're certainly not interacting with other marketing channels because they're completely siloed. One agency does paid and one agency does organic, and they're not crossing wires or understanding things. In-house, the teams are almost pitted against each other. The paid team does this, the email team does that, and the organic team does something else.

SEO should be talking to those other teams and learning about what the user/customer wants. There's an appropriate place in the funnel for each of these channels, where they can help each other out. Organic is great at top-of-funnel where users are curious about something. Paid is great at mid-funnel because they have ad copy to draw the user in. Email is better at bottom-of-funnel or retention. Social is good at top-of-funnel and retention. All of these channels should be working together so that everyone is building toward that final conversion.

I don't think that has changed in the current world. Marketing teams should work together to acquire the user. It doesn't matter who wins and, more than likely, it won't be the SEO channel.

That's a big problem with the way SEO is measured. CEOs or whoever's hiring an agency is always looking for the win: 'I hired this SEO agency, and it didn't work out because I didn't get any conversions.' It's not necessarily designed to get conversions. If you're top-of-funnel and people need some time to buy and learn, then you're not going to get the conversion. That doesn't mean it didn't work."

What are some better ways to measure the financial value of SEO today?

"It's going to be hard. In a perfect world, you should be doing blended attribution and understanding how each channel works for the end goal. That's an ideal but I've never seen a company achieve that.

The reality is you have to better understand the user and the buyer's journey, then you can approximate some sort of value. If you're selling e-commerce products, SEO probably does win. You can say that whoever got the last piece of the conversion for each product is the channel that wins. If you're selling a long-sales-funnel product or service, where there are many different touchpoints, you can try to approximate how SEO contributed by understanding and talking to the user.

The good thing about SEO is that it's relatively cheap compared to every other channel. If you're trying to approximate some sort of value and SEO only contributes 10%, SEO is typically only 10% of the expense. Paid is expensive and there's a cost for every email sent out. With Organic, you're creating content and it amortises over time as it drives conversion. Even if you're more truthful about the contribution, it's still highly profitable."

With AI becoming incorporated into search results and an ever-increasing focus on the number one position, is there still value to being on the bottom of the first page?

"I think so. I always target being on the first page because you have the user, but it depends on what you're doing.

If you're talking about a product or service where it takes a long time for people to understand what they're buying, being on the first page means that they will see you. It doesn't matter whether you're number one because it's not direct to conversion. As they do their research, they'll change their query and, eventually, you'll end up higher and they will see you. That's what SEO still needs to do; make sure the content is seen.

If you're trying to replicate what could easily be pulled out of pages and put into a generative AI response, then that was designed to go away, to begin with."

If an SEO is struggling for time, what should they stop doing right now so they can spend more time doing what you suggest in 2024?

"SEO always has a sense of urgency over everything at the same time. Something I use with all of my clients is called the RICE format. It's a way of project managing based on Reach, Impact, Confidence, and Effort.

You take each of your initiatives and you score them. You can score 1-10, high/medium/low, or however you want. When you score things you discover where you're spending your time and where you are getting results. Taking the time to understand where your efforts are being placed will help you to prioritise.

No SEO wants to come in and say, 'Just change the title tag and that's it. That's my job today.' but if you see that there's going to be a high impact from it, it's easy, and you're fairly confident it will have an impact, then do it. You will get your win and earn your political capital. On the other hand, if you want to change the privacy policy and you need to go to legal and do all these things, maybe that's not as important.

Take a step back to score, prioritise, and understand what each of the initiatives you're working on is going to do. The things you should focus on will bubble up to the surface."

Eli Schwartz is a Strategic SEO Consultant and Growth Advisor and Author of Product-Led SEO, *and you can find him over at EliSchwartz.co.*

Leverage natural language processing to unpack user intent on a whole new level - with Nik Ranger

Moving into the more technical side of things, Nik Ranger from Dejan tells you how to use the increasing power of AI to elevate your ability to understand what your users are actually looking for.

Nik says: "In 2024, we have a remarkable, uncharted ability to unpack user intent at a level we have never been able to see before. My tip is to prioritise natural language processing so that you can do just that.

With the evolution of search engines and their algorithms, along with the increasing sophistication of AI-driven models, we're seeing SGE placing even greater emphasis on understanding the context and intent behind user queries. We can reverse engineer these mechanisms to create better high-quality, valuable content, understand our pages far better, and create internal linking methodologies that outstrip anything that we've been able to do previously."

In a post-SGE AI-influenced world, is SEO changing forever?

"I don't think it's completely changing forever; it's our approach that needs to change. With the rise of AI tools at our disposal, we can leverage this to empower ourselves. We can delve into new depths with code and start to answer questions that were previously difficult to answer.

For example, if natural language processing helps search engines understand, interpret, generate, and utilise machine translation, sentiment, and recognition, we can leverage that to perform a suite of new tasks. With ChatGPT-4 and Code Interpreter, in particular, we can give custom instructions. We now have much greater access to a wealth of information that we've never had access to before. Using things like Hugging Face, which Google themselves have generated, we have access to even greater semantic understanding.

We can look at different frameworks, look at text embeddings, and capture more of the semantic content of web pages. We now have a whole new level of access and capability.

How do you leverage natural language processing techniques for information retrieval?

"An SEO can leverage this by using a suite of different natural language processing libraries – libraries like spaCy, TensorFlow, and Hugging Face. We can utilise BARD to create amazing visualisations. We can carry out text pre-processing; we can crawl a whole piece of content, prepare that text or that content for web pages and processing, and strip them down to their text embeddings.

We can create different mathematical representations for this text, at either the page level, the sentence level, or even the query level. We can strip them down, tokenize these things, remove any stop words, and convert these so that we can use this now-clean data to do many different things.

We can use this to unpack the actual intent of the page. If we have a whole corpus of text, we can see what that actually looks like for a search engine and how it would be perceived. We can extract things like entities and attach semantic meanings to those. We can utilise different pages and map them to each other to create nice internal links – or even 301 redirects to map an old page to a new page. We are now able to do all of this and more by calculating things like similarity matrices or by looking at the different related pages to one another.

9 User Intent

This is something that I've only ever dreamed of being able to do. In the past, I would have needed to utilise people smarter than me in computer science and data science but now, because of AI, we can use these types of libraries, create Python and create text, and unpack this at a rate that is just unprecedented.

Get in there. Try and ask some really intuitive questions. You will be able to answer questions in a way that was never possible before."

How do you use this process to score what you're currently doing and compare it to your competition? What software do you use?

"TensorFlow is pretty awesome. TensorFlow, and a whole variety of other visualisation tasks, allow you to map them out using Search Console APIs. We can take the Search Console API, take all of the queries, look at the JSON content, and unlock that to find similarities within the data. This allows us to see the deviation and correlations between data (maybe over a period of time; based on last year, or based on this year), and now we can start to map whether or not there are any strong correlations or any patterns.

Let's talk about an event as an example. Maybe an event from last year was starting to generate some interest and we've seen more impressions, more clicks, go towards this cluster of queries. We are now able to detect that and predict, based on what we've seen from the historical data, that we might see the same kind of patterns being generated around the same time this year. This is the level of detail we can pull out. It is really easy to do as well, by building deviations from traffic baselines and identifying strong correlations from Search Console data. We can ask and build custom Python scripts that will do this for us.

If you haven't done this before, this is something that's now been made a lot easier and a lot more accessible. That's great because a lot more is going to come from this wider accessibility."

How does this practically impact your SEO strategy?

"By having a really good grasp of the core concepts, you can now perform tasks at a rate that is a lot faster, and hopefully a lot more intuitive. Now, you're able to graphically show a visualisation of what you're trying to express to a client or a team, and you are able to build certain models to help extrapolate what you're trying to say.

That makes it so much easier to scale your work. It doesn't necessarily take away from the core aspect of what you do on a day-to-day basis as an SEO, but the time it takes and the amount of data that you can merge and create, utilising the same processes that a search engine would, is something that is completely unprecedented."

Should every SEO be researching this and finding out more about it, or is it only a certain type of SEO that can and should be doing this?

"I think everyone can, which is really amazing. Electronic music completely revolutionised the music world and levelled the playing field. It allowed a lot more people to get in there and start creating music without a formal musical background and training. Now we're seeing this in the tech world. More people are able to create custom scripts, create ways to talk to and integrate with different APIs, and build models that replicate, showcase, and transform the way that search engines work.

Say, for example, I want to use the Knowledge Graph API to pull in a whole bunch of information and attributes about specific entities. I can do that, and I am able to link in my Google Search Console data and get a deeper level of extraction – just based on pulling two APIs together to build something unique. This is something that we can do quite easily now. There is now a platform for putting these methodologies out there and it has given people the opportunity to go and explore.

My biggest tip is to go play. In previous years, I've said, 'Let's look at crawlability before we even worry about whether it's going to rank or not. If it can't crawl, if it can't index, and it can't render, then it's probably not going to rank and it's probably not going to be effective.' That was my recommendation last year. We have learned so many great things from the past – from what I and other people have been able to recommend – but this year is the year for play. That's a really empowering way that we can look at all the things that are now available to us.

Instead of saying, 'Maybe see what comes out of this and be a passenger', I say, 'Get in the driver's seat.' Let's start exploring our options. Let's test a few things and build a few things. It has given us a wide-reaching array of opportunities. Starting with natural language processing, at the very core of how search intent works, is really bread-and-butter stuff. The way for an SEO to begin to learn about what they need to do to make a page effective is by understanding user intent.

Now, we can utilise a whole variety of different libraries that help do that work for us and give us really great clues to follow. We can combine these clues with our own lateral thinking, and say, 'This is what it's presenting to me. Does this match what I think this page should be about?' If it's a 'no', then maybe you need to tweak things. If it's a 'yes', how can you build something from this understanding of what the page represents?

You can now look at not just one or two, but maybe 2,000, 20,000, or 200,000 pages. You can start to build it into a model and do things like pull out specific anchor text from the page and build internal links that link up these pages. This is something that we are now able to do, and I think that's just awesome."

Where should an SEO go and play, to begin with, and what are the first few steps of the game?

"I would say that the first step of the game is looking at a particular task that you want to do. Do you want to unpack the sentiment? Do you want to take a whole corpus of text and truly understand it?

For one of my first tasks, which I really loved, I built a crawler and tried to mimic the way that Screaming Frog (one of my favourite tools) works. Hats off to Screen Frog. It is actually incredible what they do and how they've been able to build this tool. There's a reason why it's so awesome and it's really, really hard to replicate.

I wanted to be able to crawl a whole bunch of pages, extract as much value out of that as possible, and start to build a way that I could use this as an array. I wanted to be able to say, 'How are we pulling all of this for all of these pages?' I wanted to break down each of these pages into their own mathematical representations and see what that mapping looks like."

If an SEO is struggling for time what should they stop doing right now so they can spend more time doing what you suggest in 2024?

"Stop getting so distracted with the number of changes that are happening. Try to go back to more fundamental work and understand more about how a search engine works, how things are built, why you would crawl a page, why pages would be picked up, and why some pages would be chosen over others.

Go back, understand the core aspects of SEO, and ask 'Why?' Asking yourself 'Why?' is such a valuable question because if you don't understand these things then you can get off the track really quickly."

Nik Ranger is Senior SEO Consultant at Dejan, and you can find her over at DejanMarketing.com.

10 Content

10 CONTENT

Return to the basics with your content strategy – with Begum Kaya

Once you understand your user intent, how do you determine what you serve them? Opening our chapter on content and the strategies behind your use of content, Begum Kaya from Uprise Up favours a human-centric approach.

Begum says: "Go back to basics. Focus on content and making sure it resonates, sounds reliable, and attracts the right audience.

There used to be a lot of fluff content back in the day. We should be going back to the humane basics. We should understand and acknowledge that SEO is talking to the user about the website, and remember the basics of effective communication."

How do you know that you're talking to the right user?

"You should be identifying what you want to say and what you want to communicate. Firstly, you need to know who you are to connect with the right audience and embrace their style of communication. As long as you understand what you are doing and are solid in your strategy, you can find the right audiences that will be attracted to what you are offering."

Is there a particular style or type of content that you find to be effective at the moment?

"In general: not AI-generated content. All the fluff being created recently is making us feel very pressured as SEOs. There is so much fluff going on that we cannot really get to the point where we want to be. Cut that fluff out and clear the fog so that you can present yourself as you are. That's the best thing that you can do, both for your audience and yourself.

There is a very, very deep pool that you have to go through right now, and it's extremely frustrating. We have to make it easier for our audiences.

From my perspective, fluff is all the marketing that uses jargon like, 'Get it now!', 'You deserve this!', etc. It's marketing that doesn't really offer anything for the user and is just trying to steer them in a direction that will leave them frustrated in the end. Provide value and communicate your value well. Do it without generic AI content and reveal your brand's personality in every communication that you have with the client."

Does AI only produce fluff?

"AI increases fluff, which is why I'm trying to avoid it. It is already proving to be very helpful because content is one of the most time-consuming SEO tasks. However, many brands have been leaning towards automating content production and optimization, but AI doesn't really make optimized content. You still have to be you.

You can enter keywords and it will very easily come up with an article brief, and even outline everything for you, but you still need to provide some sort of value for the client from your perspective. Otherwise, they will be frustrated with what they read on your website.

AI can help at the beginning of content creation and during the ideation process. It gives a much faster pool of content that you can take advantage of. However, this still has to go through your heads of strategy and digital marketers to be able to resonate with the users.

You don't write an article just to put it out there. People should be engaging with it and there has to be some sort of target for it. It has to serve your goals. To be able to do that, you can take advantage of AI, but it still needs to go through an editorial process."

What makes a piece of content resonate with a user?

"Providing your perspective and appealing to the users, as long as it touches them on a personal level or solves a problem for them. If it provides value, it's applicable, and it's information-rich, that's going to resonate with your users."

What makes a user feel that you're likely to be reliable?

"It's about being trustworthy and consistent in all your communications. You should have a stance and you should not be saying X in one place and Y in another.

When it comes to AI, it doesn't really know what it's talking about. When you leave the content creation up to AI without any editorial input, it just goes nuts, and you can end up in a very weird position. It has a lot of bias and a lot of the information that it has been fed is unreliable.

If the information you are providing on your website is very heavy on the content side of things, rather than facts and data, you are going to need to be very strategic instead of just publishing everything AI has generated for you."

How do you attract the right audience?

"It is about speaking the same language. There isn't going to be any change on that front. Good SEOs still find ways to identify what their users are looking for and the keywords they are using.

If you're catering to Gen Z, the wording that you use would be very different from when you're communicating with Gen Y or millennials. You need to understand those differences and know when your audience is familiar with the jargon, is from different countries, speaks different languages, etc. Identifying those differences will help your business to really cater to the right audience."

Do people make the decision to convert themselves or can you assist the process with sales writing, UX functionality, etc.?

"All of those elements definitely have their own input, but you follow some sort of sales funnel with your clients when they come to your website. That funnel relies heavily on the content that is on your website and how you engage with the user as a brand.

Not every communication that you have with your users will be on the website. Your online presence, your offline presence, and any space where you provide information and engage with your users is an input that may help them convert. On that front, we come back to identifying who you are. As long as you know yourself and you know what your users like, you can tweak your messaging and craft your sales model based on that."

How does a brand establish who it is, how it talks, and what it represents?

"It's all about the messaging, the values, and the mission. Whatever you are trying to do and whatever you feel your values are, you should be able to communicate them and stay true to them in order to be reliable.

Changing perspectives and providing different things on different fronts is not going to make you a very reliable brand. In recent years, we have seen that users are actually looking for a human connection. They want to be understood and they want to be heard.

As long as you are putting your core values out there and ensuring that your communication is wrapped around those, that will resonate with your users a lot because all the purchasing and conversion patterns have changed in the past few years."

What does human connection look like?

"It can be having an individual associated with each article you produce, having social profiles that are easy to follow, video content, etc., but it can also be simple, subtle tweaks like providing the information in the right place.

It could be something as simple as having size guides or FAQs on your pages for the sake of being useful for the client, not for the sake of SEO. Be a step ahead of them and think about what they might need throughout the journey they are taking on your website.

To do this effectively, you will need to have different inputs from different users. You should be in connection with your users to be able to identify what they want and what they need. Then, you can tailor your messaging, and even your whole strategy from time to time, if need be. Lay it all out there with subtle tweaks and useful information.

When it comes to measuring the value of improving your human connections, reviews and social engagements are definitely a great way to do that."

If an SEO is struggling for time, what should they stop doing right now so they can spend more time doing what you suggest in 2024?

"Throughout this conversation, I've had a little bit of a war with AI-generated content that doesn't get any editorial input. Take advantage of AI, but don't try to make it the core of your SEO offering. Use it as a tool that makes your job easier but stop focusing on AI. Keep focusing on people and providing for them.

You can still use AI tools to check your content. For example, Grammarly has AI-based grammar checkers which you can certainly take advantage of. At the end of the day, though, you need to be personally checking your content – particularly if it was generated or altered by AI."

Begum Kaya is SEO Manager at Uprise Up, and you can find her on Twitter @begumkayaseo and at upriseup.co.uk.

Develop a user-enriched, strategic approach to content – with Fabio Embalo

Fabio Embalo from Viaduct Generation also believes in building human connections with your content, and he says that being more strategic will help you focus on what your users really need.

What's your number one SEO tip for 2024?

Fabio says: "Now, more than ever, you need to be strategic with your content.

I was at BrightonSEO not too long ago and approximately 80% of all the talks were about AI. Everyone is macro-focused on creating as much content as possible with these new tools that allow you to create 200 articles a month. We're forgetting that the most important aspect of a website is to provide real value to your potential visitors.

That strategy shouldn't go anywhere; it should always be at the forefront. It shouldn't be about quantity, and it should be always about quality. A lot of SEOs out there focus on having as much content as possible on their sites, but I've always disagreed. I've worked on websites with less than 50% of the pages their competitors have, and outranked them greatly, just through quality, strategic content.

You need to be more strategic than ever before. Home in on what the user needs and what they want to be reading about, rather than creating as much content as possible using the power of AI."

What does an effective, user-led content strategy look like?

"I was talking about this with a client a few hours ago. He is a business owner with an e-commerce shop, and he is very passionate about the products that he sells. He receives new products and he believes that, because he's the first one in the market to have them, he's going to be able to sell them easily. However, three months down the line, there might not be enough demand for that product. If that is the case, it almost doesn't matter how good the strategy is and what sort of product we're trying to sell.

From an SEO perspective, demand is important. We can always try and target those long-tail keywords with less search volume behind them and less keyword difficulty, but demand is so important. When it comes to preparing a user-enriched strategy, we have a lot of tools at our disposal. I find Google Search Console extremely helpful for all of this. It's so interesting to marry up your performance over the course of six months and understand what's bringing impressions onto your site, what's bringing clicks to your site, what is dropping, and why.

Normally, when you look at it, it's not dropping because the demand is no longer there. It's normally dropping because competitors have created something new, in terms of content, that is more recent than what you have – which has overtaken your content. As I was telling my client today, you can instantly tell that the demand is there. Your competitors are writing about it, and you can see the traffic that those competitors are getting, so the demand is certainly still there.

That can help dictate your strategy moving forward. A lot of your clients will come to you with demands on what they think is best for their own websites, but you need to be making data-driven decisions. Making decisions based on that data, and your content, will be key going forward."

How do you determine what's going to be successful in the future and what you need to focus on from a content perspective?

"Understanding whatever market you're serving is key. The client I was just speaking about has been a client of ours for about three years now, so we understand the industry really well. We understand what the future trends will be based on what's going on today.

Having conversations with the client will always help because they are ingrained in the industry. If they're a business owner, more often than not, they will know more about the industry than you do. The collaboration element is important

At the same time, the more that you're working on an account the more you get to find out about that industry. You are constantly analysing the competition and you're constantly reading about what's going on in that specific industry, so your future strategies are based on real-life trends that you are identifying through your research.

The collaboration side of things is important because I could easily come up with some ideas based on the competitors I've analysed and the articles I've read. However, the client may have an insight that I don't.

If you're trying to define something for the future without quite knowing the demand that may generate, or without really having the data, sometimes it's important to take risks. You can identify something that you predict will work, based on past experiences – for example, a product that improves on a previous product that has recently come into the market. That allows you to go ahead and create that strategy and those articles without waiting 3-6 months to see if it will work or not. Taking the risk and being the first to put something out there is often a good way of doing it."

How will SGE impact content strategy and should SEOs be taking risks in order to rank for questions that will likely be popular for their industry?

"Understanding user behaviour will be important when it comes to those sorts of questions. The way content is going to be presented on Google is going to change completely in a lot of industries. Based on my experience testing it so far, it doesn't look like it's going to affect all industries. For those industries where SGE is present, the way content is presented will be completely different.

It places complete emphasis on user experience and engagement with the articles on your website, as well as how relevant it is for the user. The introduction of SGE means that traditional SEO techniques need to be adapted to align with the evolving search landscape.

When you have an AI writing tons of content, you will always miss the user experience aspect and the human side of things. SGE will really account for that, which is why we've had so many updates like the helpful content update and the EEAT update. Everything is placing emphasis on the user experience, and the human experience. SGE will home in on that. For that, we need to adapt and change the way we do things in the SEO industry."

What sort of metrics will demonstrate to SGE that your content offers a great user experience?

"I am actually not sure that Google themselves know the answer to that yet. Right now, based on my experience, it still gives some answers that don't feel very relevant.

However, going forward, things like the trustworthiness behind whatever you're writing on your site will be important. Having things like reviews on specific products will become ever more significant than they were before because it adds a level of credibility to the product that you are describing on your site. Things like case studies and quotes within the specific articles that you're writing are also going to be important.

If you are writing an article about the best restaurants in London, having quotes from real people for those specific articles will really help. We need to start thinking outside the box, and AI will always miss the mark with that. Bring real-life experiences into the articles that you're writing, whether it's through quotes or videos that you're creating to get their point across.

Right now, a lot of case studies feel disingenuous, so we may need to change the way we create those case studies. Perhaps it needs to be a lot more interactive, with a quick 30-second video plus the text, to add that level of credibility to the article that you're writing. I think things like that are what Google will be looking for when they are taking their answers for SGE."

Would you ever advise a client to block AI from accessing and using their content?

"Right now, I want to say no because I always want my clients to come across as the thought leaders in their space. I'm just hoping that Google takes a leaf out of Bing's book and starts giving credit and citing sources more. It's important to give props to those who they're getting the information from. So far, they're not doing that. They're doing it in some instances, but it's not good enough. They really should cite where they're getting that information from because then no SEO would ever advise a client to block it.

If they don't give more credit, we're likely going to be heading that way. Everyone works extremely hard to create what we believe is really good, quality content – just for Google to then come in with an extremely powerful and expensive robot, steal the content away from you, and get all the clicks for themselves. It's not fair to what we're trying to do, but things aren't always fair when it comes to Google, are they?"

If an SEO is struggling for time, what should they stop doing right now

so they can spend more time doing what you suggest in 2024?

"Stop doing the little things and focus on what's to come. It's very easy for us to focus on the present and then, when we have something new in front of us, we try to scramble and adapt to it.

We should be proactive. We know it's here. We know it's coming. We're living in it right now. Let's ensure that we're proactive about it, we're learning as much as possible about it, and we are starting to adapt our strategies ahead of it right now – rather than waiting until it's in front of our faces and all our competitors who have done their homework are beating us on the SERPs."

Fabio Embalo is Chief Executive Officer at Viaduct Generation, and you can find him over at SEO.ViaductGen.com.

Have conversations and listen to your customers before turning to SEO research – with Martin Huntbach

To better understand the user needs that Fabio discussed, Martin Huntbach from Jammy Digital tells you to be better at communicating with your customers and hearing what they have to say.

Martin says: "Listen to your customers first and then validate it with SEO research."

There are a lot of ways to listen to your customers, and it obviously depends on your business. A SaaS company might have to dig through their customer support tickets or run regular workshops, webinars, or Q&As to get to the bottom of what their clients, customers, and potential customers are truly having problems with.

It should help dictate what activities you do as an SEO. We're often too reliant on keyword research tools and data rather than just picking up the phone and speaking to our clients, customers, and the people who are interested in the overall topic. It's a huge mistake that a lot of SEOs fall into

– which is understandable because who wants another Zoom call? Who wants to pick up a phone?

However, when you're more ingrained in the conversations that are happening with your customers, you're able to create better content and have a bigger impact. You'll be creating important content that gets to the nooks and crannies of the problems they're facing in their day-to-day. SEO tools won't always give you all the information."

What kinds of questions should SEOs be asking their customers?

"You don't need to track the customer journey in terms of clicks, visits, where they found you, or even what keyword they typed in. You can find a lot of that information using tools. Instead, you want to understand what their goals are.

When someone buys some software or wants to work with a company, what's the problem they want to solve? What's keeping them up at night? What is it about the product or service you have that can solve that problem? The missing piece of the puzzle is how you can communicate that.

If someone is trying to rank their business on the first page of Google, what do they want from that? Do they want more revenue, more customers, or to increase the value of each customer? When you get to those kinds of questions and understand their goals, then you can say, 'Here's why SEO is going to help you achieve that goal, and this is the kind of content we need to create.'

Then, on the back end, you want to use SEO tools to validate that people actually search for that. They might say one thing on a call or in an email, but what they type into search might be different. Take the ideas from the client and then use SEO tools to do the research, validate it, and make a plan.

On the SEO side, the tools will give you the information you need. However, without the initial insight from that client or potential client, how are you going to reach them and how do you know that content is going to help them achieve their goal?

You want to help people, not just rank on the first page of Google. They don't care about rankings, ultimately. Rankings are just an indication of the work that you've done. What they want is for you to solve their problems, and SEO is a way to get there, but you need to understand the goals originally."

Do you need to have direct conversations, or can a form/questionnaire be as effective?

"Recently, we launched a survey about how the mental health of entrepreneurs and business owners is affected by dealing with clients. We used what we call a 'gifted survey'. We sent it in an email and said, 'If you fill out this survey, you'll get a free copy of our book, and you'll be entered into a prize draw.' That can work remarkably well. We had an 83% conversion rate, and you can ask really specific questions.

You can do this in any niche in any industry. Then, if you want to create a piece of original research (which is great for SEO), you can do that on the back end as well. Collect data from your ideal clients by giving them a gift in exchange for some insights. Then, on the back end, produce that original research, get links to it, and share it. The PR-friendly nature of that is so much better than traditional content.

You could also do regular workshops. Email your potential clients and ask if they want to join a free 30-minute Q&A. You can say, 'What problems are you facing right now? I'd love to understand your position and answer your questions.' Then, you can go away and create loads of content based on those questions.

Sometimes, as SEOs, we rely too much on tech when we're struggling with content ideas or what to rank for. Why not do it the old-school way and have some real conversations? The content will come flooding back to you.

We used to run a content marketing challenge where we would review people's content from an SEO point of view. Everyone who submitted blog content would say, 'Your headings/subheadings need to switch to this, you've got images here, the structure of this is a bit strange, etc.' After that call, we would have a flood of content ideas, new keywords, and new topics that we could talk about to rank for those keywords. We know that people who need support are searching for these things because they've just told us.

The energy you get from a real conversation is completely different from using tools. There are so many keyword research tools that I can't even reel them off now. I try to avoid them until I start crafting that content and targeting specific keywords.

Learn what your audience wants first, and what they need help with, even if they're not aware of it. You can uncover so many hidden content ideas based on one single conversation. What they say and what they don't say will allow you to create a series of articles to help more people."

How do you identify which people to talk to first?

"If you have a community element to your product or service, then start there. One of our clients has a Facebook group. When a customer joins and buys some software, they get added to a Facebook group where they will be asking beginner questions. That's great.

If you've got a business, there's probably a Facebook group out there with boatloads of questions about your topic. If you don't have an email list or a community, but you want to create helpful content, go and join some Facebook groups, communities, or forums that talk about those things. The same basic questions will come up all the time. That's valuable information that you can answer. You might not want to answer it there for one person, but you definitely want to answer it for the 1,000 people who come to your website through search results.

There are so many avenues. You've got customer support tickets, your own Facebook groups, topical Facebook groups, or even Facebook groups for SEO tools. There are a ton of SEO Facebook groups you could join to learn the beginner questions that people are asking.

Use those to your advantage and try to craft a website that is the best resource on that topic. Craft the best version of that resource that's transparent, open, and honest. Answer those questions as if you are the Google of your industry, and you can only really do that by listening to your clients."

How do you validate your customer research with keyword research?

"Once you've got the questions, throw them in a Google Doc to see what it would look like. If you had to think of 5-10 bullet points to answer this question or the considerations that it brought up, what would you put? Then, use keyword research tools to make sure that people are searching for those things. Collect lots of other keywords that people are typing in too, even if you don't use them.

For each article we create, it's pretty common for us to collect 30-50 keywords. They might not have the greatest search volume so you may need to consider that if people search for X, they might be searching for Y. Use tools like Majestic and SEMrush to find different channels. Keep clicking and see where the keywords lead you. Look at the competition and what they've tried to target for the same question. That's vital.

You won't struggle to find research to back it up. It'll take you 10 seconds to verify that people search for this and lots of people are concerned about this problem. However, you might not get there without speaking to that person first. Get the conversation started, then do your own research and use your own initiative before you touch a keyword research tool. Then, use the keyword research tool to help you formalise a plan and a structure for that piece of content and create it.

As an agency, we use blogging to try and rank for those keywords. It might be different for you. You might have a static page that you want to drive traffic to through links. You still have to optimize it, and use keyword research tools and data to back that up."

Do you ever need to start with keyword research to make sure you're not missing out on opportunities?

"With our clients, it changes partway through the relationship. When we first take on a client, we have a huge call about their business, their goals, and what they think people are struggling with based on the conversations they've had. Then, we go over to keyword research tools to verify what they've told us and have a look at their audience and their research.

After three months of creating long-form content, we get to understand that business and we will start to rely more on the SEO tools. We start collecting our own content ideas before speaking to the client. We will come up with a series of articles based on what we've found out since working with them, using keyword research for every article.

We start by doing a lot of the research verbally and over emails, then in Facebook groups, forums, etc., to really get into the nooks and crannies of that niche. If we were to just ask what keywords they want to rank for, put them into SEO tools, and make that content, we would still pick up rankings. However, for us to really have an impact on this business, we need to understand everything there is to know about their day-to-day, their conversations, and everything that they do. That enables us to plan content much better, and we're not relying on the client. We take ownership.

Speaking to customers, looking on forums, and using keyword research tools are all methods for finding out what people are searching for. It's just that keyword research data is more verifiable. Imagine you never considered SEO or keywords, and your only job was to answer every single question that you've ever been asked as a business owner – going into depth and giving them clarity through honest transparent content about every question you've ever been asked before. Chances are your SEO would be far better than your competitors because Google genuinely wants to provide the best results to their users.

If you only focus on keyword research, you might not get there. If you only focus on what your client is telling you, what people are searching for, and your own research, there's a good chance that you will get some long-lasting results. There are pros and cons to each, so you need both. However, you can come up with a lot more content ideas when you have real conversations with people and customers. Then, use SEO and research tools on the back end to verify the best direction for that piece of content."

If an SEO is struggling for time, what should they stop doing right now so they can spend more time doing what you suggest in 2024?

"Stop checking your rankings. It's a bit of an addiction for SEOs. Almost every morning I log into my rank tracker and check to see if the graph's gone up or down.

Checking rankings has zero impact on the client's rankings. What does have a big impact is putting in the work, creating content, building backlinks, etc. When you check rankings and Google's had a bit of a shift in the night, that's going to affect you mentally. It creates a little bit of frustration when you're just about to hit the ground running for your day.

When I was in sales, I used to check my numbers whenever I wasn't with a client, instead of finding a new client or a new way to improve a client. Avoid checking your rankings too frequently."

Martin Huntbach is Co-Founder at Jammy Digital, and you can find him over at JammyDigital.com.

Recognise the value of creator-led SEO – with Ashley Liddell

Guiding you towards a specific form of content that can unlock many doors, Ashley Liddell from Reprise Digital favours what creator-led SEO has to offer.

Ashley says: "Embrace creator-led SEO, and everything that entails.

That means working with content creators on other platforms, such as TikTok, YouTube, etc. It could be the MrBeasts of the world – but even on a much smaller scale, working with hyper-localised or smaller community creators.

It depends on your budget. MrBeast is a grand example; that's the one that grabs people's attention because as soon as you mention his name people instantly know who you mean.

For most brands, you'll be looking at the lower end of the scale and working with people with smaller followings, leveraging their expertise and their community to further your brand's SEO efforts."

Should every brand work with creators?

"I think so. There are going to be instant connections between people and brands in a B2C space, but this is also effective in the B2B space and across other industries. This isn't just something for fashion or high-consumer brands to leverage. There is an opportunity for other types of brands across various industries here as well."

How do you find and reach out to creators?

"Generally, it should be quite simple. If you understand your brand and your audience, then you're probably already following these types of creators in your space – or you at least know who they are.

If you need to do something massive on YouTube, MrBeast instantly comes to mind. For brands in fashion, there will be thousands of fashion influencers you could think of that you would want to work with. It's up to the person on the brand side, or SEO agency, that's leveraging this. You need to understand which creators already have an established relationship with your audience.

Then, it's about doing the work. Usually, you will reach out to their management or agency and say, 'We want to work with your client. Is this a brand that they feel they could have a relationship with?' That is super important. You shouldn't just be saying, 'How much do you charge? Here's a paycheck.' It needs to be very much relationship-led and audience-led.

If the creator does want to work with your brand, then you can start building that relationship and exploring it. Understanding the finances is important, but you really want to understand what the creator is going to get out of the situation (in terms of helping their community and providing useful content to their community) and what the brand is going to get out of it. Do they have an established community that you can work with? Are you going to get results?"

Do creators have pre-determined rates, or do you approach them with a budget?

"It varies. We're still establishing what that's going to look like in the long term. If you look at the influencer marketing space, as with SEO, there are always going to be people looking to cut corners and do things as quickly and cheaply as possible. When they're doing that, it's a race to the bottom dollar – finding the cheapest influencer to work with where they're still going to get awareness. That's where bad influencer marketing has really lacked.

You should focus on doing good work, and doing effective work. You want to explore those relationships and make it a positive experience for both sides, instead of just being concerned with how much it's going to cost.

In terms of the campaign idea, I will often instantly think of a creator that's perfect for the projects that we are working on. It's likely that they're going to want to do it as well, particularly if they get passionate about it. You should be saying to a creator or their agency, 'We've got a really good idea that we think you/your client's going to love. Would you like to be part of it?'

A lot of the time, if you show up with something that they're going to be really passionate about, and that they think they can get good content from, then they're going to be more willing to work with your brand anyway."

Why are these kinds of long-term relationships so important in SEO now?

"We're starting to see a transition into a new era of search and SEO. New signals are emerging, such as the new E in EEAT and the experience and expertise around that. If you can position an influencer as the authority on a topic and leverage them for your SEO content, it makes sense to take advantage of a long-term relationship rather than only working with them for a month or a single campaign.

They could be authoring content for a longer period of time which would allow you to build their authority, whilst positioning your brand in a position of authority at the same time. Brands need to develop longer-term relationships with authors for the EEAT benefits and the topical authority that comes from it.

There is still an element of link building where you are looking to gain X number of links from X and Y publications. However, when you're working with a creator, you can say to those publications, 'Your audience cares what this influencer does so you should cover this topic and link to our page.'"

What level of influencer should you aim for, and is there a budget you would recommend?

"It would be irresponsible for me to provide a blanket approach when it comes to budget because different brands are going to have different budgets.

Focus on your goals for the campaign. If your big goal is to build brand awareness, then it might make sense to go with a slightly bigger creator, which may incur a bigger budget requirement. If your goal is acquiring really qualified leads, then you might work with a smaller creator. Understand what you want from the campaign and let that drive what your budget becomes. Be really strategic.

Once you've done that, it's a matter of understanding your goals and what the creative is going to be, and then making sure that you get the most out of the relationship to justify the expense.

If you're going to work with a creator on TikTok to create TikTok content, don't just leverage TikTok. Repurpose that content and put it on your website. Make sure it's part of a blog or a landing page, or turn it into a testimonial. Get it on your website so you're immediately getting more bang for your buck. Then, get that video onto your other social platforms as a YouTube Short or an Instagram Reel. Getting the most out of the content that you create is a really effective way to justify the expense of creator-led SEO."

How do you measure the SEO value of the content an influencer produces for you, particularly when it's posted on their social media?

"It's important to remember that, when we talk about SEO, that doesn't just mean Google anymore. For the longest time, it's been really easy to say that the SEO benefit is ranking in position one, getting X number of clicks every month and X number of impressions, and going through those metrics that we all know, love, and hate.

When we start embracing TikTok SEO, for example, there are different metrics that may mean different things for your brand. How many people have watched that TikTok? How many people have then gone onto your landing page? If you know that you released the campaign in January and traffic went up by 1,000, you can assume that around 1,000 people have come through from the TikTok content you've produced (alongside everything else you've got going on). Then, you can look at the bottom dollar. How much money have you made off that increase in traffic? What's the business advantage, profit-wise?

In terms of SEO benefits, you should consider the visuals on the SERP. When you create that influencer content and get it covered by publications, is that appearing in the news features on the SERP? If so, your brand could be ranking position one and also ranking in the news feature above that, and then all the publications that have covered you are there on the SERP as well. Your visibility goes from just one blue link to having a news feature, all those publications underneath, and the position that you are ranking.

You can dominate a SERP in ways that weren't possible before, which gives you a big advantage over your competitors. You're visible on the SERP and they're not, which is fantastic."

Can you retain the same visibility once the relationship has ended?

"The news features at the top of the SERP are always evolving. As new people put out content, that's going to change. Your content will very quickly disappear from that section of the SERP after it's provided its initial value.

That's where it becomes really important for you to leverage the influencer relationships that you've built and paid for with on-site content. A really good way to do this is to take a keyword that you know is going to have long-term value (e.g., an informational query or a longer tail query) and build the creative for the influencer relationship around that query.

Then, once the influencer relationship ends and you've faded from the news publications listings, people are still searching for that query. Therefore, they're still being exposed to the content you've created and you're still getting long-term benefits from that relationship.

Over time, you can expect the initial effect to dissipate. However, in typical SEO fashion, if you can do it strategically you can extend the amount of time that content is going to be working hard for your brand."

Would you recommend creating long-form articles from creator-led videos, perhaps using AI?

"I would definitely create a long-form informational content piece based on that influencer content. However, I wouldn't necessarily say that you should utilise AI to do so, at this point in time. We'll see how AI develops.

Creating a longer piece of content that can leverage snippets – transcribing the video, taking the best bits, editing that, and making it work for your brand – is absolutely going to give you longer-term benefits.

When Google's Perspectives filter starts to roll out, influencers are going to start gaining a lot more credibility as authors. Saying, '[X feature], contributed by [influencer name]' is going to help your SEO authority as well."

If an SEO is struggling for time, what should they stop doing right now so they can spend more time doing what you suggest in 2024?

"Stop spending as much time on keyword research in its archaic form. Stop spending time developing strategies based wholly on keyword research, search volumes, and the old metrics that we've leaned into for years. It's becoming out-of-date.

Instead of building a strategy based on that, base your strategies around what your audience is interested in. You know your community best. Leverage creator-led SEO to do that, and build your strategies that way, as opposed to relying solely on keyword research."

Ashley Liddell is SEO Content Strategist at Reprise Digital, and you can find him over at AshleyLiddell.co.uk.

Influence organic search by working with influencers – with Maria White

Maria White from Kurt Geiger also knows how valuable well-known content creators can be. She believes that collaborating with them can impact search as much as it impacts your users.

What's your number one SEO tip for 2024?

Maria says: "In a cookieless future and an age of AI Work, with influencers to influence your consumers and, more importantly, search.

Influencers do not influence search directly but they do affect search. Before making a purchase, consumers tend to go to social media to find out more information about the product. In the case of luxury and fashion, they want to find out how that product looks on someone else. For example, how does that handbag look on someone? Does it suit certain body frames? What can you put inside? It's information that, as a brand, we can put together on the landing page.

Also, they want to see directly from the influencer and live that experience through them. In most cases, a small influencer tends to have more influence on the consumer. We have achieved sell-outs working with huge celebrities this year, however, it's the smaller, more friendly, and more one-to-one influencers who create content that matches the intent of the user – and that intent is to find out more information about a product.

Once the consumer is influenced, and they've seen your brand, they will then go to Google to complete the action. They go to search to engage with a brand – whether that's an ad or organic – and complete a purchase on Google."

How can SEOs or marketers influence organic search with influencer marketing?

"One of our preferred techniques is to create content with influencers that will become visible to your target audience. It doesn't have to be super viral and break the internet with a TikTok video; it's just good content supported by insights or data. Then, you can create a content hub or a collection of content resources that you can seed out to the appropriate media. This way, you can get coverage on important media outlets that your target audience reads.

Create content with influencers and then use it in your ads or on mainstream media. That's when you get the link that is going to influence organic search.

Any brand in any niche can work with the right influencer, and it's not necessarily just video or TikTok either. It's about understanding the consumer and going to the channel where they are. It's not about going straight to TikTok because that's a trend, or that's what some marketing influencer is telling you to do. First, understand your audience in particular."

Do you need to understand the influencer and what's important for them?

"Yes. In SEO software, for example, we see that new software vendors sometimes get a big SEO influencer to try the tool and give a guide on how to use it and the benefits of it. Then, people start getting to know that tool via that SEO influencer.

Influencer marketing is still important for influencing your consumers, but also for influencing search via the content you create. That content can then go into longer articles online or into relevant media channels with links, that can have an effect on organic search."

How do you identify the influencer that's most appropriate for your brand?

"This is one of the most interesting and fascinating exercises I've done for our brand this year. We had to sit down and identify influencers in new countries where we are going to expand. Even in Mexico, where I was born, I might have assumed that a singer like Belinda would be a target. However, as we looked at the data and where our target audience engages the most and starts their journey – in terms of the response to ads or searches for our brand – a handbag enthusiast might be more appropriate.

From there, we had the pleasure of working with influences such as Jennifer Lopez and Paris Hilton. We achieved sell-outs within hours, and all it took was a picture. When you see Jennifer Lopez walking on the red carpet wearing a super glamorous gown, with Ben Affleck by her side, emphasising a beautiful clutch, everyone searches for that clutch.

Even if the name of the product isn't tagged, every brand has a logo. For us, they see the eagle, and they know it is Kurt Geiger. They search for, 'Kurt Geiger clutch', 'black clutch', and other terms until they get to what they want. Then they buy the product, and it's gone within hours. We've had that a couple of times this year.

In the case of Paris Hilton, it was just one picture of her on holiday. It was published on Instagram she was all glamorous and beautiful on one of her yachts, with a little white handbag on the side. The reason why our target audience goes crazy for this is because these huge celebrities can afford the most expensive handbags in the world, but they are choosing an attainable luxury brand: us. People go, 'I can get that look'. Now, that little white handbag is also sold out.

To influence consumers and search for our regular collections that are produced more frequently, like a timeless classic collection, we might work with smaller influencers. They can offer an intimate experience and a connection with the audience that describes why they should buy that handbag, what you can put in it, how it will look on you, and more."

If you've identified the ideal influencers you want to work with, how do you persuade them to work with you?

"It depends on the type of influencer. For the bigger influencers and celebrities, that is 100% through your PR team. The traditional PR team does amazing, incredible things. They have their own way of approaching that type of celebrity.

It's easier when you work for a brand that your target audience loves. It's likely that some of the influences that we want to work with will immediately say 'yes' when we approach them, because they love the brand.

We have even approached influencers through a comment. There is a girl who has bought over 100 handbags, and she's a big fan of our brand. A few months ago, we just commented on one of her videos, 'We love your content!' She was really happy and we started working with her. It's easy when the influencers your target audience engages with already love the brand.

However, if that's not necessarily the case, brands should still utilise influencer marketing. In the world of SEO, I find out about a lot of new tools and new software because of SEO influencers. Aleyda Solis, for example, writes beautiful content, and she's incredibly trustworthy because she gives a lot to the industry. She's a drama-free influencer who creates great content and has dedication and passion for the industry. When she recommends a piece of software, you're likely to explore it – even if you've been in the industry for years.

Influencer marketing can work in almost any industry. You just need to find the influencer that can establish that connection between the user and the brand. The work that influencers do is about connection and emotion. It's up to us as SEOs to sell the facts and the flawless journey on our website through search. Let the influencer sell the dream, the emotions, and the connection. You sell the facts, the numbers, the content, and the rest."

Are SEOs often too focused on the technical side of the job?

"SEOs think that we should start super technical, that it's all about Google, and we need to learn all the different algorithms. The new breed of SEOs say it's all about consumer journey and they use jargon like 'omnichannel' that they don't necessarily understand.

It's much easier to just have a look at Google Analytics and where your traffic coming from is. Have a look at tools, like Glimpse which connects to Google Trends, which can give you an initial idea of how people are searching for you and where their searches are starting – TikTok, Instagram, etc. Have a look at your data and have a look at how your users come to you and engage with your website.

If they're coming mostly from TikTok, that means your users are looking to get information and influence on TikTok before they complete an action on Google. There is a myth out there that TikTok is replacing Google because Gen Z is using TikTok first. It's not that people are using TikTok or video more, it's that people are always going to seek information before making a purchase that they really value – which has been true as long as marketing has existed. People will look for information from video, word-of-mouth, newspapers, or any other source before making an impactful purchasing decision.

Understand that users start their shopping journey with information. Then, create content and a content hub or collection of resources that the target media for your target audience can use for a longer article, so that you can get a link. Also, 'target media' doesn't just mean national publications. If you are an SEO tool, you're not going to go to the Telegraph and advertise your new SEO software. If you manage to get a link on the Guardian, what is the value of that link? Who is going to come from the Guardian to buy your software?

Target media can be an influencer blog or a newsletter. You want to get the link in the right place. When you invest a lot of money on media links, you need to make sure that those links are placed where your target audience is going to engage, not just because it's a link."

If an SEO is struggling for time, what should they stop doing right now so they can spend more time doing what you suggest in 2024?

"Stop dedicating all of your time to one sole strategy. In an age of AI and a cookieless future, how are you going to create more relevant and personalised campaigns? Influencer marketing is a great way to do that. Don't focus only on technical SEO and understanding the algorithm, how Google works, SGE, etc. We know SGE is going to happen and, thanks to some incredible researchers like Lily Ray, Marie Haynes, and Aleyda, we know what might happen.

You don't need to understand how Google or the TikTok algorithm works to be the best content creator. The most complex machine you have to understand is the human brain and how people behave. I'm not telling you to become a neurosurgeon or go into neuroscience. Understand people and what type of content your target audience consumes, where, and how. That should drive your strategy.

Stop obsessing. Don't become too technical, too video, or too TikTok. You need a bit of everything. Also, get out of the SEO world and try to understand paid media, digital PR, etc. Get out of your head and go and understand how other marketing channels impact SEO."

Maria White is Search Lead at Kurt Geiger, and you can find her at

KurtGeiger.com.

Pan your business for thought leader gold - with Paige Hobart

While Maria and Ashley talked about the influential figures you could work with outside of your business, Paige Hobart from Unily suggests that you to look closer to home for inspiration.

Paige says: "For 2024, I want you all to get to know the thought leaders in your businesses. Go and get to know them, bake them cakes, and build a friendship. They are gold dust."

I thought SEOs didn't have to talk to people?

"I wish that was the case. There is a lot that can be done in isolation, but if you want to be proactive and unique and push a business to the heights that it can reach, then your thought leaders are amazing resources.

Your sales reps are talking to prospects and customers day in and day out. They know your FAQs and they know the common themes that are coming up right now. There are also your product evangelists. I am lucky enough to have someone in my company with this as their job title. Product evangelists are the people who work on your product and are always trying to improve it. They will have loads of influences that they're building from. There are people in your company who are advocates on social media, always talking about how great your company is on LinkedIn. You want to know why they think that way. Your CEO should be your number-one advocate for your business. They should always be looking at the competition and what the business should be doing next to stay ahead.

All of these people are such a valuable resource for an SEO, so you can be more proactive than reactive."

Where does this type of content fit into your overarching content marketing strategy?

"It can fit into lots of places. We've spoken before about the Pump and Funnel Marketing Model (If you haven't already, go and check out *SEOin2023* and David's LinkedIn Learning course!). As we know from EAT and EEAT, you want to be genuinely helpful and produce content that is genuinely helpful throughout that model. Utilising your thought leaders can add incredible and unique value.

In SEO, we tend to rely on search volume but search volume is inherently reactive. It looks at previous months and how many people have searched for a query in the past, but it isn't very good at looking forward. Your thought leaders, on the other hand, are on the pulse.

For example, we've just launched a piece of 'AI-Powered Intranet' content. It doesn't really have any search volume at all, but we're getting a lot of traffic because it's something people are looking for right now. It hasn't been picked up in terms of search volume yet but there is a demand. My product team told me that it is really hot right now. We got that page up, it is getting traffic, and it is getting conversions. From my perspective, it didn't look like it had any value, but my thought leaders knew that it did."

Is targeting zero search volume keywords the way to go?

"Not for everything, but maybe when you're looking for the next thing.

If you've been in-house for a while, you know what your core pages are, and you know where the volume is. High search volume doesn't necessarily mean high intent. It doesn't necessarily mean that you're going to convert because it could be that people are just at the start of their journey especially if they're looking for big broad search volume terms. That doesn't mean you shouldn't be visible there, but there is a lot of value to be had in zero search volume terms.

Sometimes search volume can be misleading. One of the things I used to say to my team is, 'Google it.' Don't go after a keyword just because it's got a big number next to it. Search for it, because it's not always what you think it is. Sometimes, what Google's actually serving isn't appropriate for you and you're not going to rank there even if you really try to. You should always be looking for those other opportunities."

Can you change the type of content that Google serves up for a particular keyword phrase, or should you just accept it?

"I think you should do both. If you believe that what you're putting out there is genuinely a really good result for that query, you've got to try. If you produce something that's exactly the same as the other successful articles, you still might not get in. You might as well try and do your absolute best, even if it is slightly different. It might not work, but we're nothing if not a little bit experimental in SEO. If you think that it is going to be the best answer for that query, put it out there.

If that format isn't working for you, take elements from what is doing well. Maybe blog content is what's coming up, but you want to serve a product page. Maybe there are elements from those blogs that you can take and tweak.

Eventually, you might just give up and produce what is getting ranked for everybody else to get onto page one. However, I think you should always be optimistic and try to produce something that is unique and better than everyone else, rather than just doing the same."

How do you identify who to speak to and how do you reach out?

"Identifying people and getting them to want to speak to you is sometimes quite difficult. The best strategy I found was inviting them to critique what I was doing and give me their input. I would set up collaboration sessions on individual topics I was covering.

For example, that might have been Accessibility in the Digital Workplace. Creating a digital workplace that works for everybody is really empowering for people who have certain requirements or experience barriers in the office environment. It's a good thing to have in a big business. I was able to talk to sales teams who have clients and customers with specific requirements and I was able to speak to our own digital accessibility manager. Then, I was able to get all of their points of view onto a page that I was creating. It was really insightful.

I would run this for every single topic. I would have different people show up for different things because people care more about some things than others, which is fine. You start to build a network of people who know who you are, know what you care about, and know that you're interested in what they have to say. When you invite people to help you, they're more likely to come to you later when they have new insights and observations.

I'm also lucky enough to have a Competition Analyst in the business who purely focuses on our competition. She said, 'We're a Microsoft Gold partner. None of our competitors are saying this and it's something we're not taking advantage of.' In two seconds, I put it on the website. Now, that USP (that no one really knew about) is being promoted, and it is because of those relationships.

In terms of FAQs, the sales team is constantly talking to customers. If they're getting the same questions all the time, help them out and put those questions somewhere so people can easily find that information. It saves them time in their pitch because they're not talking about stuff that can easily be answered."

What type of content should you be producing as a result of conversations with product evangelists?

"Our 'AI-Powered Intranet' content was product-led, and the product evangelists were really helpful. They noticed that our competition was talking about AI, but they weren't saying much about it. They were just saying that they use it. I worked with them to pull out all the features of the AI we work with and explain how we use it. We have AI that will help you write an article, we have AI that will translate the captions on a video into another language, etc.

AI can seem a bit scary. It affects all of us in all of our industries, and explaining how we are utilising it is super helpful for our customers. They can come and read about all the tangible things that could benefit them, as an internal comms manager or an internet manager, for example. They can then identify where it can save them loads of time and see that our software already has that capability.

The product team has a roadmap of all the things they want to do to improve the product. They're already looking ahead and being proactive. Pick out what they're thinking and talking about and turn those ideas into landing pages. Do a little bit of tweaking here and there and keep an eye on it and the keywords that come in after you go live. Obviously, when it's zero search volume, you can't identify the H1 and the title tag as easily beforehand. Sometimes you have to put it live, monitor it, and see which phrases are getting picked up more than others. It's a learning curve."

Would you also partner with paid search and test by driving paid traffic to those landing pages?

"Absolutely. My paid search counterpart is incredibly helpful, and we work together on quite a lot of things. They are really helpful with simple things like adding 'award-winning', 'best', or other little phrases into your title tag or meta description, which is going to improve your click-through rate.

The other day I had a page go live that wasn't quite ranking for what I thought it would rank for. There's a selection of terms that could all be relevant. I said to lovely Hanna in PPC, 'Could you please test these and tell me which ones work best?' Then, I was able to use that data. In this instance, the topic was collaboration software, but there are loads of different ways that you can describe that in the industry.

I give PPC 10 or 20 keywords that are all saying the same thing, they go and test those, then they tell me which one I need to optimize for. I can sit back, drink a cup of tea, and go over the results."

Are you using author schema to try and build a profile of the individuals that you're featuring on your pages?

"It is a work in progress. I don't have it currently, but it is on the roadmap. Watch this space.

We have identified our thought leaders who are being promoted on LinkedIn, they are doing webinars, and they are speaking at conferences. Those are our people, and we want to make sure that, from a Google perspective, they have author pages, and they are at the bottom of the articles we want to have a bit of clout behind. It can't just say, 'published by Unily'. No one cares. No one cares what a company has to say. People care what humans have to say.

I was thinking about Dragon's Den earlier. Why is that such an interesting TV show? Why is that even a TV show at all? It's because it's really interesting to watch people who are passionate about the topic, the business, the USPs, and the market. It's what makes good television."

If an SEO is struggling for time, what should they stop doing right now so they can spend more time doing what you suggest in 2024?

"I'm going to reiterate part of what I said last year because it echoes what I'm talking about today: stop creating content for content's sake. If you are a content writer and your KPI is to do four articles a month, or two articles a week, or post X many things – if it is a number, it is a rubbish KPI.

It is a rubbish KPI if it is an amount because you should be thinking so much deeper than just getting it out the door. Each piece of content needs to have a KPI – whether it's traffic, conversions, or shares – aand you want to achieve those. Write for that, not just because you have to. Stop creating content for content's sake."

Are all metrics equally accepted by marketing directors nowadays or do marketing directors still prefer certain metrics for SEO?

"I was really hoping I wasn't going to have to say this today, but it depends. It depends on the boss. Ultimately, conversions are what counts. However, if you have a good strategy in place that is looking at things like shares and coverage, then that's absolutely important.

If your strategy doesn't care about that, and it's more about getting traffic because you know that some of it will convert, then those are the KPIs that are important. It really depends on the overall strategy of that business and the marketing strategy."

Paige Hobart is SEO Manager at Unily, and you can find her over at Unily.com.

Invest in creativity and make your copywriting more human – with Bibi "The Link Builder" Raven

Bibi "The Link Builder" Raven from BibiBuzz also has a strong belief in the power of the people. She says that investing in the humans behind your content is what will make it truly great.

Bibi says: "Make your copywriting human-focused first.

A lot of people are using AI and trying to have it pass AI detectors. However, most language models are based on similar copy and they overuse phrases that are cheesy and obvious.

It's become very easy to start detecting what's written by AI – not necessarily by using AI detectors, but by human readers themselves.

If you want to have a unique brand voice or you want to stand out, it's really important that you still invest in creativity – whether that's in a really good editor or a great copywriter."

Is it possible to prompt AI to write with a brand's voice and a personality, without using repetitive, generic phraseology?

"It is. If you like a specific writer (like Samantha Irby who is one of my favourite writers), you can prompt the AI to write in the style of that copywriter. The problem is that, once it gets into more long-form content, all those phrases and structures still start to creep in.

I'm sure it's possible to use AI in that way, but a lot of blogs and websites are going to use it blindly, and all those things are going to pass through. Then it's going to be very easy to detect, and humans are going to get tired of that as well."

What do you think about the legality/morality of an AI copying a popular writer's style?

"If I was a writer and I saw everybody writing in my style, I think that would be horrible. At the same time, it's also part of creative evolution. People learn first by copying the masters and then trying to give it their own twist.

As a writer, you should trust that it is really hard to copy your creativity. As you're evolving, all the people who are stuck at the mediocre level, the only thing they can do is make a watered-down version of you.

If I was a writer, I would sue the AI, because I want to know what they are trained on and whether they are using your copy without permission. However, it's also unstoppable, so I wouldn't be too anxious about it. You're not going to be outdone by other people using AI to copy your voice."

What does human-first copywriting mean in terms of using AI?

"I use AI all the time, but I don't lose my creativity and critical thinking. I always apply that as a layer on top of any work that I am doing with AI. I use it as a bouncing partner as well, for ideas, because AI is sitting on a huge mountain of knowledge. I think I would be stupid if I didn't use it.

I don't always use it to embellish the ideas that I already have. It depends on the situation. Sometimes I don't have an idea yet and I just start talking to the AI. In that case, it's more like a conversational partner. If I don't have an idea, I might ask it what kind of stuff people would be interested in if they like Taxi Driver or something like that. Then they come up with those ideas and we go back and forth. It's more of a conversation."

What kind of content are you looking to get out of the AI?

"I don't use AI for long-form stuff, I still use human writers, but I do use AI for email copy – like for outreach emails. When you have an email, it is made up of certain elements: you have an intro, a segue, a subject line, etc. An intro can come from different types of ideas. For instance, it can come from a trend that's going on in a specific niche. I'll ask Bing what the trends are for popcorn right now, or something like that, and then I can use that for the intro.

However, an intro can also be a different type of thing. It can be a shower thought. Maybe I'll ask Bing or BARD to come up with shower thoughts around electric cars. It's a really cool thing because the shower thoughts are usually less obvious and, in that way, more creative.

I have the element, like the intro, and then there are all these different methods I can use to make that element interesting. I'll just talk to AI and ask it to create jokes, shower thoughts, or deep questions about that topic. Then it just goes back and forth. That's how I build the template up."

How can you be confident that your human writers aren't using AI and would that concern you?

"I use a writing agency for the guest posts that we write for the clients, and I have worked with them for years. I know the owner, and she's not a huge fan of AI. She does use it sometimes, but she doesn't use it for the articles.

Of course, you never know, but I trust her so I know that she's not letting her writers use a one-click AI writer. They might use it for parts of the copy or to come up with ideas but they're not producing it in one go with an AI writer.

I don't use AI detectors. They work for a couple of weeks, and then they stop working because AI is evolving so fast. You could still do it. In the end, though, you have to be able to recognise good copy. An average writer can also produce a rubbish piece of content. Use your critical thinking.

We also have an editor within the company who does the last proofing of all the articles, and a human writer can be just as bad as the AI. Google are saying that you can use AI content if you want but you need to make sure that it's great for the user. In the future, AI might actually start producing outstanding content, but it's not there yet."

Do you define an individual brand voice when you create articles and how do you ensure that the voice is consistent and appropriate for the client?

"I do a lot of guest post pitching, so it's more about where the guest post could be published than it is about the voice of the client. The writers that we use always check what kind of style or voice the prospect site is using – and that's nothing new.

You can prompt AI to write in a specific tone of voice or style but our writers are not using AI."

Are there any trends in the type of content that clients prefer at the moment?

"There are two different types of content that I create. One is for the clients themselves, like a linkable asset that can attract passive links and is easy to build links to. The other type is guest posts, which are published on other people's sites.

When we talk about guest posts, it's usually very simple. People are happy with plain text articles, and then they add their own stuff to it. For clients, one thing that works really well, which is more dictated by me, is stats and trends pieces. Those are very easy to build links to and can attract a lot of passive links every year. I come up with that idea, and then they will have some visuals or something, but nothing too fancy.

I use Ahrefs for a lot of content ideation for linkable assets and, in particular, their Content Explorer. When I do research, I reverse engineer the type of question that people have, not necessarily the topic. Then I look at the results and see if it's applicable for the client's audience or if it's something that I could translate to the client's audience.

For instance, when you go to the Content Explorer and you type in 'how many', you can start filtering by 'how many backlinks is it getting' or 'how many Pinterest shares', etc.

Then things start popping up and you can see which topic people are looking for or linking to the most that is related to something countable – a statistic, a piece of data, or a fact. That gives me an idea for a stats or trends piece where I can combine all those different things together.

Sometimes, I do some link-building for it and the client boosts it with some ads. The cool thing is that, once it starts picking up links, that stats piece or trends piece has many different data points within it. The people who are linking to it will usually only concentrate on around three of those. That gives you a lot of insights into what people find most interesting. You will see that it often has to do with money, like how many dollars there are in a specific niche. People are really interested in that.

It was something I was already doing but I was inspired by Stacey MacNaught, and she has spoken a couple of times about how to use these stats pieces as linkable assets. Definitely look her up because she has some great ideas."

Do you tend to search the phrase that you're thinking of writing about and then look at the results on the SERP to see what else exists there?

"Yes. I would start to look into which keywords you have for that phrase, variations of that phrase, etc. For every keyword, look at who's ranking on it, and that becomes part of the brief.

The writers that I use do their own research, but I can just give them all these examples, inspiration, and sources, and then they start putting the whole piece together."

If an SEO is struggling for time, what should they stop doing right now so they can spend more time doing what you suggest in 2024?

"What has helped me is working within my own schedule. I can't concentrate for too long and sitting for a long time is really unhealthy for me because it hurts my knees and I have to go to physical therapy. Now, I use a Pomodoro timer. I work for 25 minutes, then I take a 5-minute moving break, and then every hour I go outside and play basketball or something for 15 minutes. If possible, I only work from 11 till 3.

The cool thing about that is that I am way more focused and productive in my work than I would be if I worked 8 hours. Everybody has to figure it out for themselves, but I think the 9 to 5, 40-hour work week is a construct from the Industrial Revolution because they wanted to have kids in school and people in the factories. We should let it go as the only possible schedule.

It's also really unhealthy when you combine that with desk work. If you ask an SEO about their health problems, so many of those are related to spending too many hours behind the screen. You should try to focus more on your health.

Don't let other people dictate your schedule, you need to find a way to work that is best for you. Nothing is set in stone; make it clay and mould it to your own needs."

Bibi Raven is Head Chicken at BibiBuzz, and you can find her over at BiBiBuzz.com.

Put the human and the author first to differentiate your content – with Lidia Infante

Lidia Infante from Sanity suggests that the rise of AI is only making the human more important when it comes to content. Her advice is to focus your attention on both the human reader and the human writer.

Lidia says: "Embrace and accept that AI has changed the economics of content. Being able to create loads of content that meets user intent and responds to high-search-volume queries is no longer a competitive advantage.

Differentiation is key. You either have to provide the best possible content and understand your audience the best, or have an extremely recognisable brand. Creating content is just table stakes now. Anybody can go and ask ChatGPT to write content for them.

This is not necessarily a negative for good SEOs. If your whole strategy has revolved around copying whatever the top 10 ranking people are doing and regurgitating it into a blog post of your own, then you are in trouble. However, if you're creating strategies that put the user first, then you can really benefit from the flood of bad content we are about to see on the web and differentiate yourself by making truly audience-led content."

How do you put the user first when you're creating your content?

"It's not just the user, it's also the author. Try to bring out the particular opinion and specific anecdotes and examples that your subject matter experts have. Make that shine through in the content. You need to strike a delicate balance between brand voice guidelines and the tone of voice that these people have. Make your authors shine.

Recently, I was part of the Blue Array Academy Summer of SEO giveaway, where a lot of people applied to get a scholarship for a Blue Array course through me. I decided that I wanted to read all of the applications and go through them.

So many of them were written through ChatGPT and they didn't let the human shine. I read those applications about 'how passionately they feel about their training', and it was very obvious that there was no human behind it. The applications that actually touched me and ended up successfully receiving the scholarship were the ones that told me a story about them – with a genuine, unique differentiation of the human that was talking to me.

You can use AI for content repurposing, editorial tasks, improving readability, and even creating the content in some cases – if you're doing very good user research, to begin with. However, you need to be speaking from a human to a human."

Can you prompt an AI to create more human content, and incorporate things like anecdotes within the text?

"You can, if you give it those anecdotes. If you don't, it's going to be using the same ones that everyone else is getting. This is more evident when you're working at scale. Everybody has their own tone of voice and their own inflexions when they speak. Personally, I get very excited, I make a lot of faces, my voice goes up and down, and I convey a lot of emotion when I speak.

A generic, unprompted, plain AI is going to be outputting boring sludge. However, an AI that's been prompted to be funny in the way that I'm funny, or that's been shown my humanly written content before, can output something that replicates my tone of voice. You can create good content through prompting an AI, and you can even create content that channels the human.

When I was reading all of those applications, when I read the first one that was created by AI, I thought that person had put a lot of work into it. Then

I read the next one, and it was the same, and the next one was the same as well. They had the same structure and the same tone. They had literally just copy-pasted the list of questions from the application into ChatGPT and it had regurgitated those same standard answers.

I create some of my social media content through ChatGPT because it helps me scale my own content repurposing and content distribution. What I do, however, is prompt it very clearly and use examples of my tone of voice and previous content to say what I want to say. I give it instructions like, 'Be friendly, be approachable, be warm, be helpful.', which are all part of my unique tone of voice."

Do you need to be thorough and not rely on the AI to create content without input?

"It's not just about being thorough. Anybody can prompt it thoroughly and offer it a very extensive, detailed list of facts that they want to incorporate. You want to brief it to speak like you and have a voice. Brief it to replicate the things that make your voice unique, and brief it to let your human experiences shine.

I work with a ghostwriter who interviews some of my subject matter experts so that we can accelerate the amount of content by subject matter experts we're creating. Instead of dedicating two weeks to writing something that they're not good at writing and don't want to write, they dedicate one hour to get interviewed by my ghostwriter, and 20 minutes to review the content. I had to brief my ghostwriter to speak in the first person, as if they were the author, and to not remove their anecdotes and specific examples from their extensive working experience.

You don't just want to describe the type of content they're working on or their theory on multi-site CMSs. If you have an expert who's had one mishap they'd like to talk about, don't remove it just because it's not on the brief. It's adding colour. Include that human element in your content strategy, whether you're creating it with AI or with something else. Bring the human author into it.

In a year's time, I might be using an interviewer or a reporter who asks the questions, and then a transcript AI that identifies key phrases and structure and transforms it into an article. That's going to take a lot of prompting, a lot of prompt engineering, and a lot of work. Maybe I'll still be using a ghostwriter in a year but I don't think I will in 3-5 years."

What is the role of schema now?

"I use schema markup in combination with AI, and that's really fun. To put the human at the centre, for the sake of both the author and the reader, I like to highlight my author's expertise. In order for their expertise and their author bio to be as EEAT-friendly as possible, I give them a template, they fill out some questions, and I build out a very EEAT-friendly bio.

I have a GPT-driven engine read those bios and output knowsAbout schema and detailed person schema that includes their qualification and their job role. If I just published that, it wouldn't do great. It does not pass validation standards at all. It needs an extra layer, so I go on to schema.org validation and I tweak the JSON because it's making that up, for the most part. I tweak the JSON and feedback the warnings and errors from the schema validator into the AI until the schema is perfect.

This is my very first iteration. When I manage to do it at scale, it's going to be huge – and you can do this for authors. You want to nest that author's schema into the article so that search engines don't have to jump to the author's URL to explicitly learn what they know about and their EEAT. Nest it into the article and be as explicit as possible with your schema.

Then, in the article, you can also combine different tools and different uses of AI to output what this article is about using schema. That combination of AI, the expertise of the author, and schema markup is going to really win for you in 2024."

Are you using ChatGPT natively for this or is it in combination with other software?

"You can use the ChatGPT API within a piece of software that you write yourself. You can connect the API to systems that you're making for yourself, which is what I'm doing. If you want to do it at scale, then that's what you should do. There is some third-party software that can approximate this, but

I'm not currently using it at the moment.

You can also ask for help. I married a developer, so I will bring him over and ask him to install Node.js for me or how to get my Python going. With a little bit of curiosity, perseverance, and some assistance (especially free assistance), you can get those apps running.

Something that people don't understand is prompting over prompts. When I was developing tone-of-voice guidelines for my personal brand (for me, as a human), I fed it a bunch of articles as examples. However, if I were to re-feed all of those articles to the engine every time, I would run out of tokens or it would become too costly to run the API. You can tackle this in many different ways but there are two that I prefer.

First, give it your content and ask it to create a prompt for itself that would make it speak using your tone of voice guidelines, then it does, and you can just copy-paste that prompt rather than inputting those articles each time. Once it's outputted the prompt, you can also ask it, 'What fragments of the text did you use that were most relevant for creating these prompts?' Then, you take those fragments and you now have two layers: the prompt and the fragments. With both, you can ask ChatGPT to integrate them together so that it provides its own examples of your tone of voice."

If an SEO is struggling for time, what should they stop doing now so they can spend more time doing what you suggest in 2024?

"Stop writing content for the sake of writing content. Search volumes are a guideline but a lot of the searches that happen every day are completely new. You need to understand your audience and what they need – and talk to them. You can even use AI to interview them and extract key phrases from that conversation. Make the content that they say they need, not just the content that has volume.

Don't sacrifice quality and helpfulness for quantity. Maybe reduce the number of blog posts that you think you're going to write from 10 to 5 – and make those 5 better researched.

If you have started in an organisation that already has thousands of articles that don't really get much traffic, then evaluate why those articles aren't driving profit. First, figure out why that content is not performing and classify it into groups based on the cause. Is it very outdated? Does it not matter anymore? Put that in a group. Is it not performing because it's not optimized? Put that in another group. Is it not performing because the search intent for the query has shifted, but it performed in the past? Also, what does 'not performing' mean? Is it not performing organically? Do people navigate to it from the site? Does it get any engagement? Does it get any links? You want to know all of these things.

Out of that information, you can make informed decisions on what to do for each group. If the search intent has shifted, you might be able to rebuild the content to fit the new search intent. If it's not optimized, you can try to optimize and evaluate it in three months' time. Take the right approach but understand why that content isn't working first.

You might find that somebody has started writing nonsense content that's not related to the core concepts of the brand. They might just have created it because it had high volume. In that case, you want to map what the brand is about. What is the core product? What is the problem that the product solves? What is the audience that you are solving this problem for? What other problems does this audience have? That would become your content universe. Anything that doesn't fit that content universe needs to go."

Lidia Infante is a Senior SEO Manager at Sanity, and you can find her over at Lidia-Infante.com.

Harness informational content on your e-commerce site – with Jack Chambers-Ward

Jack Chambers-Ward from Candour has spotted an un-tapped market for people working in e-commerce: informational content that helps users research, understand, and explore the products they are buying.

Jack says: "We should be harnessing more informational content for our e-commerce sites.

When we're working in e-commerce, a lot of us focus on product pages, category pages, and lovely transactional search intent pages. However, there's so much value in offering content for people in the research stages, both pre-purchase and post-purchase. There's so much value in offering informational content for people looking to buy and people who have already bought something and are looking to make comparisons to other products. There is a lot of opportunity there.

With the ways Google has been shifting, with things like EEAT and talking more about building trust, experience, expertise, and authoritativeness, we need to rethink our overall content strategy. Don't just chuck blog posts onto your e-commerce site and hope for the best. You need a longer-term, more thought-out strategy."

Can informational content help at every stage of the customer journey?

"It can help across the journey.

For pre-purchase, pros and cons articles are a good example. Google has been pushing for content that is honest about your products, not just saying, 'We have the best product in the world. This is why you should buy it.' Being honest about the pros and cons establishes trust with search engines, but that honesty also builds up trust with your users and customers as well.

If you read an article that is very preachy about a particular product or service compared to an article that is very honest (perhaps explaining what you don't do that competitors do well while highlighting what you are good at), you will gravitate towards the more honest brands.

For post-purchase, how-to guides are great: how to use the service, how to get the most out of it, and how to use the products. I've been doing a lot of DIY since I bought my house earlier this year, and so many e-commerce sites have content explaining how to use their products in specific situations. That has been really useful for me. It makes me think that, if they've got really good guides, they know what they're talking about – so maybe I should buy from them in the future.

The really big value of this is the lifetime value of that customer. Returning customers is a nice thing to have, and it can be pretty competitive and challenging in a lot of different niches. Then, they might become brand evangelists who say, 'I read this fantastic article on this website about how to use this product, you should buy it from them as well.' Getting that word-of-mouth and having people talk about your brand because you're offering informational, unbiased content is a really powerful tool."

How does informational content fit into how-to articles?

"How-to is an important part of the post-purchase journey. You may have bought the product, but you need to learn how to use it. Things like FAQs are a huge part of that. There are so many easy ways to find these kinds of questions, like People Also Ask (PAA) data on Google search. That is a rich well of content. You know people are asking these kinds of questions so you should be answering them.

At any given stage of the potential purchase journey for a user, you should be there to answer their question. If you're not, somebody else will be.

Something I've been really pushing for recently is having your content across multiple formats. If you have a text article, you should have a video version or an embedded video within that article. People are going to be looking for video. I talked about DIY earlier; people are going to search for DIY content on YouTube.

You need to be available on other platforms, like podcasts. We're creating content through audio, video, and text right now. It's especially important from an accessibility standpoint. Audio and video versions of your articles will allow more people to access, understand, and process your content."

Is there an ideal length for how-to articles?

"I'm not going to give a specific word count. It should be as long as it needs to be to cover all of the questions you can find. This is an important part of the research stage. Have a conversation with your sales team or your client's sales team and understand what kind of questions customers are asking from that point of view. Combine that with PAA data, feedback forms, Google reviews, Trustpilot comments, and any other sources of information. Answer as much as you can and cover as much as you can.

There's always an opportunity to update it later on. A lot of people post and forget, but PAA data changes so swiftly, and sales change a lot too. Sales teams receive new complaints and questions every day. It's worth going back and updating those articles as you go. Don't just answer five questions and leave it for another year."

How do you determine which are the most ideal articles to start writing first?

"From an SEO perspective, the PAA data is important. Then, it's about understanding what the most common questions are. If you have a few dozen salespeople, ask them, 'What are the top three things customers are asking for?' If you can narrow it down to a handful, that's always useful.

You've got to prioritise using the data you've got, and PAA is a great place to start. Over the last few years, we've been learning how powerful PAA data can be."

How do you incorporate EEAT into informational content for e-commerce sites?

"You've got to assign an author. Make sure you have about pages for any writers and list their expertise, their qualifications, why they're relevant to this business, and why they're relevant to the product and the service.

I worked with a client who deals with medical supplies, and you need to know that they are quality products. It's on the YMYL side of things. You need to clearly demonstrate that you know what you're talking about. You can show your expertise with things like pros and cons articles, explaining your first-hand experiences with the products. Real-life expertise and experience go a long way. Google have added that extra E to EEAT for a reason."

How do you deal with seasonal landing pages where the search volume fluctuates over time?

"Keeping a year-neutral URL is key, so you can maintain that single URL when the season comes back around again. If you're building up to Black Friday, you can have a page like 'yourdomain/BlackFriday' as a single neutral landing page that doesn't include '2024' or '2025'. As soon as you change that, you lose some of the power of that page. Essentially, if you can avoid changing that URL, you should. You want to have neutral, evergreen pages that will work year after year, that you can keep coming back to.

Keep them up to date as well because people start searching for things way earlier than you think. People are searching for Christmas stuff as we're speaking, in September. My mother-in-law brought a Christmas present through the door the other day, and I was horrified, but people are already searching for this kind of stuff.

I was talking to a client the other day about getting ready for Christmas and they were already on it. They're ready to go 3/4 months in advance; they're planning stocks and buying all of the necessary things. There's a lot of lead-up to it. You could just work on seasonal pages all year long and keep yourself busy with the amount that goes into big sales days and big holidays."

What do you do with a seasonal page after the event?

"Keep it linked but don't highlight it. When the season is coming up, you really want to highlight it and link to it on the home page. If there's an option to link to it in the main menu or highlight it in the central nav, do that.

However, once the season is over, don't noindex it or orphan it. You will lose traction over the long term, and there is a reason to keep those links healthy. Just don't shout about it as much. If there are already internal links from product pages or articles, and people can still purchase through that page, there's no harm done.

A lot of people would completely remove that page and 404 it, or even 410 it. Then you lose a lot of traction. You don't build up that consistent evergreen content you want. There's a lot of value in keeping that URL going, even if it is just bubbling away in the background while it's not the primary focus of the business.

I was working on this for a client earlier this year. We created a little sales section which included everything that was currently on sale, but it also included links to seasonal deals that come up each year. We had wedding season deals, Easter deals, Valentine's Day deals, etc. You can still buy those products year-round, so the links are still valid, but you're not necessarily shouting about it.

That central landing page is a hub page for all the different promotional and seasonal things, which works well for people if they do end up there. It also lets people leave if they land there by accident somehow, and want to access other products and find the rest of your range."

How do you optimally structure FAQ pages?

"FAQ page schema is hugely important. Google have shifted their focus on a lot of what is going on with FAQ schema, but it's still incredibly relevant. You are still marking up that data and information to make it easier to find. You're giving Google a little waypoint.

Even if they're not going to be part of featured snippets as much, and they're reducing their overall visibility, there is still a lot of value in FAQs. There are quite a few different places you can go with FAQs, particularly in regard to search intent. There's value to having FAQs on your product pages and there's value to having standalone FAQs.

If they're for the overall business, having an FAQ page covering a bit of everything is a valuable approach. You can also have categories and include them in your blog posts, and then link to those product pages where they answer product-specific questions. If you think there is transactional intent behind a query, and they're probably wanting to buy this product, then it's reasonable to include those FAQs on the product pages themselves. You're targeting that transactional intent with that page already."

If an SEO is struggling for time, what should they stop doing right now so they can spend more time doing what you suggest in 2024?

"Stop disavowing links. Chances are Google already knows about them and has already discredited those bad links. A lot of sites will get false positives from third-party tools, so don't worry about disavowing links.

Unless you know you've been hacked and you have some serious problems, like a security flag on Search Console, don't worry about disavowing links in 2024."

Jack Chambers-Ward is Marketing & Partnership Manager at Candour, and you can find him at WithCandour.co.uk.

Reduce, reuse, and recycle the content that you have already produced – with Natalie Arney

It's not all about stocking up on brand-new content, though. SEO Consultant Natalie Arney wants you to think more sustainably and spend some time upcycling the content you already have.

Natalie says: "Don't neglect the power of reducing, reusing, and recycling content that already exists. This doesn't mean just content on your site, but any kind of content that you've produced."

Are these all part of the same thing or would you apply them to different pieces of content separately?

"It varies. One way to look at it is to think about it as part of your traditional content audit – and to think about content decay. A lot of people talk about content decay and think about whether to remove or repurpose content when you're using a content audit template. A lot of the content auditing templates out there refer to keep, remove, reuse, etc. This is the kind of depth that you can go to.

However, we're not just looking at the content audit itself. We're also looking at other things around it. It's aimed at all different kinds of businesses. It can be applicable whether you're seeing the signs and impact of content decay already, whether you have been hit by a helpful content audit or a content quality audit, whether you're worried about either of those things, or whether you just want to gain a competitive advantage over your competition."

How do you determine what needs to be done?

"With reducing, you're thinking about whether you want to remove the content altogether rather than shortening it. When you're auditing content, there are some very long guides on the web that might be better off split into separate articles, for example. You might have created that long guide as a piece of skyscraper content for link acquisition or to try and rank for as many keywords as possible. Now, intent is so important, and making sure that there is a clear intent for a piece of content is key.

If you've got a massive piece of content, the intent might be confusing – not just for Google but also for the user. That's especially true if things like the H1 and heading don't align with what is actually covered in the article. Look at what is covered in that piece and think about what you want the intent to be, then consider whether everything in that article meets or fulfils that intent. If it doesn't, are there ways that you can break that content down into separate pieces that fulfil their own intents?

The user might be looking for more informative and educational content at the top of the funnel, but you've got a lot of conversion-led content on that page. You need to think about whether you should have that piece of content as something more educational, with clear calls to action for conversion points, then create a separate conversion-led piece for the user to approach when they're at the bottom of the funnel. Obviously, the user that's going to be hitting your site could be at any stage. They might come back to your website, or they might not, but you need to make sure that the intent of that content is aligned. That is the first thing to have a look at and see whether you can split that piece of content up or refresh it."

Do you still look at things like whether the URL has been indexed, whether the page gets any traffic, or whether it has any backlinks?

"That would be part of it. Besides looking to see whether this content needs to be refreshed or not, content audits are key and there are loads of different templates out there that you can use. If you're agency side, you might be able to use a template that's standard in your agency or you might be able to get some from different sources across the internet and tweak them to make it your own.

While you're doing this, make sure that you don't just look at search content. Look at search and social content, and look at search and social stats as well. That will allow you to then pick and prioritise what you do or don't want to optimize and keep.

Then you're asking, should this piece of content be indexed? Is it indexed? How much traffic is it getting? How many keywords is it ranked for? How many shares on social has it had? Has it got any traffic from other sources, like email? You also want to look at things like whether that piece of content has acquired any backlinks.

Then, on top of your content audit, you may also want to analyse the content for EEAT. Again, there are some really good templates out there (Aleyda Solis' one is fantastic). Make the existing content, and also any new content, meets those EEAT guidelines. That includes making sure you've got quotes. Look at what your competitors are doing and do better than them by adding in your own business insights, etc. Those are the kinds of things that are included in those EEAT templates.

However, it's really key to look at how your current content is performing. It might not be indexed but it might be getting some social traffic. That gives you an insight. It tells you that the content is helpful but, at the same time, there might be an additional reason why it isn't in Google. For example, it could accidentally have a noindex on it, or it might be missing something key that all of your competitors offer. It's down to you to figure out how you are going to get this content indexed and how you are going to add value to it from there."

Do you determine whether or not that piece of content is providing value to your user by comparing it against the EEAT guidelines?

"Partly, but there are a lot of additional things that you need to consider here. For example, if you've got a customer service or customer support department in your business, there's a lot of value to get from there.

However, it is really important that your content meets those guidelines, and there are lots of different ways that you can make sure that it does. You can add your own insights and sure that, if you speak about a study, you link to that study. These are simple little things that you can do to make sure that you're supporting what you're saying. It's like writing an essay at university. If someone were to mark that, they would be asking where you got that information from.

Obviously, a lot of people are talking about LLMs at the moment. A phrase that I often use is about how LLMs are stochastic parrots and humans are not – meaning they are good at generating convincing language, but they do not actually understand the meaning of the language they are processing. Emily M. Bender wrote a fantastic article about it that you should read, and she coined this phrase.

Basically, you need to make sure that whatever you say is supported and that you're not just linking to things but bringing in quotes from authoritative sources – like someone in your business or an external person of interest.

Tereza Litsa gave a really fantastic talk at BrightonSEO about providing value and how to maintain the human element while using AI for content marketing. We're talking about good quality, helpful content, with the deluge of LLM-generated content that's flooding the internet at the moment. Even if you do create content with an LLM (with ChatGPT, BARD, Jasper, etc.), how are you providing that human value within that piece of content?

At the end of the day, it's all about whether your content provides value. Does it meet intent? Is it quality? That's not just from an SEO standpoint, but also thinking about it being shared across multiple channels. If you're wondering how to tell whether a piece of content is good enough quality, ask yourself whether you would be confident sharing that piece of content on your CEO's LinkedIn profile. Why? It should be cross-channel too. You need to be creating content that serves beyond SEO as well."

How often do you review your content?

"It depends. I've worked for lots of different businesses and, to build a workflow, we usually make sure to look at content at least once a year. Have a look and see whether that piece of content has been refreshed within the year and, if not, whether it needs refreshing.

Refreshing a piece of content doesn't mean changing that date. Google are clamping down on that because a lot of people have been getting away with it for too long. Look at things like search trends and how different phrases have changed. Look at social trends. There are lots of different ways that you can refresh that content.

Overall, you should look at it on a yearly basis, but you should also keep an eye on trends related to your business or your niche. Use tools like Google Trends, Exploding Topics – and AlsoAsked to see how People Also Ask questions and queries have changed. If there's been a demand increase related to the topic your article was about, you may need to add a paragraph or include a subheading about that, and build it into your article, to provide that extra value so that you're not left behind."

Is it ever worthwhile focusing on evergreen content that you never have to update?

"Even evergreen content should be refreshed, because things change. If you were creating an evergreen content piece about what SEO is, SEO changes a lot. You might have created a piece of content explaining what SEO was a few years ago, and you may want to have that on your website. However, because of the competitive landscape and changes in searcher's needs and the search ecosystem, even the content that you think is more evergreen should be refreshed.

Even evergreen content suffers from content decay. It's such a dynamic world, and your competitors are always going to be looking at you. If you look at bigger players in the financial publishing space, like NerdWallet, they continue to update their evergreen guides. Of course, not everyone has their budget or their SEO focus, so you need to make sure that you prioritise the correct pieces of content and what provides value.

If you see any decrease in traffic or rankings, or you see specific pieces that have been affected by an update, then focus on those. Then, think about prioritisation and what your business aims (or your client's business aims) for the year are. Take those pieces of content and prioritise them."

If an SEO is struggling for time, what should they stop doing right now so they can spend more time doing what you suggest in 2024?

"Stop putting out rushed, poor-quality content that provides little to no value. Focus on what provides value – not just from an SEO standpoint, but for content that is going to be shared across multiple channels.

If you're putting out five short, unresearched, poor-quality pieces of content that don't fulfil any search intents or answer the searcher's questions, they're not going to rank well. Reduce that to one or two pieces of content that are really great quality, rather than rushing content out just to tick the boxes."

Natalie Arney is a Freelance SEO Consultant, and you can find her over at NatalieArney.com.

Validate your long-form content with the help of AI assistants – with Mark Williams-Cook

Whether you're improving what you have, as Natalie suggested, or building new content in the ways that other contributors in this chapter proposed, Mark Williams-Cook from Candour and AlsoAsked says that AI can help ensure that you're doing it the right way.

Mark says: "Use AI assistants to validate your long-form content at scale and see if it's answering your users' intent. The kind of content can include any pages with lots of content on them – even if they're e-commerce category pages.

Generally, companies that have invested in producing content for many years have focused on content quality and understanding what users are searching for. Essentially, this process is for anywhere where you're trying to match complex user intent, which now includes pretty much any business that has a website."

Are you using the validation process to match user intent?

"Yes. If you take on a new client, you'll often do a content audit to try and work out if the content they already have is good.

You can find loads of information about expertise, authority, trust, experience, and knowing what we need to look for in content. You will also have reams of keyword research from all kinds of tools that give us hints as to what users are searching for – and you've got a wealth of experience within the company of what they know about their customers and what they regularly ask.

It's great having all that information but trying to work out if the content that you've got for a particular subject answers all of those questions is a very long, manual task – or it has been. One of the best uses of LLMs now (which leans into their strengths, especially now that they can access live URLs), is using them to feed in that research.

If you put the article title into AlsoAsked, you'll get a few hundred People Also Asked questions out, and you can load those into something like ChatGPT. You can then say, 'Does this URL answer those questions?', and you can very quickly get an idea of where you need to improve that content. It would have taken a very long time to manually go through and pick apart.

You can do this with all different types of keyword research, whether it's People Also Asked data, suggest data, or even content briefs that you're building when you're looking to improve the content. With ChatGPT, there are also opportunities to use things like their API to scale it. If you've got 1,000 or 5,000 pages you need to check, it's possible to make very quick strides into that."

Is ChatGPT your preferred AI tool?

"At the moment, for this particular task, yes. To be honest, I've been very cautious about the use of AI. ChatGPT is built on GPT-4 which is a large language model. The generative part of these algorithms can lead to what's commonly called hallucinations. How they work is they take tokens and make statistical guesses about what comes next.

I've seen people try and use LLMs for things like analysing SEO data and forming strategies, which I don't think they're really capable of doing yet. You'll certainly get an answer that sounds convincing a lot of the time because that's what LLMs do. They give you what sounds like the most probable answer, so they're great at fooling humans.

This particular language analysis task is something I've found, through testing, that LLMs can do with a high level of accuracy. It's useful, and it saves a lot of time and money."

Could you go into more detail about how the validation process works?

"Let's take People Also Ask research as an example. We'll have a public URL which has our keyword research data in. Then, if it's an optimized title, you can just drop the title of the page into Google or AlsoAsked to get a list of nearest intent questions around that topic. You can also amplify that with other things that you know manually or even other suggestions from something like ChatGPT.

Once you have that list of questions in an accessible document online, you can then build a simple prompt by posting your target URL and saying, 'Does this URL answer all of the questions posed on this other URL?' You can also tweak that prompt to get the answers in a table that specifies where it thinks the answer is, highlights any gaps, and maybe even suggests fixes. I've seen that executed really well.

To push that slightly further, you can use the Search Quality Rating guidelines PDF and ask the LLM to evaluate the content against that. It does it well at a basic level but, when it comes down to things like page experience, it gets a little bit confused. It might say that there isn't anything about page experience on the page because it's looking for the content rather than the user experience. You have to be careful where you draw the line.

However, it's really useful for that initial task of going through 2000 pages of existing content for a new client, using some quantitative data about that content from analytics (how many visitors it's getting, how well it ranks, what the engagement metrics are, etc.). At this stage, you've got no idea what the coverage is, and this process can really quickly give you an action plan to start moving things in the right direction."

Would you create a Google Sheet with all those URLs and ask ChatGPT to go through them and see what the content is and what's missing?

"Absolutely. Normally, there will be a pattern on the website for the type of URLs you want to use. You can use a tool like Sitebulb or Screaming Frog to get a list of those URL patterns.

We tend to prioritise them. You can do as many as you like but, when it comes to updating content, there's no point giving someone a work list with three years' worth of content for them to update. You should focus on particular areas of the site because it's good to have a control when you're testing and qualifying the results of what you're doing.

If you've got a website that covers several different categories, you might focus on one particular category and work on improving that content. Then, you can compare that against things you haven't worked on to see the impact you've had (number of keywords ranked for, impressions, organic clicks, etc.), and separate that from something like a Google update."

Would you focus on a category of content first or identify pages that are ranking on page two and aim for quick ranking changes?

"You can't avoid the quick wins; that's always a really good place to start with content. If you have stuff that's not quite in the top few rankings and it's possible to get there, you absolutely want to start there. That's where you'll see an impact.

However, if you want to scale it, you've got to keep track of what you're working on. If you want to work on 50 disparate URLs that fit those criteria, that's fine – as long as you still record them.

There are advantages to having a topical approach because, when you look at rankings, Google will generally favour websites for particular types of categories that are inside one topical area. If you did a Venn diagram, there's normally significant overlap between those URLs that are performing well and are topically related."

Are there any current trends in terms of the type or format of content that might improve an existing page?

"Right now, we're about one week out from the end of the helpful content update, which has seen some massive shifts in how websites have been ranking. Some sites have lost 70/80% of their traffic from what they claim are good pages, but it's too early for me to draw conclusions on that latest sprint.

Personally, I wouldn't focus too much on the pattern of the algorithm or what the algorithm is looking for and instead focus on a higher strategic goal. Do you have a genuine expert answering these questions and are you posing the right questions?

I have seen some patterns in the sites that have been impacted by the latest helpful content update in that they tend to lay out their content too much like an SEO: question-answer, question-answer, question-answer.

The advantage of using an LLM for precisely this kind of task is that, when you ask it whether a specific question is answered within that page or document, the question doesn't need to be explicitly written on the page. If the answer is embedded within a paragraph, the LLM seems to be more than capable of finding that and identifying whether it's been answered.

That's a more natural way of writing but I don't know whether that's a pattern Google's picked up on. It's certainly something that's on my mind when we're giving content briefs to the people who write the content. At Candour, we produce almost no content. We always try and get the correct person to write about it – whether it's an in-house client expert or a freelance writer who has a lot of experience in that topic."

Would you ever allow ChatGPT to also write the content for you?

"You can use it as a starting point for incredibly generic things that you might need to phrase in a certain way. However, I don't think it's a good long-term bet.

Firstly, being an LLM, if ChatGPT can generate a suitable answer for that question, then that question is already objectively solved somewhere else. You are just re-wording it, so you're not adding any additional value.

If you consider the SGE that Google is working on, their strategy has historically been to try and keep users on the SERP – because that's how they can best monetise them. If you, as an SEO or a company, have access to an LLM that can generate an answer to a question, why would Google choose to rank your content when they could generate that answer themselves?

You have to be very careful about where you use AI-generated content. You may not be worried about whether some content ranks and it might still be helpful to users. That's where you can use it. However, for things that you're trying to rank for, I don't think that's a good long-term strategy. You are essentially getting in the way of Google making additional revenue which, in my experience, isn't a good place to be."

If an SEO is struggling for time what should they stop doing right now so they can spend more time doing what you suggest in 2024?

"Stop analysing, auditing, and disavowing toxic or spammy links. In conversations with the SEOs I speak to regularly, that's just taken as read. However, when I share that point of view in other places, I have quite a number of people telling me that I'm wrong and it's really important to look for spammy links.

You will see AI-collaborated articles on LinkedIn that say things like, 'toxic links can harm your website and your brand' and, 'you need to be looking at spam scores and toxic link scores'. Google has very flatly said (and I don't think there's a reason for them to carefully word this) that they discount rather than penalise those kinds of links.

That makes perfect sense to me because, if they put a negative value on what they class as bad links, there would be a whole economy for doing that to your competitors. We've also just seen Bing depreciate their link disavow tool because they're so confident that they can identify them.

In my book, there are a lot of other things you could do that would provide value. I'd rather have another good link than get rid of 10 of what someone says are bad links."

Mark Williams-Cook is Director at Candour and Founder of AlsoAsked, and you can find him at AlsoAsked.com.

11 Internal Links

11 INTERNAL LINKS

Stop neglecting internal links and your link profile – with Bill Hartzer

You can't talk about SEO without discussing links, and Bill Hartzer from Hartzer Consulting takes us right to the roots of your internal links and your link profile with the first tip for this chapter.

Bill says: "We still have to be looking at links and links from other websites. I really love to optimize and increase the number of internal links, but we need to talk a little bit about the link profile of your website and the links from other websites as well."

How deep do you go with links? Are you talking about tier 2, tier 3, or even deeper than that?

"For years and years, we were always looking at just the tier 1 links. Tier 1 is basically another web page out there linking directly to us. In 2024, we need to start looking at tier 2: who is linking to that website that is then linking to us? That would be tier 2. We can even go further beyond tiers 3 and 4, and so forth.

When Trust Flow, Link Juice, PageRank (or whatever you want to call it), passes from one website to the next, your web page gains that credit. You build up a little more authority and trust through those links.

In 2023/24/25, let's go beyond that and start thinking about the next step. Who is linking to that website? How are they getting their trust and authority? In a lot of cases, you can bypass that and go directly to an even higher authority that's linking to a website that would then link to you. You can get even better links by looking at tier 2 and tier 3.

Not to mention the fact that the tier 1 links may be looking good, but, to really evaluate that website you need to know: are they part of a blog network? Are they part of some other kind of link network? Are the links that are linking to you natural? It's about looking at the profiles of competitors and the profiles of the links that you currently have and potentially can get."

If a website that's linking to you lives in an environment that contains links that aren't highly trusted, could that negative authority impact the perception of your site?

"It could definitely have an impact. I think the more likely case, though, is simply the fact that search engines might just be ignoring those links.

If you have a healthcare-related website, you want to get some on-topic links from other healthcare websites. However, one healthcare website might look great at tier 1, but if you look at tier 2, it could contain mostly computer and IT-related websites that are linking to that health website. Trust is being paid forward, but it's not necessarily topical trust or it's not on-topic from tier 3 to tier 2 to tier 1.

You ideally want the network that lives around that site that's linking to your healthcare website to be natural and to be in the appropriate niche."

If you establish that a network that links to you is an environment that you don't want to be in, is disavowing links still an option in 2024?

"Sure, you could disavow them. I would say there's probably a better chance that Google's just ignoring them.

They're now officially saying that disavow is only really for cases where you have some kind of link penalty, unnatural links, etc. We're at the point where Google recognises most link situations and, frankly, they are essentially disavowing certain links already."

How do you use Majestic, and do you use any other tool to dive into the multiple tiers of links that you're reviewing?

"I pretty much have Majestic open all day long, and there are so many different tools that I'm regularly using in Majestic. Anything from Bulk Backlink Checker to Topical Trust Flow, but also exporting links into spreadsheets and sorting them when there are a lot to deal with.

I look at anchor text a lot and, in many cases, that's a very good clue. If it's a certain domain, I want to look at the link graph to make sure that the network or link profile looks more natural than unnatural. Let me tell you, I've seen my share of really unnatural-looking link profiles. Once you get past tier 2, it can be very interesting."

What's the biggest red flag for an unnatural link profile?

"If you're looking at a link graph, you're specifically looking at the dots and the connections between them. If there is a cluster of links anywhere in that view, that's going to be something you want to zoom in on and see.

Maybe there's one website (or two or three websites) from that whole cluster of dots that are very close to each other, that is then linking over to you."

What traits are you looking at to try and establish whether the links have been built unnaturally?

"I'm mostly looking at the fact that there actually is a cluster. It's fairly rare that those are natural links. There are some cases where, let's say, there's a news website and the company or website was linked to from some kind of news source. In today's media environment, a lot of media websites link to each other. In the United States, we have ABC, NBC, Fox, and different local stations, so they all link to each other and they all link to the parent company – CBS, NBC, and so forth. That would be a network and that would typically be fine.

More and more, however, smaller business websites and medium-sized websites (like attorney websites, home inspector websites, real estate websites, and even some healthcare websites) tend to have these unnatural link profiles where there are clusters of links. It can be possible to sever those links or get them removed in certain ways."

Would you ever try to build your own tier 2 links, by building links to the tier 1 links that point directly to your website?

"The more natural (or more 'white hat') way of doing that would basically be through traditional social media. Let's say you write a new blog post on your blog, then you go to your socials and share it.

I did this today. I wrote a blog post for a client and posted it on their website, then I went to their Facebook page, their LinkedIn, their Twitter/X, etc., and created social media posts. Those are links that you're linking. I take a section of that blog post and put it on as a LinkedIn article, then I'm actually sharing and building links to that LinkedIn article that then links back to the original blog post. That's the more natural way of using social media to create links.

There are other ways too. If you're mentioned in the news, you would want to build some links to the article that then some links back to your website to make sure. Mostly, my reasoning behind building those additional links and mentions is to make sure that the search engines crawl those particular pages."

How often should you be analysing your tier 2 links, as an SEO, to see if any clusters appear to be unnatural?

"My process is to analyse the link profile anytime I do a mini SEO audit of a site, where you pull out the crawlers and you crawl. It could be once a month, it could be every three months, or it could be every six months. Also, any time that there's a Google update.

We are going through a Google core update right now, as we're talking about this. When that's done, and you've noticed any ranking changes or you've noticed less traffic, or you look at Google Search Console and you've seen that data start to go down, that's the time to pull out all the tools.

First, crawl the website and make sure that there aren't any issues with the website itself. Then, you go over to Majestic. Are there any new links? Look at the link graph. Are there any clusters that you are not familiar with? Zoom in a little bit and check out some of those."

If an SEO is struggling for time, what should they stop doing right now so they can spend more time doing what you suggest in 2024?

"A lot of people are thinking that they have to build a lot more content. Content, content, content. First, deal with the content, pages, blog posts, and articles that you currently have.

Build more internal links and put a pause on some of that content generation for now. Use a tool like Majestic to see all the pages on the site that Majestic knows about. There are inevitably going to be certain pages that have some links from external websites. Spend some time increasing the internal links to those pages that are a bit more powerful."

Bill Hartzer is CEO at Hartzer Consulting, and you can find him over at Hartzer.com.

Take greater advantage of internal links through a complete internal linking strategy – with Anna Uss

Annu Uss from Synthesia might be even more of an internal links evangelist than Bill, and she has some great advice on how to build a strategy and a framework that you can rely on for years to come.

Anna says: "Take full advantage of internal links and build a full, complete internal linking strategy.

It is important to create an internal link strategy once, build a framework, and then constantly refresh it.

There are also a few elements that can help you incorporate that strategy, like sharing with your team and automating internal links. However, the groundwork needs to be done, and then you need to continuously add to it."

How often do you need to add to your linking strategy?

"You need to add to your linking strategy every time you launch an important page that you want to rank. If you launch a page that targets a high-priority business value keyword, you need to add it to the cheat sheet (which I will talk more about later) and the system.

Then, once you have launched the page, you need to optimize your internal links straight away, if you want that page to be lifted up and served."

How important is having your target keyword phrase within each internal link?

"It is very important. It's a well-known fact that anchor text needs to be descriptive, but we sometimes forget that there can be two, three, or even four variations of the same keyword. All of them are semantically relevant, and they are all equally important.

Don't stop at just selecting one keyword. Select those four combinations and go the extra mile to introduce those variations in your internal linking strategy.

You should even link to your homepage using optimized anchor text that contains those relevant keywords. Use 'homepage' where it is relevant for user experience – in breadcrumbs, navigation, etc. However, within the text and even the rich text on the footer, then link to your homepage using that optimized anchor text."

Is the footer the best place to start your internal link strategy or do you get better value by having those links within the body content?

"Both are very important. A common obstacle for SEOs is that you can't link pages that are very important, SEO-wise, from the top navigation. However, the footer element is your own SEO-owned asset that you can use to make those pages discoverable. Take full advantage of it.

Make sure that footer is as descriptive as possible, by adding rich text describing what your company does. It is also very relevant for the user, who will land on different pages of your site and can always find that snippet of information about what the company does and why they are there.

Also, make sure that you structure the footer nicely. Group the pages and make sure that the groupings make sense. Group your assets in a comprehensive way, but don't be shy about linking your SEO assets there. Sometimes, that's one of the only opportunities you will have to make those assets discoverable from the high-traffic pages."

Is there a maximum number of internal links that you'd want to have on a page?

"I try not to exceed 100-150 links on the page in total, including all the footer links, nav links, body links, internal links, and external links."

Should you change your footer internal links to incorporate the sub-links within the category of certain pages or should they be consistent?

"The footer should be consistent across the whole site. Don't change the footer on specific pages.

Whether or not you choose to include subsections within that footer will depend on how important the subsection is for you. If you specialise in selling specific dotted cushions for blue sofas, and they're something you want to rank for because they are a key product, you may want to include them.

Think logically about how to incorporate that category into the footer in a way that makes sense. You wouldn't want to have 'homepage', 'blue sofas', 'dotted cushions', then 'help centre', etc. You could structure it logically by putting 'most popular products', 'most popular cushions', or 'types of cushions'. There is a range of ways you can approach it.

If it is important for you to rank for that business-crucial keyword, and you think it will drive sales, then add it."

How do you select the key pages to focus on as part of your internal link strategy?

"You want to be looking at both the pages that already bring in a lot of traffic and the pages where you want to increase their chances of ranking. There will be pages that are already ranking number one that you should still include, because the SERP is so competitive that you can't lose out on any aspect of your SEO strategy. You should still have that link there if it is number one and it is driving the business.

You should also include high-business-value keywords that are not ranking yet, but you know that they are core to the business and are going to bring in sales.

However, don't focus solely on traffic. Whether it is a high-volume keyword or a low-volume keyword that will drive sales, it is going to be important. They need to be very business-focused and business-oriented."

Which links do you incorporate within blog posts as part of your strategy?

"A complete internal linking strategy is about first designing the footer, the navigation, and the links that are populated throughout the site in a templated manner. The next stage is more creative and requires a little bit more groundwork.

Start by creating a list of the top pages that drive traffic and conversions. Then, identify a few variations of the keywords that are driving traffic to those pages. You can easily see those in Google Search Console, by clicking on the page that drives traffic and conversions, and looking at the top four keywords (obviously those that are non-branded). These will be your variations.

Document everything as a cheat sheet, and then follow through with it. Share that list with the team and constantly refer to it when you create new content and new pages. You can also use this list for automating your internal link-building strategy"

How do you incorporate automation into your strategy?

"There are so many new types of software that are being developed right now, particularly regarding AI. I'm currently using some software called

Letterdrop for automating internal links on Webflow.

It helps to determine the levels of certainty you can have for your internal link optimization, and I am aiming for the highest level of certainty. I have manually created that cheat sheet list of relevant keywords, uploaded it, and then I can select the number one keyword that the tool suggests for me. It will also suggest other anchor text that will be semantically relevant.

That high level of certainty means that I'm not just relying on Google Search Console. If you only rely on Google Search Console, you might get recommendations of anchor texts that are internally competing with each other – especially if your business focuses on one niche.

If your whole product is about one specific type of software, then that will obviously be mentioned on multiple pages, which is where the confusion might start. For example, 'video creation' can be linked to 'video creation guide', 'video creation feature', and 'video creation help article'. You need to avoid that, and you need to be very consistent that you link 'video creation' to the page that you want to rank."

Can you use these tools to automatically generate links every time relevant keywords are used in your content?

"I wouldn't recommend building links automatically without manual approval, but there are two awesome features of Letterdrop that I have been using recently.

First, you can fix links in bulk. You have a list, you have a page, you have an anchor text and where it can link to, you just click the box and accept 100 links. However, by hovering over those items, you can verify whether each link is in the right place, where you want it to be embedded.

The second feature is that you can replace the text. For example, if you search for the keyword 'AI video editing', but there are only 3 anchor texts like this on the website, you can select the option to replace 'AI video editing' with 'editing' and get 50 more internal links built at the click of a button.

There are many plugins for WordPress that you can start with but it's definitely worth looking into new emerging solutions. They can build custom features for you, you can request things, and they are constantly evolving. That's what I love about SEO: you can always find new exciting things that solve your daily problems."

How do you measure the success of your internal link strategy?

"It's hard to attribute SEO success to one specific thing that you did, but I have conducted specific internal link optimization campaigns and I have seen an increase in rankings for the keywords I optimized.

In one case, we had a single anchor text that linked to several different pages, which caused inconsistencies for a highly competitive keyword with a search volume of over 100,000. We fixed that, replaced the other anchor texts, added new internal links, and optimized the footer, and we moved from position four to position two for that keyword. We didn't do anything else with the page; there were no other changes.

That was just one example. I can't 100% say that the ranking change was directly a result of our linking strategy, but it clearly had an impact. That's how I measure it. I look at the rankings for the anchor text that I have optimized."

If an SEO is struggling for time, what should they stop doing right now so they can spend more time doing what you suggest in 2024?

"Stop going after irrelevant traffic. You might think that it is super relevant traffic for you, but look at the SERP, analyse the search results, and identify the intent. Don't follow the recommendations for commercial, informational, navigational, and transactional intent identifiers that you get from the tools, because they can be too generic.

Look for yourself. Look at the pages that rank, drop things that won't bring value to your business, and focus on things that convert and bring users down the pipeline."

Anna Uss is SEO Lead at Synthesia, and you can find her over at linkedin.com/in/anna-uss/.

Take your internal linking a step further by linking to subcategories from the parent category page – with Katherine Nwanorue

Guiding you even further down the internal linking journey, Katherine Nwanorue from Fusion Inbound has a very particular tip that could change your perspective on your subcategory pages.

Katherine says: "Don't underestimate the power of linking to subcategories from the parent category page.

On most websites, you would link the subcategories on the menu side under the category. This essentially means that the subcategory and other pages on the menu are linked to all pages on the website, which signals that these pages are important.

Some websites stop here but I think you can take it a step further by linking these subcategories to the actual page of the parent category page. That is essentially internal reciprocal linking (linking from the main category page to the subcategory and then from the subcategory page back to the main category page).

The category page itself is a really authoritative page. When you get these relevant keywords for the subcategory pages, mention them on the category page itself, add links to these subcategories, and vice versa, it helps you to improve rankings and clicks in most cases. You're taking advantage of link equity.

It also helps with conversion because it helps you move the visitor down the sales funnel. If you have some content on a category page that recommends a specific type of subcategory, ('consider this product', for example), users can click on that link within the main body content and go to the recommended subcategory where they are likely to convert. All of this translates to better rankings, better clicks, more engagement, and more conversions."

Does having these links in the main body content have a measurably

11 Internal Links

positive impact?

"I've seen really positive results. We worked on a wholesale swimwear brand that had subcategory pages. They were linked to the main menu bar, as usual, but they were not mentioned on the category page or linked back to from those pages. So, we found the relevant keywords that were mentioned and added links to specific subcategory pages.

Within a few weeks of just doing that, we saw really impressive results: over 710 new keywords were gained and we improved rankings for around 500 keywords. The new keywords we gained for those pages were around 43% of the total keywords. It was a really big deal.

In some cases, we were seeing ranking improvements on pages that were not ranking in the first place. We had basically no ranks for these pages and, within a short time, they quickly went to the top 10 and top 3. In some instances, there was no mention of the relevant keywords anywhere on the website. We started looking for some of these keywords, like 'swimsuits under $20', 'size 24 swimwear', etc., that we didn't really optimize for, but we saw great ranking improvements just by doing this.

You should have links in the nav menu as well, but you don't have to put those links in the menu alone. Go a step further and make it more meaningful for the user. Help them understand why they should visit that page in the first place."

How do you establish what keywords you should have within those links?

"For instance, if you have a category for women's swimwear, the subcategories might be 'plus size women's swimwear', 'swimwear for juniors', etc. You can do keyword research and target relevant keywords with relatively low difficulty and higher volume. You could target 'women's plus size swimwear' or 'plus size swimwear for women', depending on what makes sense in that context.

You can take that, and you don't even have to stuff the whole page with it. Just one or two references are enough. Then, add a link with valuable information on why this subcategory exists and where they can go if they want to check it out. That is enough to do the magic and get the results.

We've seen measurable, significant improvements in rankings just by doing this, without building any other backlinks or making any other site improvements. We make changes one at a time on the website and, for a few weeks after we made that change, we did not make any other changes. It was a really impressive result. On some websites, it might not have that great of an impact but, in this example, we are seeing tremendous results that were easy to pinpoint."

How do you determine the pages that you want to try this on?

"For this website, we focused on subcategory pages where we weren't getting many links – pages where we were only getting around 2 links in 30 days. We also focused on pages that had really low rankings, in the 20th-24th position. We focused on 4-5 per page and implemented this.

They were all indexed, and they had content. They were the same as those that were performing well, these links were just not mentioned on those specific pages."

Does this strategy assist with pages getting indexed?

"Getting pages indexed is more about making sure that the content is valuable, it's not disallowed from crawling, there are no noindex tags, canonicals, etc. Internal linking can help search engines find your pages and may improve the chances of the pages getting indexed. However, it won't particularly help a page get indexed if, for instance, there's a noindex tag on that page. For me, it's mainly an additional improvement to the performance of an already indexed page."

Should there be a certain maximum number of links on a page?

"I don't really have a set number of links in mind. In the past, some people recommended having 100 links or fewer on a page but that was mostly because search engines were only crawling and indexing around 100 kilobytes per page at that time. That limitation doesn't exist right now so there is no set number of links.

Instead, go with what makes sense, and don't overwhelm the user. Include links where they can help provide additional information or help the user to really understand that content, rather than just filling up the page.

If you take into account the menu links, the links on the footer, and the rest, it can really add up. In the content itself, just go with what makes sense to the user. Personally, I don't have a specific number of links that I would recommend."

Do you have a strategy for the positioning of links?

"The positioning of links is really controversial, especially because of the first link priority argument that keeps coming up. The theory is that, if you have two links on a page, then the first one could be prioritised. However, as Google has mentioned over and over again, there is no set rule for this. They could go with this today and tomorrow it could be something else.

For linking multiple URLs on a page in different positions, I don't think there is any negative or positive effect from that. I still stand by going with what makes sense to the user."

Can you automate the insertion of internal links, or do you prefer to do it manually?

"It depends on the size of the website. If you're dealing with a smaller website, it makes sense to do this without third-party tools. You can do it quite quickly. Go to your Google Search Console, get a list of your authoritative pages (the categories that are ranking well), put that into a spreadsheet, go to your search browser, use site operators to find related pages, and then interlink them in this way.

If you're dealing with a medium-sized website, you might want to speed things up by using a tool like Screaming Frog to run a custom search. They have a really awesome custom search feature where you can find mentions of specific keywords on a website. You can also use advanced features like searching with regex and searching for keywords that don't have an anchor tag, which means they don't have a link on them. You can also exclude keywords that already have internal links on them.

When you're dealing with a larger website that has millions of pages, it doesn't really make sense to do this research manually or put the links in yourself. You could use automation tools like inLinks. I haven't used it personally, but people I know have spoken highly of it. It can automatically find internal linking opportunities and add those links to specific areas of your website."

What types of pages would you not want to be ranked or linked to within your own site?

"It depends on the specific pages. It could be a page for a product or a category that is retired. If you retire a category, it doesn't make sense to link to that and try to rank it. Also, it doesn't make sense to rank for out-of-stock products. If users come to your website and see that almost all of the products in a specific category are out of stock, that wouldn't create a good user experience.

In this case, you might prioritise the pages that are in stock, the pages that are available, the pages that have a higher profit margin, and those that it would make sense to present to the users."

Would you try and remove all the internal links to an out-of-stock or retired product page?

"Not necessarily, but it depends. If you're talking about an expired product that does not exist anymore, it might make sense to remove some of the internal links and create a page where, if users hit that expired page, they can get more information. It could explain that you've retired that product and why that has happened, and offer a list of related products. If it's gone for good, you could remove some of the internal links to that expired page.

However, if you're talking about a product that is temporarily unavailable, it wouldn't make sense to remove those internal links. If you're optimizing, it makes sense to optimize pages and products that are available over those that are out-of-stock. If you already have internal links to those out-of-stock pages, and you know that they're coming back, you don't want to remove them."

If an SEO is struggling for time, what should they stop doing right now so they can spend more time doing what you suggest in 2024?

"When it comes to internal links, stop neglecting user intent. In most cases, you could add links to a page where it doesn't necessarily make much sense to the user's intent at that point. If a user hits a category page on fitness gear, and you're adding links to a subcategory that has been retired – or even your resources page – that doesn't make much sense. It won't help the user move down the funnel.

At that point, they want content that explains how to use the specific type of gear for their particular need. It makes sense to think of the user's intent. What is the user trying to achieve? What can give them additional information? Add links to the pages where they can get additional context."

Katherine Nwanorue is an SEO Specialist at Fusion Inbound, and you can find her over at TechSEOJournal.com.

Improve your internal links using Python string-matching – with Andreas Voniatis

To round out our internal linking odyssey, Andreas Voniatis from Artios explains how Python can do much more for your internal links than the humble spreadsheet you might be used to.

Andreas says: "Use Python's string-matching functions to increase the relevance of your internal links on your website."

Can you give a brief explanation of the value of using Python for SEO?

"What I love about Python is that it can scale SEO really well. A lot of SEOs will be working in spreadsheets and there are obviously restrictions or limitations in terms of what a spreadsheet can do. They are limited in the scale of the data they can handle, like the number of rows, but also in the complexity of the functions and calculations that they can perform with that data.

For example, if you're optimizing a high-traffic website with tons of pages, like Amazon, then you're going to find scalable SEO analysis in Excel or

Google Sheets pretty limiting.

Instead, you can use an IPython notebook known as Jupyter, that will allow you to run Python code. If you import string-matching functions, you can take a target keyword and compare that to the title tags of your site pages to try and find the best page to send internal links to."

Are you using this to determine whether a page or a piece of content is sufficiently optimized or just to find the most appropriate internal page to link to?

"You could also use it for measuring how optimized your content is, which is a different use case for Python. Python has many use cases for scalable and data-driven SEO.

In this case, though, we're trying to find content like blog posts where you can place internal links that will help reshape the importance of your target content for Google and other search engines."

What content elements are you looking for?

"The great thing about doing this is that there are so many different ways to approach it. On a basic level, you could take your target keyword and the title tags of all of your content, and then simply use a string-matching function to calculate the similarity between them. Based on that similarity metric, you could use a quick rule of thumb to say that anything that's 60% or above would be considered suitable pages to place internal links on, for example.

You could do it at the body content level but that's a bit more complex because you need to ingest that content into a spreadsheet cell (or what we call a DataFrame in Python language) to do that kind of calculation. That's possible thanks to Python.

If you don't know what a good rule of thumb is, you can go even deeper. You can say, 'I want to model the median' or 'I want to model the 95th percentile of what's considered relevant.' You can determine your rule of thumb on a statistical basis rather than on something that you pulled out of thin air."

Would you be able to incorporate intent into what you're looking for?

"You absolutely can. If you had the target keyword for your site content then you could create another separate column in which you've predetermined whether those two keywords share the same search intent or not."

What data sources are required for this?

"If you wanted to do this at a basic level, you could just rely on crawling data alone. If you want to get search intent involved, then you'll need SERP data so that you can determine the similarity between your target keyword and the focus keyword of the content page you're comparing the search intent of. If you wanted to look at whether Google was crawling that page live, you would obviously use server logs."

How do you clean URLs that you wouldn't want to link to?

"That's a slightly separate issue, but let's get into it. One of the things that I do is model the page rank or link equity of a website using crawl data and external backlink data, so that I get both the internal and external page rank. Then, I amalgamate those two data sources together to get what I would call the 'effective page rank', which combines both the internal and the external.

Using that, you can transform or pivot your existing site structure away from the typical catalogue/product group structure (which might make sense from a librarian's perspective) and move it more towards the type of content structure that the internet is more interested in."

Should all SEOs be doing this or is it primarily for technical SEOs?

"To me, any SEO should have a holistic view, and all SEOs should understand it. If you call yourself an SEO generalist or an SEO consultant, then you should have a level of competency, if not experience or understanding, in the holistic elements of SEO.

You should be competent in your technical, your content, and your backlinks/off-page SEO. Technical SEOs should know how to do this themselves, but SEO content strategists might not need to."

How can you use statistical distributions to model relevance and highlight under-served target content?

"If you look at the median number of internal links to a product category on an e-commerce site, for example, those will be very different from the median number of internal links to a product item.

I don't want to create a hard-and-fast rule. I don't want to say that any pages that have less than 10 internal links need more links, or that you should add a certain number of links to those pages. If you use statistical distributions, you're taking a smarter, more tailored approach. You're taking a segmented approach, and you're accounting for the fact that not all content is equal.

You would expect your product categories to have more internal links, so the threshold will be high. Your product items may have fewer internal links, or it might be the other way around. The point is to take a segmented approach. By using distributions, you're moving away from hard-and-fast rules."

Is this just for internal links or can this approach be used to determine the optimum landing page for external links as well?

"You can apply it to absolutely everything. That's the whole premise of being data-driven."

How do you measure the ROI of improved internal linking?

"You would benchmark the ROI beforehand and then it's almost like a split test. You would benchmark what it was before, then you could make the change following the model's recommendations and see what the ROI is afterwards. However, if you're going to make this change site-wide, then you would want to do a split A/A test because you're comparing the result of the internal linking on the same URL against itself, before and after.

If you wanted to make it truly scientific, then you would conduct a split A/B test. In that case, you would only make that change on a collection of unlinked URLs, measure the revenue before and after, then compare it to the control group."

Does providing better and more relevant internal links also enhance

usability?

"In theory (and, in many cases, in a practical sense), search engine SEO and user experience are often aligned. By optimizing your content for the search engines, you should also be optimizing it for the user. If the user knows what they're getting before they click on the link, and the link is more relevant for their needs, then that should improve their experience."

If an SEO is struggling for time, what should they stop doing right now so they can spend more time doing what you suggest in 2024?

"Stop getting better at Excel and retrain in Python.

Personally, I rarely use Excel. I use Google Sheets but only for putting together nice graphs because the ones produced by Python are a bit too sciencey for a business audience.

A more diplomatic and practical approach would be to say, 'Limit your use of Excel and retrain in Python'. You'll start noticing that you can invest ten minutes or one hour working out how to solve a dilemma in Python rather than Excel and, eventually, it will get to the point where you can do so much more in Python that you will drop Excel like a hot potato.

Python is also well future-proofed. That's not to say there won't be a language in 10, 15, or 20 years that will supersede Python. However, the great thing is that, once you learn a computing language, those skills are transferable to almost any other computing language. I started out using R, which is a statistical computing language. Once I saw that more of the SEO industry was favouring Python, it was really easy for me to switch. A lot of the function names are identical."

Andreas Voniatis is the Founder of Artios, and the author of Data Driven SEO (Springer Apress). You can find him over at Artios.io.

12 LINK BUILDING

Stay on top of both your link building and mention-building – with Debbie Chew

Of course, the kissing cousin of internal linking is external link building, and Global SEO Manager Debbie Chew says that you need to focus on brand mentions too.

Debbie says: "In 2024, it's really important to stay on top of your link and mention building."

Can you measure the value of mentions?

"I think that you can. For example, there is a link-building tactic where you can turn those mentions into links. It's mainly about the idea of getting your brand out there and getting people to talk about your brand. Of course, if you get the link that's a huge win, but there are going to be publications that just don't link out. Getting that mention can still be valuable.

For example, at Dialpad, we really like to do research reports. Sometimes, news publications mention the research report, but they don't actually link to Dialpad. However, they do talk about our study and use our name. The big benefit of that is that you're getting mentioned in a really big-name publication. You're getting your name out there and you're getting the word out about the report that you did.

However, it also means that people who might write content related to your report in the future may find out about that report through that news publication. They might be the ones who eventually link to you. It's not just about getting a link, it's about putting out the word about the really great content that you create."

Will off-site mentions also help to build the presence of your brand entity for search engines?

"Definitely. In the past, Google has mentioned that EEAT is largely based on both links and mentions. They have also recently said that links are no longer in the top three ranking factors. They mentioned this at PubCon, and it's a message that they've been trying to say more and more recently. I think it's because people are sometimes too focused on building links in high quantities, so the quality gets cut down.

People are more focused on building spammy links or links that aren't great for the website – and that causes a lot of potential problems for Google. They have to crawl all of these links but they're not good and they're not helpful.

We need to take a step back and recognize that links are just one part of the equation. They're not saying that links are not important; links still have a really important place when it comes to ranking. However, there are so many different signals that Google uses to determine what is actually going to rank for a certain query. We need to try not to overestimate the impact of links and really understand where a link fits into the whole SEO strategy."

When a search engine is comfortable with what your brand is, can a brand mention be as effective as a link?

"I wouldn't say that a mention is equally effective, however, it's good to try to seek out those mentions. Number one is trying to get those mentions, and number two is trying to seek them out and turn those mentions into links. That's when you can really benefit the most from them."

How is the process of building links influenced by generative AI results?

"This year, the whole industry has been shaken up due to AI and what generative AI has brought to the table. Generative AI is really great for more long-tail queries or things that aren't as factual and are a bit more creative. There's still a place for traditional search, where people are trying to find things that are a bit more factual.

The rise of generative AI makes link-building and mention-building even more important than before. The whole idea behind generative AI is that it's learning from a bunch of existing text and it's trying to predict whatever the next word should be regarding the question you're asking it.

If I am writing a blog post about the top VoIP providers, generative AI is very good for helping me do some research. I can ask it to send me the top 50 VoIP providers, and it'll give me a list. I can go through that list, check each one, and decide who is actually going to make it onto my final blog post. In those situations, it's really important to be able to influence generative AI. If you are an SEO at a company that provides VoIP services, generative AI should know that you exist and mention you the next time someone asks about VoIP providers. You want to make sure that you're on that shortlist.

In order to do that, it's all about figuring out how you get your brand out there, and how you get your brand mentioned more. A concrete way to do that is to do more 'listicle outreach'. Especially within SaaS, people like to make listicles for the Top X Software for Small Businesses, etc. Getting onto those types of lists, especially when they're relevant to your product or the features that you have, is really important.

First, go into the SERPs and figure out which of these lists it would make sense for you to be included on. You can also look at what lists your competitors are included on, but you aren't. Those are great opportunities for you to try to reach out to whoever wrote those blog posts and see if they can include your product in those listicles. The idea of building mentions and links is highly relevant for influencing generative AI."

What is the best way of doing that kind of outreach?

"A basic version of doing outreach would be reaching out to a blog author and saying that you appreciated their post, and you'd like to be included if they update it in the future. A lot of outreach templates tend to follow that template. One thing to try and do is personalise whenever you can.

Try to call out something very specific about their post that doesn't necessarily exist in other posts, because you want to show that you really did take the time to review their content. Show them that it's not just an email template that you're sending out to a bunch of different people.

Another way to step it up is to try and build some sort of relationship with this person. If you want a favour from them, what kind of favour can you offer in return? Perhaps you have a very large social media presence, and you could let them know that you'd be happy to share this on your social media. That makes it highly valuable to the person who is getting your email outreach.

Try to figure out if there is any way to negotiate something so that it's not just them helping you but you're also helping them."

Why shouldn't you blindly build links to pages without regularly revisiting the SERPs?

"With link building, the people who know that it is important will continuously build links to certain pages. There may be a money keyword that we really want to rank for, and every month we're building links to it. Then, the position or ranking of that page might start to stagnate.

In those situations, it's really important to take a look at the SERPs instead of continuously pouring resources into building links to that page – because links might not be the reason why the ranking has not improved. If you look at the SERPs, you might realise that the user intent of that query has changed. Then, you would need to go back to your content and see how you can adjust the content to better match what people are now looking for.

It might be that you are one of the slowest pages in the SERPs, and that's the reason why you're being held back. Then, you would want to identify if there is anything that you can do on the technical SEO side to help improve the page speed of that page.

There are a lot of potential factors that might be the reason why your page is not ranking number one. It's not always links, but links can be a factor. There's also the question of quantity versus quality. Maybe your competitor has five really good links and you've built 20 links that aren't as good. That might be a reason why. Instead of focusing on the quantity, you may want to focus on getting more quality links to help boost your page."

Are there any other link-building tactics you'd recommend focusing on in 2024?

"Going back to the basics, and creating linkable assets like guides, glossary pages, and stats pages, is still going to be really important.

It's also really important to figure out what types of linkable assets are the most effective for your industry. Think about what's working well for your competitors and what their best pages are in terms of links, then figure out whether that is the direction that you want to go in. Try it out to see whether or not that works for you.

Sometimes what works for them might not work for you and, in those cases, try to look at industries that are similar to yours and see what they're doing. Try to figure out the best tactic or the best linkable asset you can create that you can really benefit from. Similar industries might be more progressive than your direct competitors, in terms of what they're doing with their digital marketing, so learn from them."

If an SEO is struggling for time, what should they stop doing right now so they can spend more time doing what you suggest in 2024?

"With all the changes that are going around within the SEO industry, go back to the basics and the key areas of SEO – the three pillars of content, links, and technical SEO. Whenever there's some sort of issue on the technical side, and you do an audit and a bunch of different errors pop up, don't freak out. Calm down and look for the biggest, most impactful thing that you can work on that will really move the needle.

Don't focus too much on the little things. If there are a bunch of small errors that you can fix, but they're not going to give you results or help your organic rankings, don't worry too much about them. Focus on the big things and go back to the basics."

Debbie Chew is a Global SEO Manager, and you can find her over at DebbieyChew.com.

Build human connections in order to build better links – with Amit Raj

Debbie spoke about going back to basics, and Amit Raj from The Links Guy believes that developing a relationship with people is what link building has always been about.

Amit says: "Ultimately, the core essence of link building is human connection. Obviously, with AI coming to the forefront, there is a lot of talk about automation methods and using the best tools. However, your aim should always be to use a human-first and audience-first approach to link building.

Is the link relevant? Does it provide value? Does your outreach provide value?"

Does a human-first approach include building relationships with the person you're reaching out to?

"Definitely. 'Relationship building' is one of those buzzwords that gets used a lot, but it's important to do your research before you reach out to a person or certain types of websites. It's easy to lose sight of that, especially when you're trying to do it at scale.

Even if it's not an individual person that you're reaching out to, what type of website is it and who is the audience? Try to speak to that. If you do that, you can't go too far wrong in your outreach."

Do you want to have a relationship with someone prior to asking for a link?

"People have different tactics they use for building links. I talked to somebody the other day who had existing relationships with a bunch of SaaS companies because their company was already using these tools. They used that as leverage to get a link from them and create a piece talking about a specific topic. Things like that do help.

Reaching out without directly asking for the link is definitely one approach. You can then move the conversation forward to asking for a link or offering content, and you would at least have provided some context to that. It would make sense for them to link to you if you are providing the content."

Can you also reach out to thought leaders and ask them to contribute to a piece of content then offer to provide content for them in return after it goes live?

"That is one approach that works. There are obviously different ways of doing it. Some sites might not want to work on a large roundup piece, but I have seen that approach work before. If you get 10, 15, or 20 thought leaders to comment on something, you can leverage that. Then you have quite a few people who could potentially link back to you.

Another approach is doing it on a one-to-one basis. You can reach out to businesses that are in related sectors, ask them to contribute to a piece and you can get a link back. Industry news sites that are in your own industry are also quite hungry for content. Of course, an approach we're utilising right now is interviewing thought leaders for your own podcast, which is a great way to build relationships."

How would you define a valuable link in 2024?

"There are different degrees of relevance. What you would define as a relevant link to you is quite a wide spectrum. What everybody really wants is links within their own industry. That can be hard if it's a particularly tight niche. You might run out of sites to reach out to, and not everyone will give you that link.

Then, you have to think about crossover sectors and industries that are related to your own. They might not specifically be in your industry but that is a valuable link, and I believe that's what Google is looking for.

12 Link Building

There are different schools of thought and different theories about how it really works but your ultimate goal should be to get relevant links that are, if not from within your own industry, at least from industries where it makes sense for that link to be there. When you do that, the link quality should go up in tandem.

A crossover sector could be a feeder sector, a sector that does some of what you do but not all of what you do, or a business that is likely to appeal to the same sort of audience. You can sometimes get an idea from analysing competitors in terms of who's mentioning them. That gives you some insight as to where you might reach out to get a link.

You should also think about linkable audiences. If you have a way of relating your business to the wedding sector, for example, newlyweds could be a target audience. You could reach out to sites targeting that audience and get them to link to your content piece or publish content that could link back to you. Analyse your competitors.

A lot of people know their core business and they know who the target audience is. Sometimes that gives you an idea as to who you should be reaching out to. It could be the wedding industry, sites aimed at parents, female entrepreneurs, etc. Whatever target audience you would deem relevant can give you some seed ideas to work with."

Could you try to approach customers one step before they get to your particular service?

"We do that for clients in terms of looking at their business and thinking about what their products or services are, who they service, who their target audience is, etc. You can get a lot of ideas there.

Even if competitors don't have a lot of links from a specific sector, it's still worth trying because it might just be that they've not tried that sector before – as long as it's relevant, of course."

Are websites likely to charge money for valuable links or are they happy to link to good content for their audience?

"We've seen everything. People are saying that they are finding a lot more people asking for money for links that they wouldn't have before. You particularly find that with bloggers. It is a revenue source, and it's expected with certain types of websites. That's why we do try to reach out to other businesses, particularly small to medium-sized businesses, because we tend to find that they are more hungry for content.

As long as you serve that purpose, and it is valuable content, they're usually quite happy to publish it. Of course, they may link to you and they may not, but it's always good to establish that beforehand and look to see if they've got any guidelines.

You will have people asking for money as well. There are different schools of thought on that. You have to vet the site quality, of course, if you are going to use paid link strategies.

Small and medium-sized businesses may become bigger businesses in the future and low-authority websites may become higher-authority websites in the future. At the end of the day, they still have a target audience of some sort. There will still be some traffic there as well. It's a relevant link. With time that site could also grow so, if it's a good link, it's worth going for it."

How do you stand out with your outreach to ensure that you're not being labelled as spam?

"There are a couple of things you can do. One good way of doing it, which ties in with your strategy and prospecting, is to really think about who you're going to be reaching out to. If you do have a particular target audience in mind, make sure you have tight prospecting lists. They should actually be from that industry or a particular type of website. Then, frame your outreach and segment or theme your template so that it looks like it's very specific to them.

Also, leave room to personalise. You want to at least show that you've done some kind of research, whether it's a personalised icebreaker or you specifically mention a content idea that you know they'll find valuable. I find that works, as opposed to generic icebreakers.

I've seen a lot of AI first-line writers and I don't feel it gives you a good human-first approach to link building. I'm not always keen on AI line writing.

Having a bit of a human touch on the emails, whether it's one line or a few phrases, does make a big difference.

Even things like email deliverability on the technical side of things can help as well. You want to keep your bounce rate low and, when you frame your outreach a certain way and it comes across well and is personalised, you'll be less likely to have people marking you as spam. More of your other emails will get to the inbox as well, just from a technical deliverability point of view."

If you are using software to automate the sending of your emails, are you better off using a different domain name from that of your website?

"There are different ways of doing it, but I would always recommend using a separate domain if you are trying to do it at scale. Use a secondary domain that is related to your brand name. Obviously, it can't be your main domain, but something that's related to it.

If your main domain is brandname.com, you could use brandname.co.uk or brandname.net. I've seen people use trybrandname.com or something else that is related to it. That way, you're protecting the emails from your main domain.

Do you have a preferred piece of outreach software at the moment?

"We use Pitchbox. We've tested a few over the years, but I find that Pitchbox is really good for tracking things like success rate, win rate, etc. It gives you a lot of detail and you get some great reports. We also find it really useful in terms of doing things at scale."

If an SEO is struggling for time, what should they stop doing right now so they can spend more time doing what you suggest in 2024?

"Find a balance with outreach. The 'spray and pray' approach doesn't work. Don't take a generic single template and blast it out. The kind of numbers you would need to do to get decent links is huge. That's the first thing to avoid doing.

At the same time, have enough personalisation so that it serves the purpose of what you're trying to achieve. Don't overly personalise to the point where it's not relevant to the outreach or to the value you're trying to provide. Otherwise, you can get too bogged down in the personalisation and you start to overthink it. That's important, especially if you're trying to do it at scale.

If you're genuinely helpful and you're adding value to people when you're reaching out to them – you're showing them the right type of content and you've got the right content ideas – that will come across. That's where using themed, segmented templates can be really helpful because you can do things at scale while still relating your content to a particular type of website or group of websites."

Amit Raj is CEO of The Links Guy, and you can find him over at TheLinksGuy.com.

Find ethical backlinks and better content by leveraging happy customers – with Alan Silvestri

Examining the connection between your links and your users from another angle, Alan Silvestri from Growth Gorilla says that organic, ethically-sourced links come direct from your customers.

Alan says: "Leverage happy customers for building ethical backlinks – and there are a few different ways that you can do this.

Most companies essentially stop at just asking for a review or a testimonial. They slap it on the website, and they don't really do much with it. The key point here is to think about your customer as a whole person. They have different hobbies, they have different interests, and they have a network of people that they know that you can leverage to gain more reach and more engagement for new content and backlinks."

How can case studies help you to do this?

"Case studies are a fantastic opportunity. HubSpot is a great example of a company that's doing this really well right now. They have a case studies hub page that you can take a look at, showcasing different case studies for different companies.

The first thing I noticed when I popped the page into my SEO tool is that a lot of those case studies are ranking for the company brand terms. That's traffic that you can get if you optimize your case studies. However, the main thing I noticed is that each case study talks about a specific problem that the software has solved for that customer. That's a really good way for the company to leverage their happy customers.

For example, in one HubSpot case study, they explain how they helped a company achieve 44% social media growth using their marketing hub tool. As soon as I put that case study into my SEO tool, it showed me that they have around 70 referring domains, and most of them are from other websites linking to this one statistic. That's very useful.

To reverse engineer that, you can essentially use the KPIs that you have helped your clients improve as sources for other websites to reference. You could reach out to every article that talks about how to use marketing tools to increase social media growth and say, 'We helped this client increase their social media growth by 44%. This is the case study showing how we did that.' Chances are, you will get a very nice backlink from that page because you have provided a great, unique data point. Nobody else has that data, and it's very useful for proving that specific point."

When is the right time to ask for a case study?

"Straight away – as soon as you have some data to prove that you have helped the company. You want to create the page as soon as possible. You don't want there to be too much time between when you get the results and when you ask for the case study.

There are specific processes and best practices that you should use when asking for a case study, as well. I talked to Joel Klettke from Case Study Buddy, and he gave me a gold mine of processes and best practices to follow. If you are asking for case studies in the best possible way, that will get you the best-written experiences as well.

There is a format, but I would suggest studying companies that are doing it well, like HubSpot and Salesforce. You can get a good feel for how you should go about it by looking at those examples."

How can testimonials also help in this way?

"Testimonials are very similar to case studies. At the end of the day, most people just slap a testimonial on the homepage because it's nice to see.

However, I would suggest that you create a specific testimonials page. That is a better way to showcase your authority and your social proof, making your whole website more authoritative, which helps when you are negotiating for backlinks. You can demonstrate that your product works, and show that you have a lot of happy customers.

Companies that have a stronger brand and stronger authority typically find it easier to get backlinks. If someone who is negotiating with you for a link goes to your website and sees no case studies, no testimonials, and a very low domain rating, they'll be wondering, 'What's in it for me?' If you have more authority, with more testimonials on your page, that will make a difference – particularly if you have testimonials from people who are well-known in your niche.

The best thing about testimonials is the fact that the people who write them are often willing to share them on social media. They might even share the same testimonial on their website to showcase that they have used your product."

What is user-generated content and how can you benefit from it?

"User-generated content is essentially about creating true advocates of your brand so that they create content about your product or service. For example, I'm a huge fan of Vivo Barefoot, which is a brand that makes barefoot minimal shoes. I have a personal site where I talk about my running, and I wrote an article about my transition from normal shoes to these types of shoes. I talked all about the brand, their principles, and their core values.

It's about sharing your mission and your values so that your customers actually become true advocates of your product and the ethos behind it. That is what makes them want to create their own content.

User-generated content can be blog articles and it can be social media posts as well. It's great for social proof, but it can also rank and attract backlinks. In fact, the article that I wrote about Vivo Barefoot is now ranking for keywords like 'barefoot running' and 'transitioning to barefoot shoes'."

Should you ask your customers to write an article and include a link or do you want that content and link to be created more organically?

"Don't be too pushy. Make it as enticing as possible for them to create content about your brand. 90% of the time, the link will come naturally because it makes sense for happy customers to want to point people to the specific product.

That's exactly what I did in my article. I actually want people to try out these shoes, so I linked to the company website, and I even linked to some of the training courses that they have.

Maybe, after a month, you could do a link campaign focused on brand mentions. You could go after some of those articles that mention your brand and find ways to incentivise them. If you have a software product, you could say, 'Hey, I saw you mentioned our brand, thanks a lot for the shout-out! We are offering a free one-month subscription if you add the link to the website so that other people can find us and enjoy the product too.'"

Is guest blogging as effective as it used to be?

"Guest blogging still works. The main thing is having a creative pitch when you reach out. What I'm talking about is essentially having your customer create a guest blog article on your own website. If you have a software product, you can have a customer write an article about how they are using the product.

For example, I use Pitchbox as my main outreach tool. They asked me to do an article on their website and I wrote about how I transitioned from using a bunch of different tools for a lot of different things to just using Pitchbox as my one main tool for everything. That's useful for their customers and for new people finding out about the tool, and it's a backlink as well.

The other good thing about it is that I have now written an article on

Pitchbox. It's a great link that goes back to my site, and I can share the article too. It's one of the main pieces of content that I send over to prospective customers when they are interested in seeing my process, the kind of tools that we use, and how it works. The content keeps giving, and it's evergreen."

Do you also advocate for creating webinars and podcast content?

"These are great, as you know. Companies could create their own show and invite their customers to come on and talk about the company or the product, which is similar to a guest blog but in a video or audio format. This kind of content is really good for distribution. Video or audio snippets that you create from this content can have a lot of reach – potentially even more than a simple blog article would.

It's also important to understand where your customers hang out and the types of media that they consume. If the podcast or video format is best for them, then that might be the way to go.

It's all about featuring the specific way that your product or service has helped your customer. If it's done in their own words, it's more credible and more authoritative, and they will be more incentivised to share it back to their digital communities or network."

Would you suggest using affiliate programs, even though affiliate links aren't SEO-friendly links?

"That is true, but it's still a nice way to spread the word about your product. If you can get more people to buy your product or service, at the end of the day, that's more voice your product has in the market. It's also going to push people to write more content about your product, talk about it, and share it on social media.

Anything that can help you amplify your voice and get more reach is going to benefit your SEO. If you only think about SEO benefits in terms of specific links, domain rating, etc., that's very limiting. Especially in 2024, people need to look at SEO in a more holistic way and take care of everything that's going to give you more reach. That includes distribution, different types of media, and getting more people to talk about the product.

The direction that Google has been going in for years, specifically with Artificial Intelligence in the mix, is all about building trust. It's all about making true fans; real customers that really love your product and want to be ambassadors for it."

If an SEO is struggling for time, what should they stop doing right now so they can spend more time doing what you suggest in 2024?

"In short, stop creating new content. Get in touch with your customers and try to get them to create the content for you."

Alan Silvestri is Managing Director at Growth Gorilla and you can find him over at MyGrowthGorilla.com.

Focus less on quantity and more on quality, relevant links – with Jo O'Reilly

Digital PR Consultant Jo O'Reilly believes that less is sometimes more, and like Alan, she wants you to make your users happy. Nobody likes spammy links, she says, so don't waste time and effort on them.

Jo says: "Stop building huge numbers of low-quality irrelevant links and focus your efforts on a smaller number of quality relevant links.

We can all go out and build loads of links, but Google is going to start disregarding them when they realise they're not relevant to your business or your niche.

If you're not building links in the way Google wants, by using paid-for link building or other manipulative tactics that Google does not value and doesn't want to encourage, you're wasting your time, your money and your energy. Focus that energy on building a smaller number of quality links that are relevant to you and the users on your website. Hopefully, Google will reward you for that effort."

What would be an example of an irrelevant spammy link?

"We see a lot of these links in niches where it is more difficult to do SEO, like gambling and online crypto sites. They do voluminous link-building and digital PR, and they will do anything to get a link.

They will talk about any subject, despite the fact that it might not be relevant to their niche or their business. When online gambling firms are talking about motor vehicles or days out, that is not relevant to what they are selling as a service or what they're providing to visitors to their website.

They are typically links that are built en masse using dodgy, black/grey hat tactics."

How do you define relevant, high-quality links?

"Those are links that are really relevant to users of your website. Build links that talk about content that's relevant to the people who would naturally be visiting your website anyway. Know your customer base, whoever that may be, and talk about things where you have real expertise, experience (the new E in EEAT), and authority.

Anything that you can talk about with authority is going to increase that trust in what you're doing on your page and what the page that's linking to you is doing. Use that overall EEAT strategy to build relevant links."

How do you measure the potential value of a link?

"That is difficult. We know various metrics like DR and DA. We've either used them in the past or our clients use them, and we all know that they exist, but we don't want to use them alone. We want to have a more holistic view of links going forward. DA and DR, for example, can be gamed and manipulated, so we don't want to use them as our only benchmark for what a quality link is.

In the industry, we assume that Google's going to get smarter at ascertaining the value and relevance of a link, probably with the help of AI and other things it's employing. You have to be quite clever. Look at each link individually and try and work out: Is this relevant? Is this showing a source? Is this adding more context or information to a user's journey? That is what Google originally wanted links to be.

We sometimes forget the history of links. We use them as an SEO tool and forget that they are supposed to be citations. The original idea comes from how you would reference things in an academic paper. We want to go back to that. We want to go back to a link being something useful that adds context, extra clarity, or a trust marker to a website."

By holistically, do you mean things like position within the content as well as the likely traffic of the page?

"Yes and no. I try to stay away from talking about traffic, particularly in digital PR. I can't promise you that a link is going to bring through loads of traffic. I wouldn't want to sell a links-based service with traffic in mind because that's very hard to predict.

When I say looking holistically, I mean how useful the link is. That can include where it is placed in the content, but that wouldn't be a huge quality marker. Look for how useful that link is and what it shows about both a piece of content and the person providing that content.

I really like links to About Us pages when an expert is telling me something in a news article. That link should take me somewhere that will explain why I am listening to this person and why they are an expert – particularly when you're talking about YMYL sites. If someone's giving me health information or telling me what to do with my finances, I want to know why I'm listening to them and why their advice is worth taking on board. Links that take the user somewhere they can check that person's credentials are really good links."

Are links from author bios at the bottom of guest blog articles still worthwhile?

"If it shows you that the author is an expert in what they're talking about, then that's absolutely valuable. Author pages on guest posts or publications let the reader know that someone has spoken about the subject before or has a vested interest in the topic because it's something in which they have an academic or business background. It's an EEAT-friendly way of showing why this is the right person to get that information from."

In terms of digital PR, is it still likely that multiple press organisations

are going to link to you if they like a press release that you've distributed to them?

"I hope so, but the onus is really on the digital PR expert to ensure that the campaigns are relevant and they're not creating campaigns that have absolutely nothing to do with a client's overall business or expertise.

Digital PR is getting busier. There are more of us and there are fewer journalists, so it's a really hard nut to crack these days. Now, there's a higher expectation from the press that, when you present a campaign for a client or do some newsjacking and send expertise from a client when a story breaks, that client is really relevant to the news story. They should have real expertise and a real background in the subject that you are putting their content forward for.

It's all about that expertise. Are they an expert? Do they have experience in this? Do they have the authority? Can I trust them talking about this?"

If an SEO wants to incorporate more digital PR elements into what they do, what should learn they first?

"Newsjacking is a great thing to master. It is hard work, though. I'm not going to pretend it's an easy thing to learn but it is great, particularly if you work with some experts in your area.

If you're an SEO for a site that works with insurance experts, there are always news stories that need the opinion of an insurance expert. If you've got those people and you're already using them on-site authoring pages for you, then you can absolutely use that off-page to build links, build expertise, and build the brand. You've definitely got to remember the brand element of this.

Also, go and find who is writing about your space. Whatever space you're in, there'll be journalists who are dedicated to that. If you're in skincare, you'll work with dermatologists or a skincare brand. Go and find those beauty journalists whose job is to write about skincare day in and day out. Build those relationships and then, when they need a comment or some expertise, they will come to you. If you're going to do a campaign, you want to be able to send that to those journalists and know that they are going to trust you, print your content, put it on their website, and link back to you."

How do you conduct outreach and cut through the noise?

"One of the things we hear from journalists all the time is that they are inundated. Before digital PR existed the way it does now, I was a journalist myself and I would get 300 emails a day. Now, I speak to journalists who have been on annual leave for one day and come back to inboxes full of thousands of emails. That's overwhelming and scary to think about.

Cut through that noise by not sending out irrelevant press releases. Don't send out content/quotes you've generated on ChatGPT that aren't providing expert analysis and aren't trustworthy. You've just got to be doing the best you can, sending out really high-quality stuff to the relevant people. If you're a motoring journalist and I'm sending you a skincare campaign, you're not interested and I'm going to get blocked.

You want to spend time understanding who is covering your niche, who is writing about it, and who is interested in it. Don't blanket spam every journalist in the US and the UK with every campaign you do. You're going to clog up their inbox and you're going to annoy everyone."

Is it ever worthwhile paying for links?

"I don't think so. I know that people do it and I know that it works, but I'm not sure about the long-term value. Just because something works in the short term, that doesn't make it the right long-term strategy.

There are lots of things that you can do in digital PR that get you a really quick win but I'm not sure about their longevity. If I sent a press release to every single journalist, without doing my due diligence and looking into whether it's relevant, I would probably still get a link or two out of it. I'm not going to do that because the short-term win isn't worth the long-term damage it does to my reputation."

How do you determine what links you would like to get?

"You can use tools like Majestic to go and look at what your competitors have got. I like to do it one of two ways. I want to see where competitors are getting links from, to see if we can go and get those links as well, but I also look for the gaps. Who aren't our competitors getting links from and can we get links there?

A lot of people chase the big national links – they want to be in the BBC or the New York Times – but some of the most powerful links, in terms of their SEO impact, can be a lot more niche.

Getting links from smaller, specialist websites that are hyper-relevant can have a much more powerful SEO impact than big sites, even with a lower DA or quality score. Don't be clouded by the idea of getting big, glamorous links all the time. Look for the hyper-relevant niche links too."

If an SEO is struggling for time, what should they stop doing right now so they can spend more time doing what you suggest in 2024?

"Stop sending out thousands and thousands of outreach emails to try and build links. Focus on building on-site content that is link-worthy and send that out to a smaller number of really relevant journalists.

The best outreach is done manually. You can buy software that has the names of journalists. It does save time but it is expensive, and the best outreach is done through manual research."

Jo O'Reilly is a Digital PR Consultant, and you can find her over at 'Jo O'Reilly' on LinkedIn.

Stop being afraid of building category page backlinks – with Eva Cheng

Digital PR Consultant Eva Cheng believes that some links are underestimated. She suggests that category pages hold a lot of link building potential that is flying under the radar.

Eva says: "Don't be afraid of building category pages for backlinks.

There's a worry that if you build category page links it could be seen as unnatural to Google, but it's just like any digital PR strategy. When you start building links for a client, it's going to start slowly and build up from there. If you're doing it the same way as you would build links naturally, then it should be perceived as a positive thing.

It does depend on what you define as a category page, and these pages shouldn't just be a small summary on a single page.

A lot of the category page links we build are on our client's website. For example, if it's a wedding and engagement ring specialist, we would build an 'engagement rings' category page and, within that category page, it would include frequently asked questions as well as products and anything else that is useful for a customer visiting that website.

It's much more of a landing page, with a lot more substance to it, which makes it the kind of page that people would naturally link to."

What kind of links are you building to category pages?

"Ideally, it's links that are from topically relevant publications. For wedding and engagements specialists, we'd want to build links from Brides.com, Hitched, and all of the topically relevant sites that are relevant to that page."

Do potential partners often want to link to the homepage or a particular product instead of a category page?

"Not necessarily. When it comes to a particular product, that's normally done through product PR. We would send them a request with a product in mind.

In this case, you're essentially using digital PR campaigns to build those category page links. More importantly, we tend to use reactive PR for this kind of strategy. We would jump on an expert comment for these kinds of publications and offer them expert commentary around whatever they need. If it's engagement rings, that might be valuations of celebrity engagement rings, for example.

We also try and jump on requests for basic questions like, 'What's the most popular engagement ring at the moment?', so that we can try and build those category page links. That kind of content on a publication site like Brides.com would be very relevant to the content from our category page link."

Do you get requests through existing relationships or a public website?

"It's a bit of both. I've been working with an engagement client for just over a year now. Journalists looking for reactive celebrity engagement commentary come to me directly, now that they know that I'm there and I'm offering a reliable source. We also keep an eye on HARO and we have response source requests and press flows that we look at. Once you've initiated that relationship, ideally, they will come to you directly the next time they have a request.

Also, whenever we know that a celebrity engagement has come up, we do newsjacking to get involved in that conversation. We identify which journalists typically cover celebrity engagements or valuations of a jewellery piece for a celebrity. From that contact list, we can send them a request like, 'Hi! I'm working with X client, would you like to cover this valuation from the latest news on this person's engagement?' Then we ask them to link back to a category page from there.

The journalists we are targeting don't tend to ask for any sort of payment, which is good because that's against Google's guidelines. They don't typically ask for any returns besides the content."

Are people often keen to read and reply to those pitches or do you struggle to get engagement from people that you're reaching out to for the first time?

"Open rates are quite high, but then it's whether or not they'll cover the campaign or the reactive commentary. There have been instances where I've gone out with a celebrity engagement, and journalists have covered it left, right, and centre, but they never replied to let me know that they were using that commentary. It's just one of those things where you have to wait and see."

Why should SEOs focus on building category links instead of links to specific product pages for example?

"It's simply a good way to build up your search and get higher rankings on Google because it's a better way to target your keywords. If a client wants to be featured higher up for engagement ring keywords, then building category pages and category page links for 'engagement rings' will slowly build up the SERP rankings for that client and get them up to page one.

For relatively competitive keyword phrases, a category page can be an ideal target because those pages change often. Google will see that they have been updated a lot, which will help you compete.

It also supports your EEAT strategy as well. Backlink building in digital PR is part of an SEO strategy. You obviously need the tech and onsite to be on point too, because it's part of those three pillars. EEAT, however, is obviously all about experience, expertise, authority and trust.

In terms of digital PR, it's about who is answering those comments. For a wedding/engagement ring specialist, what is their background in wedding and engagement rings? Have they been in the business for a long time? Have they got any significant qualifications? The more links you build for that expert, the better.

You can show that you have X person at the company who says X, values Y at Z price, and offers expertise around the subject and topic. This ties into both the second E, expertise, and authority as well.

If you dominate the industry with forward-thinking press releases and campaigns (the latest trends in wedding/engagement rings, wedding/engagement ring shapes that are going to be the next big thing, etc.), and also with the reactive expert commentary, it builds your authority. Then, you become the go-to PR for a journalist on this topic. Also, if a journalist were to search for your expert, they would see your company and all the pieces of coverage that you've gained in the past. That builds trust.

Supply expert commentary frequently on relevant topics whenever you can. Gaining those links, and that coverage for your in-house expert, builds your website into more of an expert within that field."

How do you decide which category pages to focus on, and at what point in your SEO strategy do you choose to target specific category pages?

"It depends. Targeting something like 'diamond wedding rings' is quite niche, so that would be hard. It would be better to go with a 'wedding rings' category page rather than 'diamond wedding rings' because the 'diamond' makes it seem a bit more unnatural to Google. It might appear that you're forcing the link for 'diamond wedding rings' rather than just 'wedding rings' in general. There are so many niche topics that you can go down into, like 'sapphire wedding rings' or 'ruby wedding rings'.

Instead, you can build 'wedding rings' and, within that category page, build all of those other categories, like 'diamonds' and 'sapphires'. The authority from there should pass on to your website.

As for when you should start targeting specific category pages, it should be considered from the very beginning of your strategy. If you are onboarding a client who has no backlink profile, and you know their target keywords, start building those links now – along with homepage links and blog page links. Google can then see that you're naturally building that authority on the site."

Can you build up your links once and forget about it or is it ongoing?

"You need to consistently keep at it. If you start to jump from page three to page two, and you stop before you make it to page one, you will lose that place on the second page.

Google is constantly re-evaluating and re-indexing those pages and categorising which are most relevant for each keyword."

Besides responding to journalists who have requests for content, how else can you build links to your category pages?

"There are also the frequently asked questions you tend to have on your website. For example, you could have questions like, 'What are the most popular engagement rings?', 'What styles and shapes are there?', 'What's the upcoming trend for engagement rings?', or 'How do you choose an engagement ring?' Those are frequently asked questions by the general public.

You can even pinpoint those questions to a certain time and event. 'How do you choose an engagement ring?' is a great question to target at the most popular times for engagements, like Christmas or New Year's Day. You know that people will be searching for that query around or before that time, so that's when you can outreach that campaign to journalists who would be interested in that kind of topic."

Where would you position this type of FAQ content on your website?

"You can include it within the content you already have. If you scroll on your website and look at the products, you've obviously got the navigation bar that guides you to different pages. If you have an 'engagement ring' section, for example, the user would scroll past the selection of top products and that frequently asked questions section would be at the bottom of the page, before they click through to the second or third page – or even before categorising down through your products.

That frequently asked question section would contain the content so that it is on the same category page, which adds additional content and authority – as opposed to having the user click off and go to thinner category pages.

You can also build these links on your blog and host the content as part of the more in-depth content on those pages as well. This is just a snippet of one or two paragraphs, rather than a fully-fledged blog post. You might write one or two paragraphs answering the question directly within the FAQs on the category page, but then give them the option to click through and read a more expansive article if they want to."

If an SEO is struggling for time, what should they stop doing right now so they can spend more time doing what you suggest in 2024?

"Stop building links without a clear and robust digital PR backlink strategy. Otherwise, you're just building links for the sake of building links.

You want to define that strategy about every six months. Sit down with your client and see if there are any changes on their side in terms of the way they want to approach it. There may be other keywords or new focuses and topics that they want to expand on. Work more collaboratively with the client and understand what they need."

Eva Cheng is a Digital PR Consultant, and you can find her over at EvolvedSearch.com.

Build the right links to build brand authority – with Alexandra Tachalova

Alexandra Tachalova from Digital Olympus ties two of our chapters together, by highlighting how the links that you build have an impact on your increasingly important authority as a brand.

Alexandra says: "Being a brand is the biggest ranking factor. If Google recognises your website as a brand, then it will deem that your site deserves visibility in Google SERPs.

One of the strongest ranking signals of your brand's authority to Google is the number of authoritative sites referring to you, which means that building the right links is one of your biggest responsibilities nowadays. To put it simply, the more influential sites that link back to your brand (that are authoritative and relevant to your niche), the more valuable Google perceives you to be, and the more chances you have to rank better in Google SERPs.

This trend has become increasingly evident and visible to us as marketers with recent Google updates and the growth of AI-generated content. It's quite hard for Google to differentiate what is created by AI. A website that represents a real brand, with real people behind the content, will get a stable flow of links from the right websites. Then, you have a higher chance of ranking better."

Do you need to continue acquiring meaningful links all the time, and should they happen organically?

"A real brand will continue to get links (which you can essentially think of as recommendations) on a regular basis. If someone is recommending you, and you continue running your business, then it's safe to assume that you will continue getting those meaningful recommendations.

In an ideal scenario, or if you've reached a certain level of visibility, you would acquire those links organically. Some companies, like HubSpot for instance, are relatively fixed. They're organically influential thanks to their level of brand awareness and overall visibility.

However, even brands like HubSpot need to facilitate their link-building activities sometimes because they want to rank for particular pages that don't receive a stable flow of links. As marketers and SEO specialists, we often want to get links to very specific pages that are not as exciting, but they are the ones that will actually generate leads for the business."

What are a few examples of the right types of links that you should be building at the moment?

"The right type of link is the link that you'd love to receive organically, but you don't really get. The rest of the links are a substitution for something. If you open your backlink profile, look through the links, and think, 'I would love to get more links like that.' – that would be a great win. That is exactly what kind of links you need to build."

Is it possible to mimic what happens organically and do it yourself?

"Absolutely. It depends on your resources, though, and whether you have time to build relationships with other people in your industry and other companies. For instance, joining a podcast.

Let's imagine my main goal for joining this podcast was getting a link, then it should happen eventually. However, that is not the right way of getting things done. If you become too transactional, people won't like that. They don't want to be part of a transactional chain of relationships. You have to build stronger bonds and consider links as a part of your marketing activity, rather than just reaching out to people for links.

If you're going to be a guest on someone's podcast, for example, then provide value – and make sure to promote the episode. Invest in that content as much as they do. Then, when you do ask for that link, no one will feel that you're trying to take advantage. That is very important. They're more likely to feel taken advantage of if you're just playing a number game or trying to fulfil your own needs without thinking about the other parties that are involved.

A lot of people are trying to get links for websites that don't have any brand behind them. For example, many media outlets have a main page that is essentially a combination of different blog posts. It might be designed in different ways, but it's not a real media outlet or a real brand.

A real brand will have a social media channel and will monetise in other ways, beyond simply selling things and having very aggressive banners. They will do something on top of that to monetise their content – like run some newsletters.

HackerNoon is a good example. Even though they are not an 'excellent brand' in terms of their overall authority, they engage in other marketing activities besides just publishing content and trying to monetise that through either paid links or banners. That's why Google perceives them to be a 'real brand'."

You say that sites that have a strong domain authority can easily find excellent results in Google SERPs without building any links to individual pages. Does this apply to every type of industry?

"Yes. Of course, there are certain industries where Google is very cautious, in terms of what pages they show – like YMYL sites. There will be some scenarios where your website might not get visibility due to a variety of reasons, such as the type of content, the quality of that content, etc.

We have a client that is not a well-known brand, so no one is kind of linking back to them. On top of that, they don't do any marketing activities besides investing in their content and link-building. They don't run their social media or anything like that which would increase their likelihood of getting clicks. They strictly invest in their SEO channel, which is based on content production and link building.

We've been working with them for more than three years and, even though they don't really get any links organically, the backlinks we've already acquired have built a very strong foundation. That allows their individual pages to rank well – including pages that don't have any organic links at all.

It's more about the power of domain authority than the internal links on their own. If you build authoritative links back to your homepage, even though you are not really linking back from your homepage to your blog post, the overall link value that you have given to your homepage is going to pass on enough link juice back to your blog post page."

Is an AI-driven SERP likely to change the way that you would want to build links in the future?

"If a link is the equivalent of a recommendation, then why should it become less important? Imagine there were no links, and nothing related to links really mattered for SEO. How would Google understand that this entity – this website – has enough authority to appear at the top of the results? There would need to be something to replace links for Google to make that judgement, but there is no replacement at the moment.

Even though AI will be trying to find the most relevant answer, Google only wants to show trustworthy information. You can have a lovely piece of content on a low-authority website, but Google only wants to show information that is not going to harm the users.

To Google, only a big brand can produce content that users can trust. Of course, that is not necessarily the case, even big brands sometimes produce horrible content, but that is Google's logic. They give priority to brands that have the resources, and the legal department, that minimise the risks on the user's side."

If an SEO is struggling for time, what should they stop doing right now so they can spend more time doing what you suggest in 2024?

"Stop producing useless content that no one wants to read, and think about how to combine your activities. You still need to produce content, but it needs to be really good content that will help grow your brand authority and will have the highest chance of getting a link.

You can improve your chances of getting a link by reaching out to experts, for instance. Create a content piece by combining the forces of your brand and the experts in your niche. Then, after promoting the content of those influencers for some time, you can also ask for a link as a favour. Think strategically about what you can do together, and the activities that are even more important than link building."

Alexandra Tachalova is Founder at Digital Olympus, and you can find

*her over at **DigitalOlympus.net.***

13 Technical Health

13 TECHNICAL HEALTH

Make sure that your site is built on solid technical foundations – with Tom Pool

Tom Pool from Blue Array implies that technical SEO is more than just a pillar, it's also the foundation on which all the other pillars stand. Make it strong and stable if you don't want the rest to topple, he says.

Tom says: "Ensure that you have complete technical quality throughout your entire site.

I come from a technical SEO background, that is what I do, and it's incredibly important to ensure that you have solid technical foundations for a website. If you have those foundations, you can build quality content, cracking links, and everything else on top of that. If you don't have that foundation in place, that's where things start to go wrong.

If Google can't effectively crawl and index the content on your site, they can't get that content to perform as well as it could. You're not doing your content justice. If you don't pay attention to technical SEO, you're not giving your site the best helping hand possible."

13 Technical Health

What does good technical site quality look like in 2024?

"It's largely the same as it has been for the last few years. Make sure that Google and other search engines can access your site as quickly and efficiently as possible. Not only that but also make sure that users can access and engage with the content on your site easily and effectively.

Make sure your content loads quickly and it's easy for users to find and access what they're looking for. Have a solid information architecture, and relevant schema in place on your pages. Follow best practice guidelines and ensure that Google and users can find stuff as easily as possible."

Have SEOs taken their eyes off the ball when it comes to their technical setup?

"As SEOs, we often get distracted by the next best thing. Six months ago, everyone was raving about ChatGPT and how it's going to change the world. Then we realised that it's not actually going to change the world just yet. A lot of people will try and go for the next and greatest thing, and it can be really easy to forget about the basics.

If you get the basics right, then you can start exploring the next and greatest – but you've got to get those basics done first."

How often do SEOs need to look at their basics?

"You should never forget about the basics. Every time you launch a new section of a site, make sure it is technically sound. That should be part and parcel of the procedure. If you want to have a checklist, you would have 10/15 things on that checklist that you do on a monthly basis.

A good starting point is to use Screaming Frog's crawl scheduling. Set up a daily or weekly crawl and get data pulled into a Looker Studio report automatically. That can be a fantastic way to start implementing these reports regularly and keep an eye on the basics without forgetting about them.

Once it's set up, it just runs in the background. You don't have to manually run a crawl every day. You can just review a Looker Studio report at the start of the day, and that's that."

Should you set up alerts and what alerts might those be?

"You can set up an email alerting system. Every site above a certain size is going to have some 404 errors, so you can set up an alert for a spike in those, a spike in redirects, or anything else that shouldn't be happening. If it does happen, you want to get a report or email alert sent to you.

You can use numerous things for that. If you've got data that's being pulled into Google Sheets, you can use a short Apps Script. You can even get ChatGPT to do it for you. That script will send you an email any time it goes above a base level or has a certain percentage increase.

You can use Python if that's more your game, or you can use Zapier if you don't want to touch any scripts at all. Plug that into your sheet, and any time a cell value goes above a certain number, it can send you an email alert. If you want to level things up further, you can get it to send Slack alerts too. It will ping you a direct message on Slack saying, 'Hey, your site has seen an increase in errors.'

Having that view on the basics can be really important, especially if a client does something like adding a noindex to their home page. You can catch it on the same day and save them a lot of lost revenue."

Is it possible to set up really specific alerts, like a sudden loss in conversions from a particular device?

"Of course. If you're using Google Analytics 4 and you're pulling that kind of data into it, you could also pull that into the same Looker Studio report and you could get it to automatically sync with Google Sheets and set up alerts that way as well. You can set it to refresh at the same time every single day, pull that data into that one location, and then send alerts.

I'm a big fan of GA4. It's a subject of much debate, but I like the way it classifies everything as an event, and you can get it to track events for everything. You can set up Tag Manager to track those specific conversions that you want to be looking at and set up alerts that way too."

Does site speed still have a significant impact on user experience?

"Absolutely. As a ranking factor, it's part of the overall EEAT of experience, expertise, authority and trust. Speed is a part of experience, meaning how a user experiences your website.

If it's incredibly slow, there's going to be a massive drop-off in potential conversions and potential money that people are spending on your site. If your site loads in a second and you could do a really technical tweak to save you a millisecond, it's probably not worth it, unless you're trying to get the fastest site possible.

It's all about trade-offs. If you make the site four seconds faster, what impact on your revenue could that have? If you make it 0.01 seconds faster, what impact is that going to have? Usually, the more seismic changes are going to have the bigger impact."

How do you determine if technical underperformance is impacting user behaviour?

"Generally, you can tell pretty quickly. If you look at a site and it has a lot of technical issues, then that is probably causing a lot of problems.

It's also about experimenting. If you think something's causing a problem and it's a site-wide issue, fix it on a single page. Then, track that single page granularly, looking at every single metric: impressions, clicks, click-through rate, conversions, time-on-page, scroll behaviour, whether they spend a long time trying to find what they're looking for or immediately go to the CTA, and whether it's clear to them what the next step is."

If users are happy with your site, do you still need to make technical improvements?

"I would always say yes. Always try and get to the best possible technical version of a site, even if your users are happy. You've got to keep the users happy, but also the bots that are crawling your site (Google Bot, Bing Bot, GPT Bot, etc.).

The happier the bots are, the more they're going to crawl. The faster they can crawl your site, and the more valuable content they find, the more frequently and the faster they'll recrawl your site. That will keep the index fresh and make sure that you're serving the most relevant content to your users."

How far should you future-proof your site to cope with larger amounts of traffic?

"I would go for something that's scalable. It depends on what you estimate is going to happen. If you're running a really viral PR campaign and you haven't got your site's bandwidth set up to deal with that, you're going to be in for some problems. If the PR team is going to make a massive push, you want to increase capacity prior to that, so the site can deal with any potential bandwidth that's going to be used.

Communication is the key. Make sure that any person who is working on your site knows what's happening – whether that's the developer fiddling around with the back end or a PR person getting links and traction on an organic level. There needs to be great communication between every member."

When talking with other departments, how much technical SEO knowledge should you share?

"As much as they're happy to absorb. Always start with the basics of what technical SEO is, the three pillars of SEO, how it all pulls into the wider marketing view, how technical SEO impacts developers, etc. If they're happy with that, by all means, start training your clients on further technical topics. The only limit is their thirst for knowledge.

We offer training for a lot of our clients. If they're not particularly clued up on technical SEO, it can be very valuable to offer them training on specific topics, so they understand a little bit more about why we're doing what we're doing. That can give great fuel to the fire for getting stuff implemented."

How do you measure the financial value of technical SEO improvements?

"That's a very tricky question and it doesn't have a simple answer. If you make a change on a site, it usually comes with other changes as well. You're rarely going to have a single thing happening at a time, so it can be hard to report on specific implementations. When you change a technical aspect of something, it can be hard to attribute that directly.

It's good to understand the trends. If you removed a noindex tag and the page started going up in search, that's kind of obvious. However, if you change a few redirects around, optimize speed a little bit, and add some further structured data, it can be a little trickier to understand which change resulted in a specific impact.

But the longer you do these sorts of things, the more you understand what is likely to have a bigger impact. In regards to reporting, it's about literally tracking everything. You won't put everything in a report, but you should make sure to track every possible metric that you would like to have visibility on, so you can report on it if you need to."

If an SEO is struggling for time, what should they stop doing right now so they can spend more time on technical SEO in 2024?

"Stop faffing about with stuff you don't need. We're all focused on trying to do the latest and greatest things, and sometimes you don't need to do that. Just do the basics and then build upon those basics. If you get the basics down, 90% of the time, you'll be all good.

If something you're doing is boring and repetitive, and it's something that you would like to not do, consider finding a way to automate that and take the load off. That doesn't mean finding the latest and greatest solution, it just means finding a way to get a machine to do that work for you.

You could use Python to do large-scale data analysis. If you take an export from Screaming Frog that you typically analyse in Google Sheets or Excel, it can be rather painful once that export is over a certain size. If you use Python to do that, not only will you save yourself the time of loading it up in the spreadsheet, but it will also make that task highly repeatable in the future. You can run the same analysis for a different client, with exactly the same script, and it will run in the same way."

Tom Pool is Technical and Training Director at Blue Array, and you can find him over at BlueArray.co.uk.

Don't lose ground when it comes to site speed – with Fili Wiese

To strengthen your technical SEO pillar, site speed is where you need to be turning your gaze, shares SEO Expert Fili Wiese. He considers this a vital metric across the entirety of your site.

What's your number one SEO tip for 2024?

Fili says: "Optimize for site speed. It's not just for individual pages, you really want to optimize the entire website.

We are talking about things like Core Web Vitals, but also how you approach your codebase, like JavaScript."

Is JavaScript something that's significantly impacting site speed?

"It can. JavaScript is a great coding language, and it has gained popularity in the last few years. However, it isn't necessarily the most efficient language. A lot of people have JavaScript in the backend, not just the frontend. When they do, they need to hydrate or pre-render their pages and content in order to optimize the delivery of that content to the user. Not everyone is doing that, and that can definitely be optimized.

On the frontend, we also see a lot of JavaScript dependency. For example, JavaScript is used to render or inject critical technical SEO elements or content elements. Unless you are using it for a sophisticated app, like a game, the individual landing page should not be that dependent on JavaScript to deliver content.

A while ago, the UK government did a study to determine who has JavaScript disabled. It turns out that every user is a user without JavaScript until JavaScript is loaded, so every user potentially cannot view it. On top of that, network issues (including mobile connections), ad blockers, firewalls, and other reasons can block the occasional request. It might not be every request for every user, but as you surf and browse the web, certain JavaScript files may not always render. If your website is dependent on that, that can cause an issue.

On top of that, JavaScript also has a potential rendering cost, including on the Googlebot side. If you inject your technical SEO signals with JavaScript, and you have contact with JavaScript, Googlebot has to render the page in order to see that. Rendering a page is much more costly than fetching a page, which they do initially. Google is getting a lot better with this, but it's not perfect and you shouldn't assume that this will always be the case.

You can't make your content or our technical SEO signals JavaScript-dependent. You should always inject the critical mass of your content and technical signals into the initial HTML code that does not require JavaScript to render."

Is this an issue for SEOs working on the edge, who use JavaScript to make changes without relying on an IT team to update the CMS?

"Yes, it is. Working on the edge is a great way to test things, but you have to keep in mind that it is not the final solution. It is not the final way of presenting the content down the line. The edge is a good way to build a case and experiment to see what works and what doesn't, without having to involve the IT team. However, once you have the answer to that, then involve your IT team and try to make it part of the actual codebase, because you don't want that dependency to be long-term.

Also, you build a dependency on whichever cloud provider you use on the edge. If you make any changes there – or if they have any issues or make any changes – that might negatively impact your ability to serve the right signals. That can happen overnight without you noticing, which can have a huge impact – especially in larger enterprises."

What other elements of site speed would you highlight?

"A lot of SEOs optimize for site speed on the frontend – fewer kilobytes in CSS files or JavaScript files, etc. There are still things that you can improve further. For example, how do you load your JavaScript? When do you load your JavaScript? When do you load your CSS? Do you have your above-the-fold critical CSS preloaded and non-critical CSS loaded afterwards?

Which fonts do you use? How many fonts do you use? To be honest, system fonts are fine nowadays. Why load an extra font if a system font will do just as well? System fonts are often designed for readability so your content will be well-presented and very readable.

Designers want to load more custom fonts to give a unique impression of the website, the logo, etc. However, in the end, I would prefer to load that as a SVG file, rather than a cacheable one – meaning with a separate file path, rather than injected into the HTML or by using another font. If you can use a CSV file to give the same impression that the font would, that's going to be smaller and more editable as a vector, which is much more useful in the long term.

You should also look at the backend. It's incredible how many people don't actually look at the crawl stats within Google Search Console and how fast their average response time to Googlebot is. A lot of websites have an average response time to Googlebot of above 200 milliseconds. Ideally (especially for larger sites), you want this under 100 or 50. The lower it is, the faster Google can crawl your site."

How can an SEO forecast the impact that significant increases in traffic volume may have on site performance?

"It's hard to do, but you can forecast using previous data. See how your site was performing previously, measure how site speed improvements have affected conversion rates over time, and then apply that to a potential forecast of what you could expect in the future.

It's important to use a source like the Chrome User Experience Report to get real user metrics. Of course, these metrics are collected from a Chrome perspective, so this data may not be as relevant for you if you have a lot of Safari or Apple users. That being said, they are real user metrics, and you can assess how your website has been doing over time and how much things have improved.

There's always room for improvement. This report is based on Core Web Vitals, and we're getting a new major metric to optimize for in early 2024: Interaction to Next Paint (INP). Right now, about 77% of websites have a good score in that regard, which means that a lot do not. Currently, around 50% of websites do not have a good score for Cumulative Layout Shift (CLS),

Largest Contentful Paint (LCP), and INP combined. There is still a lot of possible optimization left to do."

For Core Web Vitals, how do you know when a score is good enough and how much effort you should put in?

"It's good to compare with your competitors. If they're doing better on one score, and they're ranking a lot better, then improving one of the factors where they outperform you may help you over time. It's important to keep in mind, though, that a lot of the data needs to be confirmed by Google and Googlebot. They have to recrawl your website and see that it's faster – so you need to improve the backend as well.

One of the key things that a lot of people forget is that LCP depends on how fast you load some of those resources. Also, how big do you make your packages? How complicated do you make your packages? How do you code your packages? This is where CLS and INP come in. That can all be improved.

Measuring the success that comes out of that, and deciding how much you should invest, depends on your current scores. If your scores are okay, then your primary focus may not be on site speed in Core Web Vitals, but rather on what else you can improve. That could be the back end, like your response time and Time to First Byte (TTFB). I would look at that straight away and see what your average TTFB is.

That's another web vital that is tracked. It's not a Core Web Vital, but a lot of the other signals depend on it. If your TTFB is slow, everything else is going to be slow too."

Does JavaScript impact First Input Delay (FID)?

"First Input Delay is going to be depreciated as a Core Web Vital. It will still be around, but 95% of websites are fine with that particular signal. It's not as useful anymore, which is why they have started looking at INP.

FID comes from different sources, and JavaScript can have an impact there. It depends on how the page renders, when it's available, when the forms are ready, etc."

Is CLS still going to be key in 2024?

"Absolutely. If you want to test how your website performs on that front (especially if you have some bad scores and you want to identify what the issue is), you can check out my CLS Debugger (*https://webvitals.dev/cls*)."

If an SEO is struggling for time, what should they stop doing right now to spend more time doing what you suggest in 2024?

"If you're buying pay-to-rank links, stop immediately. Use that budget to improve the site speed of your website because those links are not going to benefit you anyway. You risk a penalty, and it's wasted money. If you pay for links for pay-to-rank purposes, you're basically tossing money away. Renting links is even worse but it does happen, especially in competitive industries.

There is a distinction between what type of links you buy. If you buy links for converting traffic and you add 'nofollow', etc., then it's perfectly fine. That's the way you actually benefit from those links.

Remember, the web is built on links. Tim Berners-Lee invented the hyperlink, which is what created the web. Clicking from one document to the next is what enables the World Wide Web to exist. Before that, we had hypermedia (images, documents, etc.) and we could search on a computer. However, we did not have a way to navigate from one document to the next, from within the document itself. That was the invention of the World Wide Web.

Links are the cornerstone of what we consider to be the World Wide Web or the Internet. Without them, there is no web. That's why Google initially put a lot of emphasis on that for their page rank algorithms. It's also why we have menus on our websites to allow people to navigate.

Linking and link building is not a problem. The problem is doing it solely to manipulate page rankings. In the eyes of the search engines, it is not desirable. If you do it for converting traffic, you're not wasting your money because you're getting traffic that converts. You're generating business.

However, if you're buying pay-to-rank links, please stop. Invest that money elsewhere, like site speed."

Fili Wiese is an SEO Expert, and you can find him over at SEO.Services.

Take control over who can access your content – with Emma Russell

As many contributors have alluded to, the long-reaching arms of AI are reaching into many aspects of digital life, which is why Emma Russell from Oxford Comma Digital says that you need to be a more discerning gatekeeper.

Emma says: "Control who has access to your content and, if you do want to give them access, make it personal and personalised.

I'm talking about search engines and AI. Obviously, getting your content in front of users is the main reason why you are creating content, and you want those users to be performing an action. Controlling how they access that content is one of the most important things that you can do.

If you are a news organisation or a journal that produces original research, for example, you now have a bit more control over which companies have access to your content – specifically, with the addition of the ability to block ChatGPT in your robots.txt file.

Back when news organisations first joined Google, were getting their news articles ranking, and had people discovering that content through Google and other search engines, they missed the opportunity to develop some kind of more formal relationship with those search engines. In return for access to that content, they could have had a monetary relationship.

There is a lot of complexity around the decision of whether you want to give access or not but, at this point, we are seeing another example of that decision absolutely needing to be made. AI companies are using that content to train their algorithms and then spit it out as 'unique', even though it's not necessarily unique and they are not necessarily crediting the organisation that created that content in the first place.

This decision is vital, and you need to make it now. This doesn't just impact news organisations either; every single business should be having this discussion. At a company level, and with SEOs who keep abreast of this topic, you need to decide whether you want to give access and help these AI companies train their algorithms to create this content."

Are there any particular types of content that you should typically block ChatGPT from accessing?

"News is the most obvious one, or any kind of original research – something that might feature in an academic journal, for example. Also, event-based content. If you're an aggregator of events in a specific niche, then it might be worth blocking ChatGPT. Of course, that is a decision that you would want to involve people other than SEOs in. Personally, I would lean towards blocking at that point.

There are also lots of different organisations that would want to take a moral stand on whether you want to give them access free of charge, or at all."

Are there any downsides to blocking ChatGPT from accessing your content?

"Potentially, though it will depend on how ChatGPT and Google continue to grow and be used. If we start to see Google being used less, then you might want to see how something like ChatGPT or BARD develops because different companies are crediting sources in different ways.

Something like ChatGPT doesn't necessarily give credit. However, if a user asks questions like, 'What is a good food to give my dog with a sensitive stomach?', then you would definitely want to appear for that kind of query if that is what you provide. At a brand level, it is absolutely worth being known. Giving access, and nuanced access, to your content might be a good idea.

If you are an events company, you may not want ChatGPT to be accessing your activity listing pages. However, you might want to give it access to the marketing content on that site because you still want to appear in different kinds of searches. You probably want to be recommended in the ChatGPT results for 'I want to run a 10k. How do I book this?', if that's something you want to rank for. On the other hand, if somebody wanted a list of all the

10Ks in their area, you wouldn't necessarily want ChatGPT to be able to give a good answer. You would want them to go to the site.

At the end of the day, you never really know how it's going to develop. ChatGPT might be moving in a slightly different direction and it might start citing things more. You might want to see how these tools develop and how the use of them changes.

Essentially, you want to retain your USP. You want to be able to provide people with the value your business offers. Information isn't necessarily what your business might be doing, but the service is. You want to protect and keep that, or at least be credited and cited for it."

Why should you make your content personal and personalised, if you are giving access to it?

"With AI coming into searches a lot more, and the latest version of SGE, Google are supplementing that with a much more human feel over in the Perspectives tabs. They are also highlighting things like experience and a more personal element in the content they rank.

You've got two sides of the coin. On one side you have results that are purely informational, which can be provided by an AI tool. On the other side, the user may not trust that AI-generated information, so they want a human touch to it, so Google are building that in. We're seeing a lot of movement – from the core algorithm update that we just saw to the helpful content update that's happening now – toward making content more personal. If you want to create content and get it to rank, it's absolutely worth keeping this in mind and making your content slightly more personalised.

I don't necessarily mean through personalisation on the site, with recommendations on where they go next, etc., but thinking about how individuals want to digest information. If you have video content and you want that page to rank, have a transcription for that content because not everybody likes video. If you have written content you might need to show images and have video to make sure that it is more personal and user-friendly for the audience that is coming to your site and digesting that information."

Should you have some informative, factual content that's designed to

be accessed by AI, along with more personalised content elsewhere?

"Absolutely. If you have a website that targets small business owners to help them develop their business, you might have one hero piece of content that explains how to create a business plan for your startup. That business plan and that information aren't going to be useful for every type of business, so you might want to delve deeper. It's your classic hub and spoke technique.

You might want to create content explaining how to make a business plan for creating a new product in the food industry. Then, you will provide some information from somebody who's done it before. They can offer specific recommendations or what not to do, based on their experience. That kind of information is not only going to be much more helpful to users who didn't feel that they got what they needed from that first hero piece of content, but it's what Google are looking for now.

Google are making moves to try and be more helpful to users overall, and SEOs need to catch up. It's certainly been an endeavour over the past few years, where a lot of SEOs are saying that you shouldn't write to try and game the algorithm. We're so past that now. We need to try to look further in the future of where this is going to go – and being as helpful as possible is absolutely it."

Is there an ideal platform on which to publish more personal content?

"It depends on your business and your business goals. For my SEO agency, I probably wouldn't go on TikTok – although there are probably some people doing it really well. It's just not in our strategy. It doesn't make sense and I don't see my audience being there. Even though a video I upload to YouTube might do quite well, I wouldn't necessarily expect to see the same results on TikTok.

Each platform requires something that is personalised to the audience that uses that platform, and sometimes that will be the same. On LinkedIn and YouTube, people might want informational content about what an SEO agency does, or they might want to learn about SEO. Personally, however, if I go onto TikTok and see somebody telling me about SEO, I will skip it immediately.

You need data to inform you about where your audience is and what they want from each platform. On the flip side of that, if I saw an SEO comedian making jokes on TikTok, although it might be a little bit cringy, I probably wouldn't immediately skip that.

People want different things from social media. Your video won't necessarily be applicable to each social media platform, and you need data to help you make decisions about where you should be using the content that you're creating. You don't need to be publishing the same video on every possible platform because some people will hate you for it. That has a negative impact on your brand, so you're possibly having more of a negative impact by doing that.

However, having a YouTube video and embedding it on your page is still going to be useful (even if the data doesn't necessarily suggest that video is required) because some people might prefer to digest that through video. It won't necessarily be the thing that gets you to rank, but giving the option to digest this information in different ways on the page is still quite useful.

Again, you need to look at your own data to see if people are actually pressing play or not, and whether that's something you want to continue doing, but it helps you be a little bit more useful to your audience and their different needs/requirements."

If an SEO is struggling for time, what should they stop doing right now so they can spend more time doing what you suggest in 2024?

"I went to a talk about link building at a conference recently. This talk would have been useful if it had been presented as the speaker having done everything that you shouldn't do, and then showing the results. Instead, they said that they wanted the business to thrive, and then they went through all of the link-building techniques you shouldn't do – from link farms to reciprocal linking to paying people. Then they showed their results from that as if that was the thing that you should be doing.

Go and read up on the modern literature and the Google Webmaster Guidelines around linking. Although the person who gave that talk did see some nice results, their results would have been a lot better if they had done things differently.

Stay up to date with the things that are happening in SEO. Every so often, you'll be surprised because Google will directly give a hint like your ability to change the robots.txt file or that some form of linking is probably not the best route to go down. Stay up to date."

Emma Russell is Founder at Oxford Comma Digital, and you can find her over at Oxford-Comma.digital.

Take SEO more seriously during a migration or relaunch – with Andor Palau

There are few things in an SEO's career that are more stressful than a relaunch or migration, and SEO Consultant Andor Palau wants your voice to be louder during that process.

Andor says: "My tip is regarding migrations and relaunches. If you're a company that relies heavily on SEO in your marketing mix and you are planning a relaunch, then you should take SEO seriously from the very beginning.

You should invest in additional tools you have not yet used and get external support during that period."

Why are additional tools required?

"Additional tools will help you challenge yourself, or the SEO team involved. Sometimes you have a blind spot. You use the same tools again and again. Especially during a migration, where a lot of things are changing, it helps to add additional data layers.

Also, tools do not always show you the same things. Sometimes they interpret data a little bit differently. Some tools show things that others don't and, when you are migrating, you want to have the best possible setup.

I'm not necessarily talking about tools for performance and measuring rankings and traffic. I'm mostly referring to tools that can be helpful from a technical point of view: crawling, indexing, etc. It really is helpful to add tools and get different data layers because will see more information, or the same information presented differently. That makes you more aware of the changes that have happened.

It's not so much about the performance; that can be measured and monitored in one tool. However, if you test things, it is really important to add new tools."

How can migrations go wrong if you do not take SEO seriously enough?

"We have seen several migrations that went utterly wrong in 2023, from an SEO perspective. Some of them could have been prevented if the tool stack had been extended, in my opinion.

There was a migration in Germany where a huge e-commerce company did a relaunch on three of their websites, and they all had the same problem. 80% of their entire website got de-indexed after the migration because a second <head> section was opened within the source code that had a noindex tag. Google recognised that and simply threw them out of the index. That could have been recognisable with some SEO tools.

We also saw a relaunch where a huge loss of visibility happened because the interlinking scheme was heavily changed during their migration. If you looked at the website before and after it was quite clear that a lot of prioritisations had been moved and things like that. That can again be spotted with the right tools.

In another case, the guys from Gieves & Hawkes in Savile Row, London relaunched their website and they just placed a static 'coming soon' page on it for several weeks, and they lost everything."

Is that something that could easily be recovered from, or would it take weeks or months to get the traffic back?

"It depends on the case. In the noindex example, you can probably recover from that quite easily because, if you remove the noindex, you will be recrawled and hopefully get back to where you were before, if the migration went okay.

If you present a static 'coming soon' page, it definitely depends on what the website looks like after that. However, that page shouldn't be appearing in 2023 and beyond. If you remove entire sections of your website, though, then you will lose that organic reach and the connected traffic and revenue. That is also important during the migration process.

Make it clear to everyone that, if changes are made on content or specific sections are removed that have driven revenue before, this might be going away after the migration."

Is there a typical type of migration that tends to be an issue?

"There are a lot of different types of migration, and it's common sense in SEO that you don't want to be doing everything at the same time.

It could be essentially a re-brush that happens on the same system, which is just a change of layout. That could be one part. It could be a domain switch, where everything stays the same, but you move from one domain to another because you changed your brand or you go from a country code top-level domain to a generic domain.

There can also be a mixture of changing content, changing domains, and changing URLs. These are oftentimes the most complex migrations, and where it might make sense to do some things before the big change and some things after. That way, you can better understand what impact the changes have actually had."

What tools would you recommend SEOs try?

"It does depend on the tools that you already have, so let me explain the different categories.

You definitely need at least one, if not two, tools that are related to crawling, indexing and all of that. You also definitely need something for performance and for monitoring site speed. You definitely want log files to be involved, at least if you are a domain of a certain size.

Then, you can go deeper into tools that you have developed yourself and smaller things. There are a lot of good solutions out there. Oncrawl is a tool that I use as I'm an Ambassador, but there are so many good crawling tools and suites outside of that. Just look at what suits you best."

How can an SEO ensure that they're aware of all the changes that departments are making that could impact organic success?

"Generally speaking, clear and transparent communication is one of the most important things for a migration process. You need to communicate precisely and transparently what is actually happening, what your expectations are, and the expectations of others as well.

We often just see the website from an SEO perspective but, when a migration or relaunch happens, it's both an opportunity and a risk for the company. They may have the website as a central point at the very beginning and then decide that they could use the same data for other applications as well. They may want to move away from a monolith CMS system to a headless system.

Then, there will obviously be a lot of expectations and requirements from other departments. Every company should keep in mind that they need to get all these expectations together and they need to understand them. SEO needs to have its share of that responsibility and understand what expectations others have, which might match with your own.

SEOs definitely need to understand what the revenue driver is. If it is SEO and the website, and you are entering a process where a lot of other things get involved, you need to communicate that this is the most important channel for revenue. Let other departments know that they should have this in mind when they make decisions."

Is revenue how an SEO should communicate with a business leader about the potential downside of a migration?

"Yes, because revenue is the most important metric or KPI for C-level. There are a lot of things that come after that but, if you have the information about revenue, that is very important. If your data is good enough, you can segment revenue to specific sectors of the website (such as specific topics or products), and they can be discussed during the process.

You can always refer to that and say, 'X topic makes 20% of our revenue. If we remove that, we not only lose the revenue we have right now, but we also may lose all potential revenue within that topic.' A lot of the time, SEOs think in terms of our own internal KPIs but, at a higher level, revenue is the most important thing."

How much time do you need to plan for a migration?

"Again, it depends on the size of the domain. If your website is not that big – you are a small company and you have a highly engaged team – 3-6 months can be enough, as long as everyone is really focused. A migration or relaunch always means that resources are focused on that specific topic. That means that other projects will be on hold. For a smaller website, that time commitment can be around 3-6 months.

Bigger migrations will definitely take 12 months or even longer. There is no one-size-fits-all solution.

Some SEOs are given a lot less time than 3 months. In that case, if SEO is a revenue driver and an important part of your marketing mix, you will probably pay for it with missing revenue after the migration."

If the migration has gone relatively well, is there anything that you have to keep track of?

"From my experience, if the migration went badly, you would see that immediately – within the first few days. As long as everything looks fine during that period, I would say that you have done well. After migration, even if you have a very good project plan, you have set milestones, and you know what you want to achieve during the migration, you may still need to reschedule measures and move them to the post-migration period. That can happen.

Then everyone will be relieved, and things can often get fixed faster. At that point, you simply need to make clear what is really important; what are the must-haves and what needs to be done. Otherwise, the migration needs to be rescheduled. Whatever is just nice to have can be done after the migration.

There should at least be a certain amount of post-migration monitoring for log files, ranking, traffic, and things like that. That should always be in place."

If an SEO is struggling for time, what should they stop doing right now so they can spend more time doing what you suggest in 2024?

"First, get more tools involved as soon as possible. You will probably discover new things that can help you with your communication. If you use the same tool set, again and again, all your direct reports know them as well. There will be a lack of awareness for certain things.

If you change the way you present your data, you can get new and fresh awareness. It will help you during a migration period so, if you have a migration coming up, you should definitely do that.

You should also really stress internally that everything needs to be tested and this will take time – and that you will probably lose some of your resources and projects when you move your capacity to the migration."

Andor Palau is an International SEO Consultant, and you can find him over at AndorPalau.com.

Improve your SEO audits and make them more meaningful – with Nikki Halliwell

Nikki Halliwell believes that many SEOs are stuck in a bit of a rut when it comes to their audits, and she offers up a number of ways that yours can provide greater meaning and greater value.

Nikki says: "Create a meaningful SEO audit.

Anyone can create a website, and there are even some automated tools that can audit a website for you (which I wouldn't recommend). The biggest difference is in the outcome of that audit. It's all well and good having a list of issues for a website, which is usually all you get from these automated tools, but the website owner, the client, the stakeholders, and everybody involved needs to know what they should do about that list.

I've been refining the process of working with relevant people at all levels of the business and developing a methodology that ensures that everybody involved can get what they need. This is something that any SEO professional can do, and there's no set way that it needs to look.

Essentially, instead of having a list of issues that says, 'X number of canonicals are missing', you should also include all of the information needed to fix it. I tend to lay my audits out on a spreadsheet, and I don't go into a huge amount of detail at this stage - that comes later. For each item, I include what the issue is, why it matters, how to fix it, what type of issue it is, where it can be found, all the specific URLs, and how to replicate the issue.

I talk about how it can be fixed, who's responsible for the fix, and who's responsible for ensuring it's done correctly. There's an important distinction between those two because they can be different people or different departments. The last few elements I include are the priority level, any repercussions of not resolving the issue, the potential value of fixing it, and when it needs to be done. You're basically going through the what, who, when, why, and how of each one.

These are all laid out in separate columns on a spreadsheet, including various amounts of detail for each one. This may seem straightforward, but you'd be surprised how many audits don't include any of this information. They'll just state the issue that was found.

I find it works best to lay this out on a spreadsheet, on a separate tab from the main audit, which means that everything is in one place and it's easily accessible to everyone who needs it. If more clarification is needed, you could do that when you come to work on each issue. I use a custom dev briefing document that I've developed. That's where you can include more details about each issue, such as the technical specs and links to any additional resources.

Creating a meaningful audit is not about changing what you audit but more about how you interpret the audit. Make sure you add actions and interpretations that are relevant to your stakeholders. Most SEOs have some sort of checklist that they use for their audit. I'm talking about taking that and presenting it to the client in a way that they can actually use. It doesn't matter if you have a checklist of 20 or 200 issues – it's about what the client can take from that."

In the tabs of your audit, should you have different actions and interpretations for each stakeholder?

"Yes. I break it down at top level, to begin with. You first identify whether it's technical, on-page, or off-page, and then you can state who the stakeholders are. That dictates the level of detail that you need.

That's why it's so much more straightforward and transferable in this format. You can have the top-level details for each person, but then, if a manager needs more details, you can include them in another tab or in the briefing document.

It's a living document that everyone can work from. Department heads, C-suite individuals, and others who are only likely to be interested in the big picture need different levels of information from those working on content, and the same applies to those working in the tech space."

Can you automate the analysis of this data to create a summary or is that a relatively human-driven task?

"For me, it's still a human-driven task – and I want to keep it that way. Automated tools work for some, but they don't include any of the context that you need. They don't understand everything else that might be happening around the business.

As humans, we're able to take things into consideration, like the size of the dev queue, how frequent the sprints are, when there's a code freeze, and what resources the client has. These are all things that feed into the sheet.

I call it my RAG matrix: Red, Amber, and Green. All of the information I discussed earlier is included in this matrix, but there is also prioritisation. Red is for the most crucial issues, and green is for issues that we can come to further down the line. This is all refined based on the human elements that I take into consideration, which automated tools are not able to do."

How do you encourage dev teams to implement your recommended fixes more quickly?

"It's all about speaking their language. You can use a briefing document and make sure you've got a seat at the table with dev teams. You want to speak directly to the people responsible for implementing the fixes you recommend.

A lot of people might put in a request to fix the canonicals, but how do you want them to be fixed? Is it the same blanket fix across the site? What is it that you need them to do? When I'm creating these documents and having these conversations with the people responsible for these fixes, I make sure that I'm talking about the scope of the issue. Is it one canonical, or is it a thousand? What do you need to do about them?

Provide steps to reproduce the issue and include any specific technical specifications. You can go into more detail here than in the audit. The issues might only affect certain browsers, operating systems, or mobile devices. It can even be different between mobile and desktop. You should also discuss the success metrics, KPIs, considerations, and blockers.

The success criteria are important because that's how dev teams will know the issue has been fixed. You can specify what they need to look for to be confident it's fixed, and they can pass it back to you to validate. You can also include approvals and any sign-off they need to get.

Remember that these briefing documents are not where you're explaining what a canonical is or why they are used. These documents should speak the language of the developers. They're designed to cut out the back-and-forth and ensure they have the necessary information to crack on and do what they do best.

Make sure that you're having conversations with your dev teams and asking them what they need to know to be able to do their job. It may seem like a simple step, but it is often overlooked. Skipping those conversations creates a huge amount of frustration and back-and-forth for everyone involved.

You can even take this further and ask to be included in the handover or review calls. When the work has been done, and the developers are confident that it's been fixed and they're getting ready to push it live to production, they will often have a call where they explain what they've done and how it works. If you're on that call and have access to the staging site, you can confirm whether the issue has really been fixed or not.

It's another way to check on the progress of these issues and ensure that you're having the right conversations with the right people – before any work begins and before anything is pushed live to the production site."

How often do stakeholders want to hear from you with a refreshed or updated audit?

"I didn't want to stick to the same cliches, but it depends. It depends on the size of the website that you're working on. When I have all these items on an issue log, I plan the actions out month by month. Again, it's a living document, so the priority and the focus items change each month based on where you are and what the priorities for that month are. That roadmap usually lasts about a year, but if there are big algorithm changes or a migration that will affect things, we tend to do a refresh or updated audit.

I also have regular, scheduled crawls running on my client sites, looking for anything that's changed or been impacted in any way. I always keep the audit updated in that way. I don't want to still talk about the two canonicals that were an issue in January if I can see that it's now 22 canonicals, or whatever the case may be. We've always got the latest information when discussing each item.

It is a live Google Document that is updated all the time. They're a lot easier to share with people at all levels. Depending on their industry, some businesses don't like Google documents and might prefer Excel. However, it's easily transferable – or you can use it on calls and share it with them.

In 99% of cases, Google Documents and Google Sheets work for most people. You share the link once, and everybody can access it, especially if they bookmark it. It makes it a lot easier. It's also handy for collaboration, and they can change the status of any items if needed. If you're waiting for teams to implement a page title change, they can update the status themselves rather than you having to keep chasing them.

If nothing else comes up, I tend to do a new audit, if needed, about once a year."

If an SEO is struggling for time, what should they stop doing right now so they can spend more time doing what you suggest in 2024?

"Stop relying on automated audit. What I mean by automated are the tools that audit your site for you and try to tell you what you need to work on. They tend to say that certain items are an issue when they're not.

I've had tools say that duplicate H1s are the number one biggest issue on a website when we can see there are big rendering issues or the hreflang is broken, which will have a greater impact.

I'm not saying avoid them altogether, and automated tools can be useful, but when it comes to your audit summaries or prioritisation, they may cause you to waste time. You're much better off getting hands-on and keeping that human element in the audits that you're working on.

These tools can also miss things. The other day, I saw a chatbot that popped up on mobile devices and inhibited the user's ability to click the checkout button. That was something that we could fix quickly and easily. However, if we'd been relying on tools to audit the sites for us, we'd never have picked that issue up because that's a user experience issue – and it's a conversion issue. It was the human element we needed to be able to spot that and see which mobile devices it was happening on.

In summary, save yourself time in the long run by not over-relying on automated tools when it is clear the work can benefit from human interpretation."

Nikki Halliwell is Tech SEO Lead at Journey Further, and you can find her over at JourneyFurther.com.

14 Diversification

14 DIVERSIFICATION

Diversify your skillset beyond just organic search – with Luke Carthy

An emerging theme this year is the importance of being more than a single instrument in the entire marketing orchestra, and E-commerce Consultant Luke Carthy says that you can't just focus on banging the organic search drum.

Luke says: "We need to diversify. The potency of search is not what it was, and we need to be in a situation where we're sufficient on channels outside of the search engine.

In particular, this is an opportunity for the revival of email, as email is one of the most fascinating and profitable channels available to us. SEOs spend a lot of time and effort creating content, ranking for keywords, and driving traffic. The disconnect that a lot of brands have is connecting that to commercial impact. It's great to have traffic and give people advice, but you need to turn the wheels and keep the lights on. This is where email comes in.

Whatever space you're in, there will always be a handful of FAQs that are the top burning questions that people have. You can turn that into a valuable resource and allow people to download it for free, in addition to coming onto your blog through those juicy blog posts that you're driving via organic traffic. From top-of-funnel (asking questions research-based queries, lots of good content), you get them into your funnel, they sign up via email, and you nurture them into customers.

We're just not doing enough on email to maximise revenue, especially with a lot of what's going on with AI. The way Google BARD has taken up all the real estate, organic search is only going to get worse, so we have to diversify.

We don't need less SEO, but SEOs need to do more. Don't put as many eggs purely into the art of driving organic traffic. There are a lot more levers to pull that can drive performance, outside of organic keywords."

Do you use another channel to make users aware of the brand, so that they can opt in and continue their journey through email?

"Absolutely. Recently, I was working with a brand in the world of leather. They were in a situation where they couldn't grow organically, and they were stagnating. We pushed a lot of content – like 'leather care', 'how to choose good leather', and 'leather repair' – which drives a lot of good traffic but doesn't necessarily result in more sales.

So, we stitched that content into their email. We had a welcome series which talked the customer through the family, who owns the business, what they're about, their culture, their skills, etc. Building an idea of who the company is really helps customers to make a purchase.

Then, you can trickle that across other parts of the business, such as social channels. If you have workshops, events, or promotions that are exclusive to certain customers, that can all go on TikTok, Instagram, etc. Email just works harder at being able to drive and engage more customers.

Organic brings them in, and it's still an important pillar. There is lots of 'free traffic' to be gained. At the other end, though, you have to mop all of that up and turn that traffic into conversions, loyal customers, retention, and awareness. Organic doesn't do that very well, especially with the increasing pressure from paid, above-the-fold, the knowledge graph, and everything else."

Can email be effective for initial contact or should the user opt-in first?

"I work on the side of the buyer and the purchase funnel, so outreach is not my area of expertise. As a consumer or a potential consumer, it is wildly powerful.

You can also think about the fact that email is data. Think about lists for paid socials and building an audience on TikTok. That can happen because you have a list of genuinely engaged people who want to be involved or have purchased from you before. We're in a situation where we can begin to diversify where we spend our time and money, and where we reach our customers.

In 2024, there is going to be more organic erosion and more pressure on trying to make organic profitable. It's a real shame, but we've seen it before. Lily Ray is a great advocate of AI, and staying on the cutting edge of what Google are up to with their BARD search experience. It's all going in the same direction: less real estate and fewer buys on the classic 10 blue links. This year, we are going to get less from organic, so we have to work harder elsewhere to bring the pounds/dollars/euros to client sales.

Is social media optimization a form of SEO?

"Yes. A paying client (someone who is investing cash into the service of SEO) only genuinely cares about a couple of things. One is return on investment, and the other is increased X – whether that's revenue, leads, a bit of both, or another core KPI. They don't care about where that comes from.

With that in mind, social media could well be roped into SEO. There's been a bit of noise about TikTok becoming a competitor to Google for search. The younger generation is heading to TikTok for advice, tips, things to do, places to eat, etc. All of those local searches are starting to gain traction on TikTok. It would be crazy to leave it off the table.

Of course, it's very early on, and I'm not a TikTok expert. There are trailblazers out there, who are leaders in the space and making a difference. However, the younger audience is definitely using TikTok as a search experience and research platform rather than Google. We might not expect TikTok to become the number one search engine, but it's creating more noise, so we should be paying attention to it."

What tasks are best done by humans and what tasks can be given to AI?

"As an analogy, I like to think about self-service checkouts. We love and loathe them in equal measure. The queues are short and there are 10 of them in the space of 2/3 tills. However, there always has to be somebody there to sort it out when you scan a cabbage, and the machine thinks it's the wrong weight.

The same methodology can be applied to AI. It's an incredible thing and it's getting more and more advanced as we move forward. It's hugely powerful, but there has to be an expert in that particular field to validate the information that's been spat out of it and make sure it makes sense. That's particularly true when you're in a space where personal safety is at risk: medicine, health, etc.

AI can be really useful for efficiencies and monotonous tasks, like data analysis. If you've got 10,000 keywords, from research or supplied by a client, AI can be wonderful for helping you slice that data up to give you information and insights. It can take a day's project of running through monotonous data and creating notes, and do it for you in a handful of minutes.

It's like any other SEO tool. We all have tools that do 95% of the work, crawling URLs for us, etc. However, there has to be the right person at the other end to make sense of the data. AI needs to be applied in the same way. The downside is that it's sometimes sold as a completely comprehensive solution that can function without any intervention. That's where it gets dangerous."

Should an SEO be a specialist in a certain aspect of SEO while also knowing a bit about every other aspect of marketing?

"Yes. My experience is in e-commerce, so there may be slightly different opinions and perspectives in other sectors, but I think T-shaped marketers are wonderful people. You have a core specialist area and then you know enough about certain things to be more effective.

If we think about all of the platforms across the tech stack, there is data at the heart of them. Data is where they make their money. In a cookieless world, where privacy is becoming increasingly important, having that data is much more valuable than just having traffic by itself.

However, it's a multitude mix. It's traffic, it's data, it's social – it's a bit of everything. A good mix of everything is a lot more powerful than investing solely in one element which may erode over time."

How do you know which platform is right for a particular part of the customer buying journey?

"The SERPS hold a lot of that information and data. If you search for 'skincare', you start to get an idea of what people are looking for. If you get more social, TikTok videos, and YouTube above the fold, then that gives you a good indication. Normally, you get makeup tutorials, one-on-one basics, reviews, do's and don'ts, and more controversial things at the side. All of this screams discovery.

SparkToro is a tool that really helps you to understand where your audience exists. It can tell you what kind of podcasts they might listen to, what Twitter/X followers they have, what news outlets they read, which YouTube channels they subscribe to, etc. That can really help you identify which voices matter in their discovery phase, and how people narrow down.

Google it first, then go on TikTok and search to see what's happening there. That will give you a good idea of where you can expect to find your audience, and you can move forward from there."

If an SEO is struggling for time, what should they stop doing right now so they can spend more time doing what you suggest in 2024?

"I'm a big advocate of R&D and I think everyone should spend some time being in the 'uncomfortable'. The problem is that's normally the first thing to go because, of course, it's uncomfortable. However, there is normally something that's carrying a bit of dead weight.

Stop being in a world where you do the same thing over and over again. Analytics is incredible, but you can spend time on it until you're blue in the

14 Diversification

face. If you're not getting more insight, spend less time doing that and experiment with something else. Keyword research is vastly powerful, but you can spend days, weeks, or months going into the finite.

Think about the broader picture. Throw things into TikTok and see what happens. See what experiences you get out and where the engagements are. If you have a client who is in an industry that you're not familiar with, TikTok can be a great eye-opener. The more virality a particular video has, the more it will help – as long as the comments are positive and constructive, and it's not just controversial clickbait.

In the world of skincare, I look into all sorts of trends like the things that people are avoiding, controversial products that have been banned, and ingredients that people shouldn't mess with. That gives me inspiration, and it can feed into the content strategy beyond narrow, traditional keyword research. I can broaden my horizons and look into specific ingredients, like the negatives of peptides. I only know about peptides because I went into TikTok, searched for 'skincare', started reading, and moved on from there.

It's a wonderful place to get new ideas, kill your writer's block, give you inspiration, and get you thinking outside the box. Of course, you can get carried away and spend half an hour scrolling through stuff before realising you haven't got anywhere. It's a fine balance, as with all social media.

Ultimately, you want to get out of your comfort zone. Put the typical tools down, experiment a little bit more, and pay more attention to things that are happening outside of the SERPs to see where things are going. Also, listen to a podcast that is in your field. You can put that on in the background and learn new things as you go."

Luke Carthy is an E-commerce Consultant, and you can find him over at LukeCarthy.com.

Go holistic and work more closely with other marketers – with Izzy Wisniewska

Izzy Wisniweska has a different approach to improving the breadth of what you bring to the table, and that involves taking advantage of the talents and knowledge of the people who sit beside you.

Izzy says: "Befriend other marketers and go holistic. In today's digital marketing world, we can't focus on one channel anymore – especially for brands that want to go big in order to build their branding and target more broadly.

You can't just focus on one channel, like SEO. You have to go holistic and work with other marketers. You have to work with your brand as well, but you need to ensure that your strategies are aligned. You can't do one thing for SEO and another thing for social media or split what you're focusing on.

Align everything together. That is the only way that you're going to hit the business goals – which is always a sale. They want to make money; that's why they hired you. You have to ensure that you're working towards the same goal and, to do that, your strategies have to be aligned and you need everybody working together so that your efforts are not disconnected and going in completely different directions."

How do SEOs befriend other marketers and go holistic?

"We talk to each other; it's as simple as that. Talk to each other, and schedule meetings and regular catchups with other marketing teams. In one of the agencies I worked at, we used to have short meetings every morning with our PR people and project managers to ensure that we were working towards the same goal, we weren't disconnected, and we weren't working on something that might negatively impact other team members.

Make sure that you know each other and you know what other teams are working on because there might be things that you can help each other with. If Christmas is approaching, you might be writing some blog posts and trying to rank them. Your social media team could help by posting it on social media and boosting some of those posts.

You have to talk to each other in order to do that. If you're going to focus on Christmas and they're going to focus on one sale for Black Friday, then it's all going in different directions. You could help each other out if you just aligned your efforts."

To ensure that nothing is forgotten, is there a formal process that you would recommend for working more effectively together?

"It all depends on the company that you work for. If you're in-house or agency side, it might be different as well. You could have Slack channels, and I would really recommend having an Asana board that everyone can contribute to so everyone can see what's going on.

You can have more formal meetings, perhaps once a week. I wouldn't do it too often, though, because you might run into the trap of just talking to each other and running out of time to do the actual work.

Once a week, you could have one formal meeting to go through your strategies. The teams can explain what they're focusing on and go through their ideas together, so everyone is involved from the beginning of the process, and everyone knows what's going on. Then, at subsequent meetings, you can have a catch-up. If you have more structured management, management and department heads can make a plan and then you can involve your juniors in another meeting, so everyone knows what's going on.

The key is for everyone to know what's going on, and then you could use morning meetings to just touch base on what you're doing today and highlight any potential issues."

Instead of having an SEO team, could you have a project team that includes one marketer from each channel being represented on that project?

"I used to work like this, and I think it can work really well. There were many people in the agency, but we worked in 'pods'. Those pods would have an SEO person, a PR person, and a project manager – and then we would have our set of clients. Obviously, we could talk between different pods and share ideas, but we would focus on our set of clients. This way, we could make sure that we were aligned with each other.

I like the idea of not having different channel teams but having campaign teams instead, to make sure that you have representatives of every channel in every campaign. Then, you make sure that everyone knows what's going on.

That might be tougher in bigger organisations, but it's about coming up with a way of structuring the teams to ensure that everyone knows what's going on. It's also useful to make sure that your broader marketing team understands different channels. I don't mean specialising in different channels but, as an SEO, I know how pay-per-click works. I'm focused on technical and on-page, but I know how link-building and PR work.

If you're a T-shaped marketer, and you have an understanding of the broader marketing efforts, you know how those other channels work, what they're working towards, and how that can be achieved. Even if something gets lost in translation, you can then spot potential issues. It's really helpful to ensure that your team is educated to a certain level.

They shouldn't be specialised in everything, because we can't specialise in everything. However, they should at least know what's going on and how things are achieved in different channels. Even if it's more difficult in different organisations, there are ways to make it work. There is always a structure, and there's always someone that we're reporting to. This information can start at the top, with the heads of the departments, and they can then share it with the lower levels.

For really large marketing teams, you could have a plan drafted up so everyone can read it in their own time and understand how the different channels are going to work together. It's vital, and I've seen firsthand what can happen when things are disconnected.

Even just in SEO, we have technical SEOs, local SEOs, content SEOs, etc. If these channels are disconnected, one person will do something and another team will see that it just doesn't work for them. It can just lead to going back and changing things, and losing time fixing things instead of going forward."

Could SEOs work in a pod one or two days a week and then go to their own team the rest of the time?

"I can see the benefit of that but it might be challenging if you were working on separate clients within the pods.

The pods we worked in at Re:signal were structured really well. Outside of working in a pod, we also had something called Lunch and Learn, where different team members would give talks, so we could all learn from each other.

We also worked very closely together, so you could always go to someone and talk to someone from the same channel if you had a problem or just wanted to have a chat. We also had internal newsletters to get updates on what was happening and a very good online internal communication structure.

There are different ways of structuring things. If you worked on the same client, you could work on different campaigns as a pod to make sure that everything is aligned. Then, as a bigger picture, you could come back to your teams."

If you're in an interdisciplinary team, how do you measure which channel has the biggest impact on the customer deciding to make a purchase?

"In an ideal world, you are a marketing team and you're fighting for the same goal, so you shouldn't try to take individual credit. You can still measure your impact though.

The fact that you all work on the same campaign doesn't change the things that you do. If you're doing a Christmas sale, you would still run pay-per-click, do your on-page SEO, make sure the technical is done, and do your social ads, but you might drive them to the same page. You might advertise the same campaign at the same time that the social ads do and make a lot of noise around it because that is what's most important to the brand.

You can still see the fragments. If you go to analytics, you can see who came from pay-per-click, who came from search, who came from social, etc. You're not changing what you do so much as how you do it and how you approach it. You're making sure that strategy is aligned, and you don't go in completely different directions. If you're promoting your perfume, you want the content team to be writing a blog post on 10 Best Perfumes for Christmas, not 10 Best Christmas Gifts.

It's still possible to see who came from where and how much revenue is assigned to each channel, if you need to."

If an SEO is struggling for time, what should they stop doing right now so they can spend more time focusing on what you suggest in 2024?

"Structuring your day better is always helpful, so stop checking emails at the beginning of your day. It might sound harsh but, when you start checking emails, then you do stuff for other people, and you don't do the stuff that you should be doing right now.

If you're not making to-do lists, start making to-do lists. To-do lists are gold. Also, have blocks of time dedicated to hardcore, focused work. I try to dedicate the mornings to that. If I've got a big project to finish, or a big chunk of work to do, I try to dedicate a morning to it. Then I start checking emails, replying to people, and doing bits and bobs.

That should mean that you have more time for communication and alignment with other teams because you've already done your main piece of work for the day. You can chat with other team members and tackle the work from the emails that you didn't check in the morning.

You can even leave client emails until later in the day. If something is terribly wrong and you don't see the email, they can always pick up a phone and call. The client will appreciate you actually working on tasks for them rather than just sitting and replying to emails. Replying to emails doesn't get things done. I'm not saying leave a client's email for days, I'm just saying that you should give yourself two or three hours to dedicate to your important work.

If you were in a meeting and another client emailed you, you wouldn't stop that meeting just to reply. You wouldn't even check your emails during a meeting. Strategy meetings can last for two or three hours, so you have to leave those emails for that amount of time anyway. If you have these focused sessions of hardcore work, and you really do stuff for that client, they will see that and they will appreciate it."

Izzy Wisniewska, the director of Creatos Media, and you can find her over at CreatosMedia.co.uk.

Cut across channels with the power of multimedia – with Crystal Carter

Like Izzy, Crystal Carter from Wix thinks that you can't succeed in a silo anymore. She takes this philosophy to your content, and explains how multimedia can take you into new, more diverse spaces.

Crystal says: "Use multimedia to cut across channels in your SEO strategy. I'm talking about audio, video, images, etc. Engage with clients, customers, and users across multiple digital spaces, using lots of different types of media.

SEOs are amazing at the written word. That's something we've mastered as a community. However, we need to be thinking about different media, and optimising for all the different media across our channels. When we do that, we're able to engage with more customers who are expecting to have content in different ways.

Video is something that users absolutely love. If you look at the stats, users are watching around 84 minutes of video per day. That's the equivalent of watching all the original Star Wars movies (and enough of the prequels to remember you never liked Jar Jar Binks), every single week. One survey found that 9 out of 10 users want more videos from brands. YouTubers have known this for years. They have millions of followers and they've been getting millions of views every week, launching entire brands off their channels.

Previously, video was out of reach because of production cost restrictions. However, there are now channels that require less production and methods of creating video that are less production-heavy, making video more accessible, and the expectation for video from users higher. Users expect to see a video of what an outfit looks like on a model. If I'm looking for clothing online, I will always watch a video, because you can tell a lot about fabric by how it moves. It's completely different from looking at fabric in a photo. It's easy to make a photo look fantastic, but it's more difficult to fake it in a video. That's something that users really value.

Additionally, video gives you a great opportunity to connect with your users. Almost every streaming platform has a comment section. When you're adding those channels into your marketing mix, and adding those videos onto your website, you're creating a back-and-forth conversation with your users – which is more challenging to do on a website alone."

How do you distinguish yourself from all the other videos out there and what format should you start with?

"That will depend on your audience. It's been very public that TikTok is the go-to place for Gen Z. If you are advertising to a younger audience, TikTok is great.

YouTube is really valuable for SEO. Every single video that gets published publicly on YouTube gets indexed on YouTube. Even videos that have 25-30 views. Not every page that gets published on the web gets indexed on Google, but every video that gets published on YouTube gets indexed on YouTube. When you add information about your webpage in the description of your YouTube video, you're adding a link from an indexed page to your webpage.

If you embed that video onto your webpage, Google's recently released loads of tools for SEOs to get great data and information about video in Google Search Console. There are video pages now, and you can see whether they're indexed, how they're working, whether it's perceived as the main video or a secondary video, etc. You can get great stats to give back to your clients and show the value you're adding by embedding those videos.

There are a lot of criteria for Google to index a video as a main video within Google Search Console, but most of them default to YouTube. They set the rules, and the rules favour YouTube. If you use YouTube for a web-first SEO project, that's going to work in your favour.

Vertical videos are great for connecting with customers, and for repurposing content and driving traffic to content to help with indexing and content discovery. You can add live links in the comments of YouTube Shorts. With

Instagram, you can put a 'Link in bio'. It's a great place to keep your customers engaged.

Media is an important tool for SEO because it tends to be associated with social feeds. Therefore, users can engage with you regularly, be driven to your content regularly, and know that you're there regularly. You can also get that content out there regularly, and Google's crawling it. Google's indexing tons of content from Facebook, TikTok, Instagram, YouTube, and all of these different places.

When you're thinking about the format, it's important to think about your overall objective – whether it's to drive awareness of new content that you're creating or repurpose content to demonstrate that it will appeal to a certain audience. The title of a blog might not tell someone whether or not it's for them, but you might be able to rephrase it on social media to show them that it's really useful.

If you're repurposing content, use things like Facebook, TikTok, Instagram, etc. If you are trying to push SEO and organic traffic directly from Google, then use a standard YouTube video."

Can video work for every type of content, or is it mainly useful for 'help' content?

"I engage with video in lots of different ways. Alongside the statistic that 9/10 customers are saying they want more video from brands, Google has said that 55% of users are looking at videos when they're physically in a store making the decision to buy something. That's not when they're doing home research and late-night scrolling to buy a kayak at 3 a.m., but when they're in the store looking at the kayak. They're looking at a video review. If it's a big-ticket item, they want to know if it's going to float or sink.

It's important to engage with folks in a way that is accessible, and folks engage with video in lots of different ways. One of my favourite TikTok creators is somebody who reseals driveways. There's a special sealant that can be added to a driveway, and it's fantastic to watch. He shows up and gives you a 'before' shot of the driveway. Then he gets out the goop, spreads it around, and shows off how neat it looks afterwards. It's very satisfying.

Whatever space you're working in, there's going to be a reason why you're working in that space, and why people engage with you. You make things better for people. That might sound grandiose, but my handheld vacuum cleaner literally changed my life. I live in a two-story house, and I had a vacuum cleaner with a plug, and it was really annoying. I really hated it. Trying to do my stairs was a pain. Now, I have a handheld vacuum cleaner, and it's the best thing ever. I can do my stairs in 3 minutes, and the whole house in 20."

Can you encourage your customers to create videos like that or does it happen naturally?

"When it comes to customers, if you are social, they will be social. They will engage with you if you are engaging. Don't be shy – and don't forget to engage folks in your teams.

Hobby Lobby went viral with a video of their employees dancing around the shop. Marks & Spencer's teams do great viral videos. You don't have to be in a customer-facing and super-fun industry. People are giving really interesting and valuable advice on TikTok, about serious topics like health, law, and SEO. Take the opportunity to get in there.

The same applies to images, Instagram, Pinterest, podcasts etc. Sometimes people think their vertical's really boring. They sell industrial epoxy resin, for example. I think that's great. That's how I've always felt about SEO. When people say they work in a really boring industry, that means the bar is really low. There are going to be people wanting to hear people talk about it on TikTok, and they will all find you because nobody else is talking about it.

Someone else that I follow is the bee lady from Texas. I love her. She goes around and removes bees from different places, and she makes little videos around it. She speaks very calmly and gently explains what she's doing. She has millions of views and people love her. Don't be afraid of it being boring; be helpful and get involved.

It also helps to have a regular thing that suits what you can do. At Wix, we do a webinar every month on an SEO topic. That's really useful. We get SEO experts in to talk about different things. We were having lots of experts talking about general SEO information, and then people in the chat were asking how to do it in Wix. So, I started including a little section at the end where I explain how to implement all the great things they've heard about from all these great people in Wix. It's a two-way conversation. People are asking you for content, and you're giving them the content. We do this regularly and schedule it well in advance, so it's a lot easier to manage.

Similarly, with our podcasts, we look at the conversations that we're having with folks around SEO when we're putting our podcasts together. We look at what's happening regularly so that we can create podcasts that are topical, and those are things that work for our schedules, resources, etc.

If you have a fantastic venue, video can be really useful. Recently, I was working with someone who hadn't made videos before. During COVID, they used video to explain which days they were open, how to keep safe, what measures they were taking, etc.

Sometimes people will also check different media for a vibe check. They'll look at the images on TripAdvisor, they'll look at the beautiful images from the brand, and then they'll look at the ones that other people have taken. Does that tiramisu look the same on the plate as it does in the promo? That is really important.

Google Business Profile is a great source for getting people to engage with your media, particularly for images. Google Business Profile actively encourages users to leave reviews as a Google Local Guide, and they encourage them to add images to those reviews. When people add images for your brand, thank them. Say, 'I'm glad you really enjoyed that tiramisu, that's really awesome! We've got some more coming out next week. Hope to see you then!' Engage with those folks. People will see that you're engaging, and they'll be more likely to add more videos, comments, and content like that.

People are adding videos to Google Business Profile as well, which is particularly important for local businesses. It shows at the very top of the SERP. If you're thinking about your SEO, that's another great place for making sure that you're engaging with multimedia to cut across your channels."

Is AI changing your content production process?

"AI can sometimes be helpful, and it can sometimes be a bit of a distraction. I recently made a post about ranking and opportunity, based on Wimbledon. The thing I find interesting about ranking in tennis and SEO is that it's anybody's game. You have your big star players but, on the day, it's anybody's game. The woman who won Wimbledon this year was entirely unranked. How did she do that? With skill, determination, etc. That happens in SEO all the time. Smaller brands outrank bigger brands because they've done it better on that particular occasion.

I was looking for an image for this piece and I tried using an AI-generation tool, and it was terrible. It took me ages. Then I went on a stock photography site and found a perfect picture straight away. You have to find a balance. If you're doing lots and lots of video, there are some tools that do great video editing. For example, GoPro can do some AI edits on your videos, which can be really useful. Some of these are built-in, and they can help you with your production costs. If you're transcribing, then use AI all the way. AI can help you update your transcripts, edit them, make sure they work well, translate them, etc. Those transcripts are really useful for adding natural language to your webpage.

I haven't looked too deeply into it for video production, but there are a few tools available for that. Synthesia has some great video tools that will allow you to create video with an avatar speaker, for instance, which can be useful for teams that are looking to get started and don't have a presenter to hand.

Think about how it might work for you and how you can make it efficient, effective, and resonate with your audience. Barry Schwartz uses a lot of AI images for his posts around Google updates and Google information. They look fantastic. That's something he uses regularly, which means that they're more consistent with regard to his branding style. If you get good at it, then it can work really well. I'm still refining my image prompting skills."

If an SEO is struggling for time, what should they stop doing right now so they can spend more time on multimedia in 2024?

"Be mindful of the time you spend looking at all of the AI tools that are out there. At Wix, we have some great AI tools that are built into the platform. We have things that allow you to edit images, create text, and so much more. They're all great but don't fall into the trap of endlessly researching them. Set out with an objective to complete and try to find a tool that meets that need. Then, stick with it for a while because you need to get good at it.

Artificial intelligence should be there to amplify your actual intelligence. If you have a really messy closet and you get a closet organiser, you still have to put the clothes into the organiser. You have to use it properly. If you don't know how to use it, then it's not going to help you.

Focus on your objective and use AI as a tool. Focus on the destination rather than the journey and don't fall into using AI for AI's sake. If you need it to complete a task, use it to complete a task, but don't use it for no reason. Sometimes, you can just use your actual intelligence, and that's totally fine."

Crystal Carter is Head of SEO Communications at Wix, and you can find her over at Wix.com/seo/learn.

Learn more and do more with Performance Max – with Navah Hopkins

To give you the tools you need to diversify what you're offering, Navah Hopkins from Optmyzr is here to explain how Performance Max is contributing and what you need to be doing with it.

Navah says: "Start paying attention and harnessing Performance Max to learn the lessons you used to get from Dynamic Search Ads.

The ad networks that enabled SEOs to understand how crawlable your site was, whether the content was understandable, the auction prices and value of traffic you could expect from your organic content, and that whole side of the business, are being rolled into Performance Max.

It's critical that you understand what you used to be able to get out of Dynamic Search Ads in Performance Max, as well as the bare-bones minimum of how to make it function.

I will also say that because Performance Max is focused on video, Display, and Discover, a lot of the work you're doing to put yourself in a good spot for the generative search experience is going to carry over to these ad channels. You want to be mindful of what this change means, what you'll be able to retain, and how you'll be able to move forward."

What are Performance Max ads and why are they different?

"Dynamic Search Ads used to crawl your site, and Google or Microsoft would come up with a text headline and you would write the description. It would be based on either the feed of your site, the whole index of your site, or particular pages.

Performance Max, on the other hand, is going to encompass a lot more than just text. It's going to focus on your ideal audience, putting ads on video (YouTube), Display, Discover, local search ads (not to be confused with local service ads), etc. The main reason why this is so critical is that Dynamic Search Ads had the entirety of the search term report, which was the equivalent in-page of the search query report.

What makes it a bit of a mixed bag is that we get some, but not always all, of the data in our search term reports in Performance Max. You need to be prepared to make some logical leaps and look at cohorts of content as opposed to its entirety.

You can also see what kinds of creative you are starting to serve. Are you serving assets that resonate well with one group but maybe not with another? The most important thing that you're going to be able to harness, though, is how well you have set up your site to be understood by the search engine.

Something that paid folks get very frustrated with is when we see what Google or Microsoft comes up with in Performance Max, and we don't know where the content came from, i.e., how did Google know to pull a particular bit of text? Where did the image come from? If you don't know where the content came from, that's a sign that something's amiss on the SEO front. Vice versa, if you are immaculately happy, then you know that you've set yourself up for success. On the organic side, you know it will be very easy for you to be picked up by the search engine.

You can use those paid tools to do that test with a small budget, or you can expand that part of the business and let your SEO work pay additional dividends and PPC. Both are valid approaches."

How does Performance Max focus on your ideal audience and how can SEO learn from that?

"You have the opportunity to help Google and input audience signals. These audience signals can be based on your existing converted customers or the native audiences in the market. Even just being able to see what audiences are out there, and whether or not what you have resonates with them, is useful. You can also just let Google figure out your audience signals based on the content.

For an SEO wondering, 'Have I set up my content in the way that my ideal customer is trying to search and engage? Is my content landing?', then I would recommend not putting in audience signals and just seeing how it performs. Then you can see if the ad network can perfectly match your content with this user.

Performance Max is a paid channel, so you are going to pay for that learning, but it is really valuable learning that you can then take to inform additional content you want to put out there.

If you're on the SEO side, you're not as beholden to amazing ROAS and a perfect match as the PPC folks. You have the freedom to use Performance Max as an intelligence tool, where it is very meaningful. If you let it find those learnings you can say, 'I have created five pieces of content that didn't resonate with the audience I expected, but they resonate with these other people. That's a new way of positioning, so I want to create a whole new series of content.", or 'It resonated perfectly, so I can just keep going down that path.'

If the goal of your Performance Max campaign is to achieve sales and results, as opposed to just intelligence, you should put audience signals in. Audience signals are good; definitely do that. However, from an SEO intelligence-gathering perspective, throwing $1,000 a month at a Performance Max campaign to gain intelligence you can use for several quarters' worth of content is not a bad deal."

For creative, do ads have to be uploaded to Performance Max or can they be automatically generated from the pages on your site?

"A lot of the SEOs that I talk with are used to throwing the feed from their organic site into Dynamic Search Ads and letting it generate these beautiful campaigns. Performance Max will behave the same way with the Final URL expansion tool.

You can choose to say, 'Make all of the creative for me.' Most people have brand standards, so you have to put in something that someone signs off on. However, Google has become very clever, and a lot of their innovations have been in helping you with creating videos, creating visuals, pulling text from your website, etc. If you don't want to make creative, you can definitely get away with it.

Now, it will not create a landing page for you. In theory, you're doing this because you have a beautiful site and you're happy with your landing page and how it's laid out. You just want to gain that intelligence.

Of late, PPCs have had to shift toward using the main site as opposed to a no-index, no-follow landing page or a subdomain, so you may need to honour certain rules of engagement within Google. If you're going to do this, it's important that you know what those rules of engagement are.

Number one, you cannot make any unsubstantiated claims. Even with EEAT and wanting to have that authority, you are going to be putting yourself at risk if you make any medical claims at all. Your ads are likely going to get disapproved. There are also other industries that Google and Microsoft will not allow you to advertise. You're probably not going to be able to take advantage of this if you run a gambling site.

However, if you're in the service industry, you're B2B, you're local, etc., then this is a really useful way to go about it."

How much data do you have to run through these campaigns to get some statistical significance for your SEO and how often should you

be running these tests?

"It really depends on your company. If you cannot commit $1,000 a month to a campaign, then odds are it's not going to make sense. You're not going to get enough data to justify it.

Most folks, when you're running a proper PPC campaign that's accountable for sales, leads, etc., you're likely looking at least $15,000-30,000 a month, if not several hundred thousand dollars a month. It's a sliding scale. If it's just for data, $1,000 a month is going to give you that intelligence.

I would suggest running it twice a year; once in the middle of Q1 and then again at the start of Q3. That will set you up very nicely for both H1 and H2 so that you're able to account for seasonality and make pivots in time. You'll have given yourself at least 30 to 60 days of intelligence gathering. If you start a campaign and you run it for two days, you're not going to learn anything. You typically want to give a campaign at minimum 30 days, but ideally closer to 60."

Is it possible to do this using an agency if you do not have an in-house paid search team?

"This might be me being a PPC person, but Performance Max doesn't require a lot of changes. In fact, if you're making a lot of changes to your campaigns, you're likely hurting them. One of the reasons PPCs have become very frustrated lately is that the number of controls at our disposal has gone away.

For the initial setup you say, 'I want to create a campaign', you can allow Google to pick the creative for you, you let it do its thing, and then you just look at the data coming through. If you want to make changes, however, the changes you should be making are as follows.

You can make changes to creative, and adjust that message mapping a little bit. You can make changes to your location targeting, and adjust which markets you're testing. You might also make some changes to your budgets because, from a bidding standpoint, there is no such thing as manual Performance Max. It's always going to be maximum conversions or maximum conversion value, which means you're not making manual adjustments to bids. From an audience targeting standpoint, you're putting in audience signals. You're not necessarily specifically targeting or excluding individual audiences.

SEOs might have the idea that PPCs are making lots of manual changes, but that's no longer a thing. Performance Max is a much more automated type of campaign. That being said, it functions based on the strategy that you've put in. If you're using it for intelligence, use it for intelligence, and know that you're not expecting sales out of the campaign. You're doing it specifically to see how well your site gets crawled by Google and Microsoft and what kind of content comes out.

If you're using it for sales, you likely want to partner with someone PPC-savvy to help you craft a meaningful budget and meaningful ROAS goals. For intelligence gathering, though, it is definitely still viable. It's also still a very viable additional source of income. If you're going to run a PPC campaign in conjunction with an SEO campaign, you are now able to say 'yes' to a little bit more business.

In the PPC world, many of us have had to adapt to additional channels. On the SEO side, as well, it seems like the need to be savvy in more than just one part of SEO has really expanded. If you're really good at content, this is a way to expand that content. If you're really good at technical, this is a great way to expand the technical. For a lot of different aspects of SEO, Performance Max definitely can be a way to bolster your business."

If an SEO is struggling for time, what should they stop doing right now so they can spend more time doing what you suggest in 2024?

"Delegate, delegate, delegate. A lot of us wear the yoke of feeling the need to do everything ourselves; be the hero and the super-smart person who gets it all done. Instead, be empowered to share the load – either with a direct report and help grow their career or maybe delegate out to an AI tool.

I put a lot of content out there. I have started dictating entire articles into Voice Assistant, putting them into ChatGPT to format them, and then taking them back and editing them. That means, instead of spending two hours writing a blog post, I spend 15 minutes dictating, ChatGPT gives me my formatted blog post, and then I spend another 15-20 minutes editing. That's a lot of time back in my day. Consider delegating."

Navah Hopkins is Evangelist at Optmyzr, and you can find her over at Optmyzr.com.

Start integrating video into your SEO strategy – with Sara Taher

If you're looking for a new weapon to add to your arsenal, Sara Taher from Assembly Global says that video is the way to go. She believes that this is where users and search engines are turning their attention.

Sara says: "Integrate video content into your SEO strategy, be it long-form, short-form, vertical, horizontal, or square videos."

You want to leverage video on the SERPs themselves and also on other platforms as well – like YouTube and TikTok. You basically want to create video content that you can also post on your website. For each of those, there are values that they are going to bring to your business.

We are past the way of thinking when we were just obsessed with blog posts and ranking in search with text. We want to rank with video as well because there's a high demand for it. Therefore, we also need to leverage other platforms and optimize for them – because there's YouTube SEO and TikTok SEO as well."

What does Google's new Perspectives filter mean for video?

"Google has launched the Perspectives filter on US mobile and it shows a lot of different content there. It's a new way of trying to get different or alternative views on the topic you're searching for and a lot of the content that's shown there is video.

If someone is looking for reviews or information about your brand or product, you definitely want to be there. One of the easiest ways to try to rank in the Perspectives filter is to create good video content – ideally short video, but it can also be long-form."

Where does Google pull the Perspectives video content from and what type of video does it favour?

"It's mostly from either TikTok or YouTube, and it's mostly short videos. When I did my research, I found some people saying that it will also feature long-form videos, but I haven't seen a lot of them so far.

From what I've seen, it seems as though long-form videos might be less likely to rank but we have to be aware that correlation does not equal causation. It could just be that there are fewer long-form being created videos for certain topics."

How can SEOs optimize their videos on YouTube, TikTok, etc., to appear more in the evolving SERP?

"The first step is to look at the assets you have. If you already have long-form videos, you can cut them into shorter ones, for example.

When it comes to the assets on your website, then you have to look at the schema. You need to have the right schema and you need to make sure that the video is indexed. Then, in a perfect world, you can add a transcript of that video as well. I also like to add subtitles, but that's mainly for accessibility. Adding a video transcription is great.

If we're talking about optimizing video on other platforms, there's a lot that goes into that. One thing I like to do is audit what you already have. If you don't have any video yet, then start publishing – and all the basics will still work: tags, titles, adding more information in the description box, etc. All of these basics are still there."

Why is video becoming so much more important?

"There are a lot of reasons. First of all, Google launched the video indexing report last year, and they recently updated it with more information about issues that can impact your video indexing.

We also have the Perspectives filter, as we just mentioned, and a decent portion of that has video content. We already have an existing video filter too, and then we have YouTube shorts, TikTok, etc.

All of these things show that Google is very interested in video and they also show that users are very interested in video. TikTok has over one billion active users every month and all the content they're consuming is just video."

How do you decide what content to start producing on video, particularly when you want to be featured in the Perspectives filter?

"Doing your keyword research – looking at what people are asking for and about in relation to your products and what they want to learn – and creating content to answer that is definitely a great place to start. You can get that data from keyword research tools, and you can check forums, Quora, Reddit, etc. Start there.

You can use tools like AnswerThePublic and AlsoAsked to find long-form questions that you can answer and give your perspective on through video. That would be a good way to do it.

Should SEOs be creating more video for all different page types on the website?

"You should definitely be putting video on your product pages. A lot of users would be interested in seeing your product in a video. When you go to an e-commerce fashion website, a lot of them are adding a video preview of the product. It shows someone wearing it and walking around with it, and you see how the product would look in real life.

You can even partner with influencers on video content for your products. You can send the product out to them and have them wear it, review it, and post videos that you can put on your product pages. ASOS did something similar with a photo rather than a video a few years ago. A girl had posted pictures of herself wearing an ASOS dress and she had received some cruel comments about it. ASOS took that same photo and used it on the product page on their website.

You also want video on your blog pages as well, and it doesn't need to be the video version of your blog. That can be an SEO hack, or a shortcut, because you can create that video with AI. However, in a perfect world, it should be something related to your blog. If you put it in the right place, you can actually get a video thumbnail in search which helps with CTR.

How do you measure the impact of video?

"There are two parts to it. If the video is on your website, you can check the video indexing report and you can look in Search Console. When you check the performance report in Search Console, you can filter by search appearance and select 'video' to see how your videos are doing in search – with impressions, clicks, etc. That's a great place to start.

You can also check how many video thumbnails or snippets you're getting in search. If that number is increasing, then that's also a good sign. It's not a final business metric, it's just an internal SEO metric that would help you know that you're on the right track.

If we're talking about other platforms like YouTube or TikTok, at a surface level you can obviously look at views. However, if you go to your YouTube Creator Studio, you will have YouTube analytics that can give you some idea of what's happening on your channel and the activity there. That's definitely a good place to look as well."

How can you placate the fears of big businesses who might be concerned about adding too much personality to what their brand represents through video?

"Honestly, I would want video creators to have free reign and show more personality, but I know that's not realistic. Ultimately, there are always brand requirements for anything you create – be it a blog post, a newsletter, or whatever. There will always be brand requirements and you need to work around that.

There are going to be ways that you can integrate those brand requirements. Some B2B brands, for example, will let their internal team members make those videos because they understand a lot about the product. However, other B2B brands might not want to have a specific person hosting their videos. In that case, there are ways you can create whiteboard videos, cartoon videos, or other forms of animated videos.

There's always a way to find a balance between creating video and meeting your brand guidelines."

Do you have any pet hates when it comes to video?

"I prefer short videos, and I think most people do. That's why TikTok is very popular.

I think the biggest issue for me is that it's not as easy to create as something like a blog post, and that's a big blocker. You need a plan, and you may need a set-up that you don't already have.

There are a lot of questions that need to be answered before creating video so not all businesses have this built-in part as part of their usual processes. It's not easy to go and tell a client that you want to create video if they haven't done that before. You need to practice if you want to get better. At the end of the day, your 100th video is always going to be a lot better than your 10th.

In what ways can your video and text content complement one another?

"You don't always need to create a video based on your blog posts, you can also create blog posts based on your video content. AI can be really helpful there because you can use it to get a transcript of your video that will help you create those posts. That's a very good approach.

I don't think we're leveraging the transcripts of videos enough. We've moved past the time when you would just upload a video on a video page. You need to have text and you need to use the transcript. We're lucky now because there are tons of tools that can help you pull that transcript.

There are also tons of tools that can help you cut those long videos into shorter ones that you can leverage and repurpose elsewhere. Another tool I will give a shout-out to is called Eightify. It's for YouTube, and it actually summarises your videos. You simply upload your video and you can get a summary that you can post into the description."

If an SEO is struggling for time, what should they stop doing right now so they can spend more time doing what you suggest in 2024?

"Stop obsessing over backlinks. There's so much more that needs to be done, should be done, and will bring a lot more value than obsessing over backlinks."

Sara Taher is SEO Manager at Assembly Global, and you can find her over at Sara-Taher.com.

15 Collaboration

15 COLLABORATION

Foster a collaborative environment to achieve success – with Montserrat Cano

You can diversify your own approach and skillset, but International SEO and Digital Marketing Specialist Monsterrat Cano is a firm believer in strength in numbers. It's foolish to work alone, she says.

Montse says: "My number one SEO tip to succeed in 2024 is to foster collaboration."

Who should SEOs be fostering collaboration with?

"I am talking about both SEOs and broad digital marketers talking to each other more, particularly if they are sitting in different departments and different teams. I also mean that they should be talking to other departments such as product, finance, and development.

That is so important. I could recommend embracing Artificial Intelligence, getting to know a bit more about ML, or deep-diving into schema markup, which is so important right now. However, if we approach all of this with a collaborative mindset, it will make things a lot easier when we try to reach our goals and deliver our projects. It will also make things easier from a mindset point of view by reducing your stress."

Why should SEOs spend time talking to other people rather than doing SEO?

"Other people might actually know what you don't know. It's as simple as that. There are two main reasons for this.

One reason is that there is more specialisation these days than there has ever been before. More and more people are working only on link building, technical SEO, etc. That is very exciting, and it is how we have made so much progress. However, it also makes for a more complex working environment.

The second reason is the need to constantly familiarise ourselves with new concepts and new ways of working. For example, Artificial Intelligence tools and ML have become mainstream fairly recently, and we now have to learn all about them. It's all very uncertain, and we don't really know whether what we are learning today is going to be useful tomorrow. Why not lean on other people's knowledge?

All of this comes on top of having to upskill ourselves. By upskilling ourselves, I mean learning about other things such as GA4 or schema markup, which we may not know much about. That creates uncertainty and anxiety. We might not have the time to learn it all.

Everybody has a remit in their jobs. You might view yourself as an expert in the German market because you have worked extensively in the German market, but it's not within your remit to actually find out more and validate the knowledge you think you have. Why not ask somebody else within the extended team? Why not let somebody else know that you need that knowledge and that skill set? It's going to be really interesting from your point of view because you will be able to learn more as well.

This becomes particularly obvious when you are working internationally. It's not just about the logistics of working internationally and building up an international online business. You think about the logistics side of things, the legality, payment systems, etc. What happens behind all that? What is the story? For example, the German market may prefer certain payment systems that simply aren't used in other markets. If you don't know that, then you might be making a mistake when you are building your business. Just ask."

How much time should SEOs dedicate to learning new things?

"We need to learn all the time because everything changes all of the time, but there's a limit. We need to implement what we learn, not just read about it. We need to actually talk to others so that we can learn from each other and implement those learnings.

There's no particular amount of time that I would recommend. It's more to do with leaning on everybody's learning than anything else. Take, for example, the relationship between SEOs and PPCs. Collaboration becomes very obvious there because organic and paid are different sides of the same coin. They are both search. We may be able to use PPC at some points and SEO at others, but the friction between them has always amazed me. I think this friction comes from the outside, where more budget is allocated to PPCs whereas SEOs have traditionally needed to make do with much less."

Is it no longer possible to be successful by focusing solely on SEO?

"Collaboration has always been something useful to do. My biggest successes during my career have come from collaborating with other teams and letting them know that they can collaborate with me as well. It has always been like that.

However, the complexity of the work landscape and the high level of competition on the SERPs and in the digital landscape, at this moment in time, make it really difficult to succeed by yourself. Perhaps it was easier before, but I do believe that success has always been achieved through collaboration."

As an example, how can an SEO reach out and obtain assistance from someone else when they are undertaking a migration?

"When you are migrating your website, you need to look into various aspects. It is not just about SEO; it's about everything else. Depending on the type of migration that you prefer, you may need different professionals to look into a variety of things.

One of those professionals is definitely a development team. It's really important that this team and other professionals are on the same page at all times. What an SEO or a project manager needs to do is, first, validate the idea. Then, you need to make sure that all resources are listed. Once those resources are listed, you need to reach out to those departments and make them aware that you will be making this migration.

Those may be designers, because you may need a new website if you are replatforming. Those may be finance or sales departments if it is a transactional website because there might be some downtime. Sales might be down for a little bit. Also, developers and engineers as a whole, because there is a specific moment in time when the website becomes more vulnerable to cyber-attacks. All the engineering teams need to come together at that moment. They have to know when 'moment zero' will be happening.

Before deciding to do a website migration, one of the first people I would actually go to for advice would be a development team. They will be able to let me know what their concerns might be, the feasibility of doing that migration in that time frame, etc."

Is this kind of collaboration specific to one form of migration?

"No, I'm talking about every single type of migration. If we talk about the specific types of migration, we might need different types of professionals. For example, a designer might not be needed for a simple change of protocol, but they might be needed for a replatforming or a rebranding.

Regardless of the type of migration you are doing, you need to make everyone aware, just to be sure. That way, they know they need to plan for this. They need to be allowed to look at their pipelines for their own projects and consider whether they need to hire somebody else to help them out in case they don't have the resources they need or are working on too many projects at that time. It's a way to show communication and show that you are able to involve other people and other departments.

It's also a way to show empathy: empathy for their own projects and empathy for their work life. They're not working for you. They are working for their own boss, and they have their own jobs and their own objectives. Empathy is really, really important. This is a good way to show respect and promote a positive working environment.

A few years ago, when I started to manage people directly rather than indirectly, I ran a private session with developers, product managers, other marketers, PR people, etc. It was really interesting. I wanted to find out whether we could come up with an idea to solve issues and whether those issues were exactly the same as the ones I was coming across. I was really surprised to find out that the number one issue we all had was a lack of respect.

Respect means that, first of all, people are asked for their opinion in the first place, because they have to be able to do their job. Secondly, it means that the right people are deployed to the right jobs. Quite often, I have seen certain professionals doing a job that other people should be doing. For example, people might be in charge of bits and pieces of SEO that they don't know anything about, such as link building or technical SEO. It's not a good idea.

A developer told me privately that they found it extremely annoying and became very nervous when other people, particularly SEOs, would come to them claiming that they could code and that they knew about coding and programming. That could potentially lead to this person taking away parts of the developer's job for themselves, which should not be the case. Even when SEOs do know about coding and programming, SEO is SEO. If there is a team of developers, they need to do the coding and the programming. They need to do what they are qualified to do."

If an SEO is struggling for time, what should they stop doing right now so they can spend more time collaborating in 2024?

"Stop and think about what, exactly, is stopping you from doing what you have to do. What is draining your time? It might be a lack of deep knowledge in a key area, or it might be the fact that whatever you are doing is just too big.

In the SEO world, there are people who know a bit about everything, but their expertise lies in one particular area, and that is great. If someone is an expert in schema markup, why not ask them about schema markup? If that is what's stopping you from achieving and moving forward, then simply ask someone for help."

Montserrat Cano is an International SEO and Digital Marketing Specialist, and you can find her over at Montserrat-Cano.com.

Start thinking more like a product manager – with Gus Pelogia

Montse recommended learning from others, and Gus Pelogia from Indeed certainly agrees. In particular, he says that you can improve your impact by taking inspiration from how product managers operate.

Gus says: "Think like a product manager.

For me, it's about following a process of discovery, testing, and seeing whether the things that you're doing actually have an impact or not. Let's say you believe that you can improve indexation on a website. That's your hypothesis. Then, you're going to start with the discovery phase: what are the possible things you can do to solve this problem? There are many different ways that you can do this, depending on the size of your website and the resources that you have.

Start with a hypothesis and the ways that you can achieve this, and always put everything on paper. What is in your head is very different from what is in your CMO's head, your manager's head, or your client's head. Having all of those things documented makes what you want to do, why you're doing it, and how you want to measure it a lot clearer."

How do you start with a hypothesis and where does it come from?

"I usually start by browsing around. An easy place to start is when Google releases a new metric or a statement saying that something works or something else doesn't.

Let's say you want to add more structured data to your website because you think that's going to help you rank better. Everybody knows that Google accepts some types of structured data and doesn't read others. You might question that and say, 'I believe that using Wikipedia links on my CMS is relevant' or, 'Adding links to pages using an 'about' field will be helpful'. That becomes your hypothesis.

As a simple example, we all know that internal links help with SEO. The links you give to a page and the anchor that you choose play a role in how Google reads that page. One link is probably not enough so do you need 50, 100, or a lot more? Your hypothesis might be that you need at least an additional 50 internal links to see if that page can move up. Then, you find ways to add those links, manually, programmatically, etc.

Start with a problem you want to solve, then you can come up with a hypothesis for how you can solve it based on the size of your company and the resources that you have.

Perhaps the trickiest aspect is the actual measuring of these results. If you are doing 10 things at the same time, any one of them could have had an impact. Before I started thinking like a product manager, I would just credit everything that we were doing. If we added internal links, improved page speed, added structured data, and released a PR campaign, then I would say that all of those things together were moving the needle. That is true to some extent but, once you start thinking like a PM, you will try to isolate each one of those things and determine whether it is really driving an increase in traffic or revenue, or not. At the end of the day, your hypothesis might be wrong."

When you're testing your hypothesis, how do you decide what elements to test and how do you come to a conclusion?

"Try to test one big thing at a time. You might be adding authors to a group of pages, and creating author pages detailing who those people are and why they are qualified to write about these topics. In a separate test, you could be adding tons of links to specific high-converting pages and, in another test, you're adding pricing on titles to see if people will click and convert more if they see the price before they go to the website. Try to run one of those things at a time.

You could run different tests on different groups of pages but don't run everything with every page at the same time or you won't be able to isolate.

Running SEO A/B tests, there are several SEO tools with this capability. You can create a task group, which could be the pages where you decided to add the price in the title, and a control group, which would be an equivalent group of pages that have historically performed similarly in terms of traffic. Once you have made the change, you can compare the two groups to see whether your change actually had an impact.

Both groups might grow at the same rate, which could indicate that the change did not make a difference. Playing with that kind of mentality and trying those types of things can really prove the impact of the tasks you are doing."

How does thinking like a product manager make it easier to get buy-in for your ideas?

"Last year, I learned how to write product requirement documents. For me, that was a huge game-changer. Before that, if I wanted to explain something to a client, I would create some nice slides to explain what we wanted to do and spend a lot of time making them pretty. That wouldn't necessarily offer a real hypothesis or methodology to test.

Most stakeholders want substance, like a fully written product requirement document (PRD). You might add some images to help explain the idea, but you have a clear problem, a clear hypothesis, you have estimations of what you can achieve, and you have a section for questions.

Have your CMO, director, manager, etc. come in while you're still working through the idea on paper. They can ask questions and give feedback so that you start getting that buy-in before the idea starts moving. You might have a great idea to implement something, but your developers might say, 'Actually, we cannot do this until we improve the platform.' You need to bring everyone into the room. Physically, it can be tricky these days, but a PRD is a way to expand your idea and get that buy-in.

Before you start working, developers could let you know that you're oversimplifying or that there's a better way to do it. Getting that buy-in is very exciting and you get some clarity before you actually start building things."

Are there any downsides to thinking like a product manager?

"It can depend on the size of the company and how difficult it is to sell certain things. Occasionally, when I'm writing one of these documents, I feel as though we could just really quickly release a feature. Before I was writing PRDs, I would sometimes release something on every page and then realise that we had no way to prove that any growth happened because of that change. The feature was there, and the traffic and conversions were there, but I couldn't show that this had happened because of what I did.

If you work in a company where you don't need to prove this, or if your clients are just interested in the results, that's fine. However, you might get into a situation where you don't have the resources to do all the things that you want, or you might spend a lot of time doing something that is not really moving the needle."

Can SEOs learn something from the market awareness of product managers?

"We can learn a lot. I recently released a feature through an A/B test. It was a traditional A/B test, so we were only showing it to a percentage of users so that we could compare how people were behaving on the page in our test group and in our control group. It turns out that they were doing almost the same thing. The hypothesis that we had wasn't really accurate. It's an interesting way to look at things from a different angle.

We do internal linking because we want those pages to read better, but we might forget that real people are coming to these pages, and they might look at something and think it doesn't make sense. Then, they might lose trust in your website or your brand. Having that awareness and thinking more broadly, with an open mind, does help you to look at things in a different way."

Should SEOs be harnessing the power of measurable goals?

"I think so. I try to treat every initiative as something that has an end. That end might just be working to the point where you know that it works and you know the potential impact behind it.

Once you prove that, then you can continue iterating and release your v2 or improvements to what you're doing. Each iteration can be its own measurable goal. In the end, we will always keep doing iterations of things. If we increase the conversion rate by 2%, we think about how we can do even better. To an extent, those projects never end because we want to keep doing more things or because we are chasing more results.

It's important to ask yourself, though, whether you are actually making a difference for the company. Some things work for one specific niche but not for others. If you just take the same approach with everyone, it can be hit-and-miss."

What are the first steps an SEO can take to start thinking more like a product manager?

"There are a few places where you can go to start learning. There's a great newsletter called The SEO Sprint by Adam Gent that talks about SEO and product teams working together. There is also a course from Pendo and Mind the Product that I'm doing right now and, even though I've been on this journey for a year and a half, I'm still learning a few things that I could have learned earlier.

For example, there's a formal process that I learned on the go. Seeing a whole holistic view of the steps and how they are referred to has been really helpful. 'Discovery' is a normal term in the product management world but, for me, I would just write a requirements document for an idea and pitch it to my boss. I never thought that I was in the discovery phase, where I had to research a lot of different things and come up with a list of ideas before adding things to the roadmap. It's not just about the next idea, but how all of those different ideas stack together, how difficult they are to achieve, and what impact they could have.

Now, every difference that I see in a product – it could be a SaaS product, a website, or something else – I think about why someone was developing that one feature. It might be a small thing, but it makes the product a lot better.

I've been rehearsing for a talk, and they required us to send the final version in PowerPoint. I didn't have it, but I wanted to make sure the slides looked good. I downloaded PowerPoint and it has a feature called Speaker Coach that hears my voice, my pacing, my words-per-minute, any filler words that I'm adding, and whether I'm reading what is on the screen. It's a small product feature but, because of this little feature, I'm all in with PowerPoint and I don't want to rehearse with Google Slides anymore.

Once you start getting into the mindset of all the little product improvements you can make to hook the user up a bit more, you start seeing those things everywhere. Start studying and start paying attention to the things around you that can be framed as products or product improvements."

If an SEO is struggling for time, what should they stop doing right now so they can spend more time doing what you suggest in 2024?

"Stop doing whatever people are saying is hot at the moment. There's a very big difference between something new and something that might have an impact. Something new might have an impact in six months, or it might have no impact at all.

Everybody was adding FAQ structured data for a long time, and now Google has said they don't want it anymore. I don't know how many people actually tested whether they were getting higher CTR from it and how many were just adding it because Google gave us the option to.

Do a bit of testing and come up with a hypothesis so you can verify what you're doing and make sure that you aren't spending too much time on things that won't have an impact."

Gus Pelogia is SEO Product Manager at Indeed, and you can find him over at Indeed.com.

Ensure that SEO takes its rightful place as a strategic business function – with Helen Pollitt

Gus and Montse both suggested that you should be listening to and learning from the wisdom of others, but Helen Pollitt from Car & Classic wants you to make sure that your core expertise is being heard.

Helen says: "SEO needs to be fully integrated across the whole business. It needs to be considered as more than just a marketing channel and take its rightful place as a strategic business function.

In my experience, if you ask people in your business what SEO is, the answers tend to range from 'I have no idea' to 'It's keywords and backlinks'. SEOs tend to sit in the metaphorical back corner of the office. We do marketing things with marketing people and all we're good for is helping people find our website on Google. That's all the vast majority of businesses seem to know about SEO.

That's a huge shame because the research that SEOs do day-to-day is incredibly valuable to the wider business. It gives insight into the current market, it can measure brand awareness, levels of competition, product-market fit, and all the things that are critical to a well-functioning marketing strategy – and beyond marketing as well."

Is SEO still a marketing channel that just needs to be involved in other areas of the business?

"SEO is predominantly marketing. It's historically been a marketing channel and to completely redefine SEO would be a larger project.

However, SEO is something that touches on a lot of different elements within a business. There has been a bit of an argument as to whether SEO is a marketing channel or more of a product department. I can understand that argument because we are involved in so much, and we touch on so many different functions of the website, the marketing channels, and business development.

It's difficult to say that we're only a marketing channel but that's predominantly what we are and where most SEOs sit within a business."

Is SEO an internal product that needs to be consulted when essential decisions related to technical infrastructure changes need to be made?

"Absolutely. I see myself as a product manager/owner for SEO. As an SEO, I have ownership over that product. You can see that more when you're agency-side or a contractor/consultant because you're very much offering the product of SEO.

However, when you're in-house, that's also how you need to think. You are likely to be consulting with a lot of different teams and a lot of different departments on SEO, and showing how SEO can help them reach their end goals. You want to change that mindset so that SEO is no longer viewed as a marketing tactic but as a product or a business growth lever."

If an SEO feels that they're not involved in the conversation, how do they get more involved?

"It starts with education. If your company's overarching understanding of SEO is that it is a marketing tactic – it's something you do to get people to your website and that's all – they won't know that you should be involved in those conversations.

For example, when a company is looking to move into a new market, SEO can be very valuable. We are able to help people understand the product knowledge and appetite for that product in the new market, what the competition is like, what the current peaks and troughs are with seasonality, etc. We bring so much data, insight, and wisdom across the board. When your company's making that huge strategic decision, SEOs can provide a lot of the intelligence that is needed – but no one knows to ask us.

As SEOs, we have to educate on how we can be useful and be a little bit forceful about involving ourselves in the conversation. You might not get invited to a meeting or be included in a conversation, but if you know SEO can help them achieve their goal, then offer that.

You don't have to be aggressive about it. You can just share that information and knowledge, and explain what SEO is and what you could add to that conversation. The more that you educate people that this is something you care about, are interested in, and can advise on, the more likely they are to include you in future conversations."

Should SEOs create an internal course and market that to get as many people as possible to attend?

"Yes; use your marketing skills. I am a broken record about SEO. Every time I start a new project with a company or I'm working with a new set of stakeholders, I'm talking all about SEO. People are so unsure about what it is and what value it can add that you almost have to keep reminding them that SEO can help with whatever they are doing. That way, people have SEO at the front of their minds when they're considering data or strategy.

Education can take a lot of different forms. A course is a great way of doing it, but you are never going to get your high-level stakeholders on a course. They just don't have the time. Instead, you could offer them quick snippets of extra context or information in the conversations that you're having with them. If you're in a meeting with a senior stakeholder, and they ask for your opinion, give a little bit more context around why that's your opinion instead of just saying what it is. Try to educate in every conversation that you're having that involves SEO.

Some people don't learn well through courses and other people need to have some written material that they can refer back to. Others like to ask questions, so having a facility where people can come and ask you questions can be very helpful. I host a half-hour clinic once a month where anyone in the company can come along and ask questions. They could be as simple as, 'What is SEO?' or as specific as, 'I'm looking at selecting a canonical tag for this page, how do I go about it?'

There are many different opportunities, you just need to find what you're comfortable with and work within the existing set-up of your company so that you're educating people in a way that they're used to receiving and learning information."

As an example another area within the business, how should an SEO sell the importance of getting involved in design?

"Designers often have a preconception that SEOs are there to say 'no' to stuff. In fact, a lot of teams and departments seem to think we're there to say 'no' to things. That's something we need to work on.

For design, in particular, we have so much information and data that can be really beneficial for them. We can tell them what people are interested in, what pages people navigate between, and what the end goal for a particular set of pages might be – and we can give them that extra layer of insight that they might not get their hands on otherwise.

A lot of designers won't be using data tools like Google Analytics or Hotjar to see how people are acting on the website and what they're interested in, or even give them that wider context of who their audience is. As SEOs, we can do that. We can talk to them about things like navigation, which is hugely important to designers. We can show them what our ideal would look like compared to their ideal, and where we can find a happy medium.

You can have quarterly sit-downs with the head of design and ask them what their roadmap is, and what the design team is looking to achieve in the next quarter. Then, you can tell them how you will be able to help them achieve that. It changes the conversation from, 'SEO said 'no' to what I wanted to release' to, 'SEO and I discussed this three months ago, we've already found a solution, and we're rolling it out. Here's the data letting us know that it's going to be successful.'

It's a true collaboration, rather than parachuting in when someone talks to you about something they're working on and you saying 'yes' or 'no' to it. Design is a great opportunity to do that because these are two teams that wouldn't necessarily have a lot to talk about normally. You have to make that effort to invite yourself into those conversations."

How does an SEO work with a traditional brand team internally?

"Brand isn't what it used to be. Brand is now completely augmented by social media, for example. The concept of a brand, and society's understanding of that brand, can change in a day because of something that went viral. SEOs have a huge part to play in that. We are oftentimes the first introduction that a potential consumer will have to a brand, and we're also there along the journey.

If you are the first touchpoint that a consumer has with a brand, you need to make sure that everything about the brand in the SERPs is positive. It's traditional online reputation management. Every time someone searches your brand, the People Also Ask questions should be really positive ones. If they're not, you should be the answer to those questions so that you can turn that negative into a positive.

You want to communicate to your brand team that not only are you supplying data, but you're also there to help them understand more about their audience and communicate their brand messaging effectively in places like the SERPs.

There needs to be less siloing amongst these teams. We're all trying to reach the same end goal and we want to remove a bit of that delineation between brand, SEO, PPC, CRM, etc. For a consumer, we're all the same company. That's all they perceive us to be, so we have to be really uniform and aligned in what we're working on."

How can SEO consult and work more closely with customer services?

"Customer service is such a good ally to have within a company. They can be amazing for insights. You can hear, from customers, what resonates well with them and what pain points they have. It's also very helpful for you to get a little bit more insight into things like complaints.

I mentioned online reputation management before, and it can often fall to SEOs to make sure that the front page of the SERP about our brand is all really positive. If it's not and you've got a load of negative reviews, for example, the customer services team has heard that stuff first. They can tell you how they deal with that kind of complaint internally, which is what you should be saying to people through the search results.

They can also be a great source of information about all the questions or complaints that come through. As SEOs, we can turn that into FAQs that can be served in the search results. Then, we bypass a lot of issues for them by providing that content and making it really accessible from the search results.

It is a two-way relationship with customer service teams. They can help us by giving us the information and insight that we struggle to get otherwise, and we can help them by putting an extra layer of information and customer support online – before they pick up the phone or answer an email."

If an SEO is struggling for time, what should they stop doing right now so they can spend more time doing what you suggest in 2024?

"Stop chasing the latest algorithm updates. Every SEO says this, but we still do it. Stop chasing all those updates and all of the arguing back and forth on social media about what Google has or hasn't said recently. We spend far too much time obsessing over that and not enough time looking at our own internal data and working out what works well for our particular website in our vertical.

Secondly, we need to spend less time trying to push that one ticket through the development team or the product management team that we think is going to solve everything for SEO.

Instead, work on changing the culture of the company so that it understands the value of SEO. By doing that, those tickets get actioned a lot quicker, and it will open up a pathway for more of your tickets, suggestions, and recommendations to get implemented."

Helen Pollitt is Head of SEO at Car & Classic, and you can find her over at CarandClassic.com.

Raise the status of SEO within the business – with Ash Nallawalla

Like Helen, and many of us, Ash Nallawalla from CRM911 Digital believes that SEO deserves a bit more recognition – and businesses will benefit greatly from giving SEO managers a bigger voice.

Ash says: "Enterprises should elevate the SEO function. The person/people who manage the SEO team should have their positions moved higher up in the org chart. The SEO manager should ideally sit in the C-suite.

Ask anyone who's been an enterprise SEO, either in-house or as an external consultant or an agency, and they can give you at least one example of how the SEO team was blindsided by some website decision that was taken without their knowledge – usually too late for anyone to change it.

Let me give some examples. The re-platforming of the company's core software included a new CMS because the vendor threw it in for free or you have to use it because it's integrated with a core software. The old one would need developer resources and a budget for implementation. Maybe the timeline for implementing the new CMS is hardwired so not all content can be transitioned to the new templates.

Perhaps there was a fear that people were scraping your content with bad intent, so the company implemented a smart firewall, and web crawlers that are run by the SEO team were impacted. Maybe SEO developer requests were kept in the backlog because there was revenue-generating work that was given higher priority.

The marketing agency might have recommended they build and operate a niche website on a new domain for some campaign or that it be implemented as a subdomain – and it was already in the marketing collateral, so you couldn't change it. Do these examples strike a chord with you? They're a blend of real examples from my own experience (with details altered so you can't identify where I might have seen them).

My recommendation is an ideal scenario, so you may not get it as a first win; it might take you a bit of effort. In this perfect world, the company creates a C-level position that some companies have called a Chief Web Officer (CWO) or a Chief Webmaster (CWM). A less formal title for this person is Web Success Officer because that describes the responsibility given to them.

Nothing should happen to the website without the knowledge of the CWO. That does not mean that this C-suite executive is inserted into every website process and invited to every meeting. They analyse and modify workflows at a high level to ensure that organic traffic is not impacted. For example, they might find that the web developers need some training in HTML tags that have an SEO impact and they might need to run SEO 101 sessions at regular intervals in small group sessions. That would be the ideal situation."

Are enterprises open to the CWO role or do they not recognise it as a requirement at the moment?

"Some have definitely done it. I did a search on LinkedIn for these titles, and I found about 10 such people in the world – some of which were past positions.

One company that came to mind was Colgate-Palmolive in the US. They had a Chief Web Officer at one point, I don't know if they still do, but someone certainly thought that it was a good idea. I commend them for having done that and I hope that they have continued such a position. A few other companies have had similar titles like Chief Webmaster.

Chief Digital Officer is a relatively common title. It seems to have spun off from the title of Chief Information Officer. Sometimes the CIO does everything that is vaguely digital. However, as companies mature, they can put the CIO in charge of infrastructure and create the CDO position to look at the website, apps, data privacy, etc.

Companies have definitely made a move, and I've recently been in a structure where the CDO was the C-level suite, and he was certainly very aware of SEO. I was fortunate in that scenario, but I'm speaking for other people whom I've met and spoken to, or interacted with online. Many of them have no clue how far up the ladder their reports circulate, and some of the examples that I hear confirm that decisions are made for many reasons – and SEO is not one of them.

It's as though organic traffic is not that important to them. Even though they might say that they are trying to get more sales or more leads through other means, they are embarrassed to admit that what they decided does impact SEO.

A few years ago, I was in a situation where the CMS was changed simply because it was free and allegedly integrated with their new, very expensive, multi-million-dollar transformation project. The website was a very tiny component of it. They spent a lot of time working on this free CMS and, later on, I heard that they threw it away and went for one of the big million-dollar solutions."

How can an SEO encourage the organisation to introduce this kind of role in the future?

"You want to try and give regular presentations at senior meetings.

It all depends on how many layers of management there are. I usually find that the SEO manager role has around three levels above them. At the most, you might be presenting to your manager's level but, from time to time, you need to watch out for those opportunities and say, 'Would it be a good idea to talk about these wins?'

Initially, you want to present some wins higher up. You won't get any objections if your manager can tell their managers that they've achieved a few SEO wins. That would give the SEO manager the chance to speak at the high-level meetings, so that's where you can begin.

Later on, once it becomes a regular thing, you can slip in some of the negative discoveries that you've made and, sooner or later, someone's going to say, 'How can we improve things for you?' That's the opening you need to watch out for and that's where you need to play your cards carefully."

Could SEOs then tell their high-level managers that there should be a CWO role to prevent issues in the future?

"Absolutely. I've seen a situation where decisions were made by someone who wore the hat of an Information Architecture Specialist. We were shaking our heads in the SEO team as to how would they have the knowledge of the impact they had on SEO just because they decided to change the CMS.

It can happen that these decisions are made by completely random corners of the company. For example, information security can suddenly take an interest in the firewall and decide that no one's going to be able to crawl the website at a high speed. Hopefully, they've heard of Googlebot but, if they haven't, they might discover that they've suddenly stopped the search engines. If they did that without telling the SEO team, they might be scratching their heads as to what's happened."

If there's not a lot of buy-in or it's challenging to talk to those higher up in the organisation, is there an alternative internal route that the SEO manager can take?

"In my last role, I was very fortunate to be part of a scrum squad comprising people from different parts of the company. We had a QA person, a UX person, developers from a couple of disciplines (a mobile developer, a desktop developer, an app developer, etc.), and more. In an agile workplace, these people belong to different verticals in the company, and they've often gone back to tell them what SEO is about. Then, I was invited to speak to those different groups.

When you are invited to another vertical's internal meetings, you start to influence people from the ground up, so you don't always need to look for a C-level person. It's fortunate if you do run into them at the water cooler, or you run into the CEO's secretary — and you can have conversations and throw out the word 'SEO'. One of the happiest moments in any SEO team's life is when they start seeing other teams talk about SEO in their conversations. It shows that the word has spread — and it's usually in a positive light.

Even if they don't understand everything straight away, at least they are interested. I've had to bring a few people up to date over the years, and they appreciate that. It's all a question of how you do it.

At two different workplaces, I've created an internal wiki just for SEO. This was partly for the education of the company (anyone interested could browse the topics that we had listed), but its main purpose was for the SEO team. We would record all our learnings there.

For example, I was at companies where half a dozen brands were migrated to new CMSs, one after the other. If the first one was disastrous, we would apply the learnings from that to the next one, and there would be fewer mistakes. The last four or five transitions would be completely flawless; we did not make those earlier mistakes again.

Having an internal wiki is a great way for people to discover what you're doing, and they can ask you questions. I definitely encourage the sharing of knowledge – not just at meetings but also in a more semi-permanent form, in internal documents such as a wiki."

If an SEO is struggling for time, what should they stop doing right now so they can spend more time doing what you suggest in 2024?

"I am not sure you need to stop doing anything, but you really need to find out who has not heard about the SEO team in your company, especially at the higher levels. Try to bump into a senior executive in a corporate social context. Many companies have occasions where you can mingle with senior people over Friday evening drinks, although it all depends on the workplace culture.

Look for every opportunity to drop some SEO stories – especially the wins. Everyone likes to hear about your wins. Then just ask if they happen to have read your last report and, if they aren't aware of it, they'll ask about it. Look for those openings and then ask, 'Would you like me to include you in future reports?' They'll always say yes, even if they don't open them.

The whole point is that the more people you manage to make aware of SEO, the better it will be in the long run."

Ash Nallawalla is CEO at CRM911 Digital, and you can find him over at CRM911.com.

Get buy-in from your stakeholders despite the changing SERP – with Sally Raymer

If you want your value to be recognised, and your projects to be approved, then Sally Raymer from SEO in Motion says that you need to communicate the impact you're having in the modern landscape.

Sally says: "Achieve stakeholder buy-in in an ever-changing landscape, especially with the introduction of SGE looming on the horizon.

Stakeholders do not understand SGE at all. There's a lot of good material out there from other SEOs in the field – Aleyda Solis being one of them. She's published loads of material about SGE and the effect that it's likely to have on the SEO landscape and how we do SEO as a business, especially in the e-commerce space.

Obviously, this is an update that's going to reach different countries at different times so it might not be affecting your marketplace yet. It might be something that you're preparing for the future. It might only be affecting a small proportion of your marketplace as it is still in beta. It's not part of every user experience yet.

Use a data-first approach, keep your ear close to the ground, and be prepared for the changes that are coming. Try and keep plan B in your pocket. For example, SGE might give a product listing page (PLP) experience, and many marketplaces and e-commerce sites are actually noindexing those PDPs for canonicalization and cannibalisation issues. You might need to think about how you can change that experience without losing too much value in your site.

You may need to think about how to add first-hand experience to your site. Is your authorship tagging up to best practice? Do you have enough information about your authors? Are you tagging authors with experience within your business or copywriters who may not be an authority on the subject that your site is talking about? EEAT is an integral part of this as well."

What stakeholders are you talking about here?

"It may be marketing directors who are leading a big team in-house. On the agency side, it might be your clients, and getting them to think about how things are going to change and how you're going to mitigate losing any search volume within that process. If you do lose search to the site, how are you going to gain that back? What metrics are you going to look at? What do you need to measure to ensure that you learn something from that process?

Until we really get a tangible sense of how our content performs with SGE, it might be hard to gain search volume back through the SGE itself. There might be certain searches that are absolutely perfect for you to gain it back, with clear ways to make quick wins, or it might be looking at other parts of the site and how you can gain it back there.

It might mean optimizing for new features or adding new features to your site such as video or user-generated content, which is performing really well in the last update."

Are stakeholders feeling that the overall value of SEO is diminishing?

"From my experience, they're not at the stage where they can, or are ready to, make that decision. It's something that they don't want to think about right now.

There are a lot of priorities that they want to think about first. It's about the traffic they're getting to the site right now, rather than traffic they're getting to the site six months or a year down the line – when some of these effects trickle through.

As SEOs, we know that what's happening in a year's time is very much going to impact what we're doing now. We're not working for tomorrow's deliverables. We're working for the results a year from now."

Are many SEOs changing their focus toward optimizing for Google Perspectives?

"Not just yet. It's a very experimental space at the moment. However, I'm certainly seeing SEOs being more conscious of first-hand experience on-site and how they communicate that to Google."

How does an SEO agency make a client feel more comfortable about the future?

"If you're an agency and you're concerned about the unknown effect this could have on SEO performance in the future, it might be safe to place your eggs in more baskets. You could become more involved in other aspects of the business to mitigate the risk of losing a client.

However, you can reassure the client that this isn't going to be a massive loss for them and there are other ways to achieve their goals, even if they might see a dip while you're analysing them.

Build that relationship before you begin any of these discussions. Make sure you've proven that you can get the results and you are an authority in SEO before even broaching the subject of SGE and the effect it might have on their particular niche."

How can SEOs get better at communicating using traditional business metrics?

"SEO KPIs and our usual metrics – how many clicks we're getting, what position we are, or what share of voice we have – have a place, but they don't deliver on the end objectives for a business.

In the last year, as things have got tougher economically, businesses have turned to the bottom line and they're asking SEOs to deliver on that, whether it's in-house or agency-side. From the outset, start with what impact your efforts are going to have on them as a business, rather than what position it's going to get, or how many clicks you are going to get. If it's not turning into sales or conversions, it really isn't doing anything for the business anyway."

Should SEOs make their stakeholders aware of the longer sales cycle and the value of traditional SEO metrics?

"Absolutely, SEOs should push back on being judged solely on their impact on the bottom line, to a degree. However, you shouldn't ignore the fact that your client or your business wants to look at the bottom line.

Embrace that, but also embrace the fact that SEO does play a larger role in the sales funnel. Be clear with your communication, including in all your reporting. Segment your keyword data, segment your clicks, impressions and sessions, and paint a really clear picture of what stage those users are in and where SEO plays a role in that acquisition."

Should SEOs host regular training sessions for their stakeholders and other people within the business on things like SGE and potential changes to the SERP?

"Definitely. It's something I do quite regularly. I like to hold workshops or afternoon learning sessions within the business to help them understand an aspect of SEO, especially if it's a big move for the business.

You want them to understand what's coming when there's a big update looming. That could be SGE, or it could be the new Core Web Vitals metric INP, which is coming in 2024."

How else has the SERP changed significantly over the last few months?

"We've seen FAQs completely stripped from most businesses, and this happens quite a lot. If you look over the last 4/5 years, we've seen FAQs completely stripped from the SERP on a regular basis – and then People Also Ask coming in and FAQs being taken out. We've definitely seen this happen in some specific SERPs but not in others.

Years ago, we had one SERP for all, and now we've got very different SERPs depending on the type of search that you're putting in.

There have been a lot of changes to the SERP recently, and it might not necessarily be new features appearing for every search you're making. It might be a local search which has far more advertising than it did last year, or it might be the fact that we're not seeing as many SERP features as we used to in certain spaces."

Can SEOs do anything to future-proof their content, so it will still be featured highly and consumed by the right target audience when the SERP changes?

"If you've got good content that is comprehensive and actually talks to the user, matching user intent, it's highly likely that it's still going to perform well. In terms of the SERP features, I always optimize for as many as are appropriate for the type of content that I'm writing.

SERPs do change quite a lot. If you optimize for as many appropriate features as possible, it doesn't matter if one feature falls out and you don't see it for a few months. You will gain a different SERP feature in that place, and you'll regain the original SERP feature when it comes back in 3-6 months' time.

If you're targeting a keyword phrase for a piece of content, always look at the SERP before you start creating."

If an SEO is struggling for time, what should they stop doing right now so they can spend more time doing what you suggest in 2024?

"Stop doing tasks for the sake of doing tasks. Start thinking about what your result-driven tasks are, what's really going to drive impact, and where your highest impact lies.

Prioritisation is key. Make sure that you're focusing on the areas that are going to get you the most bang for your buck and avoid doing a lot of admin tasks for the sake of your processes.

Knowing which tasks to prioritise really depends on what type of task it is. From a technical perspective, it's always down to visibility and accessibility. You want to make sure that search engines can crawl your site and crawl the important pages so they're getting indexed, and it's meeting user intent. Prioritise from the very first step – from indexing down to users actually interacting with your site."

Sally Raymer is an SEO Consultant at SEO in Motion, and you can find her over at SEOinMotion.com.

Data and Analytics

16 DATA AND ANALYTICS

Do more SEO testing and experimenting – with Olga Zarr

Olga Zarr from SEOSLY starts our deep-dive into data and analytics by encouraging you to take a more scientific approach.

Olga says: "Start doing SEO tests and experiments, in a nutshell.

If you do tests, even simple ones, you gain valuable SEO experience. You will actually learn how SEO works. Even if you are a beginner, this allows you to gain that little bit of experience. It also allows you to make decisions based on evidence instead of just assumptions or guesswork.

The purpose of that should be to optimise your SEO performance by understanding, through your tests, what works, what doesn't work, and what may work for your specific website.

It is also something that allows you to manage risks. If you test on a smaller site that you don't really care about, if something goes wrong, you won't pay for it. You can be sure to only put the implementations into production that turned out well during tests.

This is also a way to stay updated. We all know that Google changes its algorithm basically every day and, by doing those tests, you can learn what Google is valuing more now than it was a week ago. Of course, it all depends very much on the scale and type of tests you are doing."

How do you decide what to test?

"That depends on the KPIs that you have for a specific project, and what you want to achieve. You will be able to determine what it is that you want to test.

In most cases, it will be related to what you can do to increase rankings, increase traffic, increase conversions, and increase revenue. There are endless ways of doing SEO tests and experiments.

A/B testing, or split testing, is one of the ways you can test. For example, an initial test could be changing the format of your page titles on a certain number of your pages and then split testing that against your existing pages. You can do the same kind of testing with meta descriptions, content layouts, and basically any element on the page.

Of course, there are other types of tests you can do, like split URL testing. That is when you test different URLs, implement the change, and check how those URLs react to that change. There are also technical SEO tests, like whether better mobile speed for one URL really made a difference. That is one of the famous Core Web Vitals that people were optimizing like crazy, but then a lot of tests showed that they didn't really move the needle.

You can also do simple content experiments, like putting the introduction high above the fold instead of below the fold, because it was below an image before. Those types of things can bring very interesting results.

Another test would be a schema markup test, where you only add schema and nothing else. Will adding that schema change anything? Will it change rankings? Will it change traffic? It may change the presentation in SERPs, but will that different presentation lead to better CTR? I also love internal linking tests, where you change internal links and observe.

Those are just some examples of tests, and they can be very, very simple. You don't need to take a one-million-page website and do huge tests across every page. You can simply put up a basic WordPress site and just test one thing on that new test site. I recommend having a bunch of test sites so that you can test a few things simultaneously, or have a control group."

Is there any difference between a test and an experiment?

"I was using them interchangeably, but the only real difference is that you don't need an alternative to compare against with an experiment. You can run an experiment without a split test."

What's your favourite software to use for testing?

"Again, it depends. To be as minimalistic about it as possible, you can simply use a spreadsheet where you list the URLs, the rankings for specific keywords, the changes you made, and the date. That can be all you have: just a simple spreadsheet. You can also use more advanced SEO testing tools that allow you to set up more advanced tests, and have a better eye on how they are being implemented, what the results are, and what the changes are. If you are using spreadsheets, you will have to monitor them on your own or with your rank trackers.

The tool I'm also using (which is not necessarily strictly for SEO testing) is Cora, which basically measures tens of thousands of factors and, for a specific query, it will show you which factors statistically have more meaning. For example, in the case of one URL, it might show you that the title is the most important factor. That basis is run against all 100 pages that rank for a specific keyword, and then you can test whether this is actually true for your site. In many cases, it will be. Essentially, you will have better grounds for what you want to test.

When you're tracking rankings, you have to be efficient, because rankings like to fluctuate. I use a tool called SERP Volatility so that, every time I look at rankings, it runs that check 10 times. That way, I know what the position will be in 10 separate instances, so I can make a better decision regarding the results of my tests. Sometimes, the position may go up and I might assume that was thanks to my test, but it could just have been a one-time thing. How much of the time a specific keyword is on a specific position matters. Is it

100% of the time?

Of course, there are other things to keep an eye on, like Google Core updates. If your test started the day before an update, you have to take that into account as well."

How do you determine when a test was successful? Is there a certain amount of traffic that you need or a certain percentage improvement over the initial version?

"If you carry out the same test on multiple pages, on multiple sites, and all of those instances show similar results, then you can be pretty sure that the results are reliable. You want to have a few instances of that running, including the control group and the actual pages you are testing.

You don't have to be super scientific about this – just play with it and it will start to give you a lot of meaningful insights, and a different outlook on how SEO works."

Are SEOs testing things that they don't need to be testing?

"That is not the biggest issue; the biggest issue is that SEOs aren't testing enough. I was that type of SEO for a long time as well. We read a lot of stuff, we see a lot of articles, and we watch a lot of videos where people claim different things – and we often just accept that those things are true and keep preaching about them without actually checking for ourselves.

Try testing anything. You can even test something that may not make much sense, like testing Core Web Vitals. There have been so many tests run that we can be pretty sure it won't change much, but even running a Core Web Vitals test can teach you a lot about how to run a test, what you can learn, and the entire process. It's not that SEOs are testing the wrong things, but that they are not testing enough."

What don't you test yet that you intend to test in the future?

"There are hundreds of things I still haven't tested. The one thing I haven't tested yet is schema – like setting up a bunch of pages where I add a sentence description with schema and, within that sentence, I add entities that I think would make sense for a specific query. Those are the types of things I want to isolate. I could just be doing that, but I have to do my job as well. That is something I intend to do in the future."

Should SEOs carry out testing in one batch or continue their testing over time?

"I would advise SEOs to have active tests going all the time, and you can even run some tests on your live site. You don't always have to do it on a test site. Of course, it depends on what type of live site you have, but it is totally okay to test a title change on your site, for example.

Change the title of a blog post, start tracking it in your spreadsheet, and see what happens. There will be other factors in that type of test which may influence the rankings but even this is a type of a test: you do something, you document that, and you check what's going on afterwards."

If an SEO is struggling for time, what should they stop doing right now so they can spend more time doing testing in 2024?

"Stop reading about and following shiny objects.

A huge example of that in the past was Core Web Vitals, and I was a victim of that as well. I went crazy about it, created tons of guides and tutorials, and studied the Google documentation – and it didn't really change anything for my site.

Go back to the fundamental rules of SEO and test them for yourself by simply creating a small test website (if you don't have one already). A lot of SEOs don't want to create their own sites because they think they don't have the skills and they don't know how. They want to learn the theory first, but it doesn't really matter. You can find a quick tutorial on how to set up a WordPress site in five minutes, and it is important that you do that.

You can start by testing something like how long it takes Google to index your new site when you publish it with 100 pages versus when you publish it with 5 pages. You can do anything on earth, and it can bring you valuable experience. Do more practice and less theory."

Olga Zarr is the SEO Consultant at SEOSLY, and you can find her over at SEOSLY.com.

Don't forget about the power of analytics – with Krzysztof Marzec

Krzysztof Marzec from DevaGroup reminds you of the importance of analysing and interpreting the data that you can get your hands on, and the comprehensive free tools you currently have at your disposal.

Krzysztof says: "Don't forget about analytics, and I'm not just talking about Google Analytics 4. We have lots of tools. If you don't like GA4 you can find great alternatives like Microsoft Clarity.

It is super important, as an SEO, that you check the results and effects of your content optimization in your analytics. You have to base your decisions on data. For example, you can get a report in GA4 that will tell you exactly how your landing pages gather organic Google traffic. You can check the newly defined bounce rate and sessions with interactions to see whether you are matching the intent of your users.

Other reports can give you a lot of data as well. If you have GA4 merged with data from Google Search Console or Google Ads, you can check for keywords that are performing well, which could be great candidates for your SEO campaign. There are a lot of reports that can tell you why your campaign isn't performing and give you ideas. They might tell you that you have some very hard work ahead of you because your copy doesn't match user intent.

Your text might not be well prepared for your end user, so you have to improve it by adding explanations of your products or services, adding photos, etc. You can see this in your analytics data.

With Microsoft Clarity, you can also see recordings of user sessions, which will tell you if your SXO (Search Experience Optimization) is on point. For example, you might see that a user is entering your website and they are lost. Now you have to think about what your landing page is lacking. It's not only technical SEO that you can improve with analytics data, but also the UX or usability of your website."

What is GA4's new definition of 'bounce rate'?

"You have to be very careful when comparing data from Universal Analytics with GA4 data. In GA4, the user has to enter your website and stay there for 10 seconds for it to be treated as a session with engagement. Seeing two views or making a conversion can also be viewed as a session with engagement, even though the event is totally different.

The new bounce rate is the opposite of a session with engagement. The old bounce rate was only showing sessions with one interaction. The 10-second session factor was not included.

It's important to know that you can change this 10-second period in your GA4 setting to define your own bounce rate. You can check not only if a user enters and leaves your site, but if they open a blog post and spend less than 10 seconds reading your perfectly well-made SEO copy.

You can also improve your analysis of this by using something we call micro conversions. If you have an e-commerce site, you think about conversions as transactions; where someone adds something to their cart and makes a transaction. A micro conversion, on the other hand, could be viewing three different products in your store or enlarging a single photo.

That micro conversion will show you whether the traffic is better or worse and whether it might gain you more total conversions in the future. If you don't have conversion data, or you're making predictions, then you can use a micro conversion as a sign alongside bounce rate."

Can an in-house SEO work with GA4 themselves or should they be outsourcing to a GA4 professional?

"It depends on the site. If you have a lot of data, then you should outsource. If you have a small service, you might still outsource the implementation because it needs knowledge of things like Google Tag Manager and Cookie Consent settings.

However, I think that SEOs have the technical knowledge to learn GA4. If you want Google Analytics knowledge for free, Google documentation is the best place to go. There is also a platform called Skillshop where Google specialists can learn Google Ads, Google Analytics, etc. You can take exams there and certify yourself, and it's all for free."

How do you merge your GA4 data with data from Google Search Console?

"You have to go into the administration bar and you can merge data from Google Search Console into Google Analytics by allowing it there.

If a user has permission to view data in Analytics and view and edit data in Google Search Console, you will have this option already. Just click and you will be able to use GA4 to check the data from Google Search Console.

There is one catch, though. You can't match keywords with exact conversions. You can only do that in Google Ads. If you want to test a keyword, use Google Ads for that. To check the results for SEO, you have to look at incoming traffic to a landing page."

Can an SEO use only GA4 to analyse their data or should they still be using a tool like Looker Studio to bring data sources together?

"Looker Studio is a great way to save time because, if you don't need to dig into the data, you can prepare your reports without spending hours on them. If you are sending reports to someone who is not well-versed in Google Analytics, Looker Studio can prepare great examples that are interactive for the end user and very nice to read.

Remember, if you are a good programmer, you can merge all your data sources in Looker Studio. You can take other reports from your internal agency or freelancer CRM, and you can add your notes. These reports are as good as they come. You can make them look great as well, with your logo, etc. If you don't like GA4 and it's too much of a puzzle for you, Looker Studio is the answer."

Why should you use Microsoft Clarity as an additional tool?

"We are very used to data from Google Analytics, and clients are asking for data from third parties so that we don't only provide them with our stuff. Clarity is an add-on but, if you value your time and your data, and you're concerned about the speed of your website, then you should still use both of them.

It won't affect site speed significantly and it won't waste your time because you can choose which source you collect data from when you're gathering it. You want to have the two best tools that are available to you, and they are both free.

There are differences between them, of course, but now we are in the best situation because those two companies are fighting to provide us with the best tool. They are fighting for the end user and we, as end users, are benefiting. It's a great opportunity to start testing. You can't collect data from back in time, so you have to start collecting now if Clarity is a new tool for you. When you have free time in a few months, you can use that data to dig into it."

Are you seeing analytics professionals moving away from GA4 to something else?

"We still try to keep tabs on GA4 but, of course, there are some people who have used the update as an opportunity to test other systems like Adobe Analytics.

For small websites, we are seeing that people only use GA4 and Microsoft Clarity. Maybe that's just here in Poland, but those are the two best options right now if you ask me."

In terms of UX, what metrics are you looking at and how does that impact your SEO strategy?

"One example that you can check very easily is heatmaps, and you can check how users scroll your website. GA4 has a built-in event that will tell you when a user has scrolled through 90% of your page. It's automated but you can change it if you have knowledge of Google Tag Manager.

In Clarity, on the other hand, you have reports, and you can check all of the data. They are very nice to read because they are colourful and they're easy to present to your clients or other team members.

When you're analysing this report, you can change the order of elements like text, side elements, or call-to-action buttons. If you know that most of your users aren't scrolling past 50%, then you can rearrange it to keep them on the page for longer. You can move up the most important elements that will address the user's intent.

This isn't something you do every week. When you start working with a website, gather this data, then gather new data after you have made changes to see the difference in traffic after two or three months. You might learn that you lost some users and gained some unnecessary bounce rate because it was not made perfectly. We cannot know this before. We work based on intuition, experience, and how the website looks. After some time, we have data, so we can base our decisions on that data."

Are you still using a tool like Google Tag Manager to install and manage your tracking scripts?

"Yes. It's the best tool to manage all of your tags.

For example, if you're working on a website, it might use a tag like the LinkedIn Pixel to gather demographic data from LinkedIn. You can use GTM to implement other systems too, like GDPR in the EU consent mode. It's very important to use and know this tool, but I don't recommend becoming an expert in it. You're an SEO. You don't have to know GTM completely, but you do want to know the possibilities it offers.

In GTM you can 'hack' some websites, in a good way. For example, we are working with car dealers who own a website that is made centrally. They cannot change anything on this website in the code or the CMS, but we can use GTM to change titles, descriptions, or even text – and it affects the Google index. We can change it not only for the end user but for Googlebot as well. It's a good idea to know the possibilities of GTM because there are many of them."

Is using Google Tag Manager to make these changes more of a temporary band-aid fix?

"Of course, it's best to make permanent changes, but we sometimes work with clients that have so much bureaucracy that it takes months to make any changes at all. GTM can help because it allows us to install new codes and change how we implement Google Analytics without asking the client's IT team for anything. We have access to the containers.

When you're an SEO, you want to deliver results. You don't want to wait two months for a client to change your titles, which does happen in the real world."

If an SEO is struggling for time, what should they stop doing right now so they can spend more time doing what you suggest in 2024?

"Stop making manual reports, except when they describe what you've done for a client.

I've seen SEOs wasting time copying data from GA4 and Search Console into some nicely made PDF reports. It's a complete waste of time because all of those tools are based on technology. You can use scripts, APIs, and Google Docs to merge this data, or you can use Looker Studio to make those reports for you. SEOs should read reports and get ideas from the data, but you should not waste your time copying it out.

Writing a script or using an API is hard work and it takes time but doing reports every month takes time – and it takes part of your soul as well. Automate it. There are a lot of pre-made scripts that you can use, and they will help you to share data. Google Ads teams and SEO teams should be sharing their data, for example. Google Ads teams can make those scripts and export data that is very useful for SEOs. Don't do it manually; automate it."

Krzysztof Marzec is CEO at DevaGroup, and you can find him over at DevaGroup.pl.

Focus on what really counts: fresh, relevant data – with Kaspar Szymanski

Krzysztof urged you to delve deeper into your analytics, and Kaspar Szymanski from Search Brothers wants to make sure that you're looking in the right place.

Kaspar says: "Use relevant, fresh data for your SEO. Focus on what really counts; in particular, server logs for large websites.

Do not get distracted by short-lived SEO trends. SEO really is only about relevant data, and nothing else."

Is signal input what you are tracking with data?

"There are a lot of sources of data out there that we, as SEOs, can tap into. Anything else would be guesswork. Conducting SEO, building a strategy, and introducing changes (on the content, technical, or off-page side), without a data foundation, is really just guesswork. That's a business risk, and you don't want that.

On the very basic level, every webmaster should be tapping into Google Search Console and Bing Webmaster Tools if they want their website to do well in Google Search. Bing Webmaster Tools is very important because that's another source of data that demonstrates how search engines perceive the signals from your website, but it doesn't stop there. Really large websites can do so much more.

One thing that is frequently neglected, if not completely ignored, is server logs. In my experience, large websites ignore server logs nine times out of ten. They don't record them, or they only record them for a brief period of time and subsequently ignore the data or overwrite it as time passes. That's really unfortunate because there are so many things that can be done with server logs recorded over an extended period of time.

To begin with, you can start understanding how much overlap there is between desirable landing pages that should be in the XML sitemap, and the volume of landing pages that are being frequently crawled and re-crawled by

Google in order to understand the changes that are being introduced. That's just beginning to scratch the surface."

What's the difference between Bing Webmaster Tools and Google Search Console?

"Of course, the relevance is much higher with Google Search Console, in terms of market share. The vast majority of online marketers primarily care about Google Search because the market share is so dominant; it's still around 90-95%.

That remaining 5-10% might not seem like much, but it can be a lifeline when your organic traffic from Google isn't forthcoming for some reason or another. That could be because of a Google algorithm update, because something was done on the website unintentionally, or maybe because a legacy issue is holding the website back. That 5-10% can make a big difference.

In terms of the differences between the two, the data you get from Google Search Console is much more comprehensive and interesting. However, with Bing data at hand, you can verify things – or at least look at them from a different perspective. It isn't completely one-sided.

Most importantly, it is also cost-effective. All of that data is available free of charge, and you don't have to pay for an external tool. There are great tools out there, but many of them are paid solutions, so they require additional budget. When it comes to data, Google Search Console is the absolute minimum. If you want to take a tiny step beyond that, Bing Webmaster Tools will also help you to understand how your website is being perceived, how it's being crawled, and whether there are any issues. It doesn't stop there, of course; there's so much more that can be done."

Can you automatically combine the data from Bing Webmaster Tools and Search Console in something like Looker Studio to get a more holistic view?

"It is important to export data in bulk and retain it because that data isn't going to be available to us in perpetuity. It is being overwritten. That data is a snapshot of the last 90 days or so. It is possible to export it and import it into other tools. We do it slightly differently (we have our own proprietary software and our own approach), but it can be done.

If data is being utilised, it's important that it is being done by someone who has the capacity to understand what that data actually means. If that data is being exported and utilised, you either need to have the capacity to read it, understand it, and draw conclusions based on that data in-house, or you will need a third party to help read and understand it.

It doesn't have to be done on a weekly, or even monthly, basis. There are large websites with 100 million or 500 million landing pages, where the data volume justifies the resources required to ensure that the website is being continuously improved and optimized. For smaller websites, though, it doesn't have to be done on a daily or weekly basis.

If you have a car, you take it to the garage for an annual checkup – to check the fluids, the brakes, the lights, and everything else that you want to work perfectly when you go on a family trip to the beach. You don't want to be stuck in the middle of the road because you've got a flat tire, or the fluids have run low. It is similar with websites. For smaller websites that data needs to be reviewed on a regular basis, but far from weekly or even monthly. Once per year is enough.

The important thing is that this is being done, and it is being done by somebody who is capable of understanding what the data means and how to translate that into actionable advice."

What's the optimum way to use server logs?

"Server logs are my favourite topic. I really love server logs because they allow us unprecedented insights into how the website's server interacts with bots – and not just Googlebot.

There is a multitude of things that can be understood, but a very important one is the crawl budget. You need to have server load data covering an extended period of time to verify how much of the website is being crawled on a regular basis, knowing that the homepage is going to be crawled much more frequently than other pages. Only with that data at hand can you understand how big your website is and how long it is going to take for

Google to recrawl it."

Is how often the website is being recrawled important?

"It depends. For instance, if you are in the travel industry or the retail industry then it's critically important. If Google doesn't recrawl the changes introduced to your landing pages, you're running a huge risk of having expired, unusable content that is still ranking. They can't purchase that travel package or the item they were looking for. If those landing pages still rank, it's bound to create very poor user signals, which are going to destroy your rankings.

You want to understand how much of the website is being crawled, and what is being crawled. Is it the FAQ pages and the press releases? Is it the supplemental blog that is really just filler content or is it the actual sales pages? Is it the landing pages that you want to rank because they are the cash cows? Those are just a few critically important things.

Having server logs at hand, you can also understand how much waste there is, and how often the website is being scraped and crawled by fake bots.

I penned an article on Search Engine a while ago that outlines the benefits of introducing server logs, and there are very few downsides. The only downsides, or roadblocks, originate from two departments. The first is often the legal department saying that server logs are problematic at a time when data is being protected. That's true to an extent, but it doesn't apply to server logs because you're only looking at bot data, not user data. There is no risk of utilising any data in an inappropriate way.

The other issue that is often brought to the table is that it's expensive. It is going to cost money, but very little. Hard drives are as cheap as they've ever been, and server log data is relatively small. It can be compressed and Gzipped, so it can be stored on a physical hard drive in perpetuity. It doesn't cost a lot of money, but the potential of tapping into that data in the course of conducting an SEO audit is huge."

How does an SEO define what is critically important for them to focus on?

"The honest answer is that it depends. It depends on every individual website and organisation. They're all different. If you are looking from a commercial perspective, and you want to do well in Google search, your unique selling proposition is going to be critical.

What is the one thing that makes you stand out? It could be because you have the best price ever, so your unique selling proposition would be founded on having the most attractive pricing. It could be that there is a great community behind the product, that you have the best selection of products in your vertical, etc. The important thing is to convey that message to the users and make sure they understand that this real brand has a unique selling proposition.

Then, you also need to convey that message on the landing pages, and in the snippet representations of landing pages that are being crawled, indexed, and ranked. Doing so will help you to have a massive positive impact on user signals. If your landing pages rank for relevant queries – and you can not only live up to the expectation behind that query but also meet or exceed user expectations on the landing page – that is going to translate to positive user signals for Google.

That is what's going to help your website rank well. Google shows a preference for websites that are popular with users. Putting the user first, via your USP, is a winning strategy. It's not the only thing that needs to be done, especially in competitive environments, but without a unique selling proposition, it is very difficult indeed."

If an SEO is struggling for time, what should they stop doing right now so they can spend more time doing what you suggest in 2024?

"Our industry isn't very different from others. There are a lot of myths and a lot of concerns on the client side that do not really need to be addressed. One thing you can stop doing is talking about, or even thinking about, domain authority. It is a poor allocation of your time and resources.

That is because Google doesn't care about that value. Whatever your perceived domain authority may be, it is not something that Google views as good or bad. It's of no consequence, so we can stop thinking about it in the

SEO industry."

Kaspar Szymanski is the Founder of Search Brothers, and you can find him over at SearchBrothers.com.

Use data wisely to improve your processes and prevent future damage – with Marco Giordano

Examining data is more than an exercise in analysis, says SEO Specialist Marco Giordano – it can be a pro-active way to innovate what you're doing and stay ahead of the game.

Marco says: "Use SEO data to improve processes and prevent future damage."

What SEO data are we talking about here?

"Mostly Search Console data, analytics, and crawl data from a crawler like Screaming Frog. If possible, you should be integrating non-SEO data as well.

Non-SEO data is any data that is not purely SEO: customer data, sales data, etc. It could be content information, like the author of a given article, which can still provide a lot of value for SEO."

Do you bring this into data management software, like BigQuery, alongside your Google Search Console data?

"Yes, but it mostly depends on the project I'm dealing with.

It's a great idea to have the data you care about or want to preserve in a storage system like BigQuery, where you can join the tables and combine this data. It's not always possible, but it's something I recommend if you have the opportunity. BigQuery is not expensive, in most cases, especially if you're a big company."

What is your process for acquiring data?

"My process is more of a framework for analytics as a whole and it's based on standard practices. It's not completely new. It's the same idea that you would find in any analytics book, I just adapted it to SEO.

First, you have to gather the requirements: what the client wants or what the project is about. The idea is to use data for SEO but it's not only SEO. It's also about how to use data in general, so you can apply the same reasoning in other industries. Once you get the requirements (what they want, what the best metrics are, what the goals are, what their intentions are, their capacity, etc.), you can move on to gathering your data. Try to find the proper data to analyse the problem.

Then, you clean the data. Remove what you don't care about, what creates noise, and what is not relevant to your analysis."

How do you know what you shouldn't care about?

"In most cases, you know from experience. If you have a WordPress website, tags, categories, or filler pages like author pages are not relevant for a content audit. If you want to know what pages you have to prune, it will never be those pages even if they don't get organic traffic. It wouldn't make any sense, so you can ignore them. If the goal of your analysis is to find the best articles or the worst articles, you wouldn't care about those pages because they are outside of your scope.

In other cases, it's just noise. If you have archive pages, you don't need them in your analysis, so you can just filter them out. The same applies to a lot of boilerplate pages, depending on the CMS you're using and your use case."

What's the next step in your process after that?

"Then, you're ready for analysis – which essentially means breaking things down and making them simple. You start with the complex and you make it simple.

Your analysis could involve describing data; finding the best pages of your website in terms of clicks, checking the unique query count, finding which pages are decaying, grouping pages, or creating labels for pages – for example, splitting pages into best performance and worst performance to analyse them and give actionable advice.

You are taking something raw, the data, and you are turning it into something that you or your client can use."

Is this something that AI can help with?

"I mostly use AI for writing code, where it's very good. For the rest, I don't think it's really necessary. Most of the stuff we are talking about is straightforward once you do it.

The cool thing about analysis is that it requires a little bit of abstraction and machines, especially the latest AI tools, aren't very good at this because you still need some mathematical or statistical knowledge. There isn't a lot of valid training data online for the AI to learn from. I've never got trustworthy results using AI to interpret this kind of mathematical stuff. I would only advise using AI for tactical or operational-level stuff. For strategy, abstracting, or analysing a phenomenon, then do it yourself."

What's the next step in your process?

"At this point, ideally, you would have some insights – and you usually will. Insights are essentially bits of truth: something you share with a client or with stakeholders that is actionable. Each insight should be tied to an action, something practical.

If your website got 100k clicks in August, so what? If it doesn't lead to anything actionable, then this is pure reporting. There is nothing to be done about it. However, if I tell you that 20% of your pages have zero clicks, you can implement a series of actions to improve those pages."

How do you prioritise your insights?

"I only deal with B2C content websites, so it's very easy. In other cases, like e-commerce or SaaS, it can get a little trickier.

In my case, I usually start with articles belonging to a given cluster, if I have access to this information. If I can label articles within clusters, I can recommend prioritising certain articles belonging to a specific cluster (like

'Fridges', for example) because I know that this cluster brings in more money.

Otherwise, if it's a very large website and I know there are specific individual pages that are decaying or following some kind of pattern, I can detect 5/10 pages and identify those. I judge each case and I either go by cluster and group articles to see what matters the most or I go by profit, if I have access to information like ad data, affiliate data, etc."

Are you defining processes for your clients to follow as a result of the insights that you find?

"Yes, but also the other way around. Everyone has processes. Even if you don't write them down, you have a process for everything. Most of them can be improved unless you have hit a certain threshold.

I help content websites to improve their processes, where possible. Most of them don't use data, especially if they are big. You would think they all would. Adventurous big players do, but all the other big-but-not-so-big players often don't. Even medium-sized websites don't really do it. This is a great opportunity to improve something.

Even something simple, like using data to show anomalies, identify which articles are decaying, or recognise seasonality. Maybe, during a certain period of the year, you find a strange association and you want to investigate. You might be talking about a certain product in your articles and you discover that it's popular between May and July. You don't know why so you want to investigate. To do this, first of all, you have to use your data to start investigating.

This is something that many people aren't doing at this level. They stop at Google Sheets, using the Search Console interface, or using the software without using the APIs.

What is a decaying article?

"These are mostly articles that are losing traffic rather than rankings. Traffic is the main cause for concern because, at the end of the day, you care about what gets to that page. If you lose traffic, one reason could be that you have also lost rankings.

Decay is a natural fact; everything decays in nature. There is not one thing in nature that doesn't decay or doesn't change over time, and content is the same. The difference is that, in the case of content, we have more control over it. We can measure a lot of things and it's quite easy to understand when content will decay.

If you know your niche or the type of articles you are working with, then you will already know. If you're doing walkthroughs or news content, that will decay faster compared to an evergreen informational article like 'Types of Stone'."

How do you prevent future damage?

"When you have a process, you also have some risks. This relates to the other steps in my process. The final steps are communication (communicating insights), execution (doing it), and prevention. Prevention, which is the last step, means avoiding damage in the future. Of course, you can't fully avoid ranking losses and you can't fully predict the future – it's impossible – but I'll give you a very practical example.

Let's say you have a blog that contains evergreen articles but you don't have any process for updating pages. You write articles, push articles, and you are doing well. If one day, a new competitor steals some of your traffic, it is going to take time to find which pages you need to update. You have so many of them, you have to identify the how and the why, you have to prioritise, and you have to know the process. If you tell your writers or editors to update a page, you have to give them instructions or they will get it wrong.

That's why prevention is crucial. If you already know what to do, it's easier and you don't waste time. It's like war. If you already have a plan, it's easier to attack the enemy. If you don't, you're wasting precious time and you're wasting momentum. This is essentially what I am referring to when I talk about preventing or limiting future damage.

If you know your pages will eventually decay, or that some pages in a cluster or topic are more competitive, prepare some ideas in advance. Create a simple process that can be implemented quickly to update those pages before it's too late. This is planning in advance – and you don't even need any tools.

Preventing future damage is mostly common sense. This sounds obvious because it is, but it's not so easy to implement in practice, and many people don't. Many people publish and they forget to update, or they update randomly. Then, a competitor will use this to their advantage."

Do you have a favourite process or piece of software to alert you when something isn't performing as effectively as you want it to be?

"If you want something custom, there are some custom scripts or models that will tell you that something is going wrong. They can identify when clicks for certain pages show a downward trend, and send you an email. It is possible but it's not something you will use very much unless the project allows for it. You have to consider that, usually, you also have to maintain these solutions.

If the project is small and you can do something manually once per month, then do it manually. If it is more complex, then they have these systems in place where you get notified via somewhere like Slack if something is happening.

There are methods that I prefer for measuring these problems. To measure content decay, I created a very simple script with a friend of mine, Andrea D'Agostino, who is a data scientist. It's not complex. For every page of a website, we check the clicks, and we create a straight line showing the clicks on that page over time. Then, we take the line and identify the slope, which is a number that represents the rate of change along the line. Whether the number is positive or negative tells you whether there is growth or decay. If it is close to zero, nothing really important has happened or nothing has changed.

This is one of the simplest methods you can use to give every page a score. If you want it to be more accurate, you can add some weights and you can make it more complex, but the idea is more or less the same.

You can also use a method known as anomaly detection. Anomaly detection refers to a series of algorithms that are tasked with finding anomalies in your data. Why is one page or one day abnormal? You can use this to find out which of your pages, or your days, show abnormal patterns which you can then investigate.

For putting the actual system in place, once you have the script or model running, you can just set up some notifications for Slack or any other platform or tool. What's important here is defining these problems and using the right metrics and data."

If an SEO is struggling for time, what should they stop doing right now so they can spend more time doing what you suggest in 2024?

"Stop over-analysing. In many cases, we over-analyse things we don't have control over.

For example, you can't control Google updates. Okay, there is a core update, so what? At the end of the day, if your processes are stable and you know what you're doing, you shouldn't alter your strategy – update or no update. It's something you should account for, but you can't control it.

Also, stop obsessing over small details like meta descriptions. They might be ranking factors, but you should find what moves the needle. Focus on optimization outside of an SEO context. Focus on optimizing your processes, your time, and the time of others.

Optimize your processes without becoming an automaton. We are humans, so not everything should be automated. Focusing on scaling and improving processes can be very valuable because, at the end of the day, most of SEO is boring and repetitive. Understanding how to scale and how to put the proper systems in place requires a lot of time."

Marco Giordano is an SEO Specialist, a Data and Web Analyst, and a Consultant, and you can find him over at SEOtistics.com.

Improve your ability to handle large amounts of data and perform data analysis at scale – with Pedro Dias

To help you tackle this analytics beast, Pedro Dias from Visively offers advice on how to manage the mammoth quantities of data that SEOs have to interpret.

Pedro says: "Learn how to deal with large amounts of data and do data analysis at scale. That involves developing insights into MySQL, querying databases, or even dealing with spreadsheets. You can also use tools like AI to help you."

Does every SEO need to do this or is it just for certain roles?

"As you move and your business grows, you will have more data to analyse and scale suddenly becomes important. Of course, this is more aimed at SEOs that work in-house because not many agency-side SEOs have this kind of technical approach.

It's important for SEOs that deal with big businesses and businesses that are either growing exponentially or have the potential to grow exponentially. You should be prepared to gather data and analyse data at scale because that will uncover trends, the behaviour of crawlers, internal linking, and anything else that you can pull into a database."

Why do you think this advice is so important right now?

"I started doing this four or five years ago. For some of my clients back in Brazil, we would go in-house and work as a consultant on their premises, working with their teams and helping them establish these connections.

Now, with AI becoming mainstream, it has opened a lot of doors to make better use of the data you can analyse by querying databases and pulling things into a spreadsheet. Using AI that is able to interpret code, such as ChatGPT, you can easily feed it a spreadsheet and ask it to slice the data the way you want or find trends that you would not see just by looking at it.

This opens the door for a lot of potential in terms of what's coming in the future because it's not only giant websites that can do this, medium-sized companies will be able to do it now as well."

How would you summarise best practice and/or bad practice when using automation in the production of content?

"One of my business partners in previous ventures is an automation engineer, and he always told me that the tricky part of automation is controlling the output; it's not the input itself.

Bad practice with AI and automation is letting it run loose without any kind of curated control over it. Let the AI identify what you want to analyse but be the ultimate guardian of what goes out, what gets published, and what gets seen. Use it for the surface-level things that you would otherwise miss, but don't use it to replace you or use it without supervision."

Do content creators have to use AI and automation, if they don't want to get left behind?

"Yes and no. There will always be a need for a good content creator. AI can give you ideas, it can take what's already been done and rehash it, but it lacks human inspiration and creativity. It lacks the literacy that humans have. AI can only build on what's already been created; it cannot come up with something completely new.

Sometimes you need that in the creativity process, to bring something really good and really different to the table. Otherwise, it's just going to be marginally different, and sometimes that's not enough.

You can use AI to create content at scale – and when I say, 'content at scale' that's content based on data. You can create content that is based on APIs and data, and you can use AI to create that at scale. However, it gets tricky when AI has to be creative. That's where AIs usually hallucinate but humans excel. We can be creative, and yet make sense of the creativity and make it understandable for other humans. The machine doesn't understand its own limitations in that regard."

What shouldn't be automated?

"Anything where the output is unpredictable. If you cannot predict the quality of the output, then you probably shouldn't automate it. It's a matter of testing. Test the output for a while to see whether it always comes out clean. If there's a chance that it starts to present things that don't make sense, then don't automate it.

The tricky aspect of using a fully automated system based on AI is that, when it starts to output things at a certain scale, you might be blind to what's coming out wrong.

There will be a percentage of things that come out wrong that are covered up by things that come out right. In the end, when they reach a certain level, they will hurt your business, your brand, and the way people perceive you. People will see that you didn't put effort into making these things look right. That is why you need to be the curator of what comes out of a machine rather than just letting it run loose."

Is there anything that we need to do differently to optimize for AI-driven search results?

"I don't think so. We are using AI for very specific things.

Two days ago, I was looking for a formula in Google Sheets that I couldn't remember. I was looking for a tutorial on YouTube on how to use this formula and I couldn't find one. YouTube presented me with videos that were using this formula to do other things, but not what I wanted to do. In the end, I went to ChatGPT and input what I wanted to do for my specific case, and I got the answer that I needed.

That is a very specific thing; there are maybe 100 people in the UK who want to do this. It's not something that an SEO or content publisher would go after because it doesn't have the volume to justify creating a piece of content around it.

For these cases, where the usage is very niche or specific, an automated AI can help you. It offers things that it has seen somewhere else or that it has learned by looking at things and understanding what you are after. I don't think you have to use AI to create this kind of content, but that is the need the AI is aiming to fulfil."

Is there any software that you use to help with automation?

"I use a few plugins that pull ChatGPT into Google Spreadsheets to help with formulas. You can say, 'I want to do this or that in this spreadsheet', and it does it for you. Other than that, I don't use many tools outside of the interface itself.

In my case, if I'm running an SQL query and I can't fix the error, I ask ChatGPT what's wrong with it. It will tell me if I have used a curly brace or curly quotation marks, when SQL only allows straight quotation marks. Those kinds of errors can be almost invisible to the human eye and ChatGPT really helps to spot those. I don't use any fancy software."

Does the development of AI mean that we need to move past algorithm chasing and attempting to cheat the Google system?

"I think we should have done that a long time ago, even before AI. Ever since Google moved into doing core updates, they have been putting so much into them and it all becomes part of the main algorithm. It's almost impossible to chase an update and tell what has changed.

We all know that Google has algorithms aimed at sites that abuse keyword stuffing or use thin affiliation – sites that live off affiliation but put very little effort into producing added-value content. If these kinds of sites see ranking changes after core updates, it wasn't necessarily the core update that was responsible. These algorithms have been working for a decade or more, and they have been working well. Google can improve them, but they don't really change. It should not come as a shock for a thin affiliate website, or a website that has other problems, when the algorithm is not favouring them.

What you need to understand is that the systems and algorithms that Google has in place, and always has had in place, don't stop working and are not replaced by core updates. They work in parallel. If your thin affiliate site was hit now that a core update has been released, that might just be a coincidence, and the website has already been hit by the algorithm countless times in the past. Correlation is not necessarily causation.

The industry is getting better overall, but many people who don't have good information tend to be derailed by chasing after the algorithm, which is usually a waste of time. If you're running a thin affiliate site, you should align your expectations with how much you're going to get out of it and for how long."

If an SEO is struggling for time, what should they stop doing right now so they can spend more time doing what you suggest in 2024?

"Most of all, stop chasing Google algorithms. That's certainly a waste of time. Besides that, we are often focused on what Google is changing, but we forget to work for what we think the future is. Be where the puck is going to be; don't chase after it.

For example, you might need to improve the structure of your website based on the vertical it is operating in because the vertical, the products within that vertical, and how people search those products, dictate how the site should be organised. We organise information differently according to the context, and the same applies to websites. Not all websites should be structured the same way, which is certainly not news to anyone.

We should be more vocal about teaching other people and mentoring newer SEOs in areas that are the base of the industry, like information architecture, user experience, and web accessibility. Sometimes, SEOs don't understand why they are doing what they are doing. Why are you adding alt text? Why is it a web accessibility requirement? Why do search engines see value in alt text?

Once we understand the foundations of the different areas of SEO, our mindset should work according to those foundations, not according to our own whims or according to Google. That's what you should do, and that's how you put yourself where the puck is going to be because that's what Google wants to aim for."

Pedro Dias is Founder at Visively, and you can find him over at Visively.com.

Make better use of your data by preparing a database – with Olesia Korobka

Another way that you can be effectively utilising the data you're reviewing, according to Olesia Korobka from Fajela, is by storing everything in a single place – and doing that now rather than procrastinating.

Olesia says: "Prepare a database for your brand, company, product, service, or whatever you are offering. You will be able to generate whatever you want out of it – be it a website, social media posts, a profile on a website, a Web 3.0 board, video, image, etc.

It is a good time to be doing this because we still have lots of overwhelming information that is not overly regulated. There aren't too many prohibitions and it's still affordable to put this data online. You have access to the common crawl and lots of data sets out there, which will help you to understand your marketing positioning, your voice, and how to better serve your customers.

As SEOs, we still look at search results and those guidelines, but younger people no longer want to search through 10 blue links. They want their answer straight away; they don't want useless SEO junk. Now we have a real opportunity, not only to understand our users better but also to serve them in a better way – through a knowledge base and a dictionary.

In a 'dictionary', you will have the keywords from your industry, niche terms, synonyms, and other variations. A knowledge base consists of your company's knowledge in your industry or area.

You will be able to search for the most common questions customers ask and put those into FAQs. In one of the companies where I work, we have a sales and customer support channel where the data is published in a special format and template. Templates are hugely important when you collect your data sets because, when you have a definite template for everything that you do, it's much easier to work with that information, extract meaningful data, train and fine-tune the existing models on that data, and use it accordingly.

It can be easier if you organise your knowledge base into JSON files, as long as the information load is not too big. I use fields like title, text, image, video, and metadata. I also keep databases for brand information. Those include values, voice, tone, and brand guidelines because, when you generate posts or data, you want them to fit within your brand. For your services and products, you would include customer personas, experts, testimonials, and analytics – what performs better or what posts your company prefers."

How do you create these kinds of databases and how do you organise them?

"You can do this with Python or any other tool. In a recent Google Cloud Next, they were showing how to do this with the data in Google Cloud. You could even use AI, and you might not even need the code for it to extract and work with this information.

You will usually organize this information in a hierarchy, using a tagging system so that the data is connected. Format it consistently, use templates for each data type, maintain clear naming conventions, and store all the supporting documentation. LLMs (large language models) don't usually know where they are getting their information from. You should know where you are getting your information from so that you can link to it whenever you need."

Would this database be accessible to search engines as well?

"Of course. We don't know how search engines will develop. There are so many different search engines in places like YouTube and TikTok, and we now have generative search within Google itself as well.

We want to be adaptable and serve our clients wherever they are. Maybe they won't access our website at all, but we need to supply them with information about our products, services, and companies so that they can buy from us eventually, wherever they are looking.

Clients are not specifically looking for us. They are looking to solve their pain or problem. We need to integrate our brand information into the search so that they come to us with their problem, and we can successfully help them to solve it."

Should a database be kept on your website?

"I would suggest not keeping it on your website because it should be a trading secret. You should not give anyone access to your database. Instead, you would use it to generate data in the way that you want.

That's why you have brand blogs and information blogs. You find out from the sales or customer team what questions people in your industry usually have that your product or service might help to solve. Then, you publish that information so that it's available to your users in the form that they want it. It's already personalised because you should already have information for every persona out there based on their interests, what they want, and the problems they face."

How does the information for a database get collated?

"It depends on your resources and what you are planning to do with it. Most companies simply don't have that much good information in their blog posts. They're rewritten from competitors or from somewhere on the internet, so it's unlikely that they need to collect that data at all. It's useless. They might want to generate something better.

The information that they need to collect for their databases is basically the products or services that they offer and the questions that these products or services can solve. It's an SEO's task to organise and prepare that information so the customer can find it on the internet."

How often should the data be updated?

"One of the main problems with a knowledge base is keeping it up-to-date. Whenever you have a new product or a new service, or you discontinue a product or service, you should update the database.

It's much easier to maintain when you have a good tagging or labelling system. You don't need to have a third person sitting there, manually feeding products into the database. The database should be organised. The SEO can say, 'I need this information to be stored in this way so that we can work with it.' Then, you can decide how to do that."

How does an SEO justify spending a lot of time preparing a database instead of on more conventional SEO tasks?

"It doesn't require too much time. Preparing and maintaining a database should be automated, and it's definitely not an SEO who manually inserts all the fields. SEOs use the data for their tasks – be that content, building backlinks, or analytics.

You may even integrate a chatbot into this data so that you can understand where you are, where you are heading, how many people are attracted to a page, how it's performing, etc.

It's impossible for an SEO to keep track of all this data, especially in a very big company. It will depend on the company's SEO strategy - how often you publish, which questions you answer in your blog posts, etc. For products, it's often automated. When a new product appears, you have a template for how you put it on the website, how you optimize it, how you interlink it with other products, and which category it's placed in.

It's not something that an SEO will do on a daily basis. Your job is to check and verify that everything is correct, implemented and works fine."

What software do you prefer to use?

"I use Python, but I am very hopeful about the Google Cloud services that have recently been introduced. I've already applied to several AI tools because I want to see what they're offering.

I hope these tools will make the job even faster by removing the need to write the code yourself. I want to see it first, though. Hopefully, something like that will be emerging from Google, Amazon, or somewhere else."

What's the most practical use case for a database like this?

"For me, I primarily use it for generating content and supporting content within other channels – like social media channels, press releases, and other off-page spaces.

You will keep all of that consistent by using the same database to generate it.

You will have a consistent message across all channels, and they will all support your SEO. You will have social signals for your content as well. You can fill up every channel and know that you are doing it right. If you always have a template for all of your content, it's much easier to make it, check it, and verify it within the company.

We are transforming into the age of Web 3.0, and we don't know how everything is going to look. Google is pushing the blockchain, which could be a problem for us. Whatever happens to the search next, having this information available on a database will help you to be prepared. You can be flexible and take on whatever comes. If there are websites in the future, you can build a website from it. If you need a social media profile with lots of posts, you can build that. If you need to build a Web 3.0 board, you can do that."

Are any brands doing a particularly good job of this at the moment?

"I don't think so, because it's quite new. A lot of people say they are creating these data sets and generating information out of them but, from what I've seen, most are not very successful. In the news industry, some companies are managing to generate news posts already. However, I have not yet seen big companies doing this well.

We are mostly collecting data in batches, so we have a very small portion of what we publish. So far, I have mostly created learning centers for different companies out of this content, and it's performing well in search right now."

If an SEO is struggling for time, what should they stop doing right now so they can spend more time doing what you suggest in 2024?

"As SEOs, we are given so much overwhelming information – just look at how many conferences we have and all the people saying, 'Try this!' or 'Try that!' You don't have time to listen to everything, and then someone tells you to learn Python, Looker Studio, or whatever else.

Of course, you do need to learn these things, but when you try to grab all of them at the same time, you end up doing nothing. You won't have enough return on investment for your time and resources. Stop running after every thread in SEO and stop trying to generate everything and write about everything. Concentrate on something small and start doing what you do.

The emergence and development of AI will help us to fill in the gaps where we don't have enough knowledge. Maybe you won't need to learn Python because AI will be able to generate the code for you so that you can just input it and have the same result as those who learned it. Think twice before investing your time into something because time is becoming more valuable.

I have a checklist now, for when I am trying to decide what is worth my time. The first question I ask myself is, 'Is it bringing any results or is it just keeping me active?' Then I ask, 'If I do this, what is the expected result? Do I really need that result? Are there any other priorities?' Those are the basic questions I try to ask myself.

You want to listen to Google Cloud Next, then you want to look into the new ChatGPT integration, and then there's Claude from Anthropic. You just cannot try all those things at once. You have to be focused on the results that you are bringing. It's nice to try everything, but they are not always bringing much to the table just yet."

Olesia Korobka is an SEO Entrepreneur at Fajela, and you can find her over at OlesiaKorobka.com.

Use GA4 to properly analyse and read your data – with Gemma Fontané

Krzysztof already extolled the virtues of GA4, and Gemma Fontané from Orvit Digital dives deeper into how to use it.

Gemma says: "Don't forget the importance of properly analysing and reading data for your website."

Has every website moved over to GA4 now?

"They don't have another option if they were using Google Analytics tools. Since 2023, Universal Analytics has stopped recollecting data, so everybody who wants to use Google Analytics needs to move to GA4. However, the important thing is not only to migrate to GA4 but to properly set it up as well."

What are the big changes from Universal Analytics to GA4?

"The big changes are in how Google Analytics shows and organises the data. It has changed and it's important that people know where everything is.

GA4 has also changed the way that Google wants us to analyse information. They are trying to help us more. For example, they have prepared a lot of guidance on how to organise events. However, it's only guidance and people need to understand what's really important for them and how to set it up in a proper way."

Is GA4 better?

"It's definitely not worse; I think it's more or less the same.

I really don't hate it, but it's true that it can take a long time to properly understand how to analyse all your data for different types of clients."

How can an SEO set up GA4 correctly and what typically gets missed?

"To set it up properly, there are different things that you need to take into account. First of all, you need to define what you really need to analyse for your business. It's very different for a B2B company, an e-commerce company, or a SaaS company.

Define your KPIs, and then go to the events and set up the ones that you really need. You might need to use the main tools from GA4 or you might need to use Google Tag Manager, for example. With this done, set it up properly as conversions and then it will be easier for you to analyse all of your data.

If you set this up in a proper way, then you will be able to create your audiences and your reports, and explore the data that you really want to analyse. It's important to know what you want, know where that is in GA4, and then only set up the things that you need.

It's not enough to just install the script because there are events, conversions, audiences, and a lot of things that you need to set up.

There are also other things that you need to publish. Google gives you some reports, but some are not published. If you want to see all of your Google search data, it's not published in the reports. You need to go to the library and publish it.

That's why you need to think about what you want. Do you want your Google search data to be shown on the tool? Then you need to search for where that data is and publish it. In Universal Analytics, it was already published. In GA4, you need to find it first and then make it visible."

How is the data different in GA4 compared with Universal Analytics?

"It's different and not different at the same time. It's different in the way that it is shown. Take, for example, traffic acquisition. In Universal Analytics, everything was all on one report. Now, traffic acquisition is two different reports. The user acquisition report helps you to understand how you capture a user for the first time, whereas the traffic acquisition report is more on a session level. You need to understand that it's a little bit different from before.

Something else that is different is everything related to events and the interactions that are happening on your website. Before, this was only shown in the behaviour report on Universal Analytics. Now, it's the most important thing in the engagement report. You need to understand these differences and manage the best way for your business to analyse them."

What key events might businesses be missing in GA4?

"There aren't a lot of interesting events that are not being tracked. However, there are some that happen almost automatically, like form submissions or video reproductions, that tend to be important. These should be set up automatically, however, it sometimes doesn't work the way that it's supposed to, so you need to do it with Google Tag Manager.

For example, a really important event is add-to-cart, when a user wants to add a product to a cart. For e-commerce, this is very important, and you need to set it up via Google Tag Manager. There are some important events like these that you need to take out and analyse, and they are not there."

What's the difference between an event and a conversion in GA4?

"An event is something that is happening on your website, and a conversion is something that is happening on your website that you want to highlight.

Basically, you can have a lot of different events because you think that they might be interesting for you, but the conversions will be the events that you know are KPIs for you, so you want to mark them and publish them in a different report."

How do you use all the data in GA4 to help guide your SEO strategy?

"There are a lot of different things that you can do with GA4. The first thing that I would recommend is to create a Looker Studio report and link all the information that is important for your SEO strategy in there. For example, the way that you acquire users on your website and the way conversions are happening on your website. Link this with your parameters so you have more information and you can analyse it further.

You will find a lot of things that can be useful for an SEO. You can analyse the performance of your pages, you can analyse how users interact with your content, etc. This kind of data is very helpful for understanding what's happening on your website and refocusing your strategies.

You might want to merge pieces of content or focus on a different style of content that is performing better. You will be able to see these opportunities and have even more information if you link everything with parameters via GA4.

You can also combine the data from GA4 and Search Console in Looker Studio to see which pages are ranking. You can integrate even more information than you could in Universal Analytics, so you're able to analyse all your information together and come to conclusions more easily."

Is it realistic for all SEOs to be able to understand GA4 by themselves?

"In the beginning, you might want to hire a GA4 consultant, as they will help you to set things up and organise what you really need.

You can also create your own reports in GA4. If you go through the library, you can create your own personal reports, not only use the reports that GA4 offers. Depending on your business, that might be better suited for you than using the default tool. Using a consultant will help you come to that conclusion more easily and make sure you have all the data you really need.

Then, with everything set up and knowing what you are looking for, any SEO can use it on their own."

Do SEOs need to conduct GA4 training throughout the business?

"Totally. For example, there is a report that is only focused on paid channels, so it would be necessary to explain that to the relevant team.

In Universal Analytics (especially 1/2 years ago), you would still divide the acquisition channels into five different typologies. Now, there are many more. You now have so many easy options for analysing your channels of acquisition. If all of those different departments know about this, it will be easier for them to analyse the results.

If you want to show a resource to other people within your business, don't show them the tool, because it's not very intuitive. You want to look at the Explorations report instead.

You can create your own report via Explorations or link it to Looker Studio. That's the best way to show insights from GA4 to other departments. You can show how it is working, your data, your results, and the impact of your strategies because you can play with filters in Looker Studio a lot."

If an SEO is struggling for time, what should they stop doing right now so they can spend more time doing what you suggest in 2024?

"Stop trying to do so many things with ChatGPT. The tool is very powerful, and you can do a lot of things with it but if you cannot analyse how those efforts are performing, then it makes no sense.

It's very cool to try all the new tools that are out there but it's important to know how it actually performs on your website. Try to gather all your data in a proper way and then do all the cool things that you want to do. Maybe, stop trying to do so many things with new AI tools right now!"

Gemma Fontané is Co-Founder at Orvit Digital, and you can find her over at OrvitDigital.com.

Track the metrics that actually move the needle – with Becky Simms

Becky Simms from Reflect Digital thinks that it's easy to lose sight of the wood for the trees when it comes to metrics. To keep an eye on what matters, you need to know what impact you're having, she says.

Becky says: "Focus on tracking the metrics that matter – the metrics that prove whether your strategy is moving the needle. To do that, you need to know what moving the needle means."

What are the metrics that matter?

"Sadly, this is homework for everybody because the metrics that matter are bespoke to your business.

You can't just lift what you've done for someone else and bring it over. Your audience do the hard work for you, if you are willing to listen and to understand them. If you listen well, you can start to understand the journey that they go on when they're trying to buy your product or inquire about your service. This works in B2B as well as B2C.

If you start to understand the journey they go on, you will see the little milestones. There are jobs that they do throughout the process. When you uncover what they are, those are the things that you need to be tracking.

ROI is a lagging indicator; you either hit the ROI or you didn't. It doesn't tell you how to fix anything. The leading indicators are, did they download something? Did they watch the video? Did they share with a friend? All those micro-moments are leading indicators – and you can statistically work out how many of those things need to happen, for your business, to get to a conversion. Those leading indicators tell you whether you're likely to hit the ROI or target you're trying to achieve. They're the metrics that really matter because they're the dials you have more control over, and can do something about."

Are clients interested in micro metrics or are they primarily focused on ROI?

"When they start understanding it better, then they're interested. When you start to show and model out the way that understanding these things does result in a sale or conversion, it will flip their mentality. You have to take the business on the journey. The marketing person normally gets it quite quickly but there is often someone above them who has lovely vanity metrics and big numbers and doesn't really care about the smaller things.

You need to consider how you make sure the business understands why these metrics matter. Recently, we won a client and they said that they switched agencies because their previous agency wasn't performing. We started to dig into their strategy and what we were going to be doing, and we couldn't really pick any holes in it. That previous agency had been doing a really good job.

What happened was the client had their benchmark of what good metrics looked like in their mind, and they were gunning towards ROI. They wanted to see a return for what they were spending on SEO. However, the agency had been doing upper-funnel work, driving awareness that would have assisted in a lot of conversions. They were doing a great job but they hadn't articulated that properly and the client hadn't bought into those metrics.

They lost a client over that and, if you're in-house, it could be a job that you might lose. Try to get the business to understand what metrics really matter and what the smaller things that lead to the big things are. Focus on those because they're the things you can optimize as well."

Do you have a preferred analytics tool for tracking your preferred metrics and how do you present those metrics to a client?

"From a tracking perspective, we are still finding our feet with the lovely GA4. It is working for us and we are predominantly using it because it's what most of our clients are using. We pull everything into our own dashboards and organise our dashboards and reporting against the customer funnel.

The way we present it is around what the customer journey looks like. To go on a journey to work out what the metrics that matter are is to go on a journey around your customer journey. Start with understanding the audience and where they're spending time. Look at the channels that have come up from that research to see where the opportunity lies, where the volume is, and what kind of numbers start to predict what that opportunity might look like and how the channels might play nicely together – always thinking about passing the customer through the funnel.

Then, lay that out as the customer journey, but with the tracking metrics aligned to it. You will see that the customer has told you where you should be. They've also told you what you should be saying because you understand what they're looking for at each point. They've also told you what you should track because they've told you what they're trying to do throughout the journey. That becomes a visual view of what the journey looks like as a funnel through to conversion. You see how the channels and the metrics work together, which you can roll up into the return on investment you eventually want to see."

Do you need to have face-to-face conversations with your customers to determine the customer journey or can you get the data from something like GA4?

"For us, it's a mixture. When we start thinking about the customer journey for a client, we first want to understand what they already know about their audience. Inadvertently, everyone knows something about their audience. However, we then need to know how statistically relevant, recent, and robust that information is.

Then, we look for opportunities to strengthen the data and the relevance of it. We would do that through a mixture of surveys, which could include behaviourally written surveys that go out to current customers or a potential audience. We might use a third party to help us reach a particular audience, normally with qualifying questions included to make sure we're getting to the right type of audience that would buy the product or service.

It could also include pop-ups targeting people who are actively using the site. A mixture is where you get the most robust understanding. If they've hit the website, they're already partway through the journey. If you can also get people who haven't hit the website yet, they might identify different needs. It does vary depending on who the client is, what they're trying to sell, and who their audience is.

For the questions, you want them to be behaviourally written – whether it's a written survey or an interview. Until we started to specialise more in behavioural science and brought behavioural scientists into our team, I didn't realise how biased the questions people ask are. Writing unbiased questions is a real art. You need to leave it free and open for the person to give their truthful, honest view.

Whoever's writing the questions or running the session (be it in-person, a roundtable, or one-on-one), needs to be trained and skilled at not priming the customers to say what you want them to say. You need to actually understand what it is that they're trying to do. Humans are weird. Behavioural science shows us that we don't always do what we say we're going to do and we don't always think before we do things. A lot of what we do is emotional. It's really important to try to ask the right questions and draw out the almost immediate response for what someone thinks they might do. Then, you gather all that data.

You've also got search trends, search volume, and keywords. That's an amazing voice of the customer; seeing the phrases they use and the popularity of those."

Do you need to use videos of user sessions to hear the voices of users who are less comfortable having a conversation with you?

"Definitely. We also use social listening. It's amazing what someone is willing to openly say to a wide audience on Twitter/X or Instagram that they wouldn't necessarily want to say directly to you. If they know that it's the brand themselves doing a piece of research, they might not want to tell you how they feel about your brand. However, they'll go and tell the rest of the world on social media. Social listening is a really good tool for understanding pain points and the ways that people think.

Sentiment analysis is also helpful. There are some really good AI tools out there that will take large data sets and give you data around the underlying tone of those messages and posts, without you having to read every single one of them. You can pull out things that are repeated regularly and get a feel for the mood of a particular customer, or around a particular topic they might be talking about, on social.

We use many different methods to pull that data in. It's down to what the client is comfortable with, what they've got access to, and what they've got the budget for. All of these things either cost time (if you're doing it in-house) or money (if you're working with an agency or third party). If you can't do everything at once, you want to work out where your quickest and best wins are going to be, and where you're going to get the most insight. Then, you can start understanding the pain points of your customers, and their go points: the things that drive them to move quicker.

It's one thing to know what stops someone from progressing, but you also want to know what pushes them to progress quicker on a journey and if there is anything you can do to assist that – in terms of how you create content or the type of content you create. It's not just what you say but also the format in which you say it. Does your audience want this content in video or on TikTok more than they want it as old-school written articles? Consider how they want to digest the information you're telling them to help them in the process of buying your product or service."

Do you need to insist on using these kinds of metrics for every client, even if they don't want to give you the budget for it?

"Again, it depends. For us, it always comes back to whether we will be able to add enough value. If we're knowledgeable in their area already and we can see loads of SEO opportunities, with obvious gaps that they're missing and ways we can optimize, and we know we can make an impact, we might not insist on doing this kind of research.

For these metrics that matter ahead of the final enquiry, we can make an educated guess. However, if we felt that we didn't know enough – their strategy is quite advanced and they're looking for micro increases that might make big differences at their scale – and they really need someone who's going to understand the detail of what they're missing out on, then you need to do that research.

You need to be able to prioritise and look at how the different channels are going to work together. One of my biggest bugbears in marketing is that we end up working in little silos. SEOs have keywords they're going to optimize and think they know what the customer probably searches for because of the search volume, but they haven't thought about what's next. You might get to the top position and drive thousands of visits for that keyword but, if it's not the final buying keyword, you're never going to see them buy. You need to think about what's next and how the other channels can help you drive that user through to conversion.

If you're not thinking about that, your work is a bit pointless. You will probably lose loads of people who don't go on to convert because no one held their hand through the process. If you're not thinking about the metrics to measure that – and how to work with your colleagues in paid, email, or wherever it might be to get to that conversion – then you've wasted your efforts."

If an SEO is struggling for time, what should they stop doing right now so they can spend more time doing what you suggest in 2024?

"Stop getting obsessed with the big metrics. If you're running at a metric that feels impossible, stop going for that. Break it down to something smaller that's more achievable and will eventually roll up into that bigger metric. Don't get distracted by metrics that don't matter.

Bounce rate is typically one of those. We're all done with bounce rate, aren't we? However, the metrics that don't matter are personalised to your business. Certain metrics are really important to some people so bounce rate might be significant for you. I try and steer people away from bounce rate. Instead, understand what you expect the user to do and what you think they want you to do. Ideally, they're the ones who tell you what that is."

Becky Simms is Founder and CEO at Reflect Digital, and you can find her at ReflectDigital.co.uk.

Learn how to better analyse user behaviour and conversions – with Irina Serdyukovskaya

Analytics Consultant Irina Serdyukovskaya takes a more direct look at the metrics that matter, and speaks about how data can teach you what your users are doing and why they are (or aren't) converting.

Irina says: "Learn analytics to better analyse your user behaviour and conversions.

There are two things you need to master. The first part is understanding the implementation of analytics. When you work with websites as an SEO, you are usually responsible for the results that you get from analytics, not the implementation. You need the numbers that can prove you are doing the right thing and bringing conversions, users, etc.

The first thing is to invest in analytics and ensure that they are correctly implemented on the website, and you have the data to back up your actions and investments.

The second thing is to understand how to read this data. In most cases, it's with Google Analytics 4 but it could be something else like Matomo (previously Piwik), or other tools. The goal of all of them is to understand how to prove that you are doing the right thing. You want to prove that SEO is bringing good users who are converting and engaging with the content and the website.

It's super important that you understand what reports, metrics, and dimensions you can use – and how to visualise this data for and show yourself, the client, or in-house that SEO is bringing the results that are expected from this channel."

How do you ensure that the analytics have been implemented

correctly?

"First, you need to be sure that it's implemented and collecting the traffic. The easiest way to do that is to go into Google Analytics and check that you are visible in the real-time reporting. You want to check, for example, that the data is not duplicated and none of the pages are missing.

It's good to click through the website, especially if it's on different CMSs. It might be that WordPress is implemented for the blog and you have a custom CMS for the main website. Click through the website and see for yourself that the data is collected and there is no duplication.

If you are a little bit more techy, you can use Google Tag Manager to analyse a bit more of the data you can collect in GA4. For example, you can collect more information about specific categories such as how one category of a single blog is performing or a specific category of an e-commerce website.

You can implement some additional tracking for what you are doing on the content side or the technical SEO improvements that you have made, and you can use this data to show results."

What additional tracking do you set up for your blog content?

"It's possible to set up additional tracking for specific category pages. If you have a blog with different categories like health, sport, and lifestyle, you can implement tracking so that you can see the data separately for each of those categories.

You can use that to analyse what content you can produce more of. If sport is on the rise, and it's much more engaging than health, then you may want to create more content there. Usually, you can do this using the category within the URL structure. However, if you don't have it in the URL structure, you still can collect this data using Google Tag Manager via the website code. You can build a report specifically for that category."

Should SEOs use a GA4 specialist consultant to get things set up properly?

"Either that or you can use some of the courses online – because there are already a lot of courses out there. There is one that was created by my colleague, Kyle Rushton McGregor. He prepared a course specifically for digital marketers called *GA4 for Digital Marketers* (which you can find at kyle-rushton-mcgregor-s-school.teachable.com) where he explains all the details about how you can use Google Analytics, how you can use it for reporting, etc.

You could also have some personal coaching with a Google Analytics specialist who can answer questions specifically for your website because sometimes you don't know what you don't know. For example, there is a lot of data that you might not realise it's possible to collect with Google Analytics. Having a Q&A with a specialist is a nice addition to a course.

You can ask about the data that you want to have, whether it is possible to collect that data, how you can visualise it, etc. This will help you a lot because then you will have much more data you can play with.

If the website isn't changing a lot, and you're going to be using this setup for at least a year, then it's a one-time investment. You can use this for your analysis for the whole year and maybe review this when the year is over or whenever there are changes on the website."

What are the pros and cons of using GA4 compared to an alternative analytics software package, like Matomo?

"The first difference is related to cookies. In Europe, it's still a little bit tricky with GA4 because it's collecting some data, storing it, and sending it to the USA. Matomo is not storing data in the USA (you might be storing that data on your own cloud, if that's possible for the client). That is a huge difference. For that reason, some companies, especially big companies, could not use all of the functionality of GA4.

Of course, GA4 is a free tool and you need to invest a little bit if you want to use Matomo, depending on how many metrics and dimensions you need to analyse and how much data you need to collect.

A huge pro for Matomo is that it's much easier. For small businesses, it's sometimes easier to pay around 15 euros per month to have this clear data rather than learn how to use Google Analytics. GA4 is a bit more of an advanced tool so you need to understand it better. You might need to take a course or hire somebody who understands it.

Matomo is very clean and very straightforward for small businesses. Even though you are paying, you're paying to see the data you need and you might not need any of the customisation that GA4 offers.

If you are still concerned about the complexity of your analytics package, Plausible might be another option. It is also cookieless and does not need a great deal of custom setup (compared to GA4)."

Is there a significant advantage to paying for a plan on the Matomo platform?

"Based on what I've heard from clients, they are paying because the data is very clean and easy to understand – and because of the cookies. Those are the two things that are beneficial for them.

It's also sometimes about personal preference. A lot of people don't want to learn GA4, so they move on to other tools. When GA4 was introduced (and even now) there were some bugs, so people were complaining a lot about these bugs or how some of the reporting was not working. Then, they started looking at what else is on the market.

This was not a big question before, once we had become used to Universal Analytics. Now people are asking whether they should choose something else, even if it's paid."

How do content consumption analysis and user funnels work inside GA4?

"The huge advantage of GA4 is that it's highly customisable; you can build the analytics you actually need for each project. It's not something that is set in stone, like Universal Analytics where you couldn't customise as much.

For example, you can build a funnel for B2B, and you can see how people are moving from visiting your blog page to actually making an inquiry or signing up for a free trial. You can build this funnel using the free-form report in the Explorations section.

It's quite intuitive. When I show this to clients, they usually feel that it's quite easy to do. It's not complex, it's super easy to visualise, and it's also very flexible.

The same is true for content. Some of the things that you will be used to doing in Google Sheets or Looker Studio, you can now do inside G4, also using the free-form report. You can build a table of your analysis and you don't need any third-party tool, which is also really nice."

Do you prefer to analyse your data in Looker Studio or an alternative?

"Being able to bring together data from multiple sources in Looker Studio is a huge advantage. If you need to combine the data from Google Search Console, Searchmetrics, SEMrush, your keyword tracking, etc., it makes sense to connect all of this together in Looker Studio.

The nice thing is that, if you need some quick analysis, you don't need to build a Looker Studio table. You can do that inside GA4 and already visualise what you need to check for the month to show to your stakeholders."

Is GA4 going to evolve much more over the next few years?

"I think they are preparing for a lot of changes, especially considering a cookie-less future. If a user decides that they don't want to be tracked but they do convert, GA4 can already count that as a conversion based on their prediction of what users do when they convert, even though this data wouldn't be recorded.

This is a huge difference that they have pushed a bit earlier than they might have done in other circumstances because they are preparing for the loss of cookies. Otherwise, they might be out of the market. Google needs this data. They need clients to use Google Analytics because they need that data to be collected for internal use. It's not directly about the money, because it's free, but it's about the data they have access to and the market.

You need to continue to embrace the changes with analytics – and also use this as an opportunity to invest. With a lot of clients, they got used to how Universal Analytics worked but some of their reports were created 5 years ago, so nobody knows what all of these dimensions mean. When you are pushed to learn a new tool and invest money and time into it, it's a good thing.

It can be painful, especially when it's not your priority. As an SEO, learning GA4 is typically not your number one priority. Your priority is doing keyword research, building a content strategy, or fixing technical issues. GA4 is usually more of a side thing. On the other hand, these analytics will help you to better understand what you are actually achieving as an SEO.

It's good for you, and you need to get used to it. When I started, I didn't understand any of it, because it's very different from Universal Analytics. However, when you get used to it and you understand how you can play with it, there is a lot to gain. Give GA4 some time. Some SEOs already love it because of its flexibility."

If an SEO is struggling for time, what should they stop doing right now so they can spend more time doing what you suggest in 2024?

"As SEOs, often focus too much on content creation and new content strategies. We have already produced a lot of content on the internet. Use that time to learn analytics and learn how that content is already performing. That is the combination that you should use.

You may not need to create a content plan with 100 new articles. Maybe you will find that you need to improve 50 articles that are already on the page. Invest your time improving your content – and using data and Google Analytics to understand that you actually need to do this."

Irina Serdyukovskaya is an Analytics Consultant, and you can find her over at IrinaKudres.com.

17 SEO WORKFLOW

Stop overworking and focus on the tasks that matter – with Adrijana Vujadin

Do you take the time to stop and think about whether you're doing too much on a day-to-day basis? Adrijana Vujadin, a Coach for SEO professionals, wants to help you understand when you are doing too much for your own good.

Adrijana says: "Find the reason why you are overworking – because it's just that you have too many tasks.

There is a belief that you determine your own value by all the tasks that you are doing on a daily basis. That's always negative because, in your career and your life, you should only work on the things that have the biggest impact. These things will lead you to the next level of your SEO career.

If you're running a business and you have a lot of tasks, then find the people who can help you. Your brain needs to work on the things that have the most impact on your career and your business."

Does working as much as possible early in your career help you move forward more quickly?

"It depends on the state of your mind and body.

If you are overworking every day, and you believe that your value is determined by the amount of work you have done today, that's a negative. You will never feel that you are productive enough, and you will never feel that you are good enough. However, you might be enjoying it and feel that it is the best thing you can be doing on that day.

I should define overworking here. Overworking doesn't just mean working more than 8-10 hours in a day. If you are finding joy in all the tasks you're doing, then you should definitely keep going, because that may be where you are getting your energy from. However, if you are nervous, stressed, and frustrated – and you are unhappy when you don't finish all the tasks on your to-do list, then you should stop.

If that is the case, your brain is connecting your value to the amount of work you have done today. That is a negative thing because you're not your work. How many things you have accomplished today doesn't matter; it doesn't determine your value as a person."

How do you determine when you're doing too much and when you're overworking?

"It's determined by how you feel. If you are feeling good and you are excited about new opportunities, then you can continue. However, if your body and mind are struggling, and you are feeling stress and frustration, then something is wrong. That is something you can fix.

In the early stages of our careers, we do a lot of things that we have to do. Then, it becomes very hard to actually enjoy the process because we are so overwhelmed by all of these tasks – whether it's SEO or new Google updates. It's hard to learn how to enjoy the job of SEO."

What if overworking is part of the culture in your company?

"In my company, the culture is to not overwork – but in the SEO community, and across the industry, people are encouraging overworking. People who don't want to overwork feel guilty when they aren't overworking. We need to switch that mindset. You can definitely be successful without overworking because that is connected to working smart.

Sometimes, earlier in your career, you might think that the more hours you do the better – or that you need to be seen to be working hard. There are some cultures where being the first in the office and the last to leave is perceived as being the person who adds the most value.

People love to emphasise how hard they work. They think they need to work hard, and they need to struggle. They think that, if they are not struggling, something is wrong. Get the idea into your mind that you can just work and be successful. Don't struggle. That concept blows people's minds because they think that, if they are not working hard and struggling, they are not on the correct path.

'Work smarter, not harder' may seem like a cliché. I tell my clients not to think about how to work smarter and just to focus on the things that will have the most significant impact on their careers. If you do the 20% of your tasks that are the most important, a lot of the small tasks will drop away. You will see that these things are not so important and do not benefit you as much.

Focus your mind on the top three things that will lead you to the next level – the next level of business or your career. Pay someone else to do the rest because your mind needs to be clear to have that clarity on what will bring the biggest impact to your life."

If you're the boss, how do you discourage an overworking culture when you've got deadlines to hit?

"Talk to your people about why they think they need to overwork. If that is something that is coming from their insecurities – from the feeling that they are not good enough, so they need to over-deliver, over-research, and overwork – then it's a negative.

If that feeling is coming from your deadlines, whatever they might be, remember that we are not surgeons. SEO is not life and death. Encourage your team to move the deadline back by a few days and make sure that your employees are in good mental health. If you keep pushing your employees to do one deadline after another, you are saying that your clients, your SEO, and your websites are more important than your people. That is something that I wouldn't do."

As an SEO manager, how do you support the mental health of your team?

"Firstly, always put yourself as a leader and set a good example. Take time off and take vacations, and encourage your team to do the same. I'm always talking about my team's mental health and how they are feeling. If I see that some clients and tasks are forcing them to overwork, then I push those deadlines by a few days.

Always care about your people and put them first. That will show them that they need to learn to put themselves first as well. I want to see them working in the company for the next 10 years. I don't want them to burn out and leave.

You will need to have open conversations with your clients too. I'm also an SEO consultant so I communicate directly with my clients and, whenever we have these kinds of deadlines, then I will have a discussion. We will talk about any additional resources we might need to bring in and add to our team.

Clients will sometimes have urgent deadlines, but you need to present all of these issues to them when you have that discussion. The majority of them will be okay with moving that deadline if sticking to it would be more harmful than pushing it back by a few days."

What does burnout mean and does overworking lead to burnout?

"I've been there, so I can speak from personal experience. Burnout is when you are overwhelmed by your energy and all the negative feelings and thoughts that you have on a daily basis, alongside the fact that you are overworking. You are likely to experience burnout if you are not enjoying your SEO job and the lifestyle. However, if you are giving yourself opportunities to rest, taking frequent days off, and taking things slowly, then you can avoid it.

I know it's very hard to actually tell ourselves to slow down but, when you are at a good level in your career, slowing down will make you more successful because you need some time to think. You can't just overwork, because that will not lead you to the next level. Slowing down and having a clear mind will help you focus on what you really need to do to get what you really want."

How did you personally recover from burnout?

"Firstly, I didn't know that I was suffering from burnout. I was overwhelmed and I wanted to quit my job because I didn't have a clear enough mind to identify that this was burnout. I was just thinking of quitting my job and taking some time off to identify what I really wanted from my SEO life.

Your thoughts in that moment are almost not connected to reality. You can't see that you love SEO and you have a passion for it, and it's just the way you are working, and the attitude you have while you are working, that it wrong. Personally, I just took two weeks off, not knowing that I was burnt out. I was reading the book *The Power of Now* by Eckhart Tolle and that is when all of this mindset coaching started for me. I realised that I can control my thoughts and I can change my mindset.

When I went back to work, I had different attitudes towards stress, clients, and team members. I started therapy, and then I started to move forward with mindset coaching, and that is something that helped me to work without stress and frustration – and to not overwork myself.

Of course, every person who feels that they may be overworking or suffering from burnout might need to do something different. I would definitely recommend going to therapy and doing mindset coaching, if possible. They are the two things that helped me the most and had the biggest impact.

When you are burnt out, you need to work on that immediately, because that burnout can go even deeper. You don't want to spend a year recovering from burnout, so you want to address it in the best way that you can, as soon as you can."

If an SEO is struggling for time, what should he stop doing right now so they can spend more time doing what you suggest in 2024?

"If you're struggling with time, prioritise the things that will help you achieve what you want. Not everything you are working on now will help you to achieve your goals.

Do a gap analysis on your skills. If you want to be an SEO manager in five years, what skills do you need to have? You don't need to go and do coding or deep technical things; you need to work on more soft skills like leadership. And vice versa – if you want to be a technical SEO in a specific niche, then work towards that. You don't need to work on your presentational skills."

Adrijana Vujadin is a Coach for SEO professionals, and you can find her over at AdrijanaVujadin.com.

Make the most of your time by thinking better and rushing less – with Katie McDonald

Like Adrijana, Katie McDonald from Kaweb wants you to take a step back and re-evaluate the way that you work. She says that rushing forward may actually be holding you back.

Katie says: "We should be thinking better and rushing less."

Can we use AI tools and automation to get things done more efficiently?

"We can use AI in the right way. People can get carried away with AI and think it can do absolutely everything, which I would disagree with. We can use AI to automate and do things faster once we've done the bulk of the research. However, AI is not human, and humans can do things that AI can't.

You can give it prompts and ideas, and you can brief it on a client's project and their tone of voice. You can give it the background and see what it spits out. However, without giving it that information, you wouldn't be able to get a good enough response. You need to do the research first, and that's where the experienced SEO comes in: to get to know the business, the customer's persona, etc.

You can't produce an entire SEO strategy, implement that, and get results just using AI. You need the experience of a professional SEO who knows what works and what doesn't, who has the technical SEO knowledge and the content knowledge, and who is well-rounded. They understand how things work from the base up. Having the experience of working with clients day-in day-out, doing the research, seeing how things work, and getting hands on – AI can't do that for you.

Ai can automate some of those tasks. Once you've done the research and figured out right how you're going to tackle that sector for the client you're working with, you can utilise AI to accelerate your results. It's not 'cheating' if it's done in the right way, and it's briefed correctly. When you know what schema you need to create, your H tags, your metadata, etc. – and you've briefed it correctly – you can click a button instead of spending days on all of those manual tasks.

If you've done all the wonderful research, you can feel grounded and confident in your strategy because you've spent that time thinking. You don't need to rush, and you can spend time attacking schema, meta tags, image tags, etc., more quickly and efficiently because you've done the research. That's what I mean by 'think better, rush less'."

What does the 'think better' process look like?

"I don't use AI to do the thinking for me. A better kind of thinking behind an SEO strategy comes before any SEO. When you onboard a new client, you need to talk to that client and understand how their business works and what the product or service is (getting a level of understanding that is almost as good as theirs), as well as who their customer is, what their pain points are, and what they are looking for.

Then, you need to think about how you're going to tackle that on the website, what the website needs to look like, etc. That's all part of that thinking process. Then you obviously do your competitor research to see who else is out there ranking for the terms that you should be ranking for.

You can then work out what pages you need to have on the website. Do you need a blog to support those pages? Is it more of a backlink process? How fast is the website? Is there a problem with the indexation of the website? Have Google Analytics and Search Console decided that there are serious problems, and it's suffered from an algorithm update? With that thinking done, you will be able to work out and prioritise all of the things that encompass SEO.

There are so many things that go into that thinking process, when you're planning and strategising. It can take hours, or even days, depending on the size of the website and the problems you find.

You could be doing a content strategy with wonderful keywords and great search volume that the client's really impressed with but then, six months down the line, you realise you've got a serious indexation problem and half your site's blocked by robots. Then, you've wasted your time. All of that strategising at the start, however long that takes, will help you prioritise.

You can work out whether you need to fix indexing first and make sure the website has a solid technical foundation so that you're not wasting time. You can work through what's going to get the results the fastest. Don't look at blog content and audit lots of blogs if you need to get the service pages sorted first because those are going to be your lead drivers.

Once you have a strategy and a plan, you can look at the next 3/6/12 months, and decide what you can automate to get it done more quickly. Decide what you can brief into AI and what needs a little bit more time, and plan that into your time frame. Working on a month-by-month basis is not a strategy; that's just trying to do SEO stuff each month and hoping for the best."

What tasks do you use AI for and what AI tools do you use?

"I use AI to help me with scalable tasks that need writing. If I'm working on several articles for a client as part of a strategy, I might be able to use ChatGPT. To do that, I would need to brief it and say, 'This is the kind of article we want to write. These are the competitors who are already ranking. Make sure the tone of voice is this. We want to add these internal links. Mention these sources. Don't mention XYZ.' Those are just a few of the things that I would brief into ChatGPT. There are also lots of other plugins I've used, and some are hit-and-miss.

I use ChatGPT-4 (because 3.5 tends to be a little bit less accurate) for the base content of an article. However, you don't just copy and paste it because it will obviously be using duplicate content from the internet. Once you've got that content, brief it – knowing who the client is and whether it's in line with the brief you've given – and then tweak it. Add extra things, like a new interactive calculator, a tool, or a new research paper that the client has released, which is going to add even more value to that article. Once the base of the content is there, you can add schema and internal links, and improve the SEO, which is where the client is going to get real value.

I also use AI for schema, like FAQ schema, how-to schema, etc. You can ask ChatGPT to look at the article you're working on and the part of the text you want it to focus on for schema, then ask it to write that schema. It tends to churn out some good stuff. However, there are sometimes issues with it, which is why you need that human touch. Without the human touch, it just wouldn't work. It would be inaccurate, you might have the wrong links, or you might have things in the content that are not on-brand.

Although on reflection, if you're publishing content articles or pages, with EEAT and the Helpful Content Update, any content really needs to be written by someone with real experience in that field. Google will be able to tell the difference between a piece about divorce law that Chat GPT has spit out compared to a writer who has experience in that topic and understands the terminology. It will sound better, be more helpful and flow far better than AI. And why would any brand not want to be authentic and helpful? But if your client doesn't have the copywriter or the budget to find the right one, it can be a starting point."

What's your preferred way of installing schema?

"A lot of our clients work with WordPress and we've achieved huge success from a very simple process. You go into the page or post, choose the 'text' option at the top, scroll right to the bottom of the page, and then literally copy and paste the schema in there. Of course, you need to validate it in a schema tool first, to make sure that it's correct, accurate and can be picked up.

Once you've popped it in, you can preview it to make sure it looks the way it should, get the sign-off from the client, and then go live. We've seen really good featured snippets, within days, by uploading the content and then adding in extra bits of schema. We get really good results from that so it's worth doing it, but in the right way. Don't just ask ChatGPT to write an article and paste it in."

Should every industry be using that process or is incorporating schema within an article or a blog post not appropriate for certain industries?

"I've done this across a variety of sectors; including the beauty industry, the cosmetic surgery, and the broadband industry.

For people who don't know, schema is a piece of code that essentially tells Google what that page is and gives it context about what is on the page. As soon as you add it in, you can get fantastic results.

We've added in schema that AI has given us (which has obviously been proofed to make sure it is all correct) and, so far, it has worked really well every single time. We've seen articles go from third, fourth, or fifth position to zero – getting that featured snippet literally overnight. It's a game-changer."

If an SEO is struggling for time, what should they stop doing right now so they can spend more time doing what you suggest in 2024?

"Stop trying to fill time with trivial technical SEO tasks. Stop spending hours going through a list of meta titles that are too long, meta descriptions that are too short, making sure that the H1 matches the SERP title, or trying to improve the website speed by 2% just to get a CLS score. Those can be really trivial things and your efforts can be better spent, in terms of getting actual results, seeing rankings go up, and seeing that company or client make more money that month.

Focus on your strategy and how you can carry it out more efficiently. Use your research to plan out what AI can do for you so that you can work faster. If your website is too slow to function and you physically can't use it, then of course it needs speeding up a bit. However, if you're trying to get it from a C to a B in your speed tool's metrics, then your efforts are probably better spent looking at how AI can help you implement schema or help with your articles.

If AI is getting smarter because of how we are briefing it, and it gets to the point where it can get you featured snippets without you needing to put that schema in, then that's brilliant. You can go and use your time elsewhere. You want to be doing what will get results, and AI is proving to be successful at the moment. If it figures out how to do this itself, great. I'll go and do my next priority job, knowing AI has that covered."

Katie McDonald is an SEO Specialist at Kaweb, and you can find her over at Kaweb.co.uk.

Start incorporating programmatic approaches and rule-based automation into your SEO – with Lazarina Stoy

SEO and Data Consultant Lazarina Stoy offers up a new way of thinking about the way that you do your job, that is designed to give you more time and freedom to focus on what matters most now.

Lazarina says: "Incorporate programmatic approaches. I'm specifically referring to rule-based automation for SEO best practices and AI-driven automation for process enhancements.

Mainly, this means taking some time to better understand different programmatic approaches and learning how to incorporate them in a responsible way – both for the brand voice of the company you're working for and content quality. However, you're not doing that just to put out content. You're doing it to satisfy search intent and be helpful to users.

I'm going to talk about two approaches that would be very useful to understand. The first is rule-based automation. This is very good for creating predefined instructions or conditions that dictate how specific tasks and processes should be executed without having someone intervene or monitor them.

You can apply this kind of automation for well-known, specific best practices that we are given by Google. This could be making sure that all pages have titles and headings, headings have keywords, pages have meta descriptions, images have captions, and internal links and breadcrumbs are inserted whenever certain phrases are mentioned or to promote semantically related pages. It could also be something a little bit more complex, like triggering structured data generation at the mention of certain phrases such as 'how to' in the title.

We are seeing a rise in AI models, which can be extremely helpful for a variety of tasks, but we're also seeing misuse of these models. It's important to emphasise that AI-driven automation can be extremely helpful for tasks that are not mission-critical. These tasks can be things like automating content generation, content enhancements, summaries, or content translation, but these tasks absolutely need to have someone monitoring the output and optimising it.

I'm a huge proponent of these algorithms being used, but they should be used for improving processes and not for something that is served to the end user."

How do you know when to use a rule-based automation approach?

"Rule-based approaches are things that we should seek out from Google's guidance and the guidance of other search engines. In the past, SEO as an industry didn't really have that level of guidance on how it should be done. Now, what works and what doesn't is a lot more well-documented.

Everything that we have asset guidance for – which has systematically proven that it is helpful to users, improves rankings, and is best practice – these are the things that we should be thinking of automating through rule-based automation.

The examples that I gave are very commonplace now: having a title, having headings, breaking down the text into paragraphs to ensure that it reads well on a mobile device, etc. Of course, these can be built into the processes of the people creating the content, and you can create your own checklist, but it can also be a lot more automated. You can build a system to automatically flag when something is off. These are very good examples of a rule-based automation approach."

What SEO tasks would you use a programmatic approach for without utilising AI?

"The tasks where you can apply rule-based automation without utilising AI are more about the lengths that titles should be, how many headings you should choose, and generic advice. You don't necessarily need AI for that. You can use AI as part of the process, but you don't need it in order to make that successful.

You want to make sure that you have the best practices and processes implemented before you incorporate AI to make the output better, as opposed to relying on AI to throw out a page and make it optimized for SEO by telling ChatGPT to act as an SEO consultant. The difference is that you should lead with SEO best practices when you are designing the content patterns of your pages, how they should be structured, and what is needed in order to cover a topic comprehensively. Then you can incorporate AI to help speed up the process, whether it's for generating content, translating it, or repurposing it.

The caveat here is that, if you have a very good rule-based approach, you might not need that much intervention at the final stage. When you have an approach that is entirely based on AI, you absolutely should have someone checking the output, because otherwise, there are a few things that could happen.

The first thing is that, over time, you will lose your individuality in terms of brand voice. You might see content being published that is not necessarily aligned with best practices, both in terms of how cohesive it is and how accurate it is. If you are relying on AI tools for content automation, you might see information being generated that is not factual at all.

For other tasks like translation, AI is not really a good localization exercise. Besides brand voice and a lack of cohesion, you might also see other things like losing touch with the user because they can see that the content is not based on reality, experience, or authority. Overall, while you might think that you are following a strategy and publishing content regularly, it might not be the quality content that both search engines and users are looking for. That's why you need to have human intervention when you are relying on such tools."

What are some examples of when and how you can start thinking programmatically?

"The difference with programmatic SEO, for someone unaware of this term, is that it is based on the principle of providing new information to satisfy the user, but doing that through programmatic means.

For instance, if you look at a keyword during keyword research, you might be looking at things that have a particular pattern. This could be for your category or product pages because you are organising content in a particular page template and pattern. Another example could be in blog posts and other niche site entities. When we talk about entities here, these are things that are defined with different attributes. For instance, a dog would be an entity and the food that they eat would be an attribute.

If you pivot that to programmatic SEO, you might have a keyword phrase like 'the types of food that dogs eat'. With programmatic SEO, you can take these examples and use templates to go through the different variables that your attributes have. In this case, those variables could be different dog foods or different types of dog foods, such as canned food or kibble. This would give you a very good indication of which particular elements of the page you can template.

To give a practical use case example of a programmatic issue and a rule-based approach, I recently reviewed a case study for G2 and how they do their category pages. They are a reviews website, and they have different category pages, like CRM software or ERP software. Within that, they have different ways of incorporating both rule-based automation and AI-driven automation for generating very small sections of the content.

They use rule-based approaches for templatising their headings. They might have the headings 'What is ERP Software?' and 'What Are the Benefits of Using ERP Software?', then they simply change out the category. They also use rule-based approaches for inserting particular links and organising the page template for all of these types of category pages.

When it comes to implementing this approach, multiple different businesses and niches could benefit from this. If you're an e-commerce store working on category pages and product pages, you can take that approach backwards to see what best practices you aren't currently implementing and how you can brew those into your processes for publishing pages. Also, you can use it to think about the content that you are missing or the different content elements like captions for images, meta descriptions, and titles, and how those can be improved.

Then, you can use very tailored machine learning models to help you in the execution of those tasks, but not as the final approach that you use for doing everything on the page."

How do you double-check that what you're producing actually makes sense and the entities and attributes match up correctly?

"Something that is very important when you are doing programmatic SEO and trying to create content using a programmatic approach is having a very cohesive database and strategy.

The strategy is very important because you want to know everything that you are planning to cover with this approach but it also allows you to sense-check the different avenues that you can take with your keyword targeting. The database is important because you want to make sure that you are not replicating content that is already available somewhere else just because you want your pages to look better or manipulate rankings. You want to provide new information.

Every programmatic SEO project starts with doing what you see your competitors doing. What separates successful examples from unsuccessful examples is going that step further and adding unique information to your pages to ensure that you are providing user value.

At G2, they have a graph on their category pages that shows a perception map of all of the ERP software that they have in their database and how they rank based on different characteristics. That is a great example of using your own database to provide value to the user that they could not find elsewhere.

This perception map is something unique that they have added to the page, which might be a quality signal to both users and search engines that they should prefer that page.

To make sure that you are providing value for users, you should start by creating a very well-organised database and a cohesive keyword targeting strategy, and that strategy should be aimed at covering the topic in a way that is complete and robust. You should also be focused on making sure that you provide unique value to those pages and not just replicate what everyone else is doing.

That applies to all pages that you build: blogs, products, etc. Don't just replicate what's already there. We know very well that there are sustainability issues related to that, and there are also web quality and user experience issues that come with that. You definitely don't want to be a website that is full of pages that aren't unique or helpful in any way."

If an SEO is struggling for time, what should they stop doing now so they can spend more time doing what you suggest in 2024?

"Stop doing things manually that you could be doing programmatically. I'm talking about things that are becoming low-importance factors in terms of rankings and value to users, but they are still considered best practice.

I'm talking about things like manually writing meta descriptions and image captions, especially for very large enterprise websites. These are things that a lot of people are struggling with and putting a lot of time and effort into. We have very advanced and robust APIs that can do the job to at least 90%. Having someone simply reviewing and improving those would be a much better use of your time."

Lazarina Stoy is an SEO and Data Consultant, and you can find her over at LazarinaStoy.com.

Enhance your day-to-day tasks by leveraging AI – with Aleyda Solis

Like Lazarina, Aleyda Solis from Orainti brings you an actionable way to take some of the pressure off the tasks that are cluttering up your schedule, without compromising on quality.

Aleyda says: "Start leveraging AI for the day-to-day SEO tasks within your workflow in a smart way – in a way where you take care of the quality, but you use it to accelerate the tasks that you need to do."

What SEO workflows can be enhanced with AI?

"There are now tools that use AI, like the Horseman SEO crawler, which integrates with the OpenAI API to provide you with suggestions and recommendations for the issues it finds when crawling your website. If it identifies that you have title or description issues, because they're empty, duplicated, or too long, it will give you suggestions to make them shorter or populate them with descriptive information. You can develop your SEO recommendations much faster by using these tools to support you.

There are also many integrations within Google Sheets and extensions that don't require you to have any understanding of coding or scripting. One of my favourites is Numerous.ai, which allows you to do things in bulk.

One of the main challenges that I find with ChatGPT is the interface. If you take the content from a number of pages and put it in the first two columns of a Google Sheet, and you want to generate titles, meta descriptions, headings, Q&As, FAQs, etc. in bulk, you can do so by using these extensions that integrate with OpenAI. You don't need to go back and forth with the ChatGPT interface if you don't want to. That is a hassle.

ChatGPT also has browser extensions, like KeyMate.AI. Using those extensions, the quality of the results is much better. It won't hallucinate so much as it used to. The Serpstat SEO tool also has an extension that provides accurate keyword data.

There are options that can help with all types of activities, like doing forecasts based on your historical performance data in Google Search Console. If you want to forecast, you can use the Advanced Data Analysis plugin and take the latest fluctuations, certain average positions, scenarios, etc., into consideration. It can give you the same support that a data analyst would provide."

Can AI implement recommendations without human intervention, or would you not trust it to do that yet?

"I believe that it can highly support us in the analysis and evaluation process, that's for sure. However, in order to carry out recommendations that are actually impactful and make sense from a business standpoint – based on the goals of the website and the business itself – it's important to have a proper understanding of the website context, beyond the technicalities that can be identified in an SEO audit.

For example, you may need to understand the context of certain product lines that have certain goals or need to be prioritised, or certain challenges or restrictions of the platform. There are a lot of restrictions, requirements, and external conditions that you need to take into account so that you can prioritise your SEO recommendations accordingly and make them meaningful for the organisation.

More than that, to make the recommendations actually happen, the execution is mostly done by actual developers from the website. If it is a small website, you usually try to do it with your own small platform, with WordPress, plugins, self-serve, etc. You lack that development support, so I can definitely see how AI can help you implement changes in .htaccess or develop a little script that you can use to automatically generate an XML sitemap with indexable pages for certain sections of your website. That is for a small organisation, with your own website and your own projects.

However, in bigger organisations, there's a development team that knows its stuff and specialises in executing or encoding based on the existing tech stack. Although you might want to recommend a few scenarios or suggest possible solutions, they are the ones that will ultimately implement the changes that actually make sense for the tech environment of each website.

It's important to understand our boundaries as SEOs here. What is important in that scenario, though, is having the best possible soft skills. Having really good communication will eliminate the burden of any bureaucracy at these bigger, enterprise-level organisations. At that level, it's not necessarily a knowledge problem, but an execution problem that arises from a lack of buy-in, a lack of alignment between departments, or bureaucracy and how slow everything is.

You might want to use AI to support the communication that you want to have with C-level if you find it challenging to speak in a more business-like language and use less technical terminology."

How can AI help with getting more buy-in?

"It's not about replacing your voice but supporting it. In my case, especially because English is not my native language, it is a little bit more challenging for me to come up with a very sophisticated way to say certain things in English. Sometimes I ask ChatGPT how I could say something to a C-level in a big organisation in a way that sounds a little bit more sophisticated. I might ask it how to explain something in a way that is much more straightforward, clear, and simple for a non-technical person.

It's not that AI's going to replace your job, because it won't, but it can help facilitate your communication and understanding when there might be a gap in that. Most of these are human challenges, and I don't think that AI will be able to completely replace any of those any time soon. There is no AI that will be able to push the development team better than I can with my own soft skills."

If you don't have someone who pushes other teams, can you use AI to help you better articulate what you're trying to change and the impact it will have?

"100%. The same is also true for when you are doing outreach. We were talking about different scenarios than the typical ones that we see around content generation.

If you do outreach, AI can serve as a tool to accelerate the research that you do into the people that you want to connect with. If you want to build links or get coverage for a website, you can accelerate the process. You can give an AI tool all of the articles that someone has written over the last few years and ask it to summarise what they have written about, or the three top articles that have covered a particular topic. You can ask it to create an email that would persuade them to link to your resource in a certain way by appealing to their interests.

What I like about it is that it gives you that first-step template base to build on, which is amazing. A lot of people need a little bit of initial help or a base to start building upon. Of course, I don't recommend completely automating, but it's important to accelerate that initial phase and have that input."

If AI raises everyone to the same level, how can you differentiate yourself and show that you're human?

"There should always be a human validating, personalising, and providing proof that this is not an automated email. That is something that I always ask myself whenever I receive an email. Sometimes, that proof can even be just a little image or a little reference to a previous post that I have made on LinkedIn or Twitter/X.

It is difficult to differentiate yourself because even a comment, a photo, or a video might be replicated by AI. We recently saw a video going around of someone talking in another language through AI. It makes you question what is real and what isn't right now. I was speaking in French in a video and people were questioning whether it was really me speaking French or an artificial intelligence.

How we view what is real and what is not will change over the next three years. I'm looking forward to seeing how this will impact the role of SEOs. It will be exciting. Hopefully, humans will still be required in SEO in three years' time. If not, and it's an AI version of me, at least I will be the one who trained it, so something of myself will still be there."

Will there need to be AI specialist SEO roles in the future?

"We'll have to see how much real expertise is actually needed and what long-term opportunities that can offer by itself. The 'prompt engineer' profession that I see going around looks like a big opportunity right now but, in two years, every developer, engineer, and person looking to interact with AI will need to have some prompting know-how.

The same is true for SEO and AI. If the interface changes, that will just be a new layer of understanding that we will need to develop in order to be effective in our jobs. It might not necessarily be a new specialisation, but it's something that we will all need to start doing."

If an SEO is struggling for time, what should they stop doing right now so they can spend more time doing what you suggest in 2024?

"Read SEOFOMO, my newsletter. It's the best way to accelerate your SEO knowledge, keep up with whatever is happening, and identify the updates and developments that you should actually pay attention to.

In terms of what you should stop doing, stop being so afraid. What will happen will happen. If you're afraid that SGE is going to steal all the clicks, have you analysed your click-through rate lately? Have you seen the traffic erosion that has already been happening for a long, long time because of all the SERP features, Google's verticals, etc.? You are over-worrying, and that doesn't help.

You should keep your focus on what you actually have control over and how you can make the most out of the opportunities. At the end of the day, there will always be the need for a specialist who can identify opportunities and match whatever the users need to what websites and businesses are offering. This is where our value comes in, as a specialist.

There will be challenges, but this is why we are SEOs and we are not doing paid search. SEO has always been a profession that is about going the extra mile through testing, identifying opportunities that aren't even documented, playing them out, and having a lot of curiosity about how we make our results visible to users at the end of the day."

Aleyda Solis is an SEO Consultant and Founder at Orainti, and you can find her over at AleydaSolis.com.

Learn prompt engineering and AI to improve your SEO workflow – with Si Shangase

Si Shangase from KuduHQ agrees with Aleyda's belief in the supportive power of AI. In his opinion, learning how to communicate with the LLMs can unlock all kinds of hidden potential.

Si says: "Start embracing AI and learn how to do prompt engineering. That's going to be critical for the next couple of years, particularly for seasoned SEO veterans. After that, who knows where AI can take us?

For example, if you're an SEO strategist or an SEO manager and you want to build a piece of interactive content, you might need internal dev resources and a team to support you. However, if you learn how to use prompt engineering and ChatGPT effectively, you can start to build programs that will allow you to create interactive content yourself.

On top of that, it's very difficult to get the resources you need these days, especially at a junior level. AI can help you do a lot of the heavy lifting, which allows you to focus on the strategy side of your SEO campaign."

What key AI software and skills do SEOs need to know?

"Start with prompt engineering and ChatGPT.

First, understand your processes. Take a step back and think about the main things that an SEO does. A lot of it is keyword research. We all know how to use Majestic, Ahrefs, Semrush, etc. Learn how to clean up your data, then learn what you need from your data and how to use it, and then start to put that into prompts.

Once you've done that, half the job is done. You need a process for your day-to-day activities or tasks. Get those written down and then you can scale them up."

When you're cleaning up your data, are you primarily talking about the keywords you're going to target?

"Yes. Let's say you're doing competitor analysis. Any third-party SEO tool can give you a list of keywords that your competitors are ranking for that you're not ranking for. Then, you can use OpenAI's ChatGPT tool, upload that list of keywords onto the platform, and ask it to filter out any keywords that aren't going to be relevant for your campaign. That would be the first step in cleaning up that information and data.

I also create classifications. You can ask it to group keywords by semantic relevance. That allows you to understand the different types of content entities you need to create for your landing pages. If you're doing something around holidays, when you group your keywords by semantic relevance, you can see things like the best time to visit a specific place or things to do.

Your keywords can be grouped in those semantic buckets, and AI can help you do that at scale. If you're looking at thousands of keywords, you can do that within a minute. Without AI, it would have taken you a week or more."

Can you trust how ChatGPT groups those keywords?

"When you create a prompt, the first thing that you need to do is ask it to give you an example. It will give you a sample of how the output should look and then it's up to you to refine that. You've got to think about it as if you are training someone who has some experience in SEO but not as much as somebody who's had years of SEO practice.

AI will give you an example. It's up to you to make minor adjustments and refinements before you print out the output in a CSV file – particularly with the new GPT-4 upgrade that gives you a CSV file."

Do you use AI for content creation as well?

"People are using AI to create content but, if you are going to do that, you need to learn how to make sure it has the right tone. You need to give it a specific tone in terms of how it should write content. You can ask the AI to take on a persona, and tell it what that persona should be like and the tone of voice that it should use.

It's also a good idea to give it an example of how you write as a human.

Then it would use your example to learn how to write as you, effectively cloning yourself – if you are a content writer. However, as they always say, never get an SEO to write your content for you; get a copywriter or a content writer.

Utilising AI can allow you to make a start on the content you want to create. You should then have a skilled writer going through that content and making sure there aren't any errors in it and it reads the way you need it to read. I wouldn't fully embrace creating all your copy using AI. It could help you to create about 60% of it.

One of the things it can create might be meta descriptions. They are important from a CTR perspective but they're not important from a ranking perspective. You could test that and see what the output is. Then you could start to look at description copy or landing page copy, if you are an e-commerce website.

It does depend on your use case. If you write a full 4,000-word article using AI, from my experience, it doesn't come out the way that you'd like it to. You need to do a lot of manual tweaking and it does create a bit of work."

Will you be using AI to replace some of the work that's traditionally done by junior SEOs?

"If you're coming into the profession, this should help you to shorten the learning curve. That's a positive way to look at it. If you are doing keyword research, AI can help you perform that keyword research task or that semantic clustering task.

If you can learn to work with a large language model and use it to your advantage, then it could shorten that learning curve. That's probably the best use case if you're coming into the space. Embrace it, because it gives you a competitive advantage over your peers."

Is SEO leading the way AI is used in marketing or are other channels using AI in ways that SEO can learn from?

"Within the businesses that I've worked with, it's helping with ad copy, creating ideas, and visuals. It's not just ChatGPT; DALL-E, Stable

Diffusion and other tools have come into the fold, and they allow you to create graphic content using prompts. It's enabled certain creative people to bring in new ideas by seeing their visions played out in visual formats. Other marketing and advertising channels outside of SEO are utilising it quite well.

For SEO, the most important thing is understanding your processes and slotting AI into those processes effectively. You might have a way that you want to carry out a technical audit or content audit: encode that and break it up into sections where you can use prompts and have AI fill in the gaps for things that would have taken a substantial amount of time to complete.

For instance, you could utilise AI to analyse a large list of alt tags and see which ones should have different titles based on the landing page content and the context of that page. It's often about analysing and structuring data. A lot of the work that I do, as an SEO, is with large sets of data and it helps me speed up that process and then think about the strategy and direction of the campaign."

Are there any ChatGPT plugins that you would recommend?

"There are a lot. What I would say is, if you're going to use ChatGPT, get the paid version if you can. GPT-4 gives you advanced data settings and it enables you to upload CSV files. You can do a lot more with it than you could with standard GPT-3.

The difference with GPT-3.5 is that plugins are enabled. If you're using GPT-3.5, you can use plugins but, if you use GPT-4, you can't.

With GPT-4, you can ask it to download the output in a CSV file and you can start to analyse that and bring it into your own workspace. However, there are tools like Noteable, which is a plugin for GPT-3.5 that allows you to do a lot of data extrapolation and cleansing, and use diagrams for visualisations within the ChatGPT interface.

It does depend on your use case. If you want to bring everything into Noteable, you can use GPT-3.5. However, if you want to bring everything into a CSV that you're running in your own workspace, then you should use GPT-4."

If an SEO is struggling for time, what should they stop doing right now so they can spend more time doing what you suggest in 2024?

"Stop doing everything manually and learn how to write prompts. Whatever you're doing right now, write a process for it. What are the steps that you take to get to where you need to go? Think about that and break it down into subsections.

You might be doing keyword research, and the first thing that you do when you're doing keyword research could be understanding the business. Write that down. It could be that you start with a few head terms. Write that down. When you've got that information and data, try it out with AI.

Create a prompt and ask it to think like an SEO practitioner. Once you've done that, you can give those methods for starting keyword research to the AI and see what the output is. Keep doing that continuously across all your activities, tasks, and processes – turn those into prompts. Once you've done that, you've basically automated half your work.

Then you need to think about how this fits into the bigger picture and why it matters for the business. Does this activity generate sales? Does it generate revenue? If you've automated a lot of your steps, you can analyse a lot more data and tailor your content to specific users.

When we were creating content before, it was quite generalised. Now you can create lots of variations of content for different users and demographics. You can ask your AI to think like a specific persona and create copy that is written for those users.

AI is going to open up a lot more possibilities, even just in terms of the personalisation of what we see on the internet and how websites are structured. It will help us better organise our content and our information. It won't be something that allows you to sit on the beach and enjoy the fruits of your labour, but it's something that's going to add a ton of opportunities for people.

As SEOs, we want to create new campaigns and run new pieces of content marketing. Imagine what you can do with good prompt engineering. You can ask Stable Diffusion to create different graphics and then bring those graphics into a Jupyter notebook to create an interactive infographic. You might not be working with a professional graphic designer or engineer from the get-go, but you will involve them. It means you can get to that stage a lot quicker, which will create a much richer experience for your users.

You will be able to create new ideas and new experiences for users, and I think that is going to open up a renaissance of unique content experiences online. Before, what was holding the majority of practitioners back was that they had constraints in resources and skills. Now, AI allows you to unlock those skills and resources where they didn't exist before, and that's going to create a lot more opportunities."

Si Shangase is an SEO Partner at KuduHQ, and you can find him over at KuduHQ.com.

18 Focus

18 FOCUS

Optimize for the algorithm that matters most to you – with Greg Gifford

And now we turn to your focus, and Greg Gifford from SearchLab Digital wants you to focus on the right optimization opportunity for your business.

Greg says: "Pay attention to which algorithm you're optimizing for. Most people don't even realise that Google has multiple algorithms.

If you're a business that serves people in a particular geographic area (at a brick-and-mortar location or as a service, like a plumber or an electrician), Google's going to use its local algorithm to return search results related to your business. You need to optimize differently for that algorithm.

You need to have a handle on which algorithm you are going to optimize for, at a basic level. Local SEO is my thing and, if you're doing local SEO, you really have to pay attention to Google Business Profiles. It's the cornerstone.

Is it all about Google Business Profile or are there other aspects to the local algorithm?

"A lot of people think that they just need to do regular SEO and add on Google Business Profiles to show up in local SEO. That's not really the case. The local algorithm does evaluate a lot of the same signals, like content and links, but they're weighted and evaluated differently.

You have to write content and optimize content differently. You need to get different kinds of links. You need to do the Google Business Profile stuff and include reputation management – because reviews are a big part of that algorithm as well.

It's about expanding your knowledge base and understanding that you have to optimize differently if you're targeting the local algorithm."

Have successful Google Business Profile strategies changed much in the last year?

"Not really. I'm doing a Pubcon in Austin and one of the things that I'm talking about is how to do local SEO, and it's the same things I've been talking about for over a decade. 80% of it hasn't really changed. The algorithm has updated elements, but the basics haven't changed that much.

The bits that have changed the most are related to Google Business Profile (or Google My Business, as we're all going to keep slipping up and calling it for another 5 years)."

What's changed with Google Business Profile this year?

"The biggest change is that you don't go to the Google Business Profile dashboard like you used to. You used to go to google.com/business, log in, and it would pull up the list of the business/businesses that you were going to optimize or edit. Then, it would take you to a standard dashboard that had a backend interface.

Now, it's almost like you're doing live edits to your profile in the search results. You search for the name of your business (while logged in as either an owner or manager of that Google Business Profile account), and a little row of icons will pop up at the top of the results in the main column. You just click the icon to go to what you want to do.

In the old backend, you used to have one line item for reviews. You'd click reviews, and then you'd have to go to the reviews and work on it there. Now, there's a little icon for reviews. They also put a little red badge on it if new reviews have come in since you last logged on. From an ease-of-use standpoint, it's a bit easier.

A lot of agency people are complaining about it because you used to have a dashboard that listed everything and now you just go to each individual business. You can still go to the dashboard, but it goes to the individual search result for that business, and then you've got those editing icons up at the top. A lot of people freaked out and thought it was difficult when it first happened, but they've eased into it and gotten used to it now.

All in all, I think it's a beneficial change. You don't have to dig around and it's organised a little bit better. You can complain all you want but they're not going to switch it back, so you might as well get used to it."

Can you edit the wrong Google Business Profile by mistake?

"It was actually easier to mess up and edit the wrong business before. You had your list of businesses and, if you clicked the wrong one and started editing your hours or phone number without looking at what you were doing, you could potentially edit the wrong business.

Now, it's pretty much impossible to edit the wrong business. When you click that icon, you're editing the business that you were just looking at in the search results. It's really straightforward and easy."

Is it easier to violate Google's policies nowadays, and how do you avoid doing that?

"It's not that it's easier; Google has become stricter on enforcing those policies. There are a lot of spammers and bad seeds out there who are trying to cheat and create fake listings, so Google has really cracked down. They're trying to fight those spam listings to make sure that only legitimate businesses show up. Unfortunately, they turned the dial a bit too far and a lot of false positives are happening now.

I spend a lot of time helping out on the Google Business Profile Community

Forum as a Platinum Product Expert. Over the last year, we've seen a lot more suspensions. Sometimes Google tells you when you're suspended, sometimes they don't. Sometimes every profile you're attached to gets suspended and sometimes it's only a specific business, and they won't tell you why.

It's frustrating. They tell you that you're violating policy, but you don't know what part of the policy you violated. You have to apply for reinstatement and hope that you fixed the right thing.

On the forum, I've been working with a car dealership in the south of Texas, and they've been there for 20-25 years. Google keeps suspending their listing and, when they try to get reinstated, Google tells them, 'We can't prove that you exist in the real world.' They've sent videos and photos, and you can see the dealership on Street View, yet they keep getting suspended and Google keeps saying the same thing. I think it's a problem with the script that Google support is following rather than a problem with the detection algorithm.

I know that they are working on an updated solution for reinstatement requests. For now, unfortunately, it is difficult. Sometimes you can just change your phone number, update your URL, or even change a category. Sometimes you just breathe on your keyboard, and you'll get suspended.

The best route is usually to check the Google Business Profile guidelines. There are some really basic things. If you're a brick-and-mortar with your address displayed, you have to have permanent signage, your own separate entrance, and your own staff present at the hours listed on your profile. Those are the three things that people usually mess up on: there's no signage, there's no entrance, or it's a co-working space and they say they're open 24/7 but they're never there.

Beyond that, try to fix it yourself, but the easiest thing to do is go to the Google Business Profile Community Forum and get help from the Product Experts. We spend a lot of time helping people with verification issues and suspensions. You will usually get more clear advice than you would from Google support."

Is there any form of content that will help you stand out from your

competition on Google Business Profile?

"Questions and answers and Google Posts are a really great way to stand out. There are all the standard things like business name, categories, hours, reviews, and all those main visibility/ranking factors. Then, there are the conversion factors, like the Q&A and the posts, that don't affect how you rank but do affect the conversions you're going to get.

I love the Q&A section. A potential customer is not going to go to your website, find an FAQ page, and read through 50 questions hoping their question will be there. It's too time-consuming. However, they will click 'Ask a question' on your business profile because they think it's a chat and someone's waiting to answer it. Nobody is, because it's a community discussion, but you can preload it with common questions.

They can type in their question and, if a similar question has been asked and answered in the past, Google pops up an answer as they're typing. It will auto-complete the question and supply an answer. You don't even need a live chat because most of the questions people ask should already be there and be answered. That's an extremely awesome experience for someone who has a question about your business. They get an answer before they're even done typing the question.

I also like Google Posts. A lot of people don't do much with Google Posts because they're at the bottom of the profile on desktop, but they're a lot more visible on mobile. It's a conversion factor, not a ranking factor. It will help you stand out from the competition if you do it the right way and treat it like the ad that it is. Don't treat it like social media, treat it like an ad. Put something compelling there (and don't use stock images), then you will stand out and get more conversions."

Is the search generative experience likely to have an impact on local businesses?

"There's no way to answer that question yet because the search generative experience is still so early in beta. If you have access to it and play around with it, you'll see that it changes daily. Nobody knows how it's going to change search – or if Google's even going to roll it out.

Everybody thought Bing was going to steal market share from Google because they rolled out an AI chat interface first. It didn't change anything. People played with it, but nobody started using Bing instead of Google.

I don't think it's going to have much of an effect. I think it will be more like when you had 'Dates of the World' and 'What Time is it in X Country?' websites. You don't need to go to a website to get that; you can get that from Google. From a user standpoint, you don't need to go to a website to see what holiday is happening in Zimbabwe today. You can ask Google, and Google will tell you.

There will be some queries where it will be beneficial to use generative search answers, but for e-commerce and YMYL, SGE can't handle them in its current state. Maybe 2-3 years from now that might be different but, in its current state, I just don't think it works."

If an SEO is struggling for time, what should they stop doing right now so they can spend more time doing what you suggest in 2024?

"It's all about your process. Track your time. Track how much time you're spending on things to see where your time's being used, and make sure you're using it effectively. You might have spent 10 hours on link building this month and you didn't even get a link. If you cut that in half, can you still be effective with 5 hours?

The most important things are the content on your site and how it's optimized, the links pointing to your site, your Google Business Profile, and your reviews. You don't have to do a whole lot with reviews, so you don't have to worry about that.

To spend more time on Google Business Profile, look at the time you spend on tech SEO, content optimization, and link building. Figure out whether you are efficiently using that time to get the best outcome. You don't have to spend a lot of ongoing time on your Google Business Profile. Once you have everything set up, you update your photos every once in a while and update the questions as you think of new ones.

The main time suck is doing Google Posts, and most people do them once a week. That means you need to find, at most, an hour of time a month. Track what you're doing, figure out where you're not being effective, and be better at time management.

You need to understand how to operate in a business. All SEOs and digital marketers know how to do SEO at a basic level, but they often don't think about the customer service side, the process side, the time management side, or the business side. Often, we just do SEO the way we've always done it.

It really helps to take a step back and look at the process of what you're doing. Anybody could do SEO. It's the people who can effectively manage their time and deal well with their clients that win in the long run."

Greg Gifford is Chief Operating Officer at SearchLab Digital, and you can find him over at SearchLabDigital.com.

Go deeper into managing your local knowledge panel – with Claire Carlile

Claire Carlile from BrightLocal thinks that focusing on your local knowledge panel will make a big difference for local businesses.

Claire says: "If you're a local business, you need to think about your local knowledge panel – beyond what you can manage via the NMX (New Merchant Experience).

For those who don't know, NMX is a very silly name for what replaced the Business Profile dashboard, and everyone calls it something different. Basically, businesses lost the ability to manage their Google Business Profiles via the old interface, and everything went into the SERP. Now, if you Google your business name and you are the manager of a business listing, you'll see a little box at the top. It's a bit like the CMS for your website, and a lot of editing functions exist within that box.

If the SERP isn't triggering the NMX for some reason, then go to business.google.com. You can click on the business there and it will take you directly to the NMX. However, it should be triggering now. When it first changed over, it didn't trigger sometimes because Google was still a little bit lost.

If you haven't got one, you obviously need to set up a Google business listing. Do the beginner bits first."

Why has Google changed it so that you're managing your business on the SERP instead of logging into Google Business Profile?

"Why is the sky blue? Google obviously knows a lot about what we do and will read a lot into why we do it. They know how we use all of our logins, and they know what actions we take. They probably found that smaller businesses didn't use the interface as it was before.

Hopefully, they thought that they were basically taking away a step from the process. For a small business that only manages one listing, they're going to see that as soon as they Google their business name. They probably thought that it was quicker and easier.

As SEOs, we sometimes struggle with change, and we like to make a big fuss about it. Now, you can find most things via the NMX, and we've got used to using it – unless we're managing profiles in bulk using a third-party tool via the API. The NMX is okay; we quite like it really.

It is easier to go in there and tweak things on the SERP instead of having to log into something else, especially because Google Business Profile serves a lot of small businesses. I'm sure that Google, in their infinite wisdom, decided that this would make it easier for small businesses to keep things like their hours updated, and make other important micro-changes that affect how people interface and the information they get from their Business Profiles."

If you are managing multiple businesses, can you still do that within Google or do you need to use a third-party tool?

"It depends. If you've got 10 locations in a location group then you can always update via bulk uploads, which is pretty quick and easy, and you don't need to use a third-party tool.

There are ways that you can update things without having to pay for a tool –

even if you are managing multiple locations."

What are the initial key elements that a business has to optimize within its online local presence?

"Everyone needs to go and have a little look at the Local Search Ranking Factors survey that Darren Shaw puts together every year. He surveys 30-40 people from our industry who work with a lot of local businesses, and they will talk about what they think is most important. If you're wondering what you need to do with your Business Profile, definitely go and have a look at that.

All of the things that you need to do to completely fill out your Business Profile, you can do via the NMX. That includes the basics: name, address, phone number, correct category, and correct secondary categories. Then there are all those fun things that you should be doing that give your Business Profile lots of content and encourage people to click through or take an action.

That could be photos, booking links, appointments, admissions, experiences, products, and services. It can be all singing and all dancing, and then people will take action within your Business Profile. Treat it as if it were the home page of your website and you're trying to entice people in – either to your website or to take an action on that Business Profile. You want to make sure that you look more compelling than your competitor."

How do you demonstrate more trust to Google, and describe your business in other spaces online to further influence the knowledge panel?

"Obviously, Google is also a large repository for reviews – so that's a big trust factor. You want to encourage reviews in and on Google, but there are also other elements that can get pulled into your local knowledge panel, like reviews from elsewhere around the web.

It is very important that you keep visiting your local profile to understand what is being pulled in and featured on your Business Profile. If you need to go and do a little bit of reputation triage, then you need to head off to those websites. First, learn from those bad reviews, and then try and get more, better reviews in those places to make your Business Profile look better."

How do you know where to drive customers and encourage them to write a review?

"We do keep coming back around to Google, so we know that you need reviews there. Aside from that, it is very useful to just Google your brand name. Have a look at what appears in the first two pages of the SERP (especially the ones that have got review schema of some kind), because those are the types of sites that might get eyeballs.

Aside from that, you need to know your marketplace very well so that you understand what the touchpoints in your ideal consumer's journey are going to be. Consider what else they might be consuming, in terms of reviews and content, and make sure that you've had a positive interaction at some point along that journey."

What might Google be taking from other places and incorporating within a local knowledge banner?

"This is the exciting bit. I've been looking at this for years and not really understanding where a lot of stuff was coming from. You can learn a lot about brand management from an organisation like Kalicube, and a lot of that spills over into the local marketplace. Soon, local businesses are going to be seeing more information pulled from elsewhere and you need to think about how you can manage that now.

An example we might see now would be a description coming in from Wikipedia. There are other elements that you can't control like ads and third parties that you work with, which also appear in your knowledge panels. You've got your editorial summary that Google writes that you can't directly influence as well.

More and more, you want to ask those questions. How did that get there? How do I get rid of it or how do I get one of those for myself? If your client is saying that they don't like it, and asking how to get rid of it, you may have to explain that you can't, because it's based on Google's understanding of your entity. It's a difficult conversation to have with a business.

Do a bit of a stocktake of who you are, what it is that you do, and who you do it for. That data needs to be the same everywhere – and you need to own that information on your own website."

Should a relatively small local business be trying to get a Wikipedia page if they haven't got one?

"No, because I don't think Google will be pulling in Wikipedia unless it is for educational niches, attractions, and important brick-and-mortar establishments. It appears in the type of hybrid knowledge panel that brings in information from a branded knowledge panel plus the local knowledge panel.

If you go and look at Madame Tussauds, Blackpool Tower, the Empire State Building, the Eiffel Tower, or any big university, you'll find a very extensive knowledge panel which is pulling in data from lots of different sources. Wikipedia is only really important when you are managing a brand that has brick-and-mortar as well as being a notable entity. Those are the types of businesses that are going to see a busy knowledge panel that brings in information from those different knowledge verticals."

Is it important for a local business that leads with a personal brand to build up that personal brand, and is there anything different that they need to do for that?

"You need to map it out because you can have several different 'brands'. I'm 'Claire Carlile Marketing', which is my local business, but I'm also 'Claire Carlile', which is a person, and I've got a Knowledge Graph ID for that. I've also got another one from Google Scholar for my academic writing.

I've got all of these different ways that Google is seeing me as an entity, but it isn't joining them up at the moment. My next project will be to help Google join that together a bit more. If I became a published author or released an album then that would put me in a different knowledge vertical. It's about mapping that out beforehand. If I'm being 'Claire Carlile' as an individual, then I'm a person. If I'm 'Claire Carlile Marketing', then I'm a local business. If I'm 'Claire Carlile' in Google Scholar, then I'm a scholar.

Jason Barnard's process is having an entity home, corroborating that, and then corroborating that corroboration. It's a process. This sounds complicated, but it doesn't have to be complicated. You just have to have a very clear understanding of who you are, what it is you do, and who you serve. That's key."

If an SEO is struggling for time, what should they stop doing right now so they can spend more time doing what you suggest in 2024?

"Go back to basics. We get very lost in tactics and tactical implementation, and we forget the strategic element. You should at least have some sort of strategy behind the things that you're throwing against the wall to see if they stick.

Come back to who you are, what you do, why you do it better than your competitors, and who you serve. You should have that very deep foundational marketing understanding of your business – because you should know all of those things before you take yourself online and start considering your different entities."

Claire Carlile is Local Search Expert at BrightLocal, and you can find her over at BrightLocal.com.

Research market-relevant events to stay ahead in international SEO – with Sara Fernández Carmona

Another way that you can get noticed is to focus on market-relevant events, according to International SEO Consultant Sara Fernández Carmona.

Sara says: "This year, it is important that we stay ahead in international SEO by embracing and keeping track of market-relevant events.

This can include holidays, elections, festivities, and even football matches. All of these events can have an impact on the market you work in. They can influence your traffic, your rankings and your impressions.

When I was working for a travel company, I saw a sudden spike in impressions on a Spanish domain for the query 'Sevilla Roma' in Google Search Console. However, it was not followed by clicks. Normally, in the travel context, this search query would relate to travelling between destinations – in this case, from Seville to Rome. However, this anomaly happened due to a temporary change in the SERPs on the 31st May of 2023. It coincided with the Europa League final match between Sevilla and Roma.

The users who were conducting that search weren't interested in finding flights between those cities; they wanted to find information about the football match that was being played. There was a temporary switch in the search intent. If you're working in the Spanish or Italian market and you're not aware that this match is happening, and you see that sudden spike in impressions on Search Console that's not followed by clicks, you might think that something was broken on your website. Instead, it was because the search intent had changed.

Something very similar also happened when, for one or two days, people suddenly started searching for the names of individual countries. It was not because they were interested in travelling to that country or finding more information about that country, but because the Eurovision Song Contest was happening. They were interested in finding information about the bands and the songs that represented that country."

How do you start to learn about and plan around the relevant events that are going to be happening?

"The first step is to create a calendar of market-relevant events, for each market. That should include holidays, festivals, elections, sports events, etc. If possible (depending on the size of the company), you want to have a dedicated marketer for each market. It is very useful to be able to regularly communicate with someone who is responsible for monitoring the market in any one country. Every week, if anything important is happening in your key markets, that can then be communicated via chat. It's not just about having a calendar, but also having regular communication between the different marketing teams.

The second step is to monitor industry news and trends. Tools like Google

Alerts, Google Trends, and any specialised industry news websites can be useful. They will all help you find these events that could influence search behaviour.

The third step is to use tools for data tracking, such as Google Analytics, as well as regularly performing keyword research. That will enable you to identify any shifts and adapt your content and campaigns.

You should be leveraging these events to develop content that targets these campaigns. Depending on your business, they could also benefit you and you could create special offers or promotions that are related to the event as well."

Would you recommend adding annotations to your analytics, based upon what events have impacted changes in conversion rates?

"Absolutely. It is very important that you add those annotations because, as time goes by, it's less likely that you will remember that one specific spike was due to a football match, for example.

Also, as your teams grow, these annotations in tools like Google Search Console and Google Analytics are going to be crucial for monitoring and analysing these shifts in metrics."

How do you definitively know that a particular event has caused an anomaly within your search behaviour?

"It is important that you check exactly what queries triggered the spike. In my first example, it was a football match. It was very clear that this was the cause of that spike because the query was 'Sevilla Roma', and it was on the day that the match was happening.

Something that can help you in this case is, if you see it on the Spanish website, then check the Italian website as well. Are Italian users also doing the same kind of search? You can also compare that with countries where that event is not as relevant. Generally, you can tell by checking, not just assuming. Check the actual queries that the users are searching for.

You might see queries where the search intent changes based on seasonality – and, of course, a word can also have multiple meanings. You may have a word like 'Texas', which is obviously a state in the US. However, if the band 'Texas' is doing a world tour, and you suddenly start seeing searches for 'Texas' in the countries where they're playing, that could be the reason. Those are the kinds of events that will be affecting searches.

It can be challenging to pinpoint the exact event, especially when you work with many different markets. You may not be dedicated to working in just one market; you may be managing multiple markets at the same time. If you're in that situation, communication with other marketers, and any teams that may have this information to hand, is going to be very useful.

It could also be useful for you to communicate with the sales teams. They may not be communicating with clients at a specific time of the year because there is something going on or they may be adapting their offers to events that are happening. It is very important to keep that communication open."

Is this particularly pertinent for international SEOs because SEOs operating in their own country are typically aware of the different events that are happening?

"Exactly. You could be working for a specific market because it's a country that your company wants to target, even if you're not familiar with the market that you have been given.

Of course, once you start working with this market, you will get more familiar with it. However, in the beginning, there will be other marketers and colleagues who are familiar with that market – and they may be from that country as well. It is important that you communicate with them, and they will help you quickly gain more knowledge on that market."

Do you ever try and change the content of your page, or the content displayed within the SERP, based on changes in intent?

"You can. If you're in the travel industry, for example, you could create campaigns to target that relevant event in some way.

What matters here is that you are aware of how these events can temporarily change the SERPs and that, if you see any drops, this could be the reason. You know that an event just happened and, for this short period of time, the users searching for that query were more interested in something that doesn't have anything to do with your business.

You need to be able to recognise what is happening, from an organic search perspective, so that you can identify and articulate it. When sudden changes occur, you can then communicate what is happening and demonstrate your market knowledge to your stakeholders.

If you know that some big event is happening that is related to your business, you could tailor your content, and create a dedicated campaign or landing page for that – but that would be another tip for another time."

If an SEO is struggling for time, what should they stop doing right now so they can spend more time doing what you suggest in 2024?

"Stop relying on one-size-fits-all strategies for your markets and tailor your efforts to the specific dynamics, events, and nature of each market. When you allocate time and resources to understanding these market-specific nuances, you'll get better results. If you start with a one-size-fits-all strategy, you are going to waste more time in the end. Allocate resources to research and data analysis for each market. You are going to create a better experience, and your campaigns are going to be much better.

You want to tailor the content to the market that you are targeting, but that doesn't mean that you should be creating alternative pages for every event in every market. You might have a page that talks about a specific event, like Día de los Muertos in Mexico. That event doesn't happen in Spain, so having a page for that event in Spain wouldn't make any sense.

Create the pages and content that are relevant for the users in that country, rather than applying a blanket approach."

Sara Fernández Carmona is an International SEO Consultant, and you can find her over at Sara-Fernandez.com.

Build an in-house team to elevate your game – with Luis Rodriguez

Luis Rodriguez from ComparetheMarket believes that you should be focusing inward as a business, and making sure that your internal team is fully equipped to take on future SEO challenges.

Luis says: "Elevate the value of SEO by developing internal capabilities. Building an in-house team is becoming more important than ever before, given all the movements that are happening with generative AI and all the new technology that is out there."

Should an in-house team replace your agency or augment your agency?

"It can do both. For many large and established businesses, bringing the SEO function in-house just makes sense. It's a difficult decision, given the reliance on agencies and the speed of delivery that they can offer.

However, focusing on providing a good user experience, answering people's questions through content, and driving them to the right page is a multi-pronged approach that encompasses many stakeholders, data points, platforms, and data sources. For an in-house team, that can be easier to achieve.

With outsourced teams or agencies, you can find a lot of different hurdles in terms of approvals and access to the actual data. An in-house team can own the end-to-end SEO process by using owned data, determining the strategies to create the content or the pages, and analysing the activity promptly. SEO is becoming a much faster and more dynamic environment and it's important to measure everything at each stage."

Why do you think that building an in-house team is so important now?

"After several years working with both agencies and in-house teams, I've noticed that the speed of delivery and value for the company, especially in the long-term, is elevated when you have an in-house team. Every time your team executes an SEO project, they will develop expertise within the company itself, which will lead to efficiencies.

That's not always the case with agencies. With agencies, there's always a question about who's in the background, who's handling the project, and how to communicate and execute those projects.

Developing your internal capabilities becomes more relevant right now because there is so much automation going on with generative AI. Now, you don't even know if your agency is employing people or using scalable solutions. These solutions are valid but, when you're dealing with regulated businesses or you have an international scope, your team will be better prepared to tackle those challenges."

How do you ensure that everything is accomplished as well in-house as it would be by an agency?

"Analysis paralysis is one of the biggest risks that you face in SEO when you're looking at so many data sources. There will be updates and it can become difficult to deliver on what you set out to achieve.

My advice is to stick to your plan and your goals. Even if it's a forecast or a guess, try to assign the value that you will be bringing to the company by executing certain tasks. That should help you to stay true to your goal, especially when there are updates or you see some tremors in your rankings. It can be very easy to go into panic mode and start changing all of your plans and priorities. What truly matters is that you are confident in your plan and the performance of that plan.

You have internal sources and internal stakeholders, so it's important that you are working together with the rest of the company. Generally, that doesn't get affected by algorithm changes or a change in priorities within the SEO team.

Stick to your goals and make sure that your plan considers what the output is going to be and how you are going to measure that output. That output needs to be recognised and familiar to the rest of the company."

Is there anything agencies do that in-house teams tend to forget about?

"Transparency is really important. An agency can be briefed about your company goals and the topic of your campaign, but external people won't be as connected to the philosophy of the company as your team will be.

One of the risks, though, is a lack of transparency, and things can easily be missed when you're relying on external parties. The most common of these things are how your competitors are doing, and actually visiting your own website."

If you still want to work with an agency in some capacity, what tasks might you recommend giving to them?

"A hybrid model is definitely one of the approaches that I would suggest. It helps to bridge certain parts of the project and provide skill sets that you might be missing.

The areas it would be beneficial for an agency to handle are competitors and monetary. An agency will have multiple clients, so they will have greater visibility into different industries. It's important that you're fed that information. It's almost like having a creative refresher that allows you to see a different perspective on your own conclusions.

The second task I would recommend using an agency for is as your strategic sounding board. You should always be trying to share with other SEOs and other experts in the industry to discuss new ideas and new theories. We are still in the world of figuring out how Google works. You can use your partners to give you an external point of view that has no bias to what the brand is or the actual product. That can be beneficial for making your SEO strategy more comprehensive."

If you intend to bring your SEO agency's activities in-house, what conversations do you need to have with your marketing teams?

"The most important conversation would be around the transition period and how you start reacquiring responsibility.

Recently, we started to retake the data and reporting around certain activities, and it definitely caused some tremors. You need to stay in close communication about the internal capabilities of the team and who can help you work around different challenges, particularly in terms of the data. For example, it is important to understand whether you have the storage and the software to analyse and service data points as efficiently as an external partner.

Additionally, having an in-house team requires having more people in your team, which can develop into managerial challenges and people challenges. People want to have a career so you will need to lean on your HR experts and design a career path for the people who are starting out as well as those who are already seasoned SEOs. It is difficult because there are multiple potential pathways. You can become a manager or you can become an expert in a specific area, and both are valid. It's about understanding what you need from people and then designing a path for that.

Firstly, during the transition period, pay particular attention to data migrations and reacquiring metrics. Secondly, look out for the hurdles that may arise from simply having more people within the team."

How difficult is it to build an in-house team and what trends are you seeing in terms of recruitment and what new employees are looking for now?

"To start with, the size of the team shouldn't really matter. I don't like to pinpoint a specific number of people, as long as certain areas of expertise are covered. For me, a complete in-house team will always have data people who understand and process numbers for the rest of the team. You will also need people to handle the website itself, including everything that you can tweak regarding content, performance, number of pages, and tooling.

At the tip of the sword (which is probably one of the most difficult areas to develop) you need to have dedicated team members who can understand what the next big opportunity is going to be and how to tackle it. The size of the team should reflect the responsibilities that you have and it should reflect what you are trying to achieve.

In terms of what is attracting people to new teams, providing learning opportunities upfront is really important. That's something that a lot of candidates are keen on. They want to expand their knowledge base. The market is healthy for companies at the moment, though not necessarily for SEOs. There's really good talent out there, perhaps coming out of the trend where a lot of in-house teams were really beefed up. Now the industry is entering a more normalised period, so there's definitely good talent available.

To attract the best talent, have a career plan. Everybody can be an expert and arrive at a new job already knowing a bunch of things. What matters is how you can set that person up for success in the next five years and keep them in-house. Also, be aware of the different necessities that people are bringing to the team so it can become an inclusive space. Technology isn't always inclusive, but we are becoming a more diverse industry so your team culture should reflect that."

What advice would you give regarding the use of automation and AI?

"Be cautious about automation. It's definitely very tempting because we want to make our jobs easier, and we want to make our jobs faster. However, we might be missing something in there.

I was reflecting on my own career and how I started in SEO and eventually became an expert. It was mostly through grinding keywords and grinding spreadsheets with data numbers and trying to understand how those things correlate to the SERP and how the changes become more tangible. The danger with automation is that some of the expertise developed through actually executing the work can be lost.

Try to automate the process but don't automate the task itself. You might rely on generative AI to write all of your emails, but what is going to happen when you present to a leadership team or at a conference? In those environments, you can't rely on a tool to give you all the answers.

You can use automation for the process itself – to get all of your approvals, gather everything within the same database, make data transformations, etc. – as long as you have the ability to put your effort and expertise into it."

If an SEO is struggling for time, what should they stop doing right now so they can spend more time doing what you suggest in 2024?

"Stop obsessively looking at your rankings. We've all been there, especially when there are updates. It's almost like an obsession.

The rankings are going to be there. Spend a lot less time observing something that is just there. That way, you'll have a little bit more time to spend creating your strategy, thinking about the best way to create helpful content, and distributing your product."

Luis Rodriguez is Head of SEO at ComparetheMarket and you can find him over at ComparetheMarket.com.

Learn how you can do more with less – with Adriana Stein

While Luis wants you to elevate your game, Adriana Stein from AS Marketing warns that you're not going to have every SEO resource imaginable available to you, so you have to be smart in your use of the tools and resources that you have.

Adriana says: "Do more with less. I know a lot of us have felt that across this year, but it's going to be the number one thing that we have to face in SEO going into 2024."

Is doing more with less a choice?

"In the marketing world, we are so heavily affected by what happens with the economy and what changes in technology, and all of that comes together to influence the way that we have to work.

In SEO, we wouldn't necessarily make that choice. We would love to go back to 15 years ago when it was very easy to write keywords and some text, and it worked. It was really that simple. Nowadays, there's so much more that goes into SEO, not just in a technical sense but also in the pressure to drive impact. That's what a lot of SEOs are going to increasingly face going forward, even though we've had a recession and before that we had COVID. Now, there are new standards. SEOs have to be on the ball to be worthwhile, and that's going to be a big game changer in 2024."

Do SEOs need to be more frugal with cash and more efficient with

their time to better leverage themselves in the future?

"That's a lot of it. It's not necessarily by choice, but it's the conditions that we work under. Those are going to be the conditions that stakeholders expect and what they expect SEOs to produce. It's a consequence of the circumstances and there's not really a way around it.

If you try to do inefficient SEO nowadays, it's not going to go very far. You have to accept it and go with it, and then try to learn and optimize what you can – especially related to processes. Process efficiency is going to be a major part of that."

Have these circumstances arisen primarily because of the recession, AI, or other causes?

"Those are two things, and competition and market saturation is a third. We're under these circumstances where we have the option for technology to make us more efficient. There is a question of whether that really is the case. It depends on how you use the technology – not just AI, but any marketing-related technology, as that is also rapidly changing. There is so much competition as well.

SEOs have done a really good job over the years of informing their audience of how effective SEO can truly be. Now they've got this investment, but they need to do something with it. There are a lot of companies that are producing more, especially with AI. With limited budgets and more technology, these things are coming together and you have to find a way to stand out from all of the competition.

As SEOs, we can't change any of those top-level circumstances. We have to find a way to work within them. That's the most effective way to prove ourselves in our careers going forward. Even if we suddenly had an economic explosion and everything was positive, the mindset is not going to change because that's what we've become used to.

Stakeholders – CFOs, CEOs, etc. – don't want to go and waste money. They have seen a lot of problems related to that and they're trying to condense and optimize. As a CEO myself, I have looked heavily at our technology and our processes, and I wouldn't suddenly go back just because the economy improved. It was inefficient. I would want to continue being as efficient as possible."

How does this affect someone in-house versus agency-side?

"At the end of the day, we both have the same pressure. Whether you're working in an agency, as a freelancer, or in-house, you have the same pressure to drive results.

When you're working in-house, you might have a bit less time pressure because that's inherently part of the job. From my experience, there's a whole lot less time pressure on what an employee can accomplish versus what an agency can accomplish.

If you hire an agency, you expect them to jump in straight away. Our clients expect us to start producing content within the first few weeks, so you have to onboard very quickly. Someone working in-house might take three months to learn about the company, the product or service, and how things work.

There is the same pressure to produce results, but there's often a lot more pressure on an agency in terms of the amount of time that takes. Ultimately, that's what they're hired to do. They're hired to come in and be very efficient and effective at bringing in results early on."

What is the difference between SEO in-house and agency-side?

"There are two sides to that. In the past, SEO lacked a lot of conversion-driven efforts – and I say this as someone coming from SEO who has learned a lot about PPC because my agency offers holistic marketing services. I have seen how conversion-driven PPC is. In SEO, we take time to edit, 10 people need to review everything, etc. It takes so much longer, and the processes behind it are traditionally much less efficient, compared to PPC.

An agency can come in and help you understand how to actively and effectively execute SEO. As an agency, you have broader expertise because you have applied it across a lot of different projects. You have more of an overall insight into how to do that effectively. That, in combination with the time pressure that the agencies have, typically means that things get done much faster – simply because, if you don't do your job, you're probably not going to have a client anymore.

That's a big difference between the way our team works and how our clients sometimes work. Some clients can even struggle to keep up with us, but it's difficult because we know that we have a time expectation for results. You have to move that fast because you don't want disappointment down the road. You don't want to find yourself asking why it didn't work or why there weren't any conversions. An agency has more experience to drive that forward.

It depends on where you are within your strategy, the level of investment you have in SEO, and the time you have to give to SEO. A combination of both in-house and agency can be the best option."

Which SEO tasks shouldn't be sped up too much?

"This may be an unpopular opinion, but using AI for content production should not be rushed. We've done a lot of testing with this; I did a whole series for the Wix SEO Hub where I tested using AI for full-length content production across different industries. The quality is just so bad.

I specialise in complex B2B, and I just don't see where AI can have an in-depth understanding of how to produce full-length content. Writing content from scratch, like a 3,000-word user guide or a case study, takes subject matter expertise.

You can get away with using AI for e-commerce content, SEO-wise, when it's short and simple. In terms of B2B, though, it just doesn't work. The time you have to spend figuring out all of your prompts and editing afterwards takes longer than the traditional method. Creating a strategy for a piece, working with a subject matter expert, finding a writer to help draft it out, and then using an editor may sound like a lot of steps, but the quality is so much higher.

Speeding up a piece like that using AI is going to be harmful in the end. If you start pumping out low-quality content, not only is that not helping your audience (they will see right through it) but it's also a spam indicator.

Some websites are experimenting with producing thousands of pieces of content a day. I talked to someone doing this in the finance industry, and I specifically asked whether any of it was being manually reviewed for accuracy. They said 'No, it all just goes live.' I find that truly heartbreaking. They might be finding some short-term gains but, in the long run, that is absolutely not the way to become more efficient and create high-quality content."

What does doing more with less mean for the SEO team structure? Does it mean having fewer people in your team?

"It can, but it mainly comes down to having very established processes. This stems from an issue that I've seen time and time again, and I've also heard from a lot of my SEO colleagues. There is a big struggle to simply get content or technical changes live. In the Aira State of Technical SEO Report last year, they mentioned that the average time to get technical changes to go live is six months. That's insane. Think about the amount that you can improve with SEO in six months.

Rather than just focusing on content editing (which is great, you still need to edit and produce high-quality content), look deeply at your processes and how your team is structured. Does everyone know what they're supposed to do? Do you have deadlines? Do you have a workflow with steps from A to B? Do you have the resources you need? That's especially an issue on the dev side, where a lot of the biggest bottlenecks are.

All of this beautiful content is created and then it just sits in the project management tool for six months or longer because there's no dev resource to put it live. That's such a tragedy. That content could have been ranking and converting for months already.

Those little things add up and they hinder you. That's where you can do more with less. Look at the operational background of how your SEO is established, who does what, who makes sure that things go live, and who makes sure things are optimized once they're up."

If an SEO is struggling for time, what should they stop doing right now so they can spend more time doing what you suggest in 2024?

"Look at your operational processes. Do you have too many tasks for one person that could be handled by two people? Do you need to reduce the amount of content you're creating because people can't keep up? Maybe produce a bit less content so that you ensure that it goes live.

The same could be true for technical changes. Can you make a couple of technical changes instead of a lot of changes that never go live? Break the project down into little bits and then start to see where you can optimize things.

There may be a place for AI. It can be effective for short-form writing, summaries, content ideation, and things like metadata. If that speeds you up, then great. Make sure that what you're working on actually goes live and doesn't take six months of resources with no changes. That's really ineffective SEO. Try to turn that on its head and do a little bit rather than none at all.

AI is not going to help if you're using it to produce bad content volume. With so many companies doing SEO nowadays, you have to find a way for your content to stand out. Even if you do use AI in the process, try to personalise the content as much as possible. Talk about real customers, real use cases, and real data. Get subject matter expertise from within your company or industry. If you don't have someone at your company, add quotes. Those are things that AI can't pull up.

If you're using AI to write a blog article for X topic, 2,000 other companies already have the same kind of information. You've got to put in some effort to make it a lot more personal, unique, and specific."

Adriana Stein is Founder and CEO at AS Marketing, and you can find her over at ASMarketingAgency.com.

Embrace the changes and challenges that come your way – with Sarah McDowell

To conclude our tips for this year, Sarah McDowell from Captivate and the SEO Mindset Podcast offers up a positive perspective on everything that's coming your way in SEOin2024.

Sarah says: "Embrace change and don't worry about the challenges and obstacles that come our way. It's all part and parcel of working in SEO.

SEO has always been about change to a certain degree but it feels like it's changing even faster now. In the last year alone, the number of big changes and updates that came out or were announced seems to have been constant.

We do have to remember that Google is always changing its algorithms and its search results, and it's always testing – because that's what it does. Its mission is to test new stuff, and it's all about user experience. Unfortunately, that does mean a lot of change. According to an article in Search Engine Journal, in 2021 alone, it was estimated that Google made 5,000 changes. That's what's going on; it's always changing."

Should SEOs even try to keep up to date with all the changes that are happening?

"I'm not saying that you shouldn't bother. However, most SEOs have a strategy or a roadmap. They've planned out what their projects are, and they're normally aligned to business goals and business targets. Big updates and algorithm changes happen all the time, but you don't necessarily have to jump off what you're working on right now to go and focus on them. If you do, then you're constantly playing catch-up.

If an update or algorithm change has negatively impacted you in some way, then you do need to look into it. Take a breath, have a look at what's happened, and figure out what your strategy is going to be and what you can do about it. However, if you haven't seen a massive change in the wrong direction, then don't deviate from your strategy or plan. You put that strategy and plan together for a reason."

Are you also likely to hear about big changes that might affect you anyway, like the switch to GA4 and the introduction of the SGE?

"Absolutely. There was a lot of talk when Google removed FAQ snippets from search results. I also remember that, early in the year, Google used to show carousels of podcasts in Google search results, and they don't do that any more either.

They're changing their algorithms, their ranking factors, and what matters to them. However, the things that are around now might not always be there. Google will take things away and we can't control that. Google controls it. Accept that and focus on the things that you think are going to make a difference."

When you're intending to rank for a keyword phrase, can you still look at the SERP to see what is there and what might be likely to stay?

"Yes, definitely. There will be core elements that stay the same – for example, People Also Ask, answer boxes, or YouTube carousels. I'm very aware that I've just said all these things and next week we might find out Google's removed one of them. However, you always have to look at the landscape. Look at the search results and see how you can boost your visibility.

Ranking fluctuations are important to consider as well. If you are constantly looking at your keyword rankings (especially individual ones), that's going to cause you a headache because they change all the time. We know that Google's changing its algorithms and changing what it's showing to people in the SERPs, so don't get too hung up on those fluctuations. If a keyword drops a couple of positions, keep an eye on it, and look at it in a topic to make sure that there aren't any negative trends happening.

Content and pages rank for more than just a single keyword, so it's better to look at trends on a broader scale. Don't get caught up on singular ranking fluctuations, and be more pragmatic about it."

What trends do you look at and when do you take notice and change the way you do something?

"Keep an eye on your most popular content: the pages and articles that you know are getting decent traffic a month, and giving you conversions. Those are the ones that are the most important. Obviously, you will have other articles and other content that will be ranking, driving traffic, and driving conversions – but prioritise your hero content.

It's always good to keep an eye on that on a weekly basis, but take a look at that page and have a look at the different keywords, not just a singular one. You will have a keyword that is the most important because it's the most popular, but have a look at all the keywords – and look at them over the span of a month, or a few months.

You could get caught up looking at it on a weekly or daily basis and you're constantly going to be chasing your tail thinking you have to change something when it's actually just Google changing what it wants to show people. Have a look at the key metrics, like the impressions and clicks that the page has been getting over a month.

Also, your new content might become a really important piece. After a few months of it being live on Google, it can pick up traffic and all that wonderful stuff. Keep an eye on that as well. However, you have to prioritise because even small sites have loads of articles, pages, etc. It can be a headache, especially if you're in a small team."

What do you do when Google takes something away from the SERP?

"What can you do? You can worry about it and have a little moan but be pragmatic and proactive. Have a look at how it has impacted you and have a plan for it.

For example, with the podcast carousel moving away, what can you do about that? You can't get Google to put them back because it's their decision. If you find that you're not getting as much traffic or listeners for your podcast from that, look at what you can do instead. Could you look into YouTube because YouTube carousels are still there? Have a plan B.

Also, they removed the FAQ snippets from Google, and it took some dev time and resources to put those things in place for your website. I would always recommend weighing up resources and rewards. How much time are these things going to take you and is it worth the reward, especially if Google might take it away?

There are always going to be other opportunities. As a digital marketer, you have to be adaptable. Things change all the time, and things that were working for you won't necessarily be the same in a few months or a year. You have to sort of embrace change, and embrace the new challenges that come up."

Should people be worried about AI in relation to their jobs?

"Again, it's change. It's something that the industry is going to have to adapt to. I don't think there's anything to be worried about at this moment in time. I started using ChatGPT and it's actually helped me speed up my own processes and work more efficiently.

I've just been playing around. If I'm stuck for a title for my next podcast episode or I'm writing a blog and I've just got writer's block, I go to ChatGPT, tell it what the article or episode is about, and ask it to generate some ideas for me. Then I've got some inspiration to work from. You can also use ChatGPT to help you improve your writing. I'm a blabber, and I know that I am. I've been using ChatGPT to make what I'm saying more concise by removing filler words, etc. It can also generate page titles and meta descriptions.

Obviously, you always need to check the work that ChatGPT is coming back with. Humans will always be needed, but ChatGPT can be used to make our lives easier and help us work more efficiently. The way you embrace that change is by reviewing what you're currently doing and experimenting to see if a new technology like ChatGPT can positively impact you.

Change is scary and it is hard; I get that. It is challenging but everyone else is in the same boat. I think that comparing ourselves to others is part of embracing challenges and changes. You're not superhuman and you're not going to know everything, but you don't know what challenges and obstacles someone else is facing either. We're all in this together.

Something that helps you to embrace challenges and avoid being overwhelmed is being part of a community, and I want to give a shout-out to Areej AbuAli's Women in Tech SEO community. Obviously, that is specifically for women in tech SEO but there are many others that other people can join. It's really valuable to be part of a community where you can have honest conversations. If you're worried about something or you've got a question, there are safe spaces where you can go and ask about those things."

If an SEO is struggling for time, what should they stop doing right now

so they can spend more time doing what you suggest in 2024?

"Prioritise your content. Focus on one piece of content and look at ways to improve it. There are always opportunities to increase traffic to a page, get more signups, or get more conversions.

Stop what you're doing right now, take your most important bit of content that's already working really well for you, and look for some more quick wins. What can you do with that content to boost its discoverability, get more traffic, and get more signups? It's working well, so what can you do to improve it even more?"

Sarah McDowell is SEO Manager at Captivate and Co-Host of the SEO Mindset Podcast, and you can find her over at TheSEOMindset.co.uk.

CLOSING THOUGHTS

And that completes our 101 insightful contributions to SEOin2024!

No single resource can possibly be all-encompassing, but I hope you agree that SEOin2024 is a wonderful benchmark to assist you with prioritising your SEO needs over the coming year. The

At the beginning of the book, in the Opening Thoughts, I was unwilling to suggest individual contributions that you should focus on. That's because all business requirements are different, with different strengths and weaknesses and at a different point on the journey. Therefore, each SEO department has to prioritise different things. If something's right for someone else, it doesn't mean that it's right for you, at the same moment in time.

So, take the time to decide what's right for you, based upon your circumstances. Select a handful of tips and then run with them. Then come back for more (and hopefully for SEOin2025 too!).

Based upon the '5 Knows' that I introduced in the Opening Thoughts, here are the tips that I'm personally drawn to in SEOin2024…

1) To know what to do

It seems that there are many more possibilities than ever in the world of SEO, and this makes it so hard to make a decision about what we should be doing. But decide we must – and the tip that assists me here is "Prepare for the AI-fuelled duplication epidemic" by Billie Geena.

Whether we're actively embracing AI in our content production or not, the reality is that a lot of our competitors will be. So, what do we do about it?

That brings in another tip – "Highlight your real-life authority in your online presence" by Anthony Barone. That's something that I will be focusing on in 2024 to differentiate my offering in the eyes of Google.

2) To know how to do it

This takes me on to the more practical tips about how to do what I intend to do, starting off with "Utilise AI to save you time with your content creation" by Isaline Muelhauser. Of course, I won't *rely* on AI to produce my content – but I will determine how to use AI to make my content production process more efficient.

Leading on from that, "Improve your success with AI by building a prompt library" by Garrett Sussman will ensure that I maximize relevance and enhance tonality for the content that is created.

3) To know when to do it

As a digital marketer / SEO it's so easy to get distracted by the next shiny object that reveals itself. And that's where "Stop overworking and focus on the tasks that matter" by Adrijana Vujadin comes in.

I also want to highlight "Don't lose ground when it comes to site speed" by Fili Wiese. That's because I don't want to just focus on the areas that I find the most fun (like content creation). It's important that I'm aware of when my website isn't performing effectively. Because, if I'm not delivering a good user experience, publishing more content isn't going to matter.

4) To know what *not* to do

In terms of what I shouldn't be doing – I shouldn't be focusing on the metrics that don't matter. This brings me to Becky Simms' tip: "Track the metrics that actually move the needle". Once I know the metrics that really matter to my business, this will help me to stop doing the things that don't matter so much.

Also, in terms of specific activities that I should or shouldn't be doing, Jo O'Reilly shared "Focus less on quantity and more on quality, relevant links". I'm convinced that high quality and relevance matters more than ever, especially in the age of AI.

5) To know when to review what you do

Finally, every SEO needs to take stock; to review how *what* they're doing is performing and to decide whether or not *what* they're doing is the best thing to be doing. Olga Zarr's advice of "Do more SEO testing and experimenting" hits home here because we need to be as data-centric as possible, and stop relying so much on gut instinct.

I'd like to finish off with Jono Alderson's advice of "Consider Google's incentive to index your site and prepare for the next chapter of the internet". Because, unless we hone in on what the user is experiencing today and optimize for that, we're stuck in the past.

But remember, those are the tips that resonate with me. What are the tips that resonate with you?

@Majestic #SEOin2024.

And please remember to checkout *SEOin2024.com* for the associated podcast and video series.

It's been a pleasure.

David Bain
Author, *SEOin2024*
Founder, *CastingCred.com*

Index

INDEX

Become more adaptable so that you can take advantage of change – with Rebecca Berbel...... *11*

Emotional intelligence can be your superpower – with Petra Kis-Herczegh.......................... *16*

Be human in order to sell to humans – with Jess Joyce... *22*

Keep a human eye on your AI-generated content – with Adelina Bordea............................. *26*

Stay ahead of the game by embracing AI – with Nitin Manchanda.................................... *33*

Prepare for the AI-fuelled duplication epidemic – with Billie Geena.................................... *39*

Stop worrying about the future and start optimizing for it – with Jake Gauntley.................. *44*

Consider how AI will impact user behaviour – with Annika Haataja.................................. *49*

Familiarise yourself with the capabilities and limitations of large language models – with Bastian Grimm... *55*

Use LLMs to improve your forecasting and save you time – with Arpad Balogh................. *62*

Learn how to tackle generative AI in search – with Jason Barnard.................................... *67*

Understand how generative AI is affecting SEO content – with Itamar Blauer................... *73*

Learn to think, and only automate when it makes sense – with Kristina Azarenko.............. *79*

Utilise AI to save you time with your content creation – with Isaline Muelhauser............... *84*

Employ AI to improve your quality, not your quantity – with Joseph S. Kahn.................... *89*

Improve your success with AI by building a prompt library – with Garrett Sussman........... *94*

Build your own prompt libraries for your clients – with Victoria Olsina............................ *100*

Watch out for better, AI-powered technical SEO tools – with Pam Aungst Cronin........... *105*

Keep a closer eye on the ever-changing SERPs – with Julia-Carolin Zeng....................... *111*

Consider Google's incentive to index your site and prepare for the next chapter of the internet – with Jono Alderson.. *117*

Recognise the value of visual elements in the world of SGE – with Mufaddal Sadriwala ... *124*

Consider schema markup as the language you can use to build a knowledge graph – with Martha van Berkel.. *129*

Recognise the increasing importance of brand SEO – with Miracle Inameti-Archibong...... *137*

Add a technical layer to your branding and start thinking of branding as a technical practice – with Ulrika Viberg.. *143*

Become a real entity by feeding the machine the right information – with Sara Moccand-Sayegh

Index

.... *147*

Make sure your brand-related entities are in Google's Knowledge Vault – with Austine Esezobor *152*

Accept and prepare for the fact that Schema is becoming less relevant – with Anne Berlin . *157*

Provide value by using EEAT as your starting point – with Ed Ziubrzynski *163*

Prepare for a renewed and increasing emphasis on EEAT – with Kavi Kardos *169*

Invest time and money into the EEAT of your website – with Taylor Kurtz *174*

Gain and retain visibility by demonstrating EEAT – with Kerstin Reichert *180*

Lean into long-tail search with the added value of EEAT – with Ben Howe *185*

Improve the experience you offer through high-quality content – with Dre de Vera *190*

Focus on the E, E, and A of EEAT – with Andrew Cock-Starkey *196*

Highlight your real-life authority in your online presence – with Anthony Barone *202*

Keep EEAT at the forefront of your mind – with Filipa Serra Gaspar *208*

Stand out and give people a reason to visit your site – with Gerry White *213*

Find your audience of one to cut through the noise – with Dixon Jones *219*

Always pay attention to the people that matter – with Ian Helms *224*

Future-proof by focussing on the middle and bottom of the funnel – with Myriam Jessier *230*

Stop getting distracted and go back to the basics of search intent – with Jan-Willem Bobbink *237*

Evolve your approach from SEO into HEO – with Ken "Magma" Marshall *242*

Think about the user above anything else – with Amanda White *248*

Think about the user, not the search engine – with Eli Schwartz *253*

Leverage natural language processing to unpack user intent on a whole new level - with Nik Ranger *260*

Return to the basics with your content strategy – with Begum Kaya *267*

Develop a user-enriched, strategic approach to content – with Fabio Embalo *271*

Have conversations and listen to your customers before turning to SEO research – with Martin Huntbach *276*

Recognise the value of creator-led SEO – with Ashley Liddell *282*

Influence organic search by working with influencers – with Maria White *287*

Pan your business for thought leader gold - with Paige Hobart *293*

Invest in creativity and make your copywriting more human – with Bibi "The Link Builder" Raven 299

Put the human and the author first to differentiate your content – with Lidia Infante 304

Harness informational content on your e-commerce site – with Jack Chambers-Ward 309

Reduce, reuse, and recycle the content that you have already produced – with Natalie Arney 315

Validate your long-form content with the help of AI assistants – with Mark Williams-Cook 320

Stop neglecting internal links and your link profile – with Bill Hartzer 327

Take greater advantage of internal links through a complete internal linking strategy – with Anna Uss 331

Take your internal linking a step further by linking to subcategories from the parent category page – with Katherine Nwanorue 337

Improve your internal links using Python string-matching – with Andreas Voniatis 342

Stay on top of both your link building and mention-building – with Debbie Chew 347

Build human connections in order to build better links – with Amit Raj 352

Find ethical backlinks and better content by leveraging happy customers – with Alan Silvestri 357

Focus less on quantity and more on quality, relevant links – with Jo O'Reilly 362

Stop being afraid of building category page backlinks – with Eva Cheng 367

Build the right links to build brand authority – with Alexandra Tachalova 373

Make sure that your site is built on solid technical foundations – with Tom Pool 379

Don't lose ground when it comes to site speed – with Fili Wiese 385

Take control over who can access your content – with Emma Russell 390

Take SEO more seriously during a migration or relaunch – with Andor Palau 395

Improve your SEO audits and make them more meaningful – with Nikki Halliwell 400

Diversify your skillset beyond just organic search – with Luke Carthy 407

Go holistic and work more closely with other marketers – with Izzy Wisniewska 413

Cut across channels with the power of multimedia – with Crystal Carter 418

Learn more and do more with Performance Max – with Navah Hopkins 424

Start integrating video into your SEO strategy – with Sara Taher 430

Foster a collaborative environment to achieve success – with Montserrat Cano 437

Index

Start thinking more like a product manager – with Gus Pelogia 442

Ensure that SEO takes its rightful place as a strategic business function – with Helen Pollitt 448

Raise the status of SEO within the business – with Ash Nallawalla 453

Get buy-in from your stakeholders despite the changing SERP – with Sally Raymer 458

Do more SEO testing and experimenting – with Olga Zarr 465

Don't forget about the power of analytics – with Krzysztof Marzec 470

Focus on what really counts: fresh, relevant data – with Kaspar Szymanski 476

Use data wisely to improve your processes and prevent future damage – with Marco Giordano 481

Improve your ability to handle large amounts of data and perform data analysis at scale – with Pedro Dias 488

Make better use of your data by preparing a database – with Olesia Korobka 493

Use GA4 to properly analyse and read your data – with Gemma Fontané 498

Track the metrics that actually move the needle – with Becky Simms 503

Learn how to better analyse user behaviour and conversions – with Irina Serdyukovskaya 509

Stop overworking and focus on the tasks that matter – with Adrijana Vujadin 515

Make the most of your time by thinking better and rushing less – with Katie McDonald 520

Start incorporating programmatic approaches and rule-based automation into your SEO – with Lazarina Stoy 525

Enhance your day-to-day tasks by leveraging AI – with Aleyda Solis 531

Learn prompt engineering and AI to improve your SEO workflow – with Si Shangase 536

Optimize for the algorithm that matters most to you – with Greg Gifford 543

Go deeper into managing your local knowledge panel – with Claire Carlile 549

Research market-relevant events to stay ahead in international SEO – with Sara Fernández Carmona 554

Build an in-house team to elevate your game – with Luis Rodriguez 559

Learn how you can do more with less – with Adriana Stein 564

Embrace the changes and challenges that come your way – with Sarah McDowell 569

Printed in Great Britain
by Amazon